Site Matters

Design Concepts, Histories, and Strategies

Edited by
Carol J. Burns and Andrea Kahn

ROUTLEDGE
NEW YORK AND LONDON

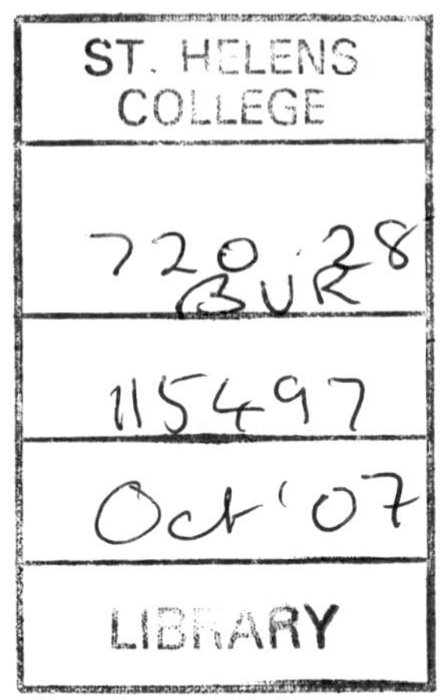

Published in 2005 by
Routledge
270 Madison Avenue
New York, NY 10016
www.routledge-ny.com

Published in Great Britain by
Routledge
2 Park Square
Milton Park, Abingdon
Oxon OX14 4RN
www.routledge.co.uk

Routledge is an imprint of the Taylor and Francis Group.

Printed in the United Stated of America on acid-free paper.

10 9 8 7 6 5 4 3 2 1

Library of Congress Cataloging-in-Publication Data

Burns, Carol, 1954-
Site matters : design concepts, histories, and strategies/edited by Carol J. Burns and Andrea Kahn.
p. cm.
Includes bibliographical references and index.
ISBN 0-415-94975-0 (hardback : alk. paper) — ISBN 0-415-94976-9 (pbk. : alk. paper) 1. Building sites—Planning. 2. Architecture, Modern—20th century. 3. Architecture, Modern—21st century. I. Kahn, Andrea, 1958- II. Title.
NA2540.5.B86 2004
720'.28—dc22 2004012430

Contents

Acknowledgments

The realization and the quality of this book depend on the efforts of many people.

For generosity in providing funded support to enhance the print quality, we are grateful to the School of Architecture at the University of Virginia along with the Office of the Dean, Graduate School of Architecture, Planning, and Preservation at Columbia University. Without their assistance the book would not have color illustrations.

Many friends and colleagues have informed the process. Even if their words are not contained herein, their ideas affect us. We appreciate the input of Marlon Blackwell and David Beuge, Renee Chow, Caroline Constant, Miriam Gusevich, Chris Reed, Michael Sorkin, and Nigel Thrift.

Excellent built work by our contemporaries concerned with site-related issues has enhanced our thinking. We particularly recognize Ed Blake, Wendell Burnette, Coleman Coker, Roy Decker, Steve Dumez, Frank Harmon, Raymond Huff, Rick Joy, Brian McKay-Lyons, David Salmela, Jennifer Siegal, Kevin Sloan, and Julie Snow.

For valuable ideas in conversation and other forms of help along the way, we thank Neil Brenner, Holly Getch Clarke, Julia Czerniak, Hope Hasbrouck, Sandro Marpillero, Eeva-Lisa Pelkonnen, and Anne Spirn. Among the many friends whose writing helped shape ours, we recognize Anita Berrizbeita and Linda Pollak, Elizabeth Gamard, Margaret McAvin, and Ellen Whittemore. We are grateful to Annette Fierro, Nancy Levinson, and Ed Robbins for consistent support and unfailingly good advice on matters large and small.

Simple good luck helped in bringing together the parts of the volume. Kate Nesbitt initially encouraged the idea and gave it impetus at a symposium at the National Building Museum. Anne Lutun created and granted use of the cover image. Robert Stern provided introduction to Sandy Isenstadt who, at a symposium on architecture by graduates of the Yale School of Architecture, presented an initial version of his paper herein on context.

For his good-humored support with the manuscript in the office of Taylor & Burns Architects, we thank Colby Lee. The patient assistance of Kimberly Parent and Emily Dixon-Ryan, interns at the office through the Tufts University internship program directed by Daniel Abramson, aided the process immeasurably.

The editors at Routledge, Dave McBride and Amanda Rice, have imparted a steady lightness of hand. Khrysti Nazzaro, project editor at CRC Press, contributed energetically to the production process, with visible benefit to the book. Thoughtful comments provided through the press by anonymous readers proved invaluable (we hope they introduce themselves, as we'd like to continue a dialogue with them) as did Matt Kiefer's insightful reading of text in draft form.

Grateful to all our authors for their contributions and commitment, we have benefited particularly from the advice of Bob Beauregard, the magnanimity of Lucy Lippard, and the generous dedication of her many artistic friends.

Finally, for their loving support and remarkable patience, we dedicate this collaborative project to our collaborators in life, David, Robert, and Rae.

Why Site Matters

Carol J. Burns and Andrea Kahn

As part of a bid by New York City to host the 2012 Olympic Games, five multidisciplinary teams of architects, landscape architects, and urban designers and planners were invited to offer design ideas for an Olympic Village. One team was led by a New York firm, three by European designers, and one by a firm from Los Angeles.[1] Proposals were requested for a particular parcel of land at the southern tip of Queens West, a waterfront area (formerly Hunter's Point) with unimpeded views across the East River to mid-town Manhattan. Publicly exhibited in the spring of 2004, all five designs were presented similarly, in three-dimensional models with graphic panels including images and text. Each team conformed to established presentation requirements, yet each nonetheless depicted their project and its urban surroundings in notably different ways. Despite common constraints regarding scale and size, the models varied widely in extent and character. One team focused on local edge conditions, conceiving the site in terms of immediate physical surroundings. In contrast, another treated the site strictly as conceptual terrain, using the proposals to engage the history of ideas about the area.[2] Some teams viewed it as belonging to the city at large, "opening the site as a New York City attraction" or "creating the largest urban waterfront park in New York City."[3] Two teams opted to construct additional models. One focused on the design of a cluster of buildings to show the proposal in greater architecture detail. The other depicted a large swath of Manhattan Island, from the East River to the Hudson, situating the Olympic Village in relation to mid-town. The different physical areas identified as relevant to each project and the distinct strategies used to see and understand these areas prompt the question: What constitutes a site in design?

For the disciplines and professions concerned with design of the physical environment, site matters. Not only are physical design projects always located in a specific place, the work of physical design also necessarily depends on notional understandings about the relationships between a project and a locale. Given that design reconfigures the environment using physical and conceptual means, articulate comprehension of site in physical and conceptual terms should be fundamental. Surprisingly, however, the design field overall has scanty literature directly addressing the subject. This is a striking omission, one that this volume begins to correct.

As exemplified by the Olympic Village proposals, a specific locale provides the material ground for action in design practice, and ideas about site provide a theoretical background against which such actions are taken. Such received understandings of the subject—even if unnoticed, unexamined, or inarticulate—inevitably precede design action.

The word site is actually quite simple; in common parlance, it refers to the ground chosen for something and to the location of some set of activities or practices. Each specialized area of physical design—architecture, landscape architecture, urban design, and urban planning—nevertheless construes the location of its activities and practices overtly and tacitly through its own normative approaches. For example, landscape architecture treats site explicitly as material terrain. Architecture's traditional focus on buildings has led to a tacit focus on the lot as the ground for design intervention. Urban planning, given its concerns beyond the purely physical, tends to construe location more broadly, incorporating social, economic, and political concerns. Urban design, more recently established as a field, tends to borrow notions about site from the other areas of design, drawing upon the material specificity associated with landscape architecture and architecture as well as the broader, less physical concerns of planning.

The multiplicity of comprehensions about the subject of site has rarely been made explicit. Within each of the design specialty areas can be found literature on specific locales and projects. However, even internally, none of the design areas has systematically treated "thinking about sites" in a disciplinary sense, and certainly not in reference to allied areas or to other disciplines, which also comprehend this fundamental topic in different ways. Little has changed in the thirty years since Amos Rapoport, noted the absence of this subject in design theory: "I am not certain that any consistent theory of site as a form determinant has ever been proposed."[4] Without making claim for consistent theory, this anthology ushers the subject of site out of its theoretical and historiographical obscurity.

While consistent in its avoidance of site-related issues, the past thirty years have, nevertheless, seen substantial changes in the direction of design theory discourse. Architectural theory, in particular, has become evermore disassociated from the consideration of physical conditions, veering toward a progressively abstract array of concerns. This shift—due in part to increased contact with other disciplines including philosophy and literary theory—has both enriched and impoverished architectural thinking. In joining, and at times initiating, a shift from modernist to postmodernist thought, architectural discourse has become more rigorous, broad, and inclusive. But at the same time, the fundamental unity between theory and practice has been discounted.

Theory specialists have emerged seeking status as distinct from professional practitioners, and design discourse has suffered from contention born of hardening the line between theorizing and practicing.[5] Stressing the fundamental integration of theory and practice, this volume engages in and promotes thinking through practices themselves. As editors we conceive of theorizing in general as "both an abstraction from, and an enrichment of, concrete experience."[6] Methodologically, concrete theorizing recognizes theoretical activity as itself a practice and considers any reflective practice to be necessarily informed by theory. Though concrete theory might derive from (or criticize) canonical texts, it can also rise from questions posed by practical activity. Concrete theory can begin by elucidating design ideas and exploring their manifestations in practice; or it might begin in the articulation of that which practice has already appropriated in reality; or it can find its sources in abstraction in order to arrive at the "reproduction of the concrete by way of thought."[7] In this approach, design action and design philosophy take place in the same realm, one not dissociable from the realm of political thought and political action. We agree with Antonio Gramsci that the philosophy of each person "is contained in its entirety in [her] political action."[8]

This book explores and critically discerns how sites are engaged by, and conceptualized through, design. As editors, our overall intention is twofold: to lay out what we think site means, and to explore how these meanings inform thinking about specific sites as places for design action. We tie thinking about site as a conceptual construct—"site thinking"—to the grounded site as a physical condition—"thinking about a site."

WHAT IS A SITE?

In design discourse, a site too often is taken as a straightforward entity contained by boundaries that delimit it from the surroundings. This oversimplified understanding has arguable basis, as every work of physical design focuses on spatially finite places. The great majority of professional commissions begin not only with a client, but also with a pre-designated lot owned or controlled by that client. In this sense, designers often receive a site as a delimited given entity. Design pedagogy traditionally has mirrored this aspect of practice. A majority of design studio courses, even those working with hypothetical problems, assign specific locations to students as fixed constraints, so that the locale for academic projects also seems delimited and pre-determined. Practice and pedagogy reinforce similar tacit understandings of site as a circumscribed physical area given *a priori*. Though generally accepted, perhaps for reasons of expediency, such an approach to the site in design misses much. It suggests that designers have no role to play in determining sites and, conversely, that the determination of a site does not bear on matters of design consideration. By implication, it minimizes the consequentiality of factors that inform site choice. By association it similarly brackets out the set of design concerns conventionally and misleadingly referred to as pre-design issues, including also program, financing, and other strategic factors that shape and structure a project. More profoundly, still, it occludes the fact that a site is defined by those holding the power to do so. Indeed, all other discussions of site follow from that structural certainty.

At the same time, existing physical conditions have an enormous influence on ensuing design proposals—both academic and professional—and the final form of built works. Landform and land itself can become the focus of design. Some projects—such as Frank Lloyd Wright's Falling Water or the Quinta da Conceiçao Swimming Pool by Alvaro Siza—gain renown for forceful, direct engagement with

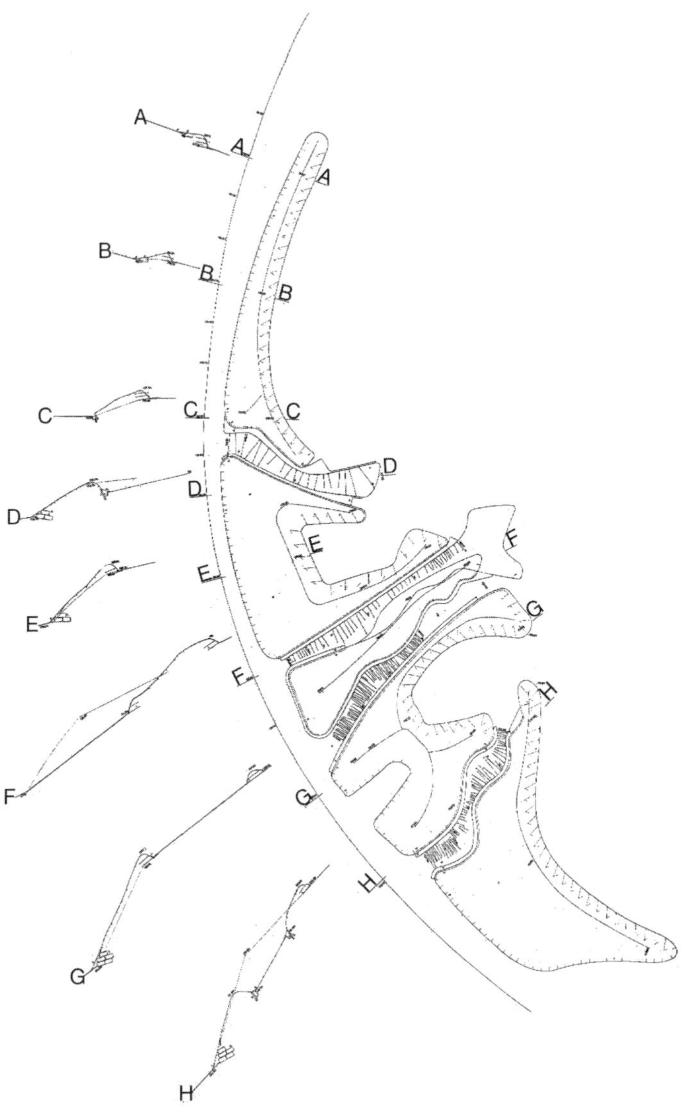

Enric Miralles/Carme Pinos, "Tiro con Arco Competition," Archery Range, Barcelona. Plan and section of entry ramp and earth berming.

geological and hydrological conditions. Such features, along with orientation, topography, and drainage, connect to larger systems that operate in various ways at multiple scales—the solar system, geomorphology, and the water cycle. Any place registers tangible certain aspects of many larger more spatially extensive patterns, orders, and systems. Design can modify site features in relation to larger patterns: vegetation can shade the sun, topographies might be altered, and watercourses might be channeled, buried, or unearthed. Cities—such as New Orleans, Prague, and Boston—reshape the edge between land and water. Channeled watercourses in the Florida Everglades create sinkholes. The *Grands Projets* in Paris, located to spur development, affect urban growth. Each built project creates new forces within its own area and also modifies and influences systems that both reach beyond the site and operate within it.

Conceived over time this way, the site has three distinct areas. The first, most obvious one, is the area of control, easy to trace in the property lines designating legal metes and bounds. The second, encompassing forces that act upon a plot without being confined to it, can be called the area of influence. Third is the area of effect—the domains impacted following design action. These three territories overlap despite their different geographies and temporalities. The area of control—most commonly referred to in design discourse by the term site—describes the most limited field spatially and temporally. Forces within it predate design action. Lying outside direct design control, the areas of influence and effect situate design actions in relation to wider processes including the often-unpredictable change propelled by design intervention. All three areas exist squarely within the domain of design concerns.

To be controlled or owned, the physical site needs delimitation; however to be understood in design, it must be considered extensively in reference to its setting. No particular locale can be experienced in isolation. Embedded in comprehension of a contained parcel is contact with something tangibly much greater. The concept of site, then, simultaneously refers to seemingly opposite ideas: a physically specific place and a spatially and temporally expansive surround. Incorporating three distinct geographic areas, two divergent spatial ideas, and past, present, and future timeframes, sites are complex.

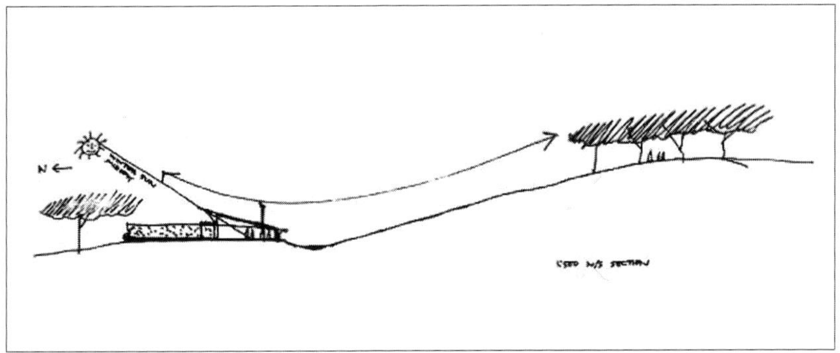

Glenn Murcutt, Meagher House, New South Wales, Australia. Sketch showing siting of house in relation to prevailing winds, topography, and seasonal changes in sun shading requirements.

Language reflects this inherent complexity. A variety of closely associated terms address different aspects of physical location. Place, property, ground, setting, context, situation, landscape: the idea of site might embrace each of these. Though often used interchangeably, none of them are exactly equivalent.[9] Neither mutually exclusive nor simply commensurate, each term invokes an identifiable region in the conceptual territory of site. With temporal, cultural, ideological, perceptual, scalar, and ontological dimensions, this territory is a culturally rich construct. Its abundant associative meanings—sponsored by many applications in design discourse, synonyms, and denotations—remain tightly interwoven. Site resonates on multiple registers and its multivalence yields varied outcomes.

On a practical level, discourse on the subject evolves independently within disciplines and their areas. Recent writings on landscape architecture have begun to open it to new depths of theoretical inquiry. The social sciences have abundant literature, particularly in urban geography, on the contested concept of place. In architecture and urban design, notions of context have received substantial critical attention since gaining currency almost forty years ago (as Sandy Isenstadt discusses in this volume). These efforts shed light on the subject of site, but only obliquely, as a secondary or corollary concern arising out of lines of investigation into other, already inherently complex design concepts or practices.

Important site issues likewise remain unearthed in current design movements. Though rarely framed as site matters per se, these movements nevertheless revolve around concerns relating to locale. Initiatives in smart growth, sustainable design, generic urbanism, or neotraditional urbanism all draw upon and propose notions of place-making. Grappling with site-based issues evokes the analogy of seven blind men describing an elephant: each depicts vivid aspects within reach but none correlates to another, and altogether they miss the sense of the overall object of study. In taking much for granted, each one leaves a great deal of knowledge unarticulated. To shape an identifiable discourse that stakes out the site as an object of design concern and a subject of theoretical study requires that site knowledge and its sources become more explicit.

This call for site knowledge echoes similar calls in other fields. In science, debate and critique of scientific objectivity have lead to lengthy explorations of standpoint theories, which argue that knowledge articulated from the standpoint of those excluded from ruling relations of power is particularly important, especially as a source of potential assessment, change, and renewal. In politics, critiques of the curious double-ness of the autonomous but universalist man constructed by the liberal–democratic social contract point out that the necessary isolation of such an entity obscures the situated condition of its existence. In philosophy, value-free assumptions in both empiricism and idealism come under critique because the notion of "value-free" denies history. In the social science debate regarding quantitative and qualitative methodology, the latter argues that verisimilitude, repeatability, and enumeration evade the contextual pressures of living. In each case, the obscured, evaded, denied, excluded, or situated knowledge has no authority, and indeed, often, has no words. The critiques delineate tacit knowledge of various kinds, and all recognize the need to work on words to bring those unspoken understandings into communication.[10]

SHAPING AN IDENTIFIABLE DISCOURSE

An inquiry into tacit knowledge about site in design, this anthology brings into evidence received ideas, embedded assumptions, and implied formulations. Creating a framework for thinking and designing begins here by foregrounding the unexamined background knowledge on which thought figures out. For example, architects know that the surrounding physical context impacts on a site; landscape architects know that ecology cannot be ignored; planners know that sites are socially produced. But have they always known these things? When and why do concerns become site matters?

Three premises inform this book. First, site knowledge, even if unspoken, exerts a powerful force in design that theoretical inquiry should acknowledge and critically assess. Second, historiography has sanctioned particular ways of engaging with site matters, and the deleterious effects of these sanctions should be recognized and countered. Third, modes of representation construe sites, and their formative role in the production of site knowledge should be revealed and expressed.

Design does not simply impose on a place. Site and designer engage in dialogic interaction. At once extrinsic and intrinsic, a site exists out there in the world but acquires design meaning only through its apprehension, intellectually and experientially. Therefore, we claim the site as a relational construct that acquires meaning and value through situational interaction and exchange. This relational condition of the site derives from uninterrupted exchange between the real and the representational, the extrinsic and the intrinsic, the world and the world-as-known.[11]

Site thinking provides the means whereby these exchanges are construed and comprehended. As a form of knowing, site thinking is concretely situated, more interactive than abstract, and less concerned with the semantic content of knowledge than with a concern for relationships among knowers and known. The site provides for a situation that guides what knowers do and how the known responds and can be understood. Site thinking understands knowledge as embedded within specific ways of engaging the world.

This collection does more than simply address subject matter related to site. Each essay herein treats thinking about site as integral to the design process, each provides insights on how ideas about site have developed historiographically or theoretically, based on where and when they arose. The various perspectives included here invite comparative reading. Some focus on formal and physical constructs, some address discursive material, and others examine processes and practices, including design strategies. All deal with examples of the ways that site knowledge arises from, and applies to, physical conditions confronted in design. In so doing, they demonstrate the ways that site knowledge is derived and concretized.

Theorizing site thinking involves critically examining ideological, historical, and disciplinary frameworks to discern the sources of unarticulated knowledge and the ends to which it is put. We begin with basic questions. How are sites defined? How is value assigned to a site? How do meanings accumulate around the notion of site? Where do they come from, how are they applied, and how are they derived?

Pursuing these questions opens up and legitimizes to serious inquiry both site thinking and thinking about sites. It elevates site (long kept out of the picture, literally) to a new level of visibility. Tracing the web of constructed relationships that ties ideas to things, this critical process scrutinizes the intertwining of conceptual and material dimensions of site. At issue is the concerted operation of concepts, instruments and methodologies that influence design disciplines and practices. Which ideas associate with the concept of site? What projects enter the historical record? How do property laws evolve? In which ways do professionals establish their expertise? How is data collected and graphically represented? The accepted meanings of site and its perceived design value depend on the answers to such questions—on the sources that produce definitions of site.

In design terms, site definition is process driven. It involves detailing physical particulars (for example, itemizing material conditions, characterizing experiential qualities, and surveying topography). It also demands specifying spatial locations—delimiting the exact areas where design activity will take place and deciding upon the contexts within which actions will be considered relevant (referred to above as areas of influence and effect and by Peter Marcuse as the "physical area of concerns"). This definitional work can occur through various means. Those explored here derive from instrumental influences that shape design ideas about site: discourse, instruments of representation, physical material contact, and forms of professional practices.

Discourse provides concepts that help shape thought. The invention—or discarding—of words in any language transforms the way speakers perceive, conceptualize, and engage their world. Language related to site continually evolves. Terminology falls out of use (as Robin Dripps points out about the Beaux-Arts term *tirer parti*) or enters the design lexicon (Kristina Hill gives the example of "resilience," a term borrowed from ecology), marking changes in the very process of defining and therefore thinking about sites.

Instruments of representation allow developments in techniques of description. Graphic tools inform and bracket how designers think. Thought is both allowed and constrained by formats (plans, sections, maps, photography, video, and use schedules), scale and scope, and informational frames of reference (types and choices of data). When a model, drawing, or diagram that includes information from outside the bounds of the plot (adjacent structures), temporal phenomena (hundred-year flood lines), or otherwise hidden factors (subterranean toxic plumes), assimilates situational influences to the site to support relational understandings. Omitting such information has the opposite effect.

Physical material contact delivers experience and perception. Direct material physical encounter with sights, sounds, smells, and textures yields yet another body of site knowledge (haecceity, as Elizabeth Meyer calls it) bracketed through subjective experiences of phenomena. Recording seasonal or daily changes in light quality, for example, introduces into site thinking a temporal dimension. The professionalized and disciplined practices of architects, planners, landscape architects, and urbanists (techniques of analysis, data collection processes, etc.) also lends identity to a site, since design actions are themselves definitive acts.

Forms of professional practice establish horizons of operation. Working knowledge of a particular place derives from abstract concepts, material conditions, and structuring practices, which are always intercalated, inflecting on and infecting one another rather than remaining separate or distinct. For a design professional, what matters about a locale slated for design action—what will be considered useful or valuable about a site—depends on how knowledge of site is framed. Developers might apply financial models, analyzing a parcel's potential to provide profitable returns in an economically construed context (the site defined in fiscal terms). Landscape architects might consider ecological measures (the site defined in terms of resilience or sustainability). Architects might focus on physical forms and built patterns (the site defined in morphological terms). Each engages in different forms of site knowledge that yield site readings. In design theory and practice, the range and variety of possible readings too rarely has been made clear.

The different perspectives these essays impart on the constructedness of site, and the challenges that its relational condition poses for design, reflect differences in the various disciplinary frameworks within the broad field of physical and environmental design. A complex interplay of forces (natural and physical, discursive and narrative, and social and cultural) brings site knowledge into being. Foregrounding this interplay underscores the constructedness of site. Opening a window onto some of the other things (places, times, instruments, and concepts) that structure the relational condition of site, situates the process of site thinking itself.

Connecting sites and settings not only bears upon the consideration of physical locales, it applies equally to theorizing genres of site thinking. That ideas regarding site come from many sources provides motive for a multi-disciplinary approach. Site thinking, like thinking in general, is necessarily situationally bound. Different stocks of site knowledge derive from recognized disciplinary settings that attribute value to ideas, practices, and things based on internalized measures. Different disciplinary backgrounds ascribe significance to specific limited perspectives, bracketing thinking according to their own interests. The placement of these brackets, in turn, signals the existence of "habits of mind," those horizons—or limitations—to imagination that *discipline* thought. The collection reaches beyond individual disciplinary confines because the subject of site is not bound to any one area, but in fact provides literal and conceptual common ground across the entire design field.

STRANDS OF SITE THINKING

The range of issues and topics touched on in this anthology reconfirms the multivalence of the concept of site. Nevertheless, three identifiable strands of site thinking stand out. The first concerns vocabulary: the terms and concepts normally drawn upon to talk about site. The second deals with history: how site-oriented issues, design processes, and the siting of specific projects are treated by the historiographical record. The third strand investigates the manifestation and derivation of site-related design practices.

Concepts, Terms, and Vocabulary

> For the most part, we do not first see and then define, we define first and then see. In the great blooming buzzing confusion of the outer world we pick out what our culture has already defined for us, and we tend to perceive that which we have picked out in the form stereotyped for us by our culture.[12]

While site discourse would appear at first glance to consist of a rich set of terms, in fact, this vocabulary has not been sufficiently examined. The idea itself commands a wide lexical domain inhabited by synonyms that are not actually synonymous. In this sense, site discourse is largely *terra incognita*, since it offers few options to qualify site study approaches or name design strategies.

Our interest in defining site does not presume to attach fixed meanings to words. The focus on language strives instead to clarify how the idea derives its meaning in combination with a host of other concepts, each of which singly suggests a region within a larger conceptual territory. This territory, long perceived primarily in terms of obvious similarities, is in fact replete with subtle distinctions that, charted out, have the potential to order new levels of theoretical understanding and new approaches to design practices.

Examining the language of site can open up existing vocabulary and add to this vocabulary. It is more than simply a linguistic exercise. The work of unpacking received terms and parsing out their different meanings forms a crucial part of a broader endeavor to nuance the conceptual foundations of design. Historical and contemporary connotations of frequently associated terms—such as "property," "landscape," and "context"—vary widely; as potent and distinct frames of reference influencing design practices, these variations beg closer examination. New vocabulary suggests new directions for future site thinking. Terms—such as "area of concern," "site reach," and "urban constellation"—challenge the very possibility of a site fully under design control. Qualifiers ("stealthy" versus "opportunistic" site strategies; site as "framework," "armature," "figure," or "fragment") add precision to accounts of specific design projects, site reading, and design practices. Inventive language enriches site discourse and, at times, promises a wider impact. New descriptors applied to existing built conditions (the inside-out site and site-sequencing, for example, coined by Paul Hess in his discussion of suburban settlement patterns) make it possible to identify features of the built environment previously left unrecognized for lack of adequate language. The notion of "site suppression" (invented by Wendy Redfield to evoke a repressive role of modern design historiography with respect to site matters) has potentially profound implications not only for the reassessment of specific modernist works of design, but for a broad critical re-appraisal of modern design practice and theory as a whole.

The Subject of Site Historically Considered

> The politics of disciplinization, conceived as all disciplinization must be, as a set of negations, consists in what it marks out for repression for those who wish to claim the authority of discipline itself for their learning.[13]

Modernist design history, and in particular that of modern architecture, is remarkable for its sustained disregard of site-related issues.[14] The written record of individual works presents countless examples in texts and graphics confined almost exclusively to the project itself or, at best, to its directly adjacent physical context. Through this extremely bracketed approach, modernist design history conveys the strong, albeit tacit, conviction that sites are simple, bounded entities.

In design history, the site has been de-natured (engaged as formal surface); mythologized (emptied of meaning); and colonized (subjected to the singular authority of design controls). This history offers few images, few tools, and few models for capturing the relationship between a project and its locale. Such accounting—or, more accurately, "discounting"—amounts to a long-standing repression of site matters. A close look at the canon in design history shows that it largely excludes tendencies toward site thinking.

A link exists between modernist design history's distaste for engaging with tradition and the omission of site-related ideas from the modern historiographical record. Revisiting projects *in situ* demonstrates that, in fact, the relationship between a project and its locale lies within the actual—if not historically authorized—array of modernist design concerns. Exposing the kind of data, methods and analytic tools that instigate specific ways of seeing (or not seeing) sites allows those methods to be recalibrated, making more accurate descriptions possible. New histories focused expressly on site analysis and site design practices bring to light long-overlooked but crucial aspects of the design process.

The received historical record puts forward a well-worn narrative that casts modernist design as predisposed to treat specific sites as idealized and universal; it consistently eschews the subject's cultural thickness and conceptual intricacy. By effectively eliminating the complexity of the subject from view, this version of history suggests that positive value adheres to sites only when they can be made amenable to simple classification and control. This predilection arises not from within design disciplines, but more broadly out of post-enlightenment thought. Site thinking throws down powerful challenge to a modern epistemological framework that privileges clear categorization.[15] At once a real construct (of nature), a narrated construct (of discourse), and a collective construct (socially constituted), site presents a potent example of hybridity. Any attempt to meaningfully address its many registers of significance demands a constant crossing of knowledge categories. Site thinking must continually oscillate between material and conceptual, abstract and physical, discursive and experiential, and general and specific points of view.

Between the Particular and the Universal

> Local uniqueness matters…Spatial differentiation, geographical variety, is not just an outcome; it is integral to the reproduction

> of society and its dominant social relations. The challenge is to hold the two sides together; to understand the general underlying causes while at the same time recognizing and appreciating the importance of the specific and unique.[16]

Twentieth-century views on modernity drew on arguments whose basic forms were established during the late-eighteenth and early-nineteenth centuries in the encounter between the Enlightenment conception of a human science and its critics. Enlightenment scholars described historical (and geographical) diversity via a de-centered, universalistic view of human nature. Critics of the Enlightenment characterized this variation in a centered, particularistic manner, emphasizing the individuality of cultural communities.

Aspects of both views were interwoven in late-nineteenth- and early-twentieth-century social thought. (For example, German liberal theorists associated with the "return to Kant" sought, in part, to accommodate the provincialism of national culture groups to the cosmopolitanism of Kant.) The tension between a de-centered universalism and a centered particularism appears in the epistemological discussions of the historical (and situated) individual. In fact, Enlightenment scholars, including Voltaire and Hume, expressed concern that the historical individuality of cultures went overlooked—obscured, in their view, by tendencies to cast the universalism of Enlightenment thought and the particularism associated with its critics in dichotomous terms. The methodological problem is to account for individuality in terms of universal concepts. Nineteenth-century critics (as well as Enlightenment scholars) failed to resolve how "historical particulars" were "to be placed within a conceptual order without violating their individuality."[17]

This same problem arises in the study of physical particulars of place, site, or region. Geographers have sought to create a science of place that recognizes both the diversity and the particularity of the way in which different cultures adapt to their environments. Geographers—as well as theorists and many designers—have valued the local and made it an object of scientific study, but generally from the cosmopolitan perspective of modern science. This neat meta-level distinction between the form and the content of investigations belies a confused relation between the universalizing and the particularizing discourses that characterize the study of places. The scientific search for universals seems to trivialize the interest in the particularity of specific sites, and the demand for universal ethical principles appears to undermine the significance of the moral particularity associated with the individual's attachment to locale and community.

Nevertheless, as agents, individuals are always "situated" in the world. The significance of place in modern life is associated with this fact of situatedness and the closely allied issues of identity and action. This aspect of human existence cannot be fully appreciated from the distant and detached viewpoint associated with scientific theorizing. To do so requires generalizing the specificity of place into a set of generic categories or reducing the richness of specific milieus as context or setting to the more limited sense of place as locations. But to understand site as context or setting forces recognition that, from the objective viewpoint of the theorist, no essence or universal site structure exists to be uncovered or discovered.

Understanding site must draw on both an objective reality and a subjective perception. From the de-centered vantage point of the theoretical scientist, site becomes either location or a set of generic relations and thereby loses much of its significance for human action. From the centered viewpoint of the subject, site has meaning in relation to an individual's (or a group's) basic worldview and social situation.

The specificity of site is understood from a point of view, and for this reason a student of site must rely upon forms of analysis that lie between the centered and de-centered view. Such forms might be described as situated knowledges or as narrative-like syntheses. Such a stance is less detached than that of the theoretical scientist and more detached than experiential or cognitive description. These distinct positions, which blend together in experience, illustrate the relative differences in the representation of site that result from the process of seeking a de-centered perspective versus one that attempts to mediate the views of the (anthropological) insider and the outsider.

Site is best viewed from points in between.

THE ESSAYS

To comprehend site requires many horizons of understanding—historical, philosophical, rhetorical, legal; analytic, formal, descriptive, aesthetic; strategic, tactical; social, economic, political. The essays included here draw upon all of these, and more. Each adopts a distinct point of departure to examine site as a culturally constructed relation. So doing, the collection provides one possible register of the range of concepts, issues, and practices that can properly be deemed site-related matters for design.

Overlapping

The book is organized around three overlapping groupings. Each functions like a lens to focus on an area of theorizing. The first addresses concepts, terms, and vocabulary; the second revisits and (re)writes history to measure the degree of importance—or irrelevance—of site matters for design; the third speaks to the relationship between techniques of representation, methods of study, and strategic approaches to design. A photo essay, curated by Lucy R. Lippard, opens the book. This portfolio of images and commentary signals the importance of creative work and critical discourse on site specificity in contemporary art. It also forecasts many of the themes developed in subsequent texts.

The opening grouping (directly following Lippard's contribution) parses the language typically used to qualify meanings of site. The first pair of essays by Harvey Jacobs and Robert Beauregard bring nuance and precision to words aligned with the most common connotation of the term site, as a localized physical entity. Hewing closely to the understanding of site as a limited place or piece of property and accepting its association with concepts of property and place, they turn attention to how the concept is constituted, and to what ends. Using history, Jacobs traces the evolving social meaning of the concept of property and, in so doing, throws the stability of property-based definitions of site into question. Beauregard problematizes the presumed synonyms *place* and *site* by interrogating narratives that set up specific locales for proposed design actions. Their examinations reveal a disciplinary predilection on the part of planning discourse to employ socioeconomic and political frameworks to construct site. Using different tactics, both authors open up contemporary discourse on site.

The next pairing augments the discourse of theory by supplementing its current lexicon with new terms. Robin Dripps revives the historical notion of *tirer parti* to qualify an approach to site thinking that assigns value to the physical ground as a font of design ideas. Elizabeth Meyer introduces notions of site as armature, figure, fragment, and haecceity. This new vocabulary, derived from close analysis of actual designed landscapes, works both as an analytical tool for interpretation and as a conceptual tool to structure design processes. Dripps and Meyer both assume a point of departure that reflects concern for the material and the experiential aspects of site, a habit of mind associated with the disciplines of architecture and landscape design. They base their respective discussions on *ground* and *landscape* in an understanding of site that reaches beyond the narrow confines of given places and legally defined property. In fact, Dripps directly challenges what Jacobs and Beauregard accept as given—that site refers to a spatially contained parcel of land. (Despite this significant difference, the attention Dripps pays to the experiential and material fullness of the ground reprises, through a different lens, Beauregard's assertion that sites are never empty.) The first set of essays concludes with two explorations of context, one from a disciplinary perspective and the other in historical terms. Kristina Hill shows how shifts in intellectual contexts shape design approaches, and in particular how recent developments in ecological sciences sponsor reconsideration of what might properly be considered the site in design. Sandy Isenstadt brings attention to what lies beyond a lot or parcel. Not primarily focused on the question of language per se, Isenstadt draws careful distinctions between context as an issue for design theory, the context as physical fabric, and, finally, the notion of site.

The six essays that examine histories of site thinking illustrate specific instances of the phenomenon identified by Wendy Redfield as site suppression (four belong as well to the first group). This second set revisits modernist design historiography to confront its depletions and expose its repressive force; this set contributes new history and new models for thinking about and acting on sites. As part of an effort to characterize sites as generative ground, Dripps retrieves a potent concept for site thinking from the early-nineteenth-century French architect and theorist, Quatremère de Quincy. Meyer delves into late-nineteenth-century and early-twentieth-century texts on landscape design to derive inventive models for interpreting, conceiving, and strategically engaging sites today. Hill writes a history of the recent past, looking at the influence of ecological science on contemporary landscape design practices. Isenstadt enlarges the historical record by tracing the lines of design debates around the issue of context, from its introduction as a corrective for the anti-historical claims in the 1960s of modernist architecture and urban design through to the 1990s. An architectural historian, Isenstadt illuminates the temporal dimension of site thinking. Both Wendy Redfield and Paul Hess (the last to focus directly on modernist history) interrogate its repressive effects with the conviction that close attention to the built historical record can bring into visibility what the written historical record obscures. Redfield takes on one of the most commanding figures in modern architecture. Her site-based readings of Atelier Ozenfant and Maisons La Roche-Jeanneret, early projects by Le Corbusier, offer a sharply contrasting view on the received knowledge of modernism to that presented by Isenstadt. Redfield raises a significant challenge to normative assumptions about Le Corbusier's self-proclaimed and historically inscribed disinterest in site-specificity. Similarly debunking a historically construed understanding of site, Hess challenges the presumption that post-war American suburban settlement fabric should be understood as comprised simply of single-family houses.

Hess and Redfield can also be read as belonging in the final grouping in the anthology, that ties a theoretical concern about site theory to the material fact that all physical design projects are situated in particular locales. These five essays consider site thinking in methodological terms, examining tools, instruments, and modes of representation through studies of specific design projects, site analysis methods, and site design processes. All the essays share a project-based approach to re-thinking site, elaborated through close attention to actual drawings, buildings, and settlement patterns, again spanning historical and present-day examples. Redfield's careful analysis of two Le Corbusier houses—the architecture, construction sites, and fabric of the urban surrounds—proffers a revised understanding of the buildings themselves, and demonstrates the substantial influence of site conditions on the process of their design. Hess makes a critique of conventional methods of census data collection as the information base that grounds received ideas of suburbs and, so doing, foregrounds the role of representation as a mode of site knowledge. Peter Marcuse examines the highly charged development site of the World Trade Center disaster. Carol Burns probes the notion of the *high performance site* to examine the site as a medium and as an agent of performance. Andrea Kahn draws on New York City to examine processes of site definition in the field of urban design, arguing for situationally derived models of site thinking.

In his Afterword, "Engaging the Field," William Sherman talks to the timeliness of a volume on the subject of site. Why does site matter now? In this era, epistemologically, knowledge is emerging with particular force in a frontier between well-established fields. Energetic scholarship today finds material in the thresholds that have, in the recent past, distinguished and separated areas of specialized knowledge. Within the modern university, new institutional structures to support emerging research between departments are called, revealingly, centers. The design fields today are undergoing such transformation, and boundaries have begun to blur between well-defined disciplinary subspecialties. Sherman describes and advocates for potential institutional innovation, drawing on initiatives at the University of Virginia to combine academic departments. Many types of new academic programs are being formed—including innovative hybrid, merged or double degree programs—that open fresh perspectives for research and teaching.[18] As new allegiances are forged, new kinds of design practices are developing.

In this context, site provides a potent locus for the production of knowledge and the redefinition of disciplines. The common ground that it affords—materially and intellectually—prompts a recalibration of relations between all whose work concerns the physical environment. Within the more specialized arena of architecture, foregrounding site as a subject of inquiry and a domain of action becomes part of a larger contemporary critique of the isolated, autonomous object in design.

The site knowledge presented here can shed new light on the past as well as provide frameworks for future developments. It also necessarily points to how much about site remains to be explored. This collection only begins to deal with the full range of ideas and things that might rightfully be deemed site matters for design. It encompasses material, conceptual, and methodological concerns to convey the complexity of site thinking. It comprehends site on the levels of theory and practice simultaneously, to abstract from and enrich concrete experience in the design field as a whole. Starting with design, these explorations reach out to encompass the world beyond design.

Notes

1. The five exhibited teams were led by Henning Larsens Tegnestue A/S (Denmark); Morphosis (Los Angeles); MVRDV (the Netherlands); Smith-Miller + Hawkinson (New York City); and Zaha Hadid Architects (London).
2. See Herbert Muschamp, "Let the Design Sprint Begin," March 11, 2004, Section F, House and Home *New York Times* http://www.nyc2012.com/village_finalists/zaha.html.
3. Descriptions from the official NYC 2012 Website http://www.nyc2012.com/village_finalists.
4. Amos Rapoport, *House Form and Culture* (Englewood Cliffs: Prentice-Hall, 1969), 28.
5. Separation of theory and practice may also be accompanied by classism, even if perhaps unconscious: "It is essential to educate the educator himself. [Their] doctrine must, therefore, divide society into two parts one of which is superior to society." Karl Marx, "Theses of Feuerbach," in Karl Marx and Frederick Engels, *The German Ideology,* ed. C. J. Arthur (New York: International Publishers, 1970), 121.
6. David Tracy, *Plurality and Ambiguity: Hermeneutics, Religion and Hope* (San Francisco: Harper and Rowe, 1987), 9.
7. Karl Marx, *Grundrisse,* tr. M. Nicolaus (Middlesex: Penguin Books 1973), 100–101.
8. Antonio Gramsci, *Selections from the Prison Notebooks,* tr. Quinton Hoare and Geoffrey Nowell Smith (New York: International Publishers, 1971), 324.
9. See Carol J. Burns, "On Site" in ed. A. Kahn, *Drawing/Building/Text* (New York: Princeton Architectural Press, 1991).
10. Lynette Hunter, *Critiques of Knowing: Situated Textualities in Science, Computing, and the Arts* (London, Routledge, 1999), 2.
11. This idea of uninterrupted exchange comes from Bahktin's work on the dialogic imagination: "However forcefully the real and the represented world resist fusion, however immutable the presence of that categorical boundary line between them, they are nevertheless indissolubly tied up with each other and find themselves in continual mutual interaction, uninterrupted exchange

goes on between them..." M. M. Bahktin, *The Dialogic Imagination*, tr. C. Emerson and M. Holquist (Austin: University of Texas Press, 1981), 254.

12. Walter Lippman, *Public Opinion* (1922) as cited by Stanley Aronowitz, "Is a Democracy Possible?" in *The Phantom Public Sphere*, ed. B. Robbins (Minneapolis: University of Minnesota Press, 1993), 78.
13. Hayden White, "Historical Interpretation," *Critical Inquiry* 9:1 (September 1982), 119.
14. For a clear omission of site as a design concept, see the "Index of Concepts," in Sigfried Giedion, *The Eternal Present Volume II: The Beginnings of Architecture* (New York: Pantheon Books, 1964).
15. Bruno Latour, *We Have Never Been Modern*, tr. Catherine Porter (Cambridge: Harvard University Press, 1993), 6.
16. Doreen Massey, *Spatial Divisions of Labor: Social Structures and the Geography of Production* (New York: Methuen, 1984), 299–300.
17. Steven Seidman, *Liberalism and the Origins of European Social Theory* (Berkeley: University of California Press, 1983.)
18. For example, at the University of Virginia, the separate departments of Architecture and Landscape Architecture were restructured in 2003 to form one faculty; at Washington University, in St. Louis, an urban design program dating back to the early 1960s has, since 1999, undergone a significant reorganization to integrate courses in landscape, architecture and infrastructure in order to establish a curriculum dedicated to the study and design of the Metropolitan Landscape; and, since the late 1990s, students can get degrees in Landscape Urbanism at various institutions, including the University of Chicago and the Architectural Association in London.

1

Around the Corner: A Photo Essay

Lucy R. Lippard

Buildings are usually constructed to be seen frontally, but sites are more elusive. Few present themselves head-on. Around the corner, in the distance, even out of sight, they conspire to illusion. The viewer's mobility is inevitable, the viewer's experience of a place is inarguable, but the site is not static either. Expectations of the site can affect what happens there. So seeing *through* a site is a necessity. A site is a half-full, half-empty container, its content(s) visible to some and invisible to others. We choose the lenses and then the frames. When a site is *exposed*, it's the last time we'll see *into* it.

When is a site not a site? When there is nothing on it? What constitutes "nothing"? Something that was or never was? The ripple effect: The best way to know a site is to move out from it in varying radiuses. When the ripples subside into the surface, or into the depths, it fades. Or, going the other direction, once you penetrate to the urban core, there may be a hole at the center: ground zero, the site *of*...

Like everything else, a site is defined not merely by its "own" qualities and quantities but by those of its neighbors. When the surroundings change, the site and what has been built on it change too. Open may become closed; closed may become open; tall may become ordinary; striking contrasts may be obliterated. Views *of* (the outside) and views *from* (the inside) can contradict each other. Every window offers a new angle on the surroundings, and the site itself is sucked into the kaleidoscope. Landscape features are notorious shape-changers.

As one comes around the corner, the site itself seems to move, or even unravel. Urban sites are seen on the run, or the fast walk. Rural sites seen from a car are a photographic blur of allusion. Walking makes them more real.

However much "place" is downplayed in favor of generic space, to ignore it means to create a placeless space. Site-specific is not the same as place-specific. The site's narrative can be downplayed but never entirely erased. The site is the past, and what will happen on it is the future. The present mediates. It makes history.

The grid is beloved by Americans for its comfort, legal clarity, and aesthetics. Breaking the grid is still acknowledging the grid as master. Around the corner, one of those modules is being filled—real estate simmering over the invisible flame of context.

Some of the following images suggest the secrets of places that are so naked or so bundled up in disguise that we can barely see their subtexts, their "true" characters. These images are fragments and/or illusions of sites, some enhanced by artists trying to see through them, contributing to the definition of site by evading it.

SOMETHING OUT THERE / NOTHING OUT THERE

Wanda Hammerbeck
Something Out There, Nothing Out There
Dunes, Idaho
1990

The "naked" landscape suggests content and lack thereof; the desert has long been perceived as a *tabula rasa* on which humans impose their greed and desires. This hole at the center is an apparently transparent site, but there may be a gas station just out of the frame. Maybe it will stay the same for millennia; maybe it will be inscribed soon. Everywhere in the West, development is just around the corner. Areas that look just like this are already, almost unimaginably, the sites of resorts, golf courses, or dams.

NATURE/CULTURE

Charles Simonds
Loisaida Growth House
(Altered photograph)
Lower Manhattan, New York
1977

This project for a "Lower East Side Museum" combines, juxtaposes, and superimposes human habitation and native flora (all the hardy vegetation that survives urban life and in turn invades the built environment) as well as fauna (rodents, roaches, feral cats...). On the upper stories, nature would reclaim tenement culture, bursting out of the windows to meet the ground of the vacant lot next door. A ruin disguised as a new landscape.

Agnes Denes
Wheatfield—A Confrontation (The Harvest)
(Two acres of wheat planted and harvested by the artist on the Battery Park landfill in Manhattan's financial district, summer 1982.)
Battery Park Landfill, Downtown Manhattan
1982

The confrontation was both geographical (city/country) and social (given the proximity to the New York Stock Exchange and the World Trade Center, Denes was making a point about world hunger and the exploitation of resources). The artist tilled, sowed, and harvested almost a thousand pounds of wheat on a landfill that was to become high-rise Battery Park City. It was a strangely prophetic homage to natural cycles in an urban landscape that seemed on its way to permanence. Less than twenty years later the Twin Towers vanished.

VISIBILITY/BOUNDARIES

Candace Hill-Montgomery
Black and White Enclosure
(Installation on found site)
Harlem, New York
ca. 1979

When Hill (then Hill-Montgomery) arrived at the site, the boat, an emblem of a certain economic status not usually associated with the inner city, was unexpectedly already on site, high and dry in a Harlem vacant lot. By adding the picket fence, she brought to bear a series of assumptions about class, race, gentrification, imprisonment, and unknown potential. Twenty-five years later that reading of the site may have been confirmed.

Sheila Levrant de Bretteville
Biddy Mason: Time and Place
(Limestone panel and "fossil" picket, details of 82′-long memorial wall)
Downtown Los Angeles
1989

A public art piece by a designer/artist, this wall creates its own memory, on site, commemorating the African Diaspora through the life of a woman born a slave who refused to leave a free state to return to slavery with her master. She remained to become a prominent citizen of black Los Angeles and to live out the Jeffersonian American dream—to own land.

INVISIBILITY

Drex Brooks
Pyramid Lake Battlefield
(Black-and-white photograph)
Pyramid Lake Reservation, Nevada
1988–1989

In May and June 1860, two battles initiated the Paiute resistance to white invasion of their lands. They were subdued and scattered to reservations, not allowed to return to Pyramid Lake until 1883. The prophet Winnemucca had dreamed three times of "women crying and I also saw my men shot down by white people...and I saw the blood streaming from the mouths of my men...." The construction of a children's playground by the descendants of those who died transforms the site of these battles, hope overcoming despair and sacrilege.

John Ammirati
The Plume Project
(Charcoal and water, tested and approved by state ecologists, 560′ × 210′)
State Park land in an industrial area bordering San Francisco Bay
Completed September 1991

This temporary site-specific installation on an urban site already in the process of unraveling was an attempt "to imagine in a giant drawing" one of the Bay Area's several major industrial plumes—invisible underground masses of toxic liquid spreading out over miles from an initial source. The drawing "flowed across property lines and beneath fences," an elusive and mobile site of an ongoing event, although the drawing itself was erased by rain five weeks after installation. (*The Plume Project* was sponsored by the Museo Italo Americano, the California State Department of Parks, the Bayview Opera House, and the San Francisco Arts Commission.)

SITES OF SUSTENANCE

Tom Jones
Ghost Meal
(Black-and-white photograph)
Indian Trust Land, Wisconsin
1999

Jones, a young Ho-Chunk photographer, examines sites of tradition and modernity in his own Wisconsin communities. The path to the jerry-rigged tent is made of sustenance. It leads to a kind of home—temporary, but traditional—a path and a tent that have occurred in this place for perhaps hundreds of years in ever-changing contexts. An unpeopled communal meal calls attention to the land, to the changing but unbuilt site that is of crucial importance to Native peoples.

Nicholas Tobier
Hot Chocolate Cart (in use)
Alfred, New York
2000

Tobier creates and enhances "everyday places" by surprise. (For instance, he has built a structure of wood, Plexiglas, wheels, and rubber floor to encase a public phone and turn it into a private office; as a comment on the ubiquitous facilities for men, he created a prototype for a Ladies Toilet, for use by all genders.) This colorful hot chocolate cart simply appeared on the "cold monochrome days" of winter in western New York State, serving free warmth and sweetness. Its resemblance to an indigenous tent or *yurt* not only transforms the site but comments on monocultural towns and perhaps makes a case for the immigration and cross-cultural vitality that is changing towns across the United States, as well as the possibility of a more caring urban life.

FREEDOMS

Mark Brest van Kampen
Free Speech Monument
Sproul Plaza, UC Berkeley
1991

A unique place that almost does not exist. The site itself is three-dimensional. The winner of a competition for a monument to the Free Speech Movement, it consists of a granite circle surrounding a six-inch circle of bare earth. The text reads: “This soil and the air space extending above it shall not be a part of the nation and shall not be subject to any entity’s jurisdiction.” In the era of the Patriot Act, this five-foot space is the site of absolute freedom, the site to trump all sites, establishing an area permanently out of control.

Blaise Tobia
Untitled (from series *Pillars of the Community*)
(Color photograph)
Detroit, Michigan
1981

Two forms of "obscenity" overlaid on the same site, which is defined by the contrasts between its past and present. Rippling out from this center, the neighborhood and its residents reflect the changes of use in this building. The former Highland State Bank, a minor monument to capitalism, is now an adult movie theater. (One can only guess at the transformation of the interior.) The freedom to profit remains a consistent theme, as does the democratic freedom to exploit others; the "all male" movies and "live show" sites are protected by freedom of speech.

CIVIC BOUNDARIES

Shawn Records
John G. Alibrand Stadium
(Color photograph)
Syracuse, New York
2000

The stadium is the focus in this photo from the series *Points of Interest*, inspired by the photographer's move to Syracuse, New York, from Boise, Idaho, and his attempts to orient himself via the official city map. Using photography and geography as tools, he cites "a mythology of exploration, conquest, and a flawed sense of objective observation…photographs that are both here and there." In this case, *here* is the foreground, an impressive sports stadium, a competitive, and decidedly male space (although a small group of girls stands on the track in the background). *There* is the unexplained pyramid looming in the background, a vanishing "point of interest," barely visible, providing a mysterious context and temporal jolt to an ordinary urban amenity. Off-center but connective, the red carpet leads back into time.

Martha Rosler
Untitled (JFK)
(Color photograph)
New York
1990

The luridly anonymous airport tunnel is a site of controlled and centered mobility, a site–nonsite, a road to nowhere. The airport is a site on the edge, channeling people into abstract space. Eero Saarinen's famous modernism has become vintage, or even primal. Rosler suggests the tunnel resembles, "a hut, a home, a temple, a dome."

NEW NARRATIVES

Michelle van Parys
Future Exhibit
(Black-and-white photograph)
Arizona
1991

A randomly discovered image in the *Scenes from the New West* series contradicts the cherished "timelessness" of western landscape. It leaves to our imaginations what the "exhibit" will be, what new agenda will be staged in this place, which at the moment is more a setting than a site.

Lucy R. Lippard
Monument Valley
(Color photograph)
Navajo Nation near Kayenta, Arizona
2001

Monument Valley has been the site of spectacle and fantasy in endless Hollywood films. Contemporary cowboy and Indian reality is introduced by the "development" in the foreground, federal housing for Navajo.

Charles Keating, Jr., began developing this planned community in the desert near Estrella Mountains while he was the chief executive officer of Lincoln Savings and Loan. In 1989 the bank collapsed due to mismanagement. Estrella was never completed.

Keating was convicted of multiple fraud and racketeering charges and was sentenced to twelve and a half years in prison. Twenty-two thousand of the bank's uninsured depositors, many of them elderly, lost their life savings.

Joel Sternfeld
Estrella Development
(Color photograph)
Near Southern Avenue, Goodyear, Arizona
1995

An apparently "natural" landscape is in fact a multileveled narrative of capitalist ambition and failure. In American myth, the palm tree stands for leisure and tropical pleasures. But this is a landscape of desolation and despair. The grid of subdivision is broken by greed and a modicum of justice.

2

Claiming the Site: Evolving Social–Legal Conceptions of Ownership and Property

Harvey M. Jacobs

When we think and talk about "the site," allowing the concept to form in our minds, we associate it with two ideas. The first is the idea that an isolatable site is owned, and that ownership is identifiable. Whether the ownership unit is a private or public entity (an individual, corporation, government, or some combination of these) is immaterial; what matters is the assumption that a legal someone has control over the site. The second idea is that the owner has a set of rights that may be freely exercised as a function of their ownership: for example, the right to keep others off the site, the right to use the site for the owner's own enjoyment, the right to develop the site, the right to extract profit from the site, and so on.

Commonly understood to be static, these two base ideas have in fact always been issues of intense social contention in the United States. What it means to own and what comprises the rights of ownership have evolved in response to changes in technology and changes in social values and relationships over the course of the nation's existence.

This essay seeks to explicate how we, as owners of, neighbors to, and people concerned about a site, claim it, given changing ideas about ownership and rights. I start deep in American history, with the debates over ownership and rights during the time of the American Revolution. Despite a popular rhetoric that often seeks to simplify this history, what I show is that any contemporary ambiguity about the ideas of ownership and rights is encapsulated in the country's founding national documents. Tracing the ebb and flow of our national social-legal dialogue about ownership and rights through to the present day, the essay closes with some speculations as to how this debate might unfold in the future.

Our ability to claim a site—to act on and toward it—is conditioned on resolving conflicting stakes upon it. Claims are proxies for expressions of ownership and understandings about rights. To the extent that ownership and rights are becoming more fragmented, more social, with more claims by more parties, the ability to act becomes ever more compromised.

The ownership and control of a site—be it an urban or rural property, a place for commercial development or the family farm homestead—is an issue embedded deeply into the American psyche and one that helps to shape and define the American character. American character is hard to summarize, but one important element has to do with the opportunity and the right to own and control land. This quality goes deep into American history itself.

The early political history of the United States is often portrayed as migrations spurred by the issues captured in the First Amendment of the Bill of Rights—a search by oppressed peoples for political freedom (of speech and assembly) and religious freedom. Though these issues were key to colonial immigrations, it is equally true that migration was spurred by a desire for access to freehold land unavailable in Europe. The United States was settled by people, first Europeans but continuing through to immigrants today, searching for religious and political freedom *and* for access to land.[1] It was the promise of land that lured people to risk crossing the ocean and to leave the communities and people that were so dear to them.

In America's early years, western European countries were still structured under the vestiges of feudalism. An elite owned most of the land, and the prospects for the ordinary person to obtain ownership were small. America offered an alternative. Here was a place where any white male immigrant could get ownership of land and use that land as capital to make a future for himself. America was the land of opportunity. To be an American was to own and control private property.

In America's colonial past, the existence of land converged nicely with the new political theories of the period, coming together into ideas about ownership and democracy. As the revolutionary period took shape, influential framers argued that it was as much for the right to own and control land as anything else that the new political experiment—American democracy—was coming into being. James Madison, writing in the *Federalist Paper* No. 54 during the debate about the ratification of the U.S. Constitution, argued that "government is instituted no less for the protection of property than of the persons of individuals."[2] Others, including Alexander Hamilton and John Adams, concurred. Adams, in a fiery set of words, noted that "property must be secured or liberty cannot exist. The moment the idea is admitted into society that property is not as sacred as the laws of God, and that there is not a force of law and public justice to protect it, anarchy and tyranny commence."[3]

According to this perspective, rights to landownership accrued through use, and freely constituted governments (i.e., democracies) existed for the protection of individual liberties, including the liberty to own and use land. The colonists utilized this idea of active use to provide the justification for taking land from America's native inhabitants. They did not understand the American natives to be using land in the European sense of active agricultural and forest management.[4]

For these founders these ideas were configured into a particular and specific relationship. Democracy required liberty (and vice versa), and both in turn required ownership and control of property. It was this sentiment that gave rise to Thomas Jefferson's idea of the yeoman farmer, one of the most enduring images from America's revolutionary period. According to Jefferson, the yeoman farmer (the family farmer who owned and controlled his own land) was the foundation and bastion of the new American democracy. Why? Because ownership of land gave the owner economic and thus political liberty. When a farmer could produce food and fuel for himself and his family on land he owned, no one could buy his vote. Thus, it was the rural landowner (in contrast to the urban wage earner) who was in the best position to make political judgments that reflected the greater public good.[5]

But this view of the relationship of property to democracy, and the fact of asserting property's primacy, was not unchallenged even in its own time. Perhaps the most articulate spokesman of an alternative perspective was Benjamin Franklin. During the constitutional period Franklin noted with force that "private property is a creature of society, and is subject to the calls of that society whenever its necessities require it, even to the last farthing."[6] Franklin was not alone in these sentiments; he shared them with Thomas Jefferson and others. (Jefferson's place in this debate is claimed by both sides; this appears to be legitimate, as he expressed statements that can be interpreted as supportive of both positions.) And in fact, if anything, what we see when we look at this issue closely is that the meanings of land and private property and their relationship to citizenship and democratic structure were and remain contentious issues—issues on which Americans did not and do not hold consensus. Rather, these are issues central to how we fight over the very nature of what it means to be American.[7]

To a large extent this lack of consensus is reflected in the country's founding national documents. In 1776 the Declaration of Independence promised Americans "life, liberty, and the pursuit of happiness." What few recall is that Thomas Jefferson drew this idea from the work of political philosopher John Locke, who called for life, liberty, and property. In the first draft of Virginia's founding documents, which Jefferson prepared and from which he drew for the Declaration of Independence, he included this phrase. Jefferson's idea was to give each free man fifty acres, to create the nation of yeoman farmers he saw as necessary for the new democracy. Jefferson lost this debate in Virginia and in Philadelphia. In its final form, the Declaration's language reflects disagreements about what was being promised to citizens of the new country.

Eleven years later, in 1787, the Constitution was adopted without any specific mention of land-related property. It was not until the adoption of the Bill of Rights in 1791 that the disagreements among the framers found a degree of consensus in the wording for the so-called takings clause, the final twelve words of the Fifth Amendment: "nor shall private property be taken for public use, without just compensation."

With the adoption of this phrase, the Founding Fathers formally recognized four concepts: the existence of private property, an action denoted as taken, a realm of activity that is public use, and a form of payment specified as just compensation. The interrelation of these concepts is such that where private property exists, it may be taken by government, but only for a denoted public use and when just compensation is provided. If any of these conditions are not met, then a taking may not occur. This constitutional provision allows for condemnation of private land for public highways, schools, parks, and other public activities, but requires that the public pay fairly for the land taken. But, as has been noted by countless scholars, our understanding of the exact meaning of these words to those who crafted them is unclear.[8] The clause does not tell us precisely when a takings has occurred, it does not define a public use, and it does not explain what constitutes just compensation. In fact, it doesn't even tell us what is considered private property.

Although some Founding Fathers did appear to want to afford property a central place in the constitutional/social contract schema, there was no consensus among the founders; their ultimate crafting of language in the Declaration of Independence, the U.S. Constitution, and the Bill of Rights reflected this lack of consensus and acknowledgment of compromise.[9] In addition, and perhaps just as important, is that the on-the-ground reality in colonial America, pre- and postindependence, was something less pure than either of the polar positions. Something akin to what we would recognize as land use and environmental regulation was common. For example, colonial Virginia regulated tobacco-related planting practices to prevent overplanting and require crop rotation, and Boston, New York City, and Charlestown regulated the location of businesses such as bakeries and slaughterhouses, often to the point of excluding their location within city boundaries.[10]

However, despite the land use and environmental regulation of colonial times, most citizens were free to use their land as they pleased, and they continued to enjoy this freedom through the eighteenth and nineteenth centuries. It was the twentieth century that brought real change to the status of property in America. This was the period when new technological developments changed how Americans lived their lives, and held and used property. In the early twentieth century, America went from a rural to an urban nation. The mass immigrations from Europe combined with the explosion of industrialization to bring waves of new citizens to the cities. As this occurred, ideas about land and ownership—management of the site—began to change.

To a large extent, new technology was responsible for a rethinking of what it meant for the individual to own land and manage a site. Under the classic definition of private property (the definition still taught to first-year law students) ownership means *cuius est solum eius est usque ad coelum et usque ad inferos*—whoever owns the soil owns all the way to heaven and all the way to the depths. This is where the idea of mineral rights, water rights, and air rights going with physical ownership of the land is articulated.

In most Western countries, and most especially the United States, land is conceptualized, fictionalized, as a bundle of rights—or, as it is commonly discussed in the legal literature, a bundle of sticks. When one owns land, ownership refers to more than the possession of the physical soil within a defined set of boundaries. For the purposes of the law and the economy, ownership means the possession of a recognizable, fungible bundle of rights. This bundle of rights is socially recognized as ownership. In theory, this bundle is comprised of rights such as the air right (the ownership of the air space above the legally defined parcel), the water right (the ownership of the water sitting under or flowing over and under the legally defined parcel), the right to control access to the property (more commonly known as the right of trespass), the right to harvest natural resources (such as trees and minerals), and the rights to develop, sell, trade, lease, and/or bequeath the land in its entirety, or to do the same with selected rights.

If an owner has complete possession of these rights—that is, if an owner owns all the rights in the bundle—the owner is said to hold the property free of obligation, to have fee-simple ownership or freehold property. However, no owner ever has all of the rights in the bundle. Society, as government, always reserves some of these rights, or some portion of these rights. For example, wildlife ownership and harvesting seasons have long been a right reserved to and regulated by the government; few owners expect to own the wildlife (fish, deer, bear, etc.) on their rural property, and thus the right to harvest at any time and in any amount as they please. Government also reserves the right to enter onto property (to violate the right to control access) to carry out necessary social functions. However, even given these reservations, private property ownership has long been thought of as consisting of a robust bundle of rights, relatively free of obligations to the state or others.

This conception made practical sense until 1903, when the Wright brothers invented the airplane. Within a very few years of its invention, the airplane went from a novelty to commercial development.

What was the property consequence? Under the commonly understood definition of private property, if I owned air rights to the heavens above, then every time an airplane flew over my property it was guilty of trespass. The airplane had entered my property without permission as surely as if the pilot had walked up to my fence, smashed the fence, and kept walking. As technological change expanded the possibilities of air travel, the pre-twentieth-century definition of private property no longer appeared socially functional. If individual landowners could claim trespass of and demand compensation for their property by airplanes, air travel would become either too cumbersome or too expensive.

What happened? During the first half of the twentieth century, the U.S. courts scratched their heads over this problem. Eventually they solved the problem by "public-izing" air rights above a certain elevation without requiring compensation under the Fifth Amendment.[11] The courts reappropriated airspace to the public sphere so individual owners no longer owned *est usque ad coelum*—all the way to heaven. In effect, the courts created a new commons where one had not existed before. The creation of this new commons responded to changing social needs pushed by changing technology.

Continuing through the twentieth century, landowners saw the very definition of property change, bend, and flex in response to new inventions and changing social values. As society understood the impact of individual land use decisions upon neighbors and society at large, and as new ideas about ourselves and others developed, Americans continued to reconfigure the foundational property rights bundle.[12] Many examples of this can be given; I offer just a few.

The first is from the Civil War period. Until the takings clause of the Fifth Amendment of the Bill of Rights in 1791, despite the passion held by some framers, there is little mention in the founding documents of the United States of private property. The one mention there is, is oblique. In the Constitution—in Article 1, Section 2—there is recognition of slaves as property. In 1863, with the issuance of the Emancipation Proclamation, President Lincoln freed the slaves, thus taking this property from these owners. When the Civil War was won by the North, a set of these owners sued in federal court for compensation over the taking of their property by the federal government. Under the terms of the takings clause their assertion seemed reasonable. Their private property had been taken for a public use but they had not received just compensation. The result of the legal action, however, did not affirm their position. Instead, the courts argued that new social values—a new view of the right of one human being to own and control another—overrode a prior, legitimate definition of property. And in fact, the codification of this view in the Thirteenth Amendment, which specifically outlawed slavery, reinforced this point.

In the 1960s, one century after the freeing of the slaves, further changes in race relations had similar effects on private property. In the popular mind, a focus of the civil rights movement was the practice of white lunch-counter owners in the American South. These owners, reflecting their understanding of their private property rights, decided who they would serve and who they wouldn't, generally refusing service to African-Americans. We have dramatic photographic images of this period, when young African-Americans sat in at lunch counters only to have food dumped on their heads. Despite the racism of these actions, these owners acted no differently than anyone does in deciding who may come into his or her home. These owners said, in effect, "It's my business, I built it with my capital and my labor, I get to decide who to serve!" But during the 1960s, as a result of social struggle, owners of commercial establishments lost their private property right to choose who they would serve or not serve.[13] Reflecting changing social attitudes on race and human relations, Americans decided as a society that the greater social interest was better served by taking this right away, and to do so without compensation to the owner.

This dialogue between changing social values and the changing nature of what the property rights bundle includes, continues through to today. During the 1990s it was perhaps best expressed through the resistance by male-only membership clubs and male-only colleges to the admission of women. What was the claim of these clubs and colleges? That the premises were their private property and they could and should decide who has access. Again, society asserted the primacy of changing social values over private property rights and changed the property right bundle (eliminating the ban on female access) without providing compensation.

In addition to the twentieth century's bringing forth a substantial reconfiguration of the property rights bundle itself, this was also the period of the rise of modern land use and environmental regulation, which themselves significantly impacted the options for site owners to exercise their property rights. As noted, the open borders and industrialization of the early twentieth century brought waves of immigrants and migrants to America's cities. In 1920, for the first time, the U.S. Census recorded more people living in cities than in the countryside. These migrations caused significant land use problems, as individual site owners sought to maximize the potential of their sites while the city found itself pressured to exercise its traditional authority to protect the public's health, safety, and welfare. This was the period of muckraking journalism, which chronicled the poverty of immigrants crowded into tenements in New York City neighborhoods with densities exceeding even that of Calcutta, India, often absent of access to sanitation facilities, clean water, light, and air. Out of these conflicts grew zoning.

Today, zoning is common. But at the time of its invention, it was revolutionary. Why? For at least two reasons. It established a public sector framework of standards for land use that proscribed the property rights of site owners absent compensation, and it did so by treating site owners differently (the very idea of establishing residential, commercial, and industrial zones). The concept was so revolutionary that the U.S. Supreme Court barely validated it in their 1926 landmark case of *Village of Euclid, Ohio v. Ambler Realty*.[14]

New York City is credited with inventing zoning in 1916. Within a decade it had spread across the United States, because it filled a need that cities had for rationalizing land use management. Until the second half of the twentieth century, most land use regulations looked similar to zoning in its initial form. But then things changed again. As America began to suburbanize, zoning was stretched to fit new land use circumstances, and new forms of site management came into being to reflect changing social values about land and natural and environmental resources. This became especially pronounced with the rise of the modern environmental movement.

Conceptually, land use and environmental planning, policy, and management (through devices such as zoning) are premised on the need for individual property rights to yield to a collective definition of the public interest. Such planning and policy argues that an unfettered right to exercise individual property rights does not serve the greater public good. As some environmentalists articulate it, land use and environmental problems arise precisely because the site and property rights inherent to it are privately held and managed. Individuals are making land use management decisions that do not take into account the broader public interest and a more expansive economic calculus—that is, their arguments update and restate those that led to the very invention of zoning.

A litany of common land use and environmental issues—farmland loss in the urban fringe, suburban sprawl, destruction of historic buildings, downtown deterioration, to name just a few—have all been depicted as issues that arise from a version of Garrett Hardin's "tragedy of the commons."[15] In these instances, the tragedy is that individual landowners make decisions that are economically and socially sensible to them, but are not judged to be as sensible to the broader public. To put the same point in the terms of classical economics, each individual pursuing his or her own self-interest does not yield the greater social interest.

For many, the legal pinnacle of this perspective was reached in the early 1970s, when the modern environmental movement was brand new.[16] A landmark case was argued before the state of Wisconsin Supreme Court: *Just v. Marinette County*.[17] The Justs had chosen to fill in a wetland in violation of state law. They argued that it was their land and they could do what they wanted with it. The supreme court disagreed; they said, you bought a wetland, you can use it as a wetland. Any other use, other than the natural use, is not something you can assume to be within your bundle of property rights; it is something that you must acquire from the community to which you belong. In the late 1990s the Wisconsin Supreme Court affirmed that this continues to be the law of the state.[18] This is one of the most dramatic examples available, but it shows the diversification and fragmentation of claims to the site.

Critics of this evolution of social control of the site ask us to take a deep breath and step back.[19] They argue that the fallacy in seeing modern society as a series of Garrett Hardin–style tragedy-of-the-commons situations is that society (government) is continually able to justify a restriction/removal of property rights every time a new land use and environmental problem is identified. Government can reconfigure who has a claim on and to the site, and there is no reasonable end in sight. From the critics' point of view there are at least two problems with this: when what I own and control is only what the government says I control, does private property really exist? And what about the literal and figurative property–democracy social contract that forged and underlies the nation?[20]

There is an additional way to frame these two phenomena: as the reconfiguration of property rights in response to changing technology and changing social values, and as the continuous expansion of regulation. Framed that way, we see that throughout the twentieth century the parties that have had claim to any particular site have been expanding. If in the eighteenth and nineteenth centuries sites were largely the purview of owners to do with as they pleased, the story of the twentieth century is that a variety of interests laid claim to the site and argued that the owner's traditional rights were to be reshuffled to include their interests and claims. Most obviously, this expansion included government (in its various forms and layers) asserting its claim upon the site through the need to protect the public health, safety, and welfare. Modern land use and environmental policy also includes a formal and informal place for parties such as neighbors, community and neighborhood organizations, and special interest organizations when the site has a special characteristic (such as historic character or unique ecological characteristics).

But this is not a one-sided story. Early in the twentieth century, at the time zoning was being born and affirmed as a legitimate exercise of governmental control, the U.S. Supreme Court took up a related issue: is there a limit to how much the government can regulate private land? In 1922, in the case of *Pennsylvania Coal Co. v. Mahon,* Justice Oliver Wendall Holmes wrote, "The general rule is that while property may be regulated to a certain extent, if regulation goes too far it will be recognized as a taking."[21] This sentiment would seem to support the concern of the critics of the evolution of social control of private land. Unfortunately, Justice Holmes did not specify the precise place where the unacceptable limits of the regulation occurred. Political, policy, and judicial practice since then has been to largely (though not completely) back public regulatory activity as not crossing the line that Justice Holmes identified. As recently as the spring of 2002, in the case of *Tahoe-Sierra Preservation Council v. Tahoe Regional Planning Agency* the U.S. Supreme Court recognized the legitimate and important role of public regulation over sites where there are conflicting claims between owners, neighbors, environmentalists, and the government.[22]

If this is where claims upon site stand at the beginning of the twenty-first century, how is all this likely to evolve into the future? We know that property is a complex social institution. People and communities have strong emotional attachments to particular places, and, for many people in industrialized countries, the ownership of private property is still one of the (if not *the*) primary economic assets acquired and managed in a lifetime. As such, individuals tend to have strong interest in the integrity of their property rights bundle. But at the same time, many people seem to have an inherent understanding of the need to limit the exercise of property rights through the use of public mechanisms (such as those used in land use and environmental management). How will these tendencies be balanced?

One prediction I offer is that the differences of policy and political opinion about the integrity versus malleability of property rights is going to deepen, rather than heal; fighting over the site will be intensified, rather than lessened.[23] Why? One reason has to do with the spread in America over political and social values and social and economic circumstances. This has been expressed and talked about in a number of ways. After the 2000 presidential election the national print media published a map that coded by red and blue the counties that voted for the Republican and Democratic Party candidates (George W. Bush and Albert Gore), respectively. The map showed a nation whose political opinions were divided largely between those who resided in the coastal (more liberal) states and in the heartland (more conservative states).[24] To some extent this division reflects social and economic circumstances. It was largely (though not exclusively) the residents of the blue states who enjoyed the economic boom of the 1990s, who were able to reposition their economic circumstances upward, and thus participate in further dividing America's economic classes.[25]

All of this has effects on property rights issues. How? While property matters to all of us, as an individual gets wealthier, the component of that person's financial profile directly tied to property decreases. This is only logical. As one's wealth increases, one tends to diversify one's holdings, and wealth is represented by real estate and other wealth instruments (stocks, bonds, art, precious metal, etc.). So it is not that the upper middle class and wealthy do not own larger homes, second homes, and so on, but rather that the proportion of one's wealth represented by this property decreases in the total wealth profile. So, while for the middle and lower middle class, the ownership of property (a house and lot) is the primary form of wealth, for the upper middle class and wealthy, property is only one part of how they own and invest to secure their wealth.

The impact of all this for claims upon the site is profound. If a proposed land use or environmental program is going to impact upon property rights, it matters how important those property rights are to those being impacted. If those being impacted are wealthier, they can, quite literally, afford the impact; it matters less to them. If those being impacted have only their landed property, then land use regulations that propose to take the value of that property for larger social values become more important to the individuals, who have significant incentive to resist such regulatory efforts and work to preserve the integrity of their property rights bundle.

Social scientists have long noted this phenomenon. That is, they have noted that those who tend to support the development and implementation of land use and environmental policies and programs are those who can, quite literally, afford them. And they have noted that an upward shift in economic circumstances, leads to a focus on the promotion of a set of quality-of-life values that can become (often become?) translated as regulatory efforts to shape the use of other people's private property in the interest of pursuing larger social values such as environmental protection, growth management, and smart growth.[26]

So if the observations and predictions offered about the way America's social and economic classes are developing are correct, what we can expect is ever more social conflict over property rights, as one group with resources seeks to secure more quality-of-life values (controlled growth, undivided farmland, pure trout streams, vibrant downtowns) and one group with some but marginal resources seeks to protect that sliver of investment they have in the American dream through investment in property (whether these be farmland owners, ranchers, wetland owners, or the owners of "blighted" downtown neighborhoods slated for redevelopment even when these neighborhoods and homes may be socially and economically viable).[27] To emphasize the point, an era of intensified social conflict over claims to the site is upon us, and one of its expressions will be heightened conflict over property rights.

The bulk of this essay tells an American story about property rights. A way to characterize the story is that, starting at some mythical point in the pre-twentieth-century period, the property bundle was fuller, thicker, and stronger than it is today. Then, beginning at some undetermined point, but taking clear shape in the early part of the twentieth century, the property rights bundle came under assault from the state, as government was pressured to make the bundle narrower, leaner, and weaker to fulfill public goals at the expense of the private property bundle.

The twentieth century was a century in which the property rights bundle experienced waves of assault. At first the assault was a function of new technology and rapid urbanization. These phenomena continued through the century and were then joined in the century's last half by an assault born of changing social values, rooted in new attitudes about racial, gender, and then environmental relationships. With each wave of assault, the property rights bundle diminished.

What is interesting about this story is that each of these assaults was a change driven by a threat. In the early part of the century city spaces were changing as a function of international and intranational immigration; traditional ideas about property did not seem to work as these changes occurred. In the midcentury, property seemed to be a barrier to ever-mounting calls for legal and social change in racial relationships. In the late century, claims to property's integrity appear to clash with new scientific findings about ecosystem functioning and maintenance.

The question is: what's next? Will there be new challenges to property analogous to those that reshaped it in the twentieth century? The answer has to be "yes." We continue technological development, and it continues to present challenges to our ways of living and our concepts of property. Exactly what these developments will be, I won't venture. But they will come, and as they do property will be asked—we will demand—that it bend and flex in response, just as we have done throughout the twentieth century. And we will continue to do the same in the social arena. As a society we will insist that property be reshaped as we discover ways in which old conceptions of property hold back the liberation and social integration of peoples and others (animals, landscapes) once deemed invisible or irrelevant, or at least less deserving than property itself. One likely trend for the future will be an increasing focus on the implications of new ecological understandings of human–land relationships. Going back at least fifty years, but gaining ever more currency with the growth of the modern environmental movement, land ethicists have been calling for a new view of land that is less commodity based and more community based, a view that gives to the land a right to existence on its own term.[28]

But as a broad set of predictions, these are uncomfortable for at least two reasons. One, it seems to suggest that there is no logical end to the reshaping of property, that instead property is always subservient to technology and social values. If this is true, then how can the premise, the promise, of property as an establisher and enabler of the individual in a democracy be realized? That is, if technology and social values always trump property (and always do so absent compensation), then what is property's value? What value does it serve as a bastion against the arbitrary power of the state? How does one prevent the tyranny of the majority? Are there first principles that are inviolate?

Also, these predictions fall into the trap of many predictions: assuming that the future will unfold as has the past. Instead, what we know about technological and social change is that there are periods of disjuncture, when something(s) happens to completely reshape our worldview and our abilities to live in the world as we have to that point. The difficulty is that few of us can imagine what these disjunctures might be and what changes they might bring. Yet we know these disjunctions have happened in the past; they will happen again. These changes, whatever they will be, will impact property and thus claims upon the site. So, for example, it is interesting to note that in this present period of history property is again dominant on the world stage as a result of one of these disjunctures. In 1989 the Berlin Wall fell, and within a few years the world experienced the dissolution of the Soviet Union and its political–economic block. Since then, the Western countries have been actively promoting democracy and capitalism throughout the second and third worlds. Often the first step in this process is assistance in the creation of private property, property registration and transfer institutions, and property markets. Private property—strong private property—is a premise of current international development policy.[29]

So, is there a future for private property in America? Yes. Private property is central to the very essence of the American experience, and it will continue to hold an important place in American economics, politics, law, and social debate. The desire to own and control a site seems to be a nearly universal human motivation. For many reasons, conflict over site management has been and will continue to be central to our dialogues—as neighbors, as members of special interest communities, as part of the larger community to which we belong, proximately, socially, and legally.

So how does any one of us make a legitimate claim to a site? To whom does a site belong? Who owns a site? It turns out that these are not easy questions to answer. If the site was ever the purview of the owner, it is no longer. In modern times, the site belongs to the owner of record *and* it also belongs to all of us. When we look at the legacy of the Founding Fathers and the documents they left us, we see a confusion about land and property, a confusion that is still with us and even more acute. Site ownership is more fragmented than we commonly acknowledge. The site has more claims upon it, and we, society, have ever more difficulty sorting out the legitimacy of conflicting claims.

So how do we—as owners, neighbors, concerned appreciators, and users—go about claiming the site? Who has the rights to act upon the site? The only way we have learned to answer these questions is to continually come together and argue it through, to use a social, dialogical, democratic process to address an issue with complex legal, economic, and cultural roots. There is no simple economic or legal formula to which we can turn. Each community in each generation decides on the balance point that respects the rights of the site owner and those of other claimants to the site. Is this is messy process? Yes. Does it guarantee that everyone will be satisfied? No. Is there is any other alternative? There doesn't appear to be.

We do know something about the future: private property will not stagnate. It never has, and it will not now. Private property will continue to evolve in America; it has to. As it does, so too will claims upon the site. Private property is a social contract. It establishes the rights of the individual *and* it binds society. The balance point between individual and social rights in property will continually be renegotiated. Each time it is renegotiated, the claimants to a site will be reshuffled.

As Americans continue to reinvent their concept of freedom, of what it means to have liberty, they will come to understand anew what it means to hold private property while living in a democratic society. Claims upon the site become one of the most obvious expressions of this ever-changing dialogue.[30]

Notes

1. James W. Ely, Jr., *The Guardian of Every Other Right: A Constitutional History of Property Rights* (New York: Oxford University Press, 1992).
2. Alexander Hamilton, James Madison, and John Jay, *The Federalist Papers* (New York: Mentor Books, 1961 (1788)), 339.
3. John Adams, "Discourses on Davilia: A Series of Papers on Political History," in *The Works of John Adams*, Vol. 6, ed. C. F. Adams (Boston: Little Brown, 1851 (1790)), 280.
4. William Cronon, *Changes in the Land: Indians, Colonists, and the Ecology of New England* (New York: Hill and Wang, 1983).
5. James Gilreath, ed., *Thomas Jefferson and the Education of a Citizen* (Washington, D.C.: Library of Congress, 1999).
6. Benjamin Franklin, "Queries and Remarks Respecting Alterations in the Constitution of Pennsylvania," in *The Writings of Benjamin Franklin*, Vol. 10, ed. A. H. Smith (London: Macmillan and Co., 1907 (1789)), 59.
7. Ely, *The Guardian of Every Other Right*; Harvey M. Jacobs, "Fighting over Land: America's Legacy...America's Future," *Journal of the American Planning Association* 65 (1999): 141–149.
8. For example, Fred Bosselman et al., *The Taking Issue: An Analysis of the Constitutional Limits of Land Use Control* (Washington, D.C.: United States Government Printing Office, 1973); Richard A. Epstein, *Takings, Private Property and the Power of Eminent Domain* (Cambridge: Harvard University Press, 1985); Ely, *The Guardian of Every Other Right*; William Michael Treanor, "The Original Understanding of the Takings Clause and the Political Process," *Columbia Law Review* 95 (1995): 782–887; Jacobs, "Fighting."
9. Bosselman et al., *The Taking Issue*; Ely, *The Guardian of Every Other Right.*
10. Treanor, "The Original Understanding of the Takings Clause and the Political Process."
11. Harvey M. Jacobs and Brian W. Ohm, "Statutory Takings Legislation: The National Context, the Wisconsin and Minnesota Proposals," *Wisconsin Environmental Law Journal* 2 (1995): 173–223.
12. Bosselman et al., *The Taking Issue.*
13. Neil Hecht, "From Seisin to Sit-In: Evolving Property Concepts," *Boston University Law Review* 44 (1964): 435–466.
14. 260 U.S. 393 (1926).

15. Garrett Hardin, "The Tragedy of the Commons," *Science* 162 (December 1968): 1243–1248.
16. Donald W. Large, "This Land Is Whose Land? Changing Concepts of Land as Property," *Wisconsin Law Review* 4 (1973): 1041–1083.
17. 201 N.W.2d 761 (1972).
18. Brian W. Ohm, "The Wisconsin Supreme Court Responds to Lucas," *Land Use and Zoning Digest* 48, no. 9 (1996): 3–7.
19. Tom Bethell, *The Noblest Triumph: Property and Prosperity through the Ages* (New York: St. Martin's Press, 1998); Epstein, *Takings, Private Property and the Power of Eminent Domain.*
20. Harvey M. Jacobs, "The Anti-Environmental, 'Wise Use' Movement in America," *Land Use Law and Zoning Digest* 47, no. 2 (1995): 3–8.
21. 260 U.S. 393 (1922) at 415.
22. 532 U.S. 302 (2002).
23. The thrust of the comments that conclude this essay are drawn from Harvey M. Jacobs, "The Future of an American Ideal," in *Private Property in the 21st Century: The Future of an American Ideal*, ed. H. M. Jacobs (Northampton, MA: Edward Elgar, 2004), 171–184.
24. David Brooks, "One Nation, Slightly Divisible," *Atlantic Monthly* 288, no. 5 (2001): 53–65.
25. Paul Krugman, "For Richer: How the Permissive Capitalism of the Boom Destroyed American Equality," *The New York Times Magazine* (October 20, 2002).
26. One set of examples focusing on a set of cases in New York State is laid out in Michael K. Heiman, *The Quiet Evolution: Power, Planning and Profits in New York State* (New York: Praeger Publishers, 1988).
27. One relatively recent and highly publicized example of the phenomenon of displacement for reinvestment is the case of the Poletown neighborhood in Detroit, Michigan, a viable ethnic working-class neighborhood whose owners had their properties condemned by the city's governing authorities to pursue an agenda of manufacturing investment-based economic development. See the documentation of this case in J. Wylie, *Poletown: A Community Betrayed* (Urbana: University of Illinois Press, 1989).
28. Aldo Leopold, *A Sand County Almanac* (London and New York: Oxford University Press, 1968 (1949)); Christopher D. Stone, *Should Trees Have Standing? Toward Legal Rights for Natural Objects* (Los Altos, CA: W. Kaufmann, 1974).
29. Hernando de Soto, *The Mystery of Capital: Why Capitalism Triumphs in the West and Fails Everywhere Else* (New York: Basic Books, 2000).
30. The interpretation of American history presented here, including the forces that shape property's form, would be characterized as "liberal" by those with a differing point of view. These opponents, self-described "conservatives," view property as the foundational base of American democracy. From this point of view, property is not subject to reshaping as a function of technological and social changes. Instead, property is *a priori* and immutable, and any challenges to or assaults upon it by society and government must be compensated under the provisions of the takings clause of the Fifth Amendment to the U.S. Constitution. From this conservative point of view, the reg-

ulatory takings doctrine articulated in *Penn. Coal* (see note 21) should be understood as requiring compensation except under the most extreme of conditions. The leading scholar of this position is Epstein (see note 8); for similar arguments see also Bethell (note 19) and Bernard H. Siegan, *Property Rights: From Magna Carta to the Fourteenth Amendment* (New Brunswick, NJ: Transaction Publishers, 2001).

Property line marker embedded in New York City sidewalk.

3

From Place to Site: Negotiating Narrative Complexity

Robert A. Beauregard

All sites exist first as places. Before places become objects of urban planning and design, they exist in personal experience, hearsay, and collective memories. Standing between planners and designers and the sites on which they hope to act are socially embedded narratives. And, while these place narratives can be ignored, they cannot be wholly erased. Places are never empty.

No place, even if unexplored, escapes this rule. Simply that we know of the jungles of Borneo or the desolate tundra of northern Russia means that a story can be told. At the least, we imagine these places as far away, undeveloped and uninhabited, as dark and mysterious. These images, in turn, prepare the way for other narrative constructions. When settlers establish wilderness outposts, for example, they enter into narratives of discovery, conquest, and the beneficence of civilization. These stories are possible only because the place has been first understood as alienated and empty, that is, because it existed in a prior narrative.

Antithetic to places unknown are places saturated with meaning.[1] Densely imagined through overlapping histories and intersecting current events, they resist being turned into "cleared" sites, that is, sites "received as unoccupied, lacking any prior construction and empty of content."[2] A multitude of stories compete for attention, and do so with conflicting interpretations and story lines. These are anthropological places whose inhabitants live in history, whose identity has not been formalized, and whose intellectual status is ambiguous.[3] The options for planners and designers to impose their singular vision are severely curtailed. At the same time, the richness of narratives constitutes a wellspring of creative possibilities.

As I write these words in the fall of 2002, the former World Trade Center in lower Manhattan, where twin 110-story towers once stood, is one such saturated place. Encased in a multitude of powerful and competing narratives, it is currently the most freighted of redevelopment sites on the planet. No plan for the site can avoid the narratives of terrorism, globalization, U.S. hegemony and cultural imperialism, victimization, and sacrifice that shape how this place is collectively imagined.

At the same time, lower Manhattan is known locally by a number of stories that began prior to that tragic day. One story tells of the recent conversion of office buildings to residential use and claims that investment in housing will release the area from its commercial doldrums and make it a 24-hour neighborhood of multiple uses and diverse activities.

Critics of the original World Trade Center tell a story that refers to a high modernist hubris that took hold in the early 1960s. This vision led to the demolition of a wholesale and produce market, the closing of Radio Row (a cluster of consumer electronics stores), and the displacement of a Lebanese merchant community. This narrative includes the abandonment of the city's port for the world of high finance. This history, of course, was buried beneath the massive foundations of the Twin Towers and layer after layer of retailing and transit paths. Now, that history lies even deeper. Amid such a surplus of narratives, the planning, design, and subsequent redevelopment of the 16-acre site seems overdetermined, awash in a turbulent sea of meanings.[4]

A site is a social construct, a representation of space. It is conceived apart from the complexity of human relations. In effect, a site is a place that has been denatured, formalized, and colonized, its meanings made compatible with the relations of production, state imperatives, and the order that both imply. Opposed to the site is a representational space—what I have termed *place*—and its complex symbolism grounded in lived experience.[5] The former emanates from professionals and technocrats, the latter from human encounters in dwellings, churches, sidewalks, plazas, markets, and the workplaces of the city.

Sites, though, do not appear initially as fully rationalized. Rather, they have to be created through the articulation of certain professional qualities (e.g., area, economic value) and the suppression of others. The place to be displaced has first to be prepared. Consequently, the site does not exist prior to the onset of planning and design. It is an integral part of these processes. The site is created through the acts of planning and design. There is no preplan or predesign stage that fixes the meaning of the site and through which one passes never to return.

Urban designers and planners, developers and engineers, government administrators, and architects have developed a variety of methodologies for making sense of place. Using variations in scale and slope, economic value and solar orientation, configuration and zoning, and other analytical and abstract categories, they turn different places into a smaller number of types of sites. First they move the specific place—with its connotations of richness, diversity, and complexity—onto "muted ground."[6] There, a limited number of qualities prepare it for intervention. To accomplish this, the untamed, overlapping, and contradictory histories, remembrances, and engagements that cling to the place must be removed and subsequently replaced (or not) with simplified, coherent, and transparent representations. In the case of the World Trade Center, the place of terrorist destruction and capitalist machinations becomes 16 acres with a gigantic floor-to-area ratio and huge development potential.

Planners and designers take control of a place by distilling its narratives. They eliminate the ambiguities that might derail the project by casting doubt that it is the best and only viable option.[7] Their intent is to create opportunities for action. Given a set of conditions or a sense of unease, they represent places in terms that enable them and others to intervene. They turn what they are given into what they know, and what they know is situations of a certain type. Presented with a client's need for solitude and nearness to nature, the architect writes a program for a house in the woods.

In effect, places are professionalized. A small number of qualities are used to situate the place in a closed, analytical discourse. Abstractions abound. Anxiety is reduced. Professionals isolate in order to control, and this hermetic move enables professionals to claim that their depiction captures the foundational nature, the truth, of the place—at least for purposes of development. Without such a site discourse, professionals claim, the site cannot be developed. Professional knowledge is thus doubly essentialist, producing a further need for site professionals.[8]

Good planners and designers recognize the compulsion to engage in abstraction and reductionism. They grapple with narratives that others might discard. They attempt to use nonprofessional understandings to add, rather than subtract, meaning. What design element would capture the tragedy of the World Trade Center terrorist attack? they ask, thus engaging a nonprofessional narrative of the site. These planners and designers attempt to negotiate the messy and multiple narratives of place and explore representations that resist the bloodless quality of professional categories.[9]

Sites, of course, seldom remain vacant. They are almost always developed and, once developed, their new use and activities create—even require—new narratives. In fact, for many development projects, whether they be suburban housing or entertainment districts, the making of the site into a place begins during the development phase. To support the investment, new images must be publicized. Examples range from resort areas, such as Cancún on the Mexican coast and Las Vegas, that were "undeveloped" prior to becoming tourist sites, to garden apartment complexes. Sites are only way stations between place and place.[10]

Two examples will be used to explore these themes. Each illustrates the difference between place and site and how these differences are negotiated. Both deal with cleared sites, but in quite dissimilar ways. The first example is the multi-site Operation Breakthrough, a demonstration project of the early 1970s developed by the U.S. government to produce industrialized housing for low- and moderate-income households. The second example is Brasilia, the planned capital city of Brazil built in the late 1950s and officially inaugurated on April 21, 1960.

Operation Breakthrough required standard sites, sites without encumbering narratives and without physical and regulatory impediments to mass-produced housing schemes. The idea was to create interchangeable spaces that would be efficient and profitable for industrialized, modular housing. Consequently, the places in which such housing was to be built were stripped of any prior history—made empty—and their physical surroundings suppressed. Rewritten as professionalized sites, they became eligible for the program.

The Brasilia case moves in the opposite direction, not from place to site but from site to place. Brasilia was located in a part of the country that was first collectively imagined as undeveloped, empty, and without history. This understanding opened the area to two narratives: one of modern architecture and design and the other of developmentalism and nation-building. The place could accommodate these narratives only by first being made empty.

FROM PLACE TO SITE: OPERATION BREAKTHROUGH

In 1969, President Richard Nixon appointed George Romney, former head of the Ford Motor Company, as secretary of the U.S. Department of Housing and Urban Development (HUD). One of Romney's first policy initiatives was Operation Breakthrough, a national program designed to demonstrate the potential of industrialized housing and modular building systems and to address a housing shortage, particularly for low-income and moderate-income households. In pursuing these goals, the program would rationalize what was viewed as a fragmented and backward home-building industry immune to innovation. The initiative was launched in May of 1969.[11]

Operation Breakthrough was designed to have three phases, only the first of which was fully realized.[12] After an initial phase in which guidelines were developed, HUD held two separate competitions: one for prototype building systems and the other for sites on which to erect those systems. In the second phase, the prototype systems were matched with the prototype sites and construction was to begin. After completion of the demonstration, HUD hoped that developers and communities would adopt these systems for large-scale production. The projected goal for the last phase was 2.8 million housing units over ten years. In the spirit of mass production, the whole process was fast-tracked. Requests for Proposals were made available in July of 1969, winners were announced in February of 1970, and contracts for construction awarded in August of 1971.

The competition phase unfolded on parallel paths: one for the building systems and the other for sites. (This was an early sign that sites would have to be standardized.) Over 600 product prototype proposals were submitted for consideration, 60 percent of which were for advanced research and development contracts rather than total housing systems. The housing system proposals were evaluated by a committee of individuals from various government agencies. The committee rated each proposal on the quality of the physical design, the availability of financing, and the management capability of the system producer. The last two criteria were particularly important, given the objective of moving quickly into and out of the demonstration phase. Secondary criteria included the geographical reach of the system (that is, the extent to which it could be adapted to different climates) and minority participation in the production and construction phases.

The housing systems were of different types: low-rise stackable boxes, high-rise stackable boxes, concrete panels, lightweight components, and "breakthrough limits" (i.e., mixed systems).[13] The systems were developed by a variety of producers: integrated building products corporations such as Boise-Cascade; diversified corporations such as the Aluminum Company of America (Alcoa), General Electric, and TRW Systems; and large home-builders such as Stirling Homex and National Homes. Almost all of the submissions were made by consortiums, the majority of which included architects. In the end, thirty-seven system producers were selected, a number later reduced to twenty-two.

Simultaneously, competitions were held for prototype sites and for planners of prototype sites. Local governments submitted proposals for 218 sites while eighty-two architecture, planning, and design firms applied to be site planners. Eleven sites and ten site planners were chosen. Four of the sites were in the inner city, four in city fringe areas, and three in the suburbs. (The intent was to develop the prototype sites at different densities, one of the only efforts to contextualize the projects.) The selected sites were spread across the country and included St. Louis in the inner city category, Sacramento in the city fringe category, and New Castle County (Wilmington, DE) in the suburban category.

Because Operation Breakthrough was meant to be a demonstration, HUD wanted to place more than one system on each site. Moreover, it also required that housing units be clustered and expected that the site would also have stores, playgrounds, parking, and other facilities.

Consequently, site planners had to analyze the site, develop market analyses, determine the number of housing units to be placed on the site using each housing system, develop a site plan, and negotiate regulations with local officials. In Jersey City, for example, the site planner (David A. Crane Associates) developed a plan that integrated the housing of four system producers with parking structures, a school, and office space. In addition, Crane Associates selected the structure types, specified the number of units to be built with each system, and worked with the system producers to minimize costs.

HUD also selected eight site developers to address the issue of market aggregation, that is, the creation of sufficient demand to support industrialized housing at specific sites. Because mass production needs to exploit economies of scale to be cost efficient and thus profitable, the financial viability of these housing systems depended on the scale of construction. The scale of construction, in turn, depended on the size of the market, that is, the effective demand. Since the consumer base was to be low-income and moderate-income households, profitability required financial assistance from the federal government. These subsidies had to be identified and allocated to the projects. They would lower the construction costs of the units, expand effective demand, and increase the scale of construction.

Because Operation Breakthrough was designed to open up the national housing market to industrialization, HUD required local governments to identify places where housing was needed and then to prepare these places to receive *any* of the mass-produced housing systems. In the third phase, HUD wanted producers to have access to standard sites. Consequently, to participate in the demonstration and the subsequent production phase, the sites had to be free of local building and housing codes and zoning ordinances. There could be no variations in regulations from one site to the next—in fact, no local regulations at all. Additionally, union work rules had to be suspended. (Factory-built housing mainly utilizes unskilled labor and thus most construction trade unions had already been eliminated from the process.)

The sites were further extracted from their physical surroundings when the adjacent street pattern was not continued onto the site. The idiosyncrasies of city blocks were viewed as incompatible with mass-produced systems. And, of course, the sites had to be fully cleared of buildings and structures before construction could take place.

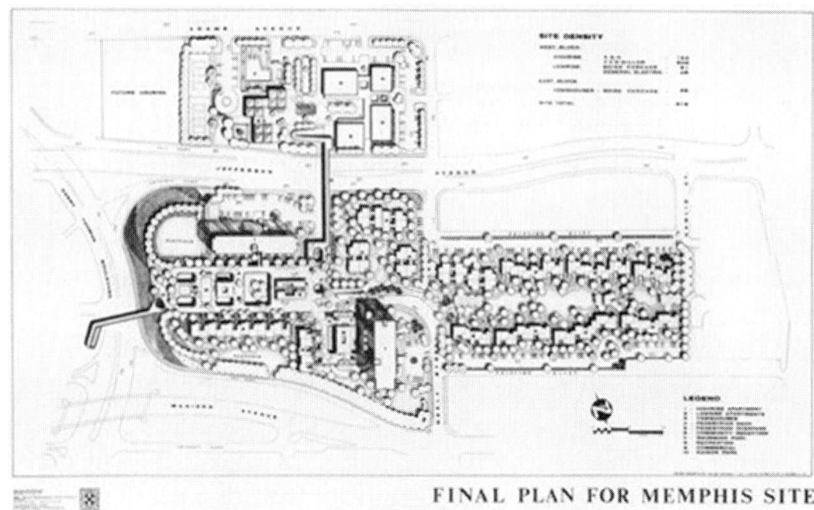

Figure 3.1. The Operation Breakthrough prototype site plan was taken from the "Final Report to Department of Housing and Urban Development for Prototype Site Design and Related Services, Memphis Prototype Site, Operation Breakthrough," dated December 1973 and prepared by Miller, Wihry & Lee, Landscape Architects and Engineers, Inc., Louisville, Kentucky.

Whatever distinctive history or identity these places had was to be suppressed. Consequently, prior narratives were not made part of the development process. Once it was determined that the place was available for residential development and that housing there made locational sense, the professional site narrative was set in motion. Stripped of rules, regulations, and street patterns, the site was then ready to receive the housing systems.

The demonstration phase began with HUD awarding twenty-two contracts for 2,796 housing units at a total cost of $63 million.[14] From that point onward, Operation Breakthrough lost momentum. By late 1972, a number of system producers had gone bankrupt. High start-up costs, inadequate economies of scale, and a lack of long-term commitment by system producers and governments were immediate causes. In addition, a January 1973 federal government freeze on all subsidized housing and the collapse of the housing market when double-digit inflation and unemployment struck the economy in the mid-1970s further contributed to the financial infeasibility of the initiative. In

1980, adding proverbial insult to injury, HUD demolished a 147-unit project in New Haven designed by the architect Philip Johnson. The long-term maintenance and repair costs simply exceeded the costs of demolition and replacement.[15]

In sum, neither the site planners nor HUD gave much value to the prior history of these sites or to how these housing systems would be articulated in relation to the surrounding urban fabric. The stories of people who had once lived and worked in these places, of the changes these communities had undergone, and of the meanings disrupted by such an abrupt design shift were ignored.

This was a national demonstration meant to transform the home-building industry, and it had all the utopian impulses that such an endeavor seemed to require. Romney and his policymakers at HUD wanted to avoid a particular scenario that seemed to pervade the residential building market. In this scenario, "[a] producer has to locate land site by site on which to build housing, then he has to deal site by site with local zoning, building and housing codes, and, of course, locate financing on a project by project basis."[16] Highly inefficient, this was anathema. It had to be changed.

Operation Breakthrough first erased history from the site. Soon thereafter, local government regulations, labor relations, and the surrounding street pattern were cast aside. The only relevant stories about the site were those that indicated its suitability for industrialized housing systems and that positioned it favorably as regards the perplexing problem of market aggregation. Only in this fashion, HUD believed, could Operation Breakthrough overcome fragmentation in the building industry.

This attitude was reinforced by the way the housing system and site identification processes occurred in parallel, only intersecting *after* systems and sites were *independently* selected. The implicit assumption was that for industrialized housing systems to be profitable, they had to be erected on sites that posed few variations from a basic model. Every place in which mass-produced housing was to be located had first to be standardized.

By contrast, American automobile manufacturers, those exemplars of mass production, learned to produce a variety of models and styles and to appeal to a range of desires and needs in segmented markets.[17] Nothing inherent in industrialized or modular housing systems precludes listening to and incorporating the narrative richness of a place.

Thus, nothing impassable stands in the way of treating the site as a bearer of meaning.[18] The designers of Operation Breakthrough thought differently; without standardized sites, mass-produced housing would not be financially viable and would not attract either producers or investors. Place had to become site.

FROM SITE TO PLACE: BRASILIA

From the late-eighteenth century, political elites in Brazil dreamed of establishing a capital city in the interior of this large and resource-rich country. Brazil then, and through to the last half of the twentieth century, was primarily a coastal country. Its major cities and most of its population were arrayed along the Atlantic Ocean. The interior—vast areas of savanna and jungle—was mostly undeveloped. The country was blessed with "boundless resources and untapped wealth."[19] Yet, its destiny was not being realized.

The dream came to fruition under President Juscelio Kubitschek (1956–1961). In 1947, a national commission had designated the Central Plateau—located in the symbolic center of the country—as the place of the new national capital. Not until 1956, however, was a competition held to produce a plan. Twenty-six proposals were submitted. (The competition was open only to architects and planners licensed in Brazil.) The jury selected the submission of Lucio Costas, a self-described "free-lance town planner" and a key figure in the modern movement of architecture and design in Brazil.[20]

Costas offered an "elementary gesture," a dual axis plan with one east–west axis of monumental buildings serving political and administrative functions and a north–south axis of residential and commercial superblocks. In effect, he proposed "one of the oldest devices of urban design," a cross.[21] The architect Oscar Niemeyer, a member of the competition jury, was selected to design the buildings. Like Costas, he was a high modernist in spirit and style.

The actual site was chosen by a team consisting of Belcher Associates of Ithaca, New York, and two Brazilian consultants. Hired in 1954, the team was asked to study a 54,000–square kilometer area on the Central Plateau and to select five alternative sites of 1,000 square kilometers that would support a population of 500,000 peo-

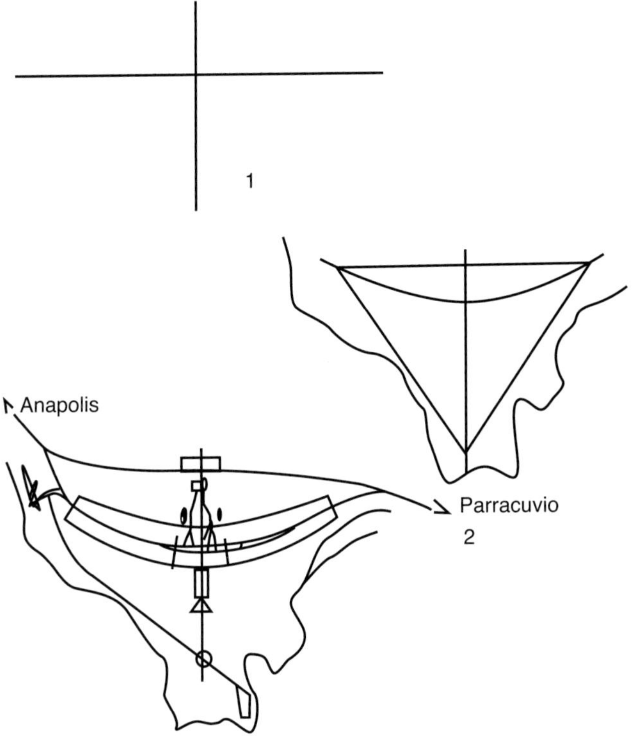

Figure 3.2. Lucio Costas's competition sketches.

ple. The chosen site would be the one that best met criteria established by an earlier government commission. These criteria included an altitude that would provide an amenable climate and reduce the incidence of malaria, moderately sloping terrain with a gradient sufficient for efficient drainage, a nearby water source with hydroelectric power potential, modest distance to an urban center for obtaining supplies during construction, and available construction materials (specifically, sand and gravel). The team made its decision known in 1955, and it was this best site for which Costas drew his highly stylized plan.

The Central Plateau is approximately one thousand kilometers inland from the Atlantic Ocean, not quite halfway across the country to the west, and between 3,000 and 3,500 feet above sea level. It is on the high plains, basically a gently rolling woodland savanna comprised of grasslands, scrubby and scattered deciduous trees, and poor soils. Despite its temperate climate, however, development lagged. In the early 1950s, there were few settlements (mostly isolated towns and agricultural stations), little economic activity, and hardly any industry. "Transportation depended on paths cut into the ground and through the bush...[and were]... almost impassable during the rainy season."[22]

Prior to construction, this region constituted 22 percent of the territory of Brazil but had only 4 percent of the country's population and generated only 3 percent of its national income. Moreover, it was sparsely populated with only one person per square kilometer. By contrast, the east coast (with Rio de Janeiro) had 15 percent of the territory, 34 percent of the population, and accounted for 36 percent of the national income. The southern region around Porto Alegre had comparable figures: 10 percent of the territory, 36 percent of the population, and 50 percent of the national income.[23] To the Brazilian government and most of the country's citizens, the Central Plateau was the undeveloped interior.

This frontier place was subsequently represented by three quite powerful and intersecting narratives. These narratives were at the root of the idea for a new capital city; they shaped the plan and influenced the architecture that came to dominate Brasilia. The first, a story of the Central Plateau as undeveloped and uninhabited, created the place as a site. It emptied it of all but its development potential. Moreover, it prepared the place to receive a highly stylized plan and ultramodernistic architecture. The other two narratives filled the site, turning it into a place it had never been. One set the site in a framework of developmentalism and nation-building that would achieve Brazil's destiny. The other juxtaposed the new capital with the existing capital of Rio de Janeiro and signaled a break from the past.

Brasilia was to be located in a place widely described as wild and undeveloped. Sparsely populated, with vast open spaces, the Central Plateau was the remote interior. One commentator labeled it an "enormous expanse of emptiness," another called the location a "no man's land," and a third referred to the planned city as being built on "virgin soil."[24] The journey from the developed coastal region—from Rio de Janeiro or Salvador or Porto Alegre—to Brasilia involved a transition from densely spaced settlements to an undeveloped interior, from urban congestion and clutter to "silent horizons," and, after the city was built, from busy markets and public conversations (and a familiar Brazil) to desolate commercial strips and an incongruous modernism.[25] The distance from the populous cities of the coast to this planned and artificial capital was more than geographic.

Initially, the Central Plateau was situated in a narrative without history. Nothing had happened there, at least nothing of significance for either the people or the nation of Brazil. That the place was considered empty, however, did not mean that it was without possibilities.

In fact, it was precisely this perceived emptiness that enabled the jury to select Costas's highly stylized and schematic gesture and that allowed Niemeyer to impose a severe and high modernist architecture on its original buildings. The site—a "clean tablecloth," Kubitschek claimed[26]—provided little resistance to an elementary and utopian idea and to a rigid and closed plan. And, since there had been so little development, an architecture characteristic of the interior had not developed. Consequently, Niemeyer could indulge his modernist ambitions and design buildings whose massing and style spoke neither to context nor history but to the future. The plan and buildings gave meaning to the empty site. High modernism was selected to typify the emerging nation. Brasilia was the "new" Brazil, a *de novo* alternative to existing Brazilian cities. It was "...a bold gesture and an act of faith in the future."[27]

The desolate place narrative also enabled a narrative of socioeconomic developmentalism and nation-building. Kutbitschek came into office touting the modernization of Brazil and its potential for becoming a world industrial power and a significant contributor to global trade. His developmentalism called for rapid industrialization, the expansion of domestic markets, and increased trade with other nations. The country was well populated, rich in natural resources, and blessed with major ports and rivers. But, the interior—"the vast expanses of the Brazilian back country"[28]—was undeveloped and its potential was being squandered.

By occupying the interior, by integrating it with the developed coastal cities, the nation could itself be modernized. The interior had to be settled, and this required a growth pole. A planned city would catapult the interior into history and the nation into the future. Quoting Lucio Costas, "Founding a city in the wilderness is a deliberate act of conquest."[29]

Brasilia was to be the wedge that would make the interior desirable to investors and settlers. Centrally located, a national system of highways would be built to connect it to cities across the country. On this 11,000–mile network would travel the internal commerce of the country. Goods would move from the interior to the coast, and from there they would be shipped to other countries. Imports from abroad would arrive at Brazilian ports and be distributed throughout the land. Industrial development and resource extraction in the interior would expand export production and create workers with incomes sufficient to purchase imports. Brasilia, though, would remain a political and administrative capital; its satellites and other cities in the region, now connected to the coast by highways, would be the poles of state-driven industrialization. Further support for industrial development would come from hydroelectric dams, schools, and other public works.

As investment increased and jobs expanded in the interior, population pressure in the large cities such as Rio de Janeiro and Sao Paulo would be reduced. Workers would adapt to the changing landscape of employment opportunities and resettle their families. National integration—economic and social—would be the result. Its spark would be Brasilia, "the symbol of the opening of a vast interior to modernization and the unification of all regions of Brazil."[30]

By occupying "the vast empty core of the nation," the new capital would serve as a catalyst for regional and national development.[31] Through modernization, Brazil would realize its continental destiny. The ultimate goal was to build a nation, an integrated political and economic space overseen from the national capital. This required an end to the underdevelopment of the interior. Only by breaking down the frontier could nation-building be accomplished. Brazil had to be written on the savanna (and the jungle) landscape. This would be progress and it was progress that made a country modern.

Keeping the capital in Rio de Janeiro thwarted this dream. Rio was known for its relaxed lifestyle and its inefficient civil service. Clientalism reigned, with patronage and social connections guiding government policy. At the same time, Rio was home to intellectuals and students, radical ideas, and (as the country's major industrial center) labor activism. Further detracting from its status as the capital city, Rio de

Janeiro still retained a European and thus colonial heritage, a symbolism that blocked the emergence of a new, independent Brazil. Brasilia would signal a symbolic end to Portuguese colonial rule.[32]

To build a modern nation would require strenuous effort, efficient bureaucracies, and an absence of favoritism and corruption. Relocating the capital would allow officials "to breathe the pure air of the plateau" rather than being forced to live "in the atmosphere impregnated with sea, air, burnt oil and cynical sensualism that weighs on Rio."[33] Isolation would provide the critical distance to resist the call of clientalism—and the beaches—and produce a different governmental culture. Brasilia would be the new beginning, lifting the burdens that had kept the country divided between an undeveloped interior and a thriving coast.

Of course, clientalism did not cease with the relocation of the capital. In fact, critics labeled the planned city a massive patronage project. The building of Brasilia was a political act. President Kubitschek wanted to leave a great legacy, and this could not be done in Rio. Any project there would be overwhelmed—both socially and aesthetically—by the existing city and its stunning landscape of beaches and hills. That Brasilia needed to be completed before Kubitschek left office, that it had to proceed as rapidly as possible, was an indication that Kubitschek's vision—"fifty years progress in five"[34]—could not be sustained politically. In fact, "[t]he full-blownness of the city plan was a partial antidote to the danger that future administrations...would succeed in undoing the [plan's] lucidity and authority...."[35]

In sum, the planning and design of Brasilia was implicated in overlapping stories about the Central Plateau. The emptiness of the area provided a "clean canvas" on which to sketch a crisp and highly defined modernist plan and construct an architecture devoid of contextual referents. The plateau's underdevelopment made it ideal both for nation-building and for hosting the anti-Rio. These qualities, though, were not inherent to the place. They were part of shared narratives created to legitimize and guide planning. Brasilia was never a utopian city; it was meant to be somewhere. A place understood as—created as—empty has to be filled with the appropriate narratives. In the case of Brasilia, place had first to become site in order to be turned into a new and different place.

FINAL THOUGHTS

We know little about how urban planners and designers actually go about the deconstruction of place and the narrative construction of sites. We do know that intervention cannot occur, development cannot happen, until the site is brought under control, situated in a professional discourse. To arrive there, prior narratives are reduced in number or, in some instances, totally eliminated. Emboldened by simplification and standardization, analytical description thrives. Such representations cast a particular place in terms of a category of "problems" that the professional knows how to solve.[36]

Places are never emptied. Rather what occurs is a form of discursive displacement. Planners and designers substitute a professional narrative for a multitude of shared histories, collective remembrances, and personal experiences. Unwieldy stories about the place are suppressed and replaced by more actionable understandings. Planners and designers abhor narrative vacuums. Even a cleared site has to have meaning attached to it. To be cleared is to be prepared for, receptive to, a particular intervention. That is what it means for a place to become a site.

The Central Plateau was not raw nature in the mid-twentieth century. Settlements existed, there were small mining operations and a few farms, and cattle grazed on the plains. To support the twin projects of developmentalism and nation-building, Brazil's leaders suppressed this understanding and portrayed the Central Plateau as in a pristine state. The Central Plateau was returned to nature. Proponents of Brasilia then naturalized the site in a second way. They made the Central Plateau seem the only possible location for the new capital. Once the narratives were constructed and publicized, it all made perfect sense.

That a site has to be refilled with narratives to realize the benefits of investment and development points to the complexity of the place–site relationship. It is not enough to establish a new national capital on the plains, build a state-of-the-art baseball stadium downtown, reinvest in housing in an old neighborhood, or turn a derelict waterfront into a park. These places must also, and subsequently, be reinserted into the respective narratives that make up the national identity, list local entertainment options, celebrate gentrification, and extol the attractiveness of city living. Investment requires narrative support.

Part of preparing a place to become a site involves the formation of new narratives. Familiar to anyone who observes real estate development is the narrative onslaught that begins almost immediately as developers and real estate brokers tout the benefits, for example, of their proposed apartment building, its compatibility with urbane lifestyles, and its prestigious address. Planners and designers are complicit in this process. Their presence indicates a seriousness of purpose and even inevitability to the project. Their reports and images portray and publicize the new place. The first act of real estate development is the narrative remaking of the site.

The most likely scenario is the turning of place into site in order then to turn site into place. The connecting element is always the site. The initial place has to pass through the site, as in the case of Operation Breakthrough, to emerge as another and different place. The scenario moves forward by the deployment of preexisting and shared understandings as well as novel interpretations. Because there is no essence to any site, no single truth waiting to be discovered, different site knowledges—of the architect, the investor, the bureaucrat, and others—need to be negotiated. Narratives are constructed and deconstructed prior to but in harmony with the physical transformation eventually to be realized.

Throughout all of this, the default position remains a site story, a story of professional categories and interventions. This is the dominant narrative of planning and design. Like all stories about place, it "weaves the tissue of habits, educates the gaze, [and] informs the landscape."[37] It is the discourse of choice, meaningful within and resonant outside the design professions.

Yet, planning and design projects are never purely analytical; they are fully professionalized only in an ideological sense. Because maintaining a boundary between professional knowledge and what one knows in general is nearly impossible, few planners and designers work wholly from within the standardized site discourse. To do so would be to abandon the last pretense of creativity as well as to misread, possibly fatally, the complexity of the design task.

Notes

1. On the meaning attached to place (and space), see Edward S. Casey, *The Fate of Place: A Philosophical History* (Berkeley: University of California Press, 1997).
2. Carol J. Burns, "On Site: Architectural Preoccupations," in *Drawing/Building/Text,* ed. Andrea Kahn (New York: Princeton Architectural Press, 1991), 149.
3. Marc Auge, *Non-Places: Introduction to an Anthropology of Supermodernity* (London: Verso, 1995), 51–56.
4. On the redevelopment of the World Trade Center site see Paul Goldberger, "Groundwork: How the Future of Ground Zero Is Being Resolved," *The New Yorker* 78, 12 (May 20, 2002): 86–95; and Michael Sorkin and Sharon Zukin, eds., *After the World Trade Center: Rethinking New York City* (New York: Routledge, 2002). On the history of the World Trade Center, see Eric Darton, *Divided We Stand: A Biography of New York's World Trade Center* (New York: Basic Books, 1999).
5. *Representations of space* and *representational space* are phrases drawn from Henri Lefebvre. See his *The Production of Space* (Malden, MA: Blackwell, 1991); and Andy Merrifield, *Metromarxism* (New York: Routledge, 2002), 71–92. On the ways in which we encounter places, see Helen Liggett, *Urban Encounters* (Minneapolis: University of Minnesota Press, 2003).
6. The phrase is Michel Foucault's, made in a comment about a famous list by Jorge Borges that eliminated, Foucault notes, the site that enables entities to be ordered. See Liggett, *Urban Encounters*, 41–42.
7. In this sense, the ostensibly empty site is not the non-place discussed by Marc Auge. For Auge, a non-place is ambiguous, a place where a person experiences a self-suspension. A site is unambiguous. See his *Non-Places*; and also *In the Metro* (Minneapolis: University of Minnesota Press, 2002), xviii.
8. On these points, see Samuel Weber, *Institutions and Interpretation* (Minneapolis: University of Minnesota Press, 1987), 18–32.
9. For a rich and evocative exploration of the relations between social meanings and urban design, see Brian Ladd, *The Ghosts of Berlin: Confronting German History in the Urban Landscape* (Chicago: University of Chicago Press, 1997).
10. Alexander Reichl tells the story of the Times Square (New York City) redevelopment from a discursive–political perspective in his *Reconstructing Times Square* (Lawrence: University Press of Kansas, 1999). See also Sharon Zukin et al., "From Coney Island to Las Vegas in the Urban Imaginary: Discursive Practices of Growth and Decline," *Urban Affairs Review* 33 (1998): 627–654; and Charles Stansfield, "Atlantic City and the Resort Cycle," *Annals of Tourism Research* 5 (1978): 238–251.
11. See Margaret Farmer, "Toward a Decent Home...For Every American Family," *Architectural Record* 146 (1969): 131–134. For a contrary view of the home-building industry, see Tom Schlesinger and Mark Erlich, "Housing: The Industry Capitalism Didn't Forget," in *Critical Perspectives in Housing,* eds. Rachel Bratt, Chester Hartman, and Ann Meyerson (Philadelphia: Temple University Press, 1986), 139–163. The precursors to mass-produced hous-

ing were the mail-order houses of the early twentieth century sold by Sears, Roebuck & Co., among others. See Dolores Hayden, *Building Suburbia: Green Fields and Urban Growth, 1820–2000* (New York: Pantheon Books, 2003), 97–127. The more contemporary version of this housing is manufactured housing. See Andy Leon Horner, "Putting the Pieces Together," *The Washington Post* (March 19, 1987): 19.

12. See Robertson Ward, Jr., "Breakthrough?," *AIA Journal* 55 (1971): 17–22; "Winners Assembled for Breakthrough," *Business Week* 2113 (1970): 35; and Marguerite Villelo and John Morris Dixon, "Breakthrough?," *The Architectural Forum* 132 (1970): 50–61.
13. Villelo and Dixon, "Breakthrough?"
14. Schlesinger and Erlich, "Housing: The Industry Capitalism Didn't Forget," 144.
15. Schlesinger and Erlich, "Housing; The Industry Capitalism Didn't Forget," 145.
16. Don Raney and Suzanne Stephens, "Operation Breakthrough: Operation P/R," *Progressive Architecture* 51 (1970): 120.
17. Hayden, *Building Suburbia*, 132, makes a similar comparison.
18. See Andrea Kahn, "Overlooking: A Look at How We Look at Site or...Site as Discrete Object of Desire," in *Desiring Practices: Architecture, Gender and the Interdisciplinary*, ed. Duncan McCorquodale, Katerina Ruedi, and Sarah Wigglesworth (London: Black Dog Publisher, 1996), 174–185.
19. Norma Evenson, "The Symbolism of Brasilia," *Landscape* 18 (1969): 19.
20. For general background on the planning, design, and construction of Brasilia, see David G. Epstein, *Brasilia, Plan and Reality (*Berkeley: University of California Press, 1973); Norma Evenson, *Two Brazilian Capitals: Architecture and Urbanism in Rio de Janeiro and Brasilia* (New Haven: Yale University Press, 1973); James Holston, *The Modernist City: An Anthropological Critique of Brasilia* (Chicago: University of Chicago Press, 1989); James Scott, *Seeing Like a Stat*e (New Haven: Yale University Press, 1998), 117–130; Willy Staubli, *Brasilia* (London: Leonard Hill Books, 1966); and Lawrence J. Vale, *Architecture, Power, and National Identity* (New Haven: Yale University Press, 1992), 15–27. This was not the first planned city in Brazil; that was Belo Horizonte, inaugurated in 1896.
21. Evenson, *Two Brasilian Capitals*, 146. Evenson notes that most of the submitted designs embraced a "rigid formality, a lack of intimacy with the site." See her "The Symbolism of Brasilia," 22. On the same page, she points out that Costas did not "set foot on the site" until after construction was nearly complete in order "to be free of the temptation to vitiate the purity of the design."
22. Staubli, *Brasilia*, 11.
23. E. Bradford Burns, *A History of Brazil* (New York: Columbia University Press, 1993)(3rd edition), 420.
24. These three phrases are from Holston, *The Modernist City*, 14; David E. Snyder, "Alternate Perspectives on Brasilia," *Economic Geography* 40 (1964): 35; and Staubli, *Brasilia*, 10, respectively.
25. Holston, *The Modernist City*, 3.
26. Quoted in Scott, *Seeing Like a State*, 118.

27. Evenson, *Two Brasilian Capitals*, 104.
28. "Brasilia," in *Encyclopedia Britannica* (Chicago: William Benton, Publisher, 1993), 108.
29. Staubli, *Brasilia*, 12.
30. Burns, *A History of Brasil*, 403.
31. Snyder, "Alternative Perspectives on Brasilia," 35.
32. Epstein, *Brasilia, Plan and Reality*, 28–30.
33. The quote is attributed to Mario Penna, a leading apologist for the capital's transfer. See Epstein, *Brasilia, Plan and Reality*, 30. On the politics of spatiality and the spatiality of identity, see Jane M. Jacobs, *Edge of Empire: Postcolonialism and the City* (London: Routledge, 1996).
34. Quoted in Holston, *The Modernist City*, 84.
35. Epstein, *Brasilia, Plan and Reality*, 52.
36. Another way to think about these issues is in terms of emplotment. How does the planner or urban designer set the site in a story of intersecting narratives, a story that brings meaning to their differences and also serves professional goals? See Hayden White, "Interpretation in History," in *Tropics of Discourse* (Baltimore: Johns Hopkins University Press, 1978), 51–80.
37. Auge, *Non-Places*, 108.

4

Groundwork

Robin Dripps

> ...If background seems inappropriately modest, we should remember that in our modern use of the word it means that which underscores not only our identity and presence, but also our history.[1]
>
> **J.B. Jackson**

The purpose of this essay is to develop an awareness and understanding of the structure of the ground so that its potential for making connection can become a part of any architecture that engages it.[2] The term *ground* will be used in a literal sense to describe the structure and processes of the earth, but also as metaphor. Metaphorically, ground refers to the various patterns of physical, intellectual, poetic, and political structure that intersect, overlap, and weave together to become the context for human thought and action. Unfortunately, things operating in the background—including the earth—have not always been well understood or valued. It is easy to understand how the earth's rough and bumpy surfaces, its uncertain and shifting fixity and its damp porosity, could be considered qualities that would destabilize physical, political, and even psychological equilibrium. But, it is not only the intense earthiness of the earth that proves problematic, but the whole question of how humans ground their thoughts, actions,

Figure 4.1. Scarperia, Italy. The structure of agricultural fields merges with and informs the political structure of the city.

and structures so that effective hypotheses can be made about relationships among things. As humans become more confident in the capacity for will to shape the world, the preexisting background contexts that support these acts of will become less compelling. The consequence of an indifference to the ground is an almost terminal insensitivity to the rich subtleties of the teeming wild, the variegated forms and materials of the landscape, the nuanced patterns of urban texture, and the rituals of the every day. This is the very stuff from which special moments emerge and distinguish themselves. It also provides the necessary complexity to promote an almost endless variety of relationships among things.

WHAT CONSTITUTES GROUND?

One could imagine that the term *site* might encompass the network of social, political, and environmental connections in operation beyond the confines of a building. Yet this is not the case. Though understanding of site and ground tend to conflate, they have distinctly different meanings. A site, in contrast to a ground, is quite simple. This is undoubtedly why the idea of a site becomes so appealing to architects and planners. A site possesses a reassuring degree of certainty, whereas the ground is always in flux. A site's edges are known and a center can always be found. Connections to the world beyond are limited and tightly controlled. Sites can be owned. In other words, the site takes on many of the qualities of an institution. As such, it reduces the complexity of both human and natural interactions to guide with assurance the polity it has gathered within. It has become a figure and has thereby reduced the potential for accommodating the fullest range of human possibility.

The spatial circumscription of *ground* into the more simply understood gestalt of *site* removes the context required to see and understand how the site is a part of something larger, and therefore limits or alters the scope of its meaning similar to the temporal circumscription of events that takes place within modern historical reporting. Comparing modern historical methodology with vernacular history offers a useful analogy to elucidate the nature of ground relative to site. Within modern history, the duration chosen to circumscribe a particular historical event has typically been short. The consequence of this limited temporal duration has been an emphasis on describing catastrophe, war, and destruction because these are bounded events that take very little time. These slices of life are objectified as autonomous events, making them difficult to reattach to the ongoing unfolding of existence beyond their limited artificial boundaries.

In contrast to modern history, vernacular history has a different view of temporal duration. Here, stories of everyday life record typical events and recurring themes whose smooth running is noticed only when disrupted. The emphasis on repeating pattern and process requires a large enough temporal context to be certain that phenomena are in fact recurring.[3] When actions repeat, they are not objectified or taken out of context, but instead become something continually taking on new meaning through participation in a larger pattern of recurrences whose cyclical nature has no discernible beginning or end. As a consequence, vernacular history gives greater weight to the background. What the modern historian would consider as a proper historical event is nothing more than the interruption or disturbance of the smoothly running background machinery of everyday life. These exceptions understandably command more attention, but as they continue to be further distinguished from their normative supporting context, they become increasingly isolated, objectified, and disengaged from everything that has given them meaning. As a further consequence, genuinely significant events become difficult to recognize as being special when removed from the background field that served to register their difference from the typical.

Comprehension of these temporal cycles can be found in Greek mythology. Homer understood the stabilizing importance of a background of recurring temporal cycles. The heroic episodes of the *Odyssey* are measured against a background ordered by the repeating patterns of external phenomena—the cycle of sunrise and sunset, the action of wind on waves and on leaves, the relationship of heavenly bodies, the movement of birds and animals, the annual cycle of change. Human life and activity are thus brought into the orbit of these natural events. The repeating patterns of simile within his poetry reveal human order by finding a correspondence between this and the order of nature. Modern poetry more typically works in the opposite way by projecting human order onto nature and then abstracting this back to human order.[4]

The valuation of the ground as part of a larger cultural proposition was an essential characteristic within Native American tradition. Speaking to a class of environmental design students, Oren Lyons, the faith keeper of the Onondaga Nation explained his tribe's attitude about the earth: "What you call resources we call our relatives." His comment puts a different perspective on how to value the ground. There is little or no distance between the ground and human artifice so that the theoretical opposition separating natural and human systems that was initiated in the Renaissance and still persists would be unthinkable. The analogy between the ground and the structure of human relationships implies a similarly intelligible pattern of relationships within the ground. It is interesting to think about the increased particularity and character that the earth must assume when imagined with such anthropomorphic qualities. This metaphorical extended family would immediately have a structure that would connect all its members in a recognizable and understandable way, making the ground an intrinsic part of the human condition.

Primitive societies were not alone in valuing the ground as part of a larger cultural construct. The painters of the Hudson River School in late-nineteenth-century America worked within a similar idea to that seen in the Onondaga Nation. Their paintings reveal their interest in representing the structure, texture, and meaning of the geomorphology and the natural history of the Hudson Valley, where a background, temporal substrate mattered more than idealized, decontextualized landscape figures. For Albert Bierstadt, Frederic Church, Thomas Cole, and other nineteenth-century American landscape painters, it was the emerging understanding of the geological structure of the earth that would ground a contemporary culture. But instead of remaining in the

Figure 4.2. Thomas Cole, *The Course of Empire: Arcadia or The Pastoral State*, 1836.

background, the earth, seen in its literal geological sense, took on a transcendent meaning. As such, it was thought to be a work capable of rivaling and possibly even exceeding the value of the cultural production of Europe. The continuing presence of such a powerful, evocative, and wild nature, something long vanished from European consciousness, became a legitimizing cultural asset with a temporal reach extending beyond history.

> ...Geology was the Great Myth of the nineteenth century. If offered Americans a past at once more recent and more remote: the wilderness, ever new in its virginity, also stretched back into primordial time. That past was crucial in establishing an American sense of identity—sought nowhere more than in landscape painting. By augmenting science with inspiration, the artist could get closer to the elusive enigmas of Creation, and also approach solutions that might confirm American's providential destiny.[5]

When valued as a cultural product as well as a natural resource the processes, connections, stories, and meanings of the ground take on a different cast. The more readily grasped social, political, and physical structures that give a culture its unique particularity are brought into relationship with the immense and less comprehensible scale of natural process. The discontinuous and fragmented intentions that always compete for cultural authority can also possess a degree of coherence by virtue of being allied with the continuous structure of systems operating over much larger spatial and temporal territory. In turn, the structure of the ground is brought into contact with human artifice and made intelligible as part of this world.

The import of understanding the ground in cultural terms is evident in ancient Greece with its earth-based system of belief. Ancient Greek faith, with its focus on ancestors as the object of worship, has been characterized as a religion of the dead.[6] The souls of the dead did not depart for a foreign world; they continued to exist underground in close proximity to the living, from whom they required regular attention. This gave to the soil a meaning of considerable personal import, suggesting an unexpected vitality. The advice to bury the dead near the front entrance of the house to facilitate consultation with one's ancestors when leaving or returning reveals much about this vitality and the grounding anticipated from generational continuity. This was not land to be easily abandoned. In fact, a man could not quit his dwelling place without taking with him his soil, or in other words, his ancestors.

Another crucial place in the Greek domestic environment, the hearth, also connects to the ground. As the central focus of the Greek house, this symbol of domesticity was also part of a familial connection to the land. The hearth was engaged in the veneration of ancestors, with its sacred fire representing their constant presence. Hearth and ground are thus intertwined in an intense relationship. The hearth's vertical extension is its most obvious visible attribute. This totem pointing to the sky gives the hearth its initial sense of figural autonomy. But its foundation tells a different story. The material of its massive structure seems to grow directly from the earth, giving the hearth its contradictory aspect of being both figure and extension of the web of relationships intrinsic to the ground. The fire within is just as ambiguous, being at once the means by which humans have kept the wildness of nature at bay, and yet a very part of that same nature.[7]

The hearth also finds special charge and connection to ground within modern history. Writing in the mid-nineteenth century, Gottfried Semper shows the same equivocal relationship between the figural hearth and its situation as part of the earth that the ancient Greeks understood. The hearth, according to Semper in *The Four Elements of Architecture*, was the catalyst and focus for the foundation of political and religious culture. It was the moral element of architecture. Protecting the hearth and mediating its relationships to nature were the remaining three elements: the mound, the enclosure, and the roof. Although few in number, these elements intersect and engage one another in an unexpectedly complex manner. The mound, a part of the earth, serves as the base for the hearth, increasing its figural autonomy but also connecting it to a context of infinite possibilities. Extensive topographic, geomorphic, political, and ecological structures are all brought into focus as they converge on the hearth and provide a substantial grounding for the humans who dwell there. The potential complexity of the ensuing interactions produces an equivalently complex response among the elements within Semper's dwelling. They change the balance between figure and ground that had been the basis for most prior hypotheses on the origins of architecture. As each of the elements become more independent, each can respond to a different aspect of nature and a wider range of human desire. Both woven mat and masonry wall handle the tasks of enclosure, but in different ways. The mat, loaded with all the connective metaphors derived from weaving, defines the social space of the dwelling, while the masonry wall provides protection and a sense of permanence. Unlike the lightweight mat, with its greater spatial freedoms, the wall is part of the ground. It grows from the making of terraces and thus reveals the underlying topographical structure of its earthen context and grounds local place in a larger world.

A curious note by Semper explains how the human being "...most probably arose from the plains as the last mud-creation, so to speak."[8] Is Semper hinting that the basis for his elemental architecture is in the relationships that the ultimate figure, the human, engages in with the earth? If the muddy ground can quicken into life, then there must be more to the earth than is currently understood to enable the level of complexity, ambiguity, and poetic profundity expected of human relationships. When humans enter into a relationship with the ground, they engage more than its extensive physical network of connections.

The structure and materiality of the ground has figured prominently in literary works as a metaphor for aspects of human consciousness that escape simple description. By reading closely from a wide variety of poetic and literary works, the phenomenologist Gaston Bachelard has proposed a set of spatial relationships common to both, enabling spatial structure and poetic content to be compared. The ground plays an important part in his conclusions. It forms one pole in a spatial construct linking earth to sky that he considers one of the fundamental relationships guiding human thought and action. The attic, with its clearly articulated structure exposed to view, its removal from the particularity of the ground, which gives it its greater sense of perspective on things, and its mnemonic capacity coming from the contents typically stored within, is considered the rational part of the house. The cellar, with walls just barely holding back the vast and formless extent of the earth beyond, is both physically and poetically the dark entity of the house. Bachelard proposes that within the cellar thoughts turn to the irrational.[9] Irrationality, however, must not be understood as negative, but instead as the source of other intuitions about our relationship to the world that complement and amplify those that come from the more transparent processes of reasoning.[10]

The special condition of the cellar, a place in and of the ground that humans can occupy, makes its structure and its unique qualities worth study. Properties of the cellar reveal much about the structure and potential of the ground itself. Equating the spatial disposition of the cellar and its loaded poetic content to the unique structure of the ground further demonstrates how architecture can engage this ground.

The cellar is only experienced from within. Without the light of day, its vague and shifting contours, its partial completion, and its many twisting passages contribute to its sense of being boundless, extending beyond easy comprehension. Without boundary, there can be no discernible form and consequently no figure. The cellar, with its actual and implied extensions into the ground, becomes the perfect counter to the figures placed upon it. Its single-sided walls hold back the earth but also make us constantly aware of the ground's immediacy. Actually and metaphorically, this ground becomes a powerful part of the cellar's territory, further extending and complicating its closure.

The cellar contrasts with a site's simple autonomy and provides the antidote to its inhabitant's estrangement with the world. Its depth(s) confound the flat, two-dimensional constraints of the platted site with its defined political and economic limits. "If the dreamer's house is in the city it is not unusual that the dream is one of dominating in depth the surrounding cellars. His abode wants the undergrounds of legendary fortified castles, where mysterious passages that run under the enclosing walls, the ramparts and the moat put the heart of the castle into communication with the distant forest."[11] The heart of the castle requires these enclosing walls, ramparts, and moat for protection, to distinguish it from its context, and give it the figural form needed to operate as an autonomous political center. But the security of human artifice is short lived unless it is capable of responding effectively to the unpredictable changes inevitably taking place outside its control. Forest and ground are just those places that tend to destabilize the authority of human artifice so that these subterranean passages connecting to the distant forest become the necessary complement to a premature foreclosing of political and personal inquiry. Concentration and extension coexist to make this complex whole. Thus, the section cutting through the castle from sky to earth extends the closed figure of the plan and connects it to possibilities not yet imagined.

WHERE IS THE GROUND?

Techniques for translating the entanglement of the ground into the cellar appear in the layered archaeological sites common in places built over a long period of time, as in Rome, for example. Successive layers of ground having distinct properties of geometry, dimension, and alignment, representing successive political and cultural moments, coexist in a dense sectional collage. The ground here, however, does not provide a stable datum. Moving across these sites, the shifting section of the terrain reveals its multiple ground planes intersecting, reinforcing, or else contradicting one another to produce a new set of volumes, linking these fragments of the past to conditions of the present. What once was the network of public life—the streets, courtyards, gardens, and squares—is now part of a vast and not easily grasped underground world that on occasion disrupts the certainty of the ground above to participate in this life as well. Contemporary scaffolding, erected as an additional layer to stabilize ancient walls and protect workers and artifacts, often becomes legible as another form of architecture—a more ambiguous set of porches, trellises, and porticos that further intersect with this other architecture of the ground.

Recurring physical and political structures operating in the background are crucial components of the urban matrix. Patterns of streets, alleys, and other urban pathways have a structure, hierarchy, and political and social coding that become a powerful stabilizing datum. The way a section of the city is platted—and the patterns, dimensions, and alignments of this—reveals relationships between public and private property. This often provides clues to conventional modes of construction, such as the repetitive pattern of masonry-bearing walls, that describe a scale of development common to many smaller American cities. The history of changes that this platting has undergone tells a story of constant negotiation between a place, its people, and the political intentions that bear on it from the outside. Not so obvious, but no less crucial, is the structure of public works that supports and determines the scope and pattern of development.

While these are mostly considered in instrumental terms, this has not always been the case. Many American and European cities have revealed rather than hidden their systems of water supply and celebrated this at critical moments through fountains and other public displays. Aside from the obvious potential for this to be a place of public gathering, this visual reminder of the source of water might extend into the private realm. Turning on the faucet might activate, with the water, an understanding of the connection to the watershed and the consequence of water usage.[12]

The pattern of manhole, gas, and water valve covers dotting streets and sidewalks often tells a story about what is there and what has disappeared. Even when obsolete, they remain witness to buildings and people who once were part of a place.

The topographical structure of many urban places is all but invisible, having undergone centuries of change as part of the process of urbanization. Being aware of the topographic past and its history of alteration provides a much broader temporal background to make

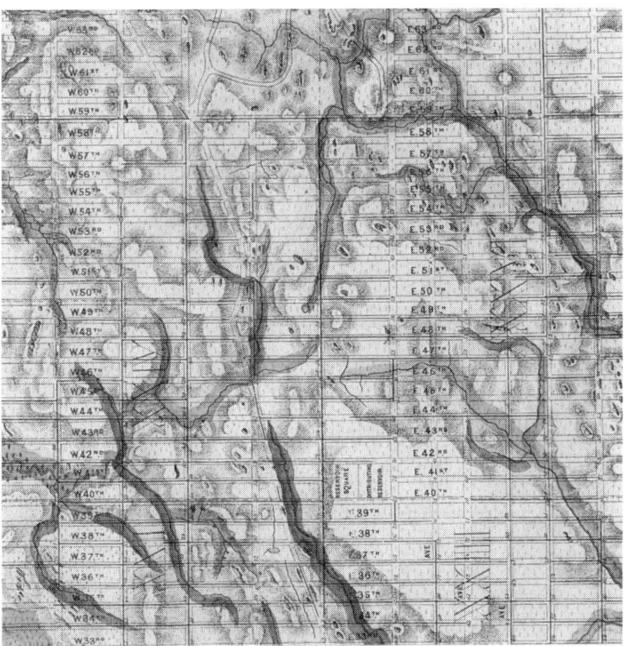

Figure 4.3. Egbert Viele, *Topographical Map of the City of New York Showing Original Water Courses and Made Land,* 1865.

effective and imaginative decisions in the present. When Egbert Viele made his topographical map of the city of New York in 1865, his purpose was to show the extent of the underground water system that was rapidly disappearing from public view as a result of leveling and filling to assist development.[13] Although Viele was primarily concerned with stopping the spread of plague, which he believed to be a consequence of the trapped water beneath the city, his recommendation to open these sources and allow them to flow again suggests a far more ambitious strategy. Using his maps, which are still the most reliable source for anticipating subsurface problems, it would now be possible to take advantage of, or make the best of, these evocative watercourses by bringing them into the design of the city as something with intrinsic value. The meandering streams running mostly diagonally through the city have a logic and pattern of connection different from the rigors of the orthogonal, cellular grid imposed over them. The conjunction of the political, which operates locally, with the extensive pattern of the hydrological structure, offers opportunities to open the bounded site to places far beyond. Along with this comes the ability to use the natural system to create local microclimates as part of a larger project of environmental control.

The movement of animals and humans is another part of the urban ground that needs to be made visible so that its patterns can be effectively engaged. These patterns extend well beyond the boundaries of the site and signal connections to other resources that merit awareness. Animals move with respect to water source, vegetation, and other crucial aspects of habitat that operate at a large scale and require continuity. The local manifestation of this will be subtle and not readily noticed but provides access to a vital source of potential ecological support. The systematic flow of information that is a by-product of human movement is another opportunity needing to be incorporated within the site. These less visible patterns need to be mapped to become part of design thinking.

Outside the city, actual and vestigial agricultural structures create a pattern of fields, hedgerows, and farm roads. This pattern can often be found in older maps and traced in current aerial photographs. When these images are compared with a present condition that has taken a different developmental turn, it is often possible to understand how many planning decisions were unacknowledged responses to these older patterns. It is clear that the original patterns were the result of very acute observations about local topographical, hydrological, and climatic structures and were modified by consequent movements of people and animals. The scale and orientation of these former agricultural patterns become reliable guides to contemporary development, connecting this to the ecological sensitivity that was a part of the prior life of the land.

GENERAL QUALITIES OF GROUND

The vast diversity and unlimited combinatorial and connective potential of the ground suggests an expansive account of the site. Perhaps rather than limiting the site to its artificial political and economic boundaries, the site ought to be considered more as a special repository of clues—an opening to more extensive and varied grounds. Here are indications of complex ecological systems too immense to be contained in so small a place. Here is provocative evidence of human purpose, often in conflict and filled with new potential. Also, here are the diverse fragments of individual stories still waiting completion. The potential of these clues lies in the suggestive possibilities that these seemingly incomplete artifacts offer and in their ability to be combined, reconfigured, or hybridized without the formal or intellectual compromises suffered by a more complete and closed entity. In this way, multiple relationships and even contrary interpretations are promoted as a means to engage a broadly diverse audience.

Grounds operate with great nuance. They resist hierarchy. There are no axes, centers, or other obviously explicit means of providing orientation. Single, uncomplicated meanings are rare. Instead, there are open networks, partial fields, radical repetition, and suggestive fragments that overlap, weave together, and constantly transform. Within this textural density edges, seams, junctures, and other gaps reveal moments of fertile discontinuity where new relationships might grow. Relationships among grounds are multiple, shifting, and inclusive. They engage the particular and the concrete rather than the abstract and the general. The rich and even contradictory context needed to enlarge our understanding of self and world resides in the elaborative potential of individual hypotheses about how to put all these pieces together.[14] In other words, discoveries made within the ground are likely to offer profound and rewarding challenges to the human intellect.

FORMAL POTENTIAL: HOW ARCHITECTURE CAN ENGAGE THESE STRUCTURES

Despite a continuing project to open architecture to the world beyond, modern architecture has remained obstinately self-contained. Although effective in housing institutions, architecture has been less successful in connecting these to the life of a place and its people through a fabric of relationships. It is not as if architecture is itself unable to make these connections. On the contrary, there have been many promising strategies to extend the interior domain of the building beyond its walled enclosure. Wright's effective breaking open of the box, the neoplastic propositions of Van de Veldt, Rietveldt and Mies van der Rohe, or Le Corbusier's purist explorations into phenomenal transparency are a few examples of inventive ways to defy the closure of conventional rooms. Recent architects have shown even more complex fractured and folded planes that claim to abolish distinctions between inside and outside. And if the modern project has legitimate parentage well before its conventional historic boundaries, then the Mannerist work of Romano, Michelangelo, and Peruzzi all demonstrate the degree to which architectural limits can be successfully breeched. But to what end? The absence of any substantial theory regarding the ground makes all of these efforts incomplete. In other words, any theory for opening up, fragmenting, or blurring distinction between inside and out must have a better grasp on the nature of what is outside.

Outside, the ground already exists as part of a broad network of political, social, and ecological systems. If these systems were able to be part of the architectural whole, then the social, political, and environmental alienation that characterizes modern life might be effectively ameliorated. The difficulty, however, is that this ground is multilayered, multivalent, open, and unburdened by the overall consistency and coherency that is the basis for institutional stability. Although an unmediated engagement of this would be problematically chaotic, its current exclusion is just as problematically reductive.

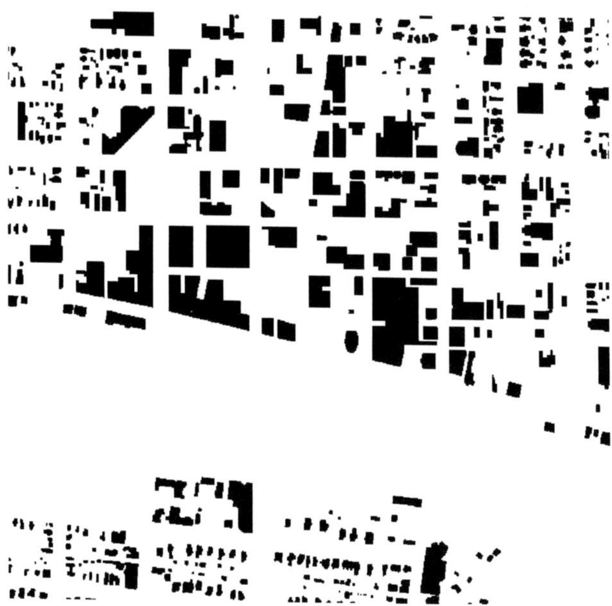

Figure 4.4. Figure–ground drawing.

For architecture to substantially engage the ground, there needs to be effective ways to make this ground as visible and compelling as buildings. Within architecture, the most common graphic for showing a building in a larger context is the figure–ground drawing. In this simple black-and-white graphic, buildings are black and all else is white. Its original intent, coming from Gestalt psychology, was to show how the vestigial space around buildings could itself be formed into a figure just as recognizable as that of the surrounding buildings. The puzzling graphic of the profile of two faces framing a void that also can be read as the figure of a classical Greek vase is a familiar example that convincingly demonstrates how the composition of figures in relationship to one another can reveal a place of value in between that was not previously recognized. The new place, in turn, grounds these same figures. Unfortunately, the common use of this graphic has strayed far from its origins and now represents little more than an unrelated aggregation of objects floating aimlessly within a void. Since this is typically rendered on standard white paper, the black buildings are not just the only thing represented but in fact the only things that are actually ever drawn. The empty white space is not a pregnant silence waiting to take on meaning from what surrounds it, but instead a space so devoid of character that even the surrounding figures seem to lose a degree of their own quality. At best, it has value as a future building opportunity: a void waiting for its architectural life. What was initially meant to demonstrate reciprocity between figure and ground now serves only to remove the building from its physical context. The ground displaced by the building can hardly be missed because it is shown as having nothing to contribute in the first place. It is easy to see why the empty spaces surrounding much of the built environment become filled with paved parking lots. The fault here lies not necessarily with what is made visible (those black buildings) but with a widespread myopia that makes so much else invisible, including so crucial a presence as the drawing medium itself, for, as Henri Foccilon has observed, although a text is invariably indifferent to the paper it is written on, paper is an essential element of life for a drawing.

As buildings accommodate human purpose, they take on enormous weight. Through these projections of individual and collective human will it is possible to take a stand against the indifference of nature to define what it means to be human. The task is so improbably difficult that when something comes of it, this is certainly worthy of notice and celebration. But returning to the pale account of the figural "other"—the missing ground—it seems that this stand (which, of course, is the original meaning of the term *object*) is hollow. When shown without substance, the ground will be easily displaced rather than offering the necessary resistance that produces constructive dialogue.

For architecture to remain a significant part of human existence, it must take up the challenge of entering into a dialogue with the ground. In so doing, architecture would then be capable of poetically and pragmatically mediating the heroic aspirations of human intent and the shadowy outlines of natural process, the shifting and uncertain structures of social formations, and the traces of inherited rituals that show earlier attempts to make sense of everyday life. But the empty, open space surrounding thoughts, actions, and places leaves these ungrounded, unconnected, and at odds with one another. Their random accumulation fails to make substantial contribution to the understanding of the human condition. It seems as though figures of all kinds have been let down, and, as a consequence, human existence diminished.

The intense interest with figures in contemporary architecture can be seen as a direct outcome of internal debate within the Ecole des Beaux-Arts at a time when long-standing conventions of putting things together were being codified into a system of composition that has overtly and covertly influenced almost all subsequent thinking about the topic. The point of friction at the Ecole arose when considering whether the figure ought to exist on its own, free of contingency, and therefore completely under the control of its author, or else give up some of this autonomy by engaging the intellectual and physical context to such a degree that both figure and ground are significantly transformed. But if the architect was to cede ground to a pre-existing context over which little control could be expected, was this too great a loss? The contested positions are revealed in the course notes of Quatremère de Quincy, where he clearly equivocated on the exact values that might initiate the process of design.[15] Quatremère uses two distinct but related terms in his discussion of the design process: *prendre parti* and *tirer parti*. *Prendre parti*, from which the more common architectural term *parti* derives, means to take a stand. As such, it becomes the starting point or fundamental premise on which a design is based. The successful *parti* must be clear, easily grasped, unambiguous, and unencumbered by attachments that might

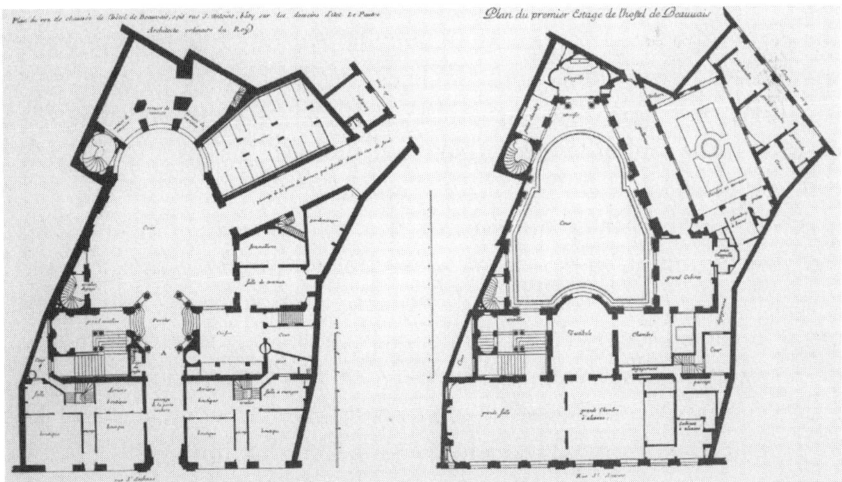

Figure 4.5. Antoine Le Pautre, Hotel de Beauvais, Paris, 1752.

compromise its formal authority. The figural object standing apart from its messy context perfectly fits this description.

But Quatremère also mentions *tirer parti* as the foundation for design thinking. *Tirer parti* means to take advantage of or make the best from what you find. This is a very different proposition. It shifts attention away from the architectural object as an autonomous, abstract formal ideal and privileges the existing physical and political context that a design would have to engage. Le Pautre's Hotel de Beauvais, built in Paris in the mid-seventeenth century, is an inventive example of this. Its site could hardly be more irregular, being made up of leftover fragments of other properties built at different times. Below ground are medieval foundations of substantial size and evocative configuration. Although a regular figure, the central court of the hotel is surrounded by a fantastic variety of rooms with alignments to at least four primary systems of order. Multiple entries respond to two streets of very different character. The typical garden has been displaced to an upper level, giving views onto yet another part of the city so that even the certainty of the ground plane is called into doubt. Although a residence for a single family, its stables and other supporting services—along with its included group of small shops—further confound the sense of clear boundary or simple divisions of public and private activity. Le Pautre did indeed make the best of what he found. The result is a building with the programmatic complexity of a piece of the city. Its architecture reveals to its inhabitants the competing histories of all that surrounds. At the same time, multiple connections, both literal and implied, are established with different parts of a large and varied neighborhood. This was accomplished with no loss to the figure, whose presence remains in the form of the principle courtyard.

Over a century later, the issue of what was to be the basis of design was just beginning to be resolved, as evidenced by Ledoux's presentation of his design for the Hotel d'Evry. In plan this too makes the most of its impacted, complex site. Yet, when Ledoux renders the building in elevation, it is depicted as a simple ideal object with no site encumbrances whatsoever. The structure appears as a freestanding pavilion in a park. *Prendre parti* was clearly becoming the dominant mode of operation. With modern education in architecture being an outgrowth of teaching within the latter years of the Ecole des Beaux-Arts, it is not surprising that the figural object has continued its ascendancy while the ground has become mute.

The rise of a theory of composition that emphasizes the independence of the building from its physical, political, and environmental context parallels a change in the understanding and valuation of the term *to invent.* With designers freed from contextual constraint, their building could now be assessed in terms of how inventive they were. To be inventive typically describes a condition of novelty or newness and places the most value on things not seen before. The consequence for architecture is an aggregation of unrelated buildings vying for attention by virtue of how they stand out from one another and from the cities and landscapes that surround them. Although this is the common understanding of the phrase *to invent,* historically the term means to come upon and implies a process of discovery in which new relationships are found for things and ideas that already exist. This is remarkably similar to *tirer parti.*

There is yet another term that should be brought to this convergence, and that is *to represent,* which literally means to reveal or to make present something that, although always there, has remained obscure or hidden. In other words, the fundamental activity of representing the world and the place of humans within it, the inventive relationships that underlie creative making, and the inventive opportunities that derive from making the best of what is found, are remarkably entangled. The common ground here is just that—the ground out of which all these relationships emerge. Think of common ground, or being grounded, as revealed by J. B. Jackson when he describes landscape serving as the background for collective human existence.

FIGURING GROUND

The consequences of our blindness to the rich and subtle structures of the ground extend to the figure. When the ground becomes abstract, general, and less articulate, there is less incentive to find subtle nuance within the figure in order for this to stand out. When so reduced, the figure loses much of its capacity to participate in the multiple conversations of which it is capable. This loss is apparent when considering the many ways figure enters into human thought. The geometrical figure, the human figure, the musical figure, and the figure of speech each have such particular and different characteristics that reliance on any one meaning fails to capture the potential of their commingled and overlapped coexistence. Instead, this expanded field of meaning can enlarge an understanding of the figure and its operations and then take advantage of the complex and multiple strategies by which figure and ground can engage one another. When the figure opens literally and metaphorically to so many forms of connection, its autonomy will obviously be diminished, but the benefits are substantial. As the junctures, seams, fissures, and gaps in the figure are revealed, these become significant moments of discontinuity, small hooks grabbing onto the world beyond. As figures become more porous and more prickly, they begin to take on many properties of the ground. A more accessible figure, in turn, promotes comparison with the ground to reveal properties there that would have been thought more the province of the figure. As distinctions involving figure and ground become ambiguous and shifting, the limitations of an antagonistic juxtaposition become apparent.

An alternative set of relationships between figure and ground is found within the Confucian yin–yang diagram, where the two are engaged and mutually dependent. If the black shape is the hierarchically privileged figure, then it ought to be found significantly distinguished from its supporting ground, and yet it is the same shape as the remaining ground, only rendered in white, giving figure and ground a shared value. The S-curve separating black from white confounds the reading of either shape as unequivocally figural. As it switches seamlessly from concave to convex to both include and exclude, the curve further compromises a simple reading. Which figure might the curve belong to? Might it belong to neither and be constituted from the juxtaposition of the two? Tracing the contour of the S-curve reveals even more troubling uncertainties. It seamlessly flows into the line demarking the circumference of the circle containing the two figures so that what once separated figures now contains them. In making hypotheses about how this diagram might have been put together, it is necessary to ask whether the black shape, for instance, was superimposed over the white ground within the original large circle or whether the ground was always black before the white shape was placed on top. Those two smaller circles residing at the center points of each part of

Figure 4.6. Juan Gris, *Still Life with Bottle*, 1912.

the S-curve begin to suggest just this sort of an overlap. Are these apertures into a substrate that reveal the presence of a contrary ground existing immediately below the two shapes that by now seem much less like figures? The point of this interrogation is to show how this simple structure can establish a framework for looking at relationships that is far richer than a reductive juxtaposition of supposed opposites.

The complex ambiguity of the yin–yang diagram and the particular properties of its construction that open the figure to engage the ground are critical components of the intellectual intentions and formal structure of the Cubist painters, poets, musicians, and filmmakers who wanted to make figures more accessible while giving a voice to pictorial, textual, and musical grounds previously operating in silence. Figures of all kinds were carefully taken apart just to the point at which the resulting fragments were the most open to external relationships but not so far that reference to the original whole was lost. The basis for this process of decomposing was the assumption that objects were articulate and assembled from recognizable elements held together by an understandable internal structure—they are not inherently closed. The violins, bottles, and stemware so prevalent in these paintings are all composed of a complex combination of the S-curves found in the yin–yang diagram and gridded rectilinear components, and thus already contain structures inherent to both figure and ground.

The Cubists perceived the figure as having a life animated by a level of complexity and ambiguity well beyond the static formal, social, and political hierarchies present around the turn of the century. This hidden life is revealed when the figure's constituent pieces are unfastened and displaced to engage the ground on their own terms. This decomposition, displacement, and recomposition shifts attention from an object to a relational view. The primary relationship was to the object's supporting ground or fields. Now valued as an articulate entity in its own right, the dense mosaic of the ground could engage the disarticulated pieces of the figure on equal terms and significantly extend the number and type of relationships among all these parts.

Ground was no longer a neutral datum to display the hegemony of the figure, but a textured and meaningful construct able to direct relationships with authority equal to that of the figure. Within this context, fragmentation becomes an optimistic and expansive process that can include a broad array of pieces—a set of open hypotheses about how things might go together.

Architecture might well draw on some of the explorations of the Cubist theorists to reconsider the closed form of the building.[16] In so doing, architecture would engage in a process of revaluing ground by opening to it. It would find not only an immensely vital realm but also processes, structure, and relationships that, if applied to architecture, would significantly transform the way it engages all that is within and around it. A revalued ground would demand much in return. Similar to the way Cubist painters tested the hold of figural closure on both object and subject while exploring open networks of relationships, architects might question assumptions about *a priori* hierarchies and other forms of premature closure that suppress legitimately dissenting voices within the program, composition, and materiality of their work.

When the ground becomes a part of the architectural project, the resultant open structure will be a more effective mechanism for increasing choices within an inevitably open program than the prior collection of closed figures and attached corridors, stairs, and circulation shafts. As the ground is understood as much more than a simple, thin, two-dimensional plane, the opportunities its multilayered structure offers for architecture become more obvious. The interweaving of different thickening and thinning layers that gives the ground such sectional complexity provides far more effective a structure for expanding the three-dimensional connective potential among places and activities than the now-common stack of undifferentiated floor plates with point connection by the elevator and fire stair. Within a structure of overlapping and intersecting differential ribbons of space, the limitations of the singular ground plane no longer hold. Multiple ground planes increase the opportunity for more parts of the architectural project to be grounded in the particularity of the larger world. Furthermore, the ground's impressive capacity to extend beyond arbitrary boundaries and its mutable and open structure give it a far greater porosity to surrounding natural and political structure.

Many assumptions about architecture need to be reconsidered when the ground becomes so much a part of its constitution. A building so limits the breadth of architectural potential that it no longer can be considered its most effective product. The increasing size and hermetically sealed situation of buildings preclude relationships with ground other than displacement and erasure. As institutional programs become more complicated and densely variegated, with more autonomy and authority for the individual, the bounding envelope of a building seems a crude mediator between institution and world. The active or verb form of *building* is more promising. Rather than the static and finished product of a building, there is a continuing open-ended and inclusive process much closer to the processes of the ground and to life itself. An even better term would be *constructing,* with its double meaning of fitting things together and, coming from the same Latin root *construere*, its more ambitious task: "to interpret, put a meaning on, to explain."[17] At least one of the things expected from this process of constructing would be a compelling interpretation of the relationship between human action and the structure of the ground.

One of the crucial pieces that will need to be "fit together" within the process of constructing is the room. The room most closely accommodates the presence of the human figure within and thus claims a considerable figural legitimacy. Its interior is a refuge, yet also the means to understand and orient oneself in the world. Its own parts, such as window, door, hearth, ceiling, and floor, are the means by which rooms mediate relationships among humans and between humans and the natural world, and therefore are the pieces that will directly engage the ground. When this articulate figure opens to and takes on properties of the ground, while simultaneously imparting its own figural identity to the relational structures of the ground, then the human can truly feel connected to the world.

A remarkable representation of the human figure evocatively incised in a room that is also fully engaged in urban life and natural process is Messina's painting of *St. Jerome in His Study*. Here is a room so responsive to its inhabitant's particular physical and intellectual needs that it seems more like a protective garment. Each surface registers the physical presence of the saint, and even without him indicates the special character of its intended task. The room is elevated above the ground and focused inward. Jerome's most explicit contact with his world would seem to be the book that is both part of the room and

Figure 4.7. Antonella da Messina, *St. Jerome in His Study,* 1475.

an extension of his body. Even the title of the painting suggests a place removed from the world to promote reflection. And yet it is just as apparent that this room is only a fragment of something larger. Its autonomy is mostly a consequence of implied, rather than actual, closure. A carefully calibrated incompleteness situates the study within an implied urban context just in front of the picture plane while connecting this to a landscape framed and ordered by multiple fields of columns, windows, and the scarcely visible network of gridding that ties everything together. To further link the study to its multiple supporting fields, the strongly felt order running in the background is eloquently revealed in the structure of the study fragment itself. The surrounding context deserves further comment. Many qualities of the ground are in evidence here. The dark presentation and obscure edges lend a sense of this space being formless, a ground that extends far into both urban and natural worlds beyond. The intense patterning of the floor, the proliferation of treelike columns in the background, and the exotic animals roaming about all contribute to a reading of this space as some form of ground. All of this lends an air of ambiguity to Jerome's situation. Is his study a fragment of the city, displaced to a landscape outside? Or, perhaps the ground itself has returned to its pre-urban condition? Within this rich contradictory setting, the actions of St. Jerome put figure and ground, and city and landscape into their multiple relationships.

The raw natural setting of the North American continent was a revelation to the first Europeans. Coming from a continent that had long ago lost its forests, where land was cultivated more as an extension of the urban field or else completely acculturated as a garden, their descriptions of the new land are telling. Writing in *The Machine in the Garden*, Leo Marx finds America praised as a bountiful garden of plenty where nothing is wanting and yet at the same time as a hideous wilderness.[18] Marx argues that the tensions within these contrasting accounts have been crucial to the formations of American culture and, by extension, American patterns of settlement. Ground would certainly be expected to have a profound presence. Early examples of architecture and urbanism demonstrate means of representation and strategies of engaging the ground of the New World that differ markedly from what had been known in Europe.

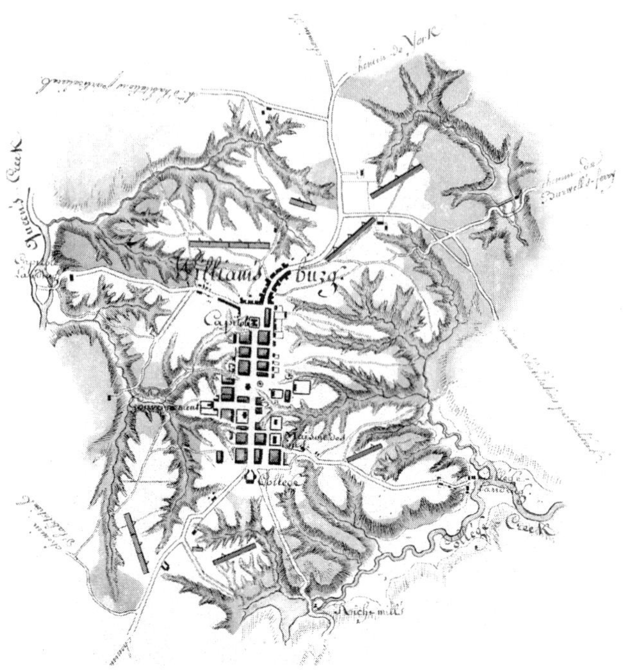

Figure 4.8. Alexandre Berthier, Map of Williamsburg, 1781.

A particularly compelling representation of city structure effectively engaging the ground can be seen in a late mid-eighteenth-century map of Williamsburg by Alexandre Berthier. Instead of the autonomous figure of the European walled city existing in a void, Berthier shows an urban pattern open to the land outside. In fact, the idea of outside seems completely inappropriate. The natural world so permeates the urban order that to refer to it as outside fails to account for just how strongly the ground has been assimilated into this new democratic order. Although there are gardens and cultivated lots, the intense presence of the natural process weaving through human intent stands out. Berthier has blurred distinctions in the way he represents political order and landform. The structure of the watershed with its articulated pattern of streams, creeks, swales, and ridges is rendered equivalent to the spatial structure of streets, alleys, public squares, and gardens that represent the then-current political and cultural aspirations. The complex interweaving of these multiple systems describes a context in which nature and culture are far more engaged than opposed, and each must be maintained for the others' good.

The same interdependent weaving together of political and ecological structure can be seen at the domestic scale of architecture. The Wythe house, built in Williamsburg around 1752, depicts a rapprochement between ground and constructed form similar to that found in Berthier's map of the same city. The house is typically photographed in a tight composition that decontextualizes it and emphasizes its objectness, but this is more the outcome of a predilection within architectural history to focus on buildings and not their settings. Rather than being contained within the confines of the colonial house, the domestic program here is parsed out and distributed over the entire site, and in some instances even beyond. Kitchen, smokehouse, well, stable, gardens, pavilions, along with fences, hedges, trees, pergolas, porches, and other liminal pieces are deployed so that the ground itself—with its swales, ridges, and other topographical features —is engaged as an active part of a larger construct. Conventional distinctions between inside and out or nature and artifice fail to capture the complexity of this place. Equally challenging is trying to understand differences between public and private activity. With the domestic program no longer constrained to a singular structure, much of the domestic enterprise becomes porous and open to public engagement. The eight separate points of entry to the site allow individual pieces of the domestic program to form their own separate relationship with one another and the town beyond.

These examples show the importance that edges play in mediating relationships with the ground. Whether made by adjacency, juxtaposition, overlap, or by things brought together by seam, the edge registers and responds to similarity and difference. Once architecture or any other figure becomes open to the ground, attention shifts away from the center and toward an increasing number and variety of edges. A less commanding center gives parity to these edges, which in turn are free to engage in their own relationships with grounds.

Edge, *margin*, *fringe*, *verge*, and *rim* are a few of the words qualifying ground. These terms, however, carry a semantic power well beyond their portrayal of the ground's physical structure. The *marginal* notes necessary to a critical reading, the cutting *edge* of new thought, or the alternate forms of community proposed by *fringe* groups are obvious examples of the rich critical potential inherent to existence at the boundary. The view from the edge is almost by definition a critical one. From this liminal vantage point, it is possible to look outward and inward and more easily recognize and assess problems at the center.

But this is not just the metaphorical construct of critical thought and action. In nature, edges are never thin and unambiguous, but instead thick, overlapping, and even generative. For instance, the ecotone where two ecosystems meet combines qualities of each system. The niches and sanctuaries within this thick boundary make it one of the richest locations for finding a broad diversity of organisms.[19]

The edge's inherently contrary quality of simultaneously separating and bringing together gives it a physical as well as an intellectual thickening at the same time that it is porous. With the edge so involved in the process of engaging ground, it will prompt a substantial reconsideration of the walls, ceilings, roofs, and even floors that define the room so that they too can participate in the expanded network of linkages revealed within the site.

At this point, it seems that the long-standing desire to erase boundaries separating inside and out might be reconsidered and reframed. Inside and out describe more than simple climatic distinctions. Intuition, which is essentially a mysterious process interior to the mind, differs markedly from the externalization needed to rationalize actions. Intimacy itself is an interior condition made powerful by comparison to the vastness outside. Finally, feelings are another part of the interior life of the human that require protection from the outside. In other words, the brain itself would seem to be structured to promote, protect, and mediate relationships between inside and out, making the desire to erase such an inherently important condition a questionable one. So instead of making boundaries disappear or nearly so in the case of the glass curtain wall, it would be logical to make the boundary even thicker. The thick edge is more able to effectively respond to the differing pressures and needs of inside and outside. And as soon as inside and outside edges become entities in their own right, this sponsors a new place in-between, capable of its own special form of occupation. The dense matrix of liminal space within the thick walls of the French Hotel, the urban house of a member of the royal court, is an evocative example of a different form of existence that contrasts with that led within the public figural rooms that these surround. The highly particular labyrinthine network of connectivity in both plan and section encourages relationships both licit and otherwise to be more freely entered into than do the limited and controlling axial routes within the public realm.[20] The configurations within these thick walls speak to a freedom of choice and consequent vitality that could never be present in those limited figures. Martin Heidegger noted the catalytic potential of these edges when he wrote, "A boundary is not that at which something stops but, as the Greeks recognized, the boundary is that from which something begins its presencing."[21]

Much of the same literal and metaphorical ambiguity is also present in the more ephemeral structure of the porch. Is this part of the landscape, an extension of the room, or a place all its own? As the porch oscillates between interior and exterior as well as between figure and ground, it further explains the nature of the edge. Edges separate things and yet they also bring things together. Thus, the apparent contradictory constructs of continuity and discontinuity are able to be present at the same time and place. With this comes the ability for the human to be part of the larger network of political, social, and ecological systems while at the same time being removed and protected from this excess complexity to reflect on how best to engage it. Are there other forms of porch, and might other constructed edges perform similarly? Like the boundaries found in nature, these thick edges of architecture bring together the different ecologies of human artifice and nature to produce a third system: a liminal microclimatic place capable of mediating inside and exterior environments. Perhaps this form of the edge finally provides the unrestricted passage linking inside and out that has been an elusive goal of architecture for so long. Now, however, it is possible to imagine a richer and more equal relationship between human artifice and natural process as humans freely move physically and imaginatively between their own intentions and the conflicting environmental, political, social, and psychological matrix.

CONCLUSION

Ground has always been a crucial part of human existence. In almost every discipline, in different form, it is the common reference among people and the world that makes shared thought and action possible. The ability to connect to a larger world is a direct consequence of the ability to effectively engage the ground and bring this within human comprehension and action. Ground is where human artifice and natural process commingle for the benefit of both. Our myopia and misrepresentation of something so essential seems inexplicable. The reductive representation of ground within architecture, urban planning, and even landscape architecture representation is just as strange. Possible explanation for the suppression of ground is complex and mostly beyond the scope of this essay. However, our ability to contend with one of the inescapable facts of being human, our mortality, tells much about how the ground is valued. When intellectually and emotionally capable of acknowledging their finitude, humans have looked to the ground for solace and support. Its patterns of repetition go on forever and thus contrast with any form of figure, which already having reached a state of conclusion, resists significant intervention and growth. But when culture is unable or unwilling to reach a productive rapprochement with its mortality, then ground, in all its manifestations, becomes an unwelcome reminder of the problematically short span of individual human existence.[22]

Irrespective of causes for this difficult relationship to ground, humans cannot continue to be blind to its opportunities. By questioning assumptions about the relationship of ground to human existence such as those embedded within the figure–ground drawing that polarizes a relationship between things that are mutually dependent, it is possible to come to a better understanding of the value of the ground in human terms. By finding imaginative means to represent what has been invisible for so long, humans can at least bring the ground to attention as something worthy of consideration. Within architecture, once the ground is revealed and its structure made visible, it is possible to give the ground a voice equal to that of the products of human artifice. At this point architecture can open to and take into its domain a rich world that can augment what architecture is capable of. In being open to the ground, architecture will also discover a wealth of means to deal with intractable problems of its own. The consequence of this intense engagement is the effective reattachment of humans to the many worlds that support them.

Notes

1. Jackson, John B., *Discovering the Vernacular Landscape* (New Haven: Yale University Press, 1984), 8.
2. This essay is an extension of material covered in my earlier book, Dripps, R. D., *The First House: Myth, Paradigm, and the Task of Architecture* (Cambridge: MIT Press, 1997). Mostly, I am developing ideas that were introduced in the epilogue, where I proposed a reevaluation of the Vitruvian Myth of the first dwelling. This myth, which has been repeated in various forms in almost every treatise of architecture, describes people driven from the forest by a fire and into a clearing where they subsequently gather around the fire's dying embers to initiate speech, political structure, and architecture. Language began here as people communicated the pleasure they found in the warm fire and signaled to others to bring logs to keep it burning. Written at a time when the forest was the predominant ground in Europe, this tale seems benign. But from our perspective, it is clear that to maintain the public realm, the forest will ultimately be consumed. I proposed an inversion of the myth where the vitality of a living forest could hold that crucial central position instead of the consuming fire.
3. See Robert Scholes and Robert Kellogg, "The Oral Heritage of Written Narrative," in *The Nature of Narrative* (London: Oxford University Press, 1966).
4. Norman Austin, *Archery at the Dark of the Moon: Poetic Problems in Homer's "Odyssey"* (Berkeley and Los Angeles: University of California Press, 1975), 116.
5. Barbara Novak, *Nature and Culture: American Landscape and Painting, 1825–1875* (New York: Oxford University Press, 1995), 49.
6. Numa Fustel De Coulanges, *The Ancient City; A Study on the Religion, Laws, and Institutions of Greece and Rome*, translated by Willard Small (1873) (Reprint, Garden City, NY: Doubleday Anchor, 1956), 22–33.
7. "What better proof is there that the contemplation of fire brings us back to the very origins of philosophic thought? If fire, which after all, is quite an exceptional and rare phenomenon, was taken to be a constituent element of the Universe, is it not because it is an element of human thought, the prime element of reverie?" Gaston Bachelard, *The Psychoanalysis of Fire*, translated by Alan C.M. Ross (Boston: Beacon Press, 1964), 18.
8. Gottfried Semper, *The Four Elements of Architecture and Other Writings* (1851), translated by Harry Francis Mallgrave and Wolfgang Hermann (Reprint, Cambridge: Cambridge University Press, 1989), 102.
9. Gaston Bachelard, *The Poetics of Space*, translated by Maria Jolas (Boston: Beacon Press, 1964), 18.
10. Dante captured the intensely paradoxical nature of this background while writing about Hell in *The Divine Comedy*: "Midway in the journey of our life I found myself in a dark wood, for the straight way was lost. O how hard it is to tell what it was like, that wild and mighty and unfriendly forest, the very thought of which renews my fear! So bitter was it that death could be no worse. But, to reveal what benefit it brought me, I shall tell of the other things I found." So beginning with a place dark and labyrinthine, a place that made death seem promising, Dante's protagonist finds within

this chaotic state of multiple orientations the means for his own spiritual redemption. Dante Alighieri, "Hell," in *The Divine Comedy* (1314), translated by Louis Biancolli (Reprint, New York: Washington Square Press, 1968), 3.

11. Bachelard, *The Poetics of Space*, 20.
12. Italo Calvino, "The Call of Water," in *Numbers in the Dark* (New York: Vintage, 1996).
13. Robert Augustyn and Paul Cohen, *Manhattan in Maps, 1527–1995* (New York: Rizzoli, 1997), 136.
14. Actually and metaphorically, forest and ground are dark. This is not only the darkness that contrasts with the clear light of rationality, but a quality essential for our most important creative actions. In *The Human Condition*, Hannah Arendt argues that the privacy of the house ultimately makes public life legitimate. "A life spent entirely in public, in the presence of others, becomes...shallow. While it retains its visibility, it loses the quality of rising into sight from some darker ground which must remain hidden if it is not to lose its depth in a very real, nonobjective sense." Hannah Arendt, *The Human Condition* (Chicago: University of Chicago Press, 1958), 71.
15. David Van Zanten, "Architectural Composition at the Ecole des Beaux-Arts from Charles Percier to Charles Garnier," in *The Architecture of the Ecole des Beaux-Arts*, ed. Arthur Drexler (New York: Museum of Modern Art, 1977), 506n46.
16. Architects might also look at the parallel strategies of the musicians who challenged the hegemony of a controlling tonal structure to reveal the musical potential of common sounds, rhythmic patterns, and other more open-ended structures that connected the piece to the everyday world.
17. See Dripps, "Constructing the Paradigm," in *The First House*, 65–75.
18. Leo Marx, *The Machine in the Garden: Technology and the Pastoral Ideal in America* (New York: Oxford University Press, 1964), 43.
19. Bill Mollison, *Permaculture: A Designer's Manual* (Tyalgum: Tagari Publications, 1988), 76.
20. In the play performed within *A Midsummer Night's Dream,* Shakespeare introduces the character Wall: "This man, with lime and rough-cast doth present Wall, that vile Wall which did these lovers sunder; and through Wall's chink, poor souls, they are content to whisper." The wall is the device that separates the two lovers yet is also the agency by which they reestablish their relationship on even more solid ground. It is notable that what we might have anticipated as an inert piece of building becomes quite literally animated as its own implicit inside is played by one of the characters and is even given a speaking role. During this brief scene the Wall is alternately hailed as sweet and lovely and then as vile, thus demonstrating the wall's double capacity to separate and bring together. William Shakespeare, *A Midsummer Night's Dream* (1595), in *Shakespeare's Twenty-Three Plays and the Sonnets*, ed. Thomas Marc Parrot (Reprint, New York: Charles Scribner's Sons, 1953), 159.
21. Martin Heidegger, *Poetry, Language, Thought*, translated by Albert Hofstadter (New York: Harper and Row, 1971), 154.

22. Hannah Arendt, *The Human Condition*. See also Robert Harrison, *Forests: Shadow of Civilization* (Chicago: University of Chicago Press, 1992).

Geological Outcrop, Central Park, New York City.

5

Site Citations: The Grounds of Modern Landscape Architecture

Elizabeth Meyer

INTRODUCTION

Site works, site specific, site-inflected, site-readings, site-seeing, site response, site conditioned, site interpretation. Contemporary landscape architecture is replete with such phrases. For many, a site's characteristics are not simply circumstances to be accommodated or mitigated. Instead, a site's physical and sensual properties are sources for design expression. Site concerns permeate the design process, leaving their compartmentalized role in preconceptual design analysis. These repositioned site concerns challenge the modern divide between rational site analysis and intuitive, creative conceptual design: design as site interpretation, and site as program, not surface for program.

Landscape architects introduced to writings and works by Carol Burns, Julia Czerniak, Robert Irwin, George Descombes, Sébastien Marot, or Peter Latz cannot imagine a design process without site immersion. How could one design for a site seen only in photographs taken by someone else? Impossible. Site analysis, at a large scale and recorded through detached rational mappings, has given way to site readings and interpretations drawn from first-hand experience and from a specific site's social and ecological histories.[1] These site-readings form a strong conceptual beginning for a design response, and are registered in memorable drawings and mappings conveying a site's physical properties, operations, and sensual impressions. Recent reemphasis on site intersects with other interests and developments in the design fields, from sustainability to phenomenology, from regionalism to smart growth, from feminist critiques of modernization to green politics, from postmodern skepticism about meta-narratives such as master planning to site-specific art.

Given the pervasiveness of contemporary writing about site, it's curious how little reflection there is on the history of site in modern landscape architecture. Granted, there has been significant scholarship on the importance of site in pre-nineteenth-century landscape theory.[2] This essay, part of a larger project of recovering modern landscape architecture theory, extends such site stories into the nineteenth and twentieth centuries in America. Site-reading and editing were central to establishing landscape architecture as a discipline separate from architecture, engineering, and horticulture. Counter to the historical narratives that reduce landscape practice to stylistic debates about the picturesque and the beautiful, or the formal and informal, I have found the written record of park reports, treatises, journal articles, monographs, and design primers replete with designers' positions about site.[3] These sources substantiate the significance of site in modern landscape design theory and, as such, in differentiating landscape architecture from other disciplines.

Awareness of this history provides a lens for contextualizing contemporary practice, understanding how landscape architecture emerged as a new profession, and partially explaining why landscape architecture struggled to maintain recognition as a fine art. In a nineteenth-century culture in which site specificity resonated at several levels—as an index of cultural and political identity as well as a source for artistic inspiration—site matters established landscape architecture as a central activity. Conversely, site matters marginalized landscape architecture a half-century later when a contrasting set of criteria such as abstraction, objecthood, uniqueness, and universality characterized modern art and design. In brief, site matters defined the core of landscape architecture, but they did not always contribute to its perceived artfulness by others.[4]

NINETEENTH-CENTURY LANDSCAPE GARDENING PRACTICE AND THEORY: SITE AND PROFESSIONAL IDENTITY

One detects in both the writings and works of nineteenth-century landscape practitioners in North America that the act of visiting a site and interpreting its essential character was fundamental to their conceptual design processes. Site structure joined, and at times supplanted, building structure as the armature of the designed landscape. Site concentration differentiated the nascent profession of landscape architecture from other fields.

> There is a large spirit of inquiry and a lively interest in rural taste....but the great mistake made by most novices is that they study gardens too much, and nature too little....the fields and woods are full of instruction....And yet it is not any portion of the woods and fields that we wish our finest pleasure-ground scenery precisely to resemble. We rather wish to select from the finest sylvan features of nature, and to recompose the materials in a choicer manner....Let us take it then as the type of all true art in landscape gardening—which selects from natural materials that abound in any country, its best sylvan features, and by giving them a better opportunity than they could otherwise obtain, brings about a higher beauty of development and a more perfect expression than nature itself offers. [5]

A. J. Downing identified the fundamental skills required of the landscape designer: the eye of a connoisseur who discerns, as well as the hand of an improver who alters the best features of a site. This connoisseur-as-creator preserved desirable features but also arranged and recombined those features, sometimes editing out or destroying others, to reveal found natural beauty. Landscape design, for Downing, required an astute ability to read and interpret found sites before creating sites. This attitude toward the found site permeated the design literature accompanying the inception of landscape gardening, and later, landscape architecture, as a profession in nineteenth-century America.

If in researching the history of site one only reviewed landscape design theory book titles, it would be apparent that site, at various scales, figured prominently. For instance, Downing's *A Treatise on the Theory and Practice of Landscape Gardening, Adapted to North America* (1841), "...probably the most famous American nineteenth-century treatise on garden design," suggested that European landscape gardening theories must be modified for a new nation's sociopolitical values as well as a different continent's physical geography and climate.[6] One of the first texts to define the role of a professional landscape architect in American town design was Horace W. S. Cleveland's *Landscape Architecture as Applied to the Wants of the West* (1873), which framed site more narrowly than Downing, at the scale of region.[7] Cleveland addressed developers, speculators, and public officials who were building new towns in a region made accessible by rail. Appealing to their sense of profit, he argued that the existing terrain—wooded ridges and stream valleys—could be a public armature around which the developer's speculative grid was arranged and from which it gained value. Later, Wilhelm Miller's *The Prairie Spirit in Landscape Gardening* (1915), building on new scientific theory about plant ecology while appealing to regional pride, called for specifying native Midwestern plant communities instead of imported horticultural species and hybrids.[8] *American Plants for American Gardens* (1929), co-authored by Edith Roberts and Elsa Rehmann, described eleven garden types based on plant communities found on eastern sites, from Maine to Georgia.[9] Their explicitly ecological perspective explained the relationship between soils, moisture, light, plants, and time in the creation of sites, underscoring their successional nature. Miller's and Roberts and Rehmann's sites were not stable spaces, but dynamic systems. These four texts, representatives of a genre, demonstrate how varied site scales and concerns were—from the social and economic to the geological and ecological, from the scale of the city, region, and continent to the specification of plant species, from the spatial to the temporal.

THE CENTRALITY OF SITE THEORIES IN NINETEENTH-CENTURY AMERICAN CULTURE

Nineteenth-century landscape architects gleaned much of their design theory from that of eighteenth-century European practitioners such as Thomas Whately, Uvedale Price, and William Gilpin. Frederick Law

Olmsted, Sr., encouraged his apprentices to read these original sources in addition to Downing, who translated that European theory into an American idiom. All these theorists described and admired landscapes characterized by site structure, and experienced sequentially through unfolding, layered, veiled, and atmospheric spaces; they were less concerned with extending a building's geometry into the designed landscape than amplifying the site's latent character. The translation of these site-nuanced theories to another continent, another century, and into an urbanizing society, raised fascinating questions. What did it mean to transpose a site aesthetic from one place to another?[10] Were the designers who read Gilpin, Price, and Whately looking to make landscapes reminiscent of the ones they described? Or were they learning to read a site, and to appreciate its particularities, in the manner of Gilpin, Price, and Whately?

These questions were examined in American art criticism familiar to landscape architects, such as that of John Ruskin, Asher Durand, Ralph Waldo Emerson, and Horacio Greenough. For instance, Ruskin's admonition that landscape painters capture "the specific, distinct and perfect beauty" of elements in a site, and suggestion that "the highest art is that which seizes this specific character, which develops and illustrates it, which assigns to it its proper place in the landscape" resonated with landscape architects as well.[11] Asher Durand's essay on Landscape Painting in *The Crayon*, expounded both site-specificity and site editing as part of the artistic process.

> I would urge any young student in landscape painting, the importance of painting direct from Nature as soon as he shall have acquired the rudiments of Art....Let him scrupulously accept whatever she presents him, until he shall, in a degree, have become intimate with her infinity, and then he may approach her on more familiar terms, even venturing to choose and reject some portions of her unbounded wealth.[12]

Thus ideas about particularity and specific sites filtered into landscape architecture practices. One approach interpreted known aesthetic theories, such as the pastoral or beautiful and the picturesque, as lenses for finding whatever was particular on a site and amplifying it through design. Another sought existing sites with the proper ground forms and woodlands/meadows to support these known aesthetic categories; the existing site was an armature or frame upon which to drape or construct known aesthetic characters. Deciding how particular or general it should be, or how much of the site to preserve or alter, varied from practitioner to practitioner, but the range of debate was narrow. How did landscape architecture reveal the site? Which site was revealed: the one at hand, or the ideal one? These questions came into increased focus concomitant with the sectional conflict leading to the Civil War and with the rise of the modernized city, as specific sites, rather than transposed idealized landscape types, came to be associated with specific cultural, national, and regional identities. The shift away from transposed landscapes, as exemplified by Olmsted, Sr.'s early works, to specific regional sites, such as those valued by Jens Jensen or Horace W. S. Cleveland, was partially explained by the meaning of specific sites to different generations and regional communities.

Gradually, landscape architects weaned away from an English form of Picturesque aesthetics as they invented another, more contaminated by, or intermingled with, cultural, scientific, and artistic trends of their own time and place.[13] Through the lens of site, one can demonstrate how landscape architecture intersected with broader cultural themes, and how this clustering of shared interests situated landscape architecture in a central place within American cultural production. Critics of the day underscored the prominent role of landscape design. For example, Ralph Waldo Emerson, who, in lecturing on the relationship of landscape and national identity in 1844, described landscape design as "the most poetic of all the occupations of real life, the bringing out by art the native but hidden graces of the landscape" and the "fine art which is left for us, now that sculpture, painting, and religious and civil architecture have become effete, and have passed into second childhood."[14]

New languages and techniques for describing sites in maps, diagrams, and paintings reinforced this cultural currency and influenced how landscape architects and their clients valued particular plots of land. Landscape painters, scientists, and cartographers produced new images that altered and, at times made more particular, the site-reading capacity of landscape architects, their consultants, and their clients. Painters, aware of the public's knowledge of natural history, especially geology, rendered individual plants, rocks, and terrain—Ruskin's vital truths and beauties—with great precision, while at the same time taking artistic liberties to reassemble, distill, compress, or intensify those elements to improve on the overall composition.[15] If landscape painters provided landscape architects with clues to the relationship between site-reading and creativity, then geologists' studies of land formation processes such as glaciation, erosion, and deposition provided both artists and landscape architects with additional lenses for appreciating and understanding specific sites. A geological cross-section, such as one included in the 1861 Central Park report, depicted deep structure below the surface. These theories and representations offered landscape architects, especially those in the northern states shaped by glacial processes, new vocabularies for understanding their canvas and medium: the earth's surface. Previously valued for its visual, surface qualities in texts such as Downing, these geological sites had sectional form, structure, depth, and content which a designer such as Frederick Olmsted, Jr., could reveal through design subtractions or additions.[16] The intermingling of aesthetic discourses and conventions with geological knowledge reinvigorated and at times transcended aesthetic categories such as the picturesque, pastoral, and sublime. This disciplinary contamination also enabled the translation of those eighteenth-century European design codes into American design dialects that valued particular local regional sites for their aesthetic beauty, geological uniqueness, and historical associations. Geological descriptions underscored the vastness of North American natural history. Such associations imbued sites with cultural and historical significance that undergirded regional and national identity. While the public's geological literacy persisted, this scientific lens enriched the site readings and practices of both designers and their clients.[17]

Later, ecology as well as geology enriched landscape architects' ability to read and alter a site. For Miller, Jens Jensen, O. C. Simonds, Rehmann, and Marjorie Cautley, plant ecology was to vegetation what glaciation theory was to rocks.[18] It gave landscape architects a different vocabulary for composing plants—and for understanding their relationship to one another and the environment—than the language of *natural*, *irregular*, and *informal*.[19] Unlike the taxonomic disciplines of botany and horticulture, ecological thinking emphasized relationships, not parts. One knew plant communities, and spatial layering and strata, in relationship to particular soil types, moisture gradients, topographic settings, and orientations. Documentation of such plant groupings was often photographic, emphasizing plants' massing, spacing, and texture. Accompanied by lists of indicator plants characterizing certain communities, these photographs enabled the translation of scientific fact into design vocabulary. The ecological lens for site-reading entered public consciousness and the profession in the early-twentieth century when popular interest in geology was waning.

One should not underestimate the importance of a literate audience in the reception of designed landscapes. Landscape architecture was a design practice, and yet it was also a cultural practice that projected Americans' desires for cultural identity into designed landscape form. The site-reading skills and interests of politicians and cultural critics as well as geologists, ecologists, poets, cartographers, and painters, propelled landscape architecture into prominence as much as the talents and tenacity of its practitioners. These non-designers appreciated landscape art and design in relationship to particular sites made legible through art, science, myth, and literature. They understood the landscape's particularity as meaningful in relationship to urbanization and industrialization. Site appreciation was born of a cross-disciplinary perspective, the likes of which were not matched until the "blurring of boundaries" in late-twentieth-century cultural practices. That a similar intersection of art, science, and politics recently propelled landscape architecture out of the margins of design practice suggests that this reassessment might be a source for contemporary as well as historical reflection.

DIFFERENTIATING LANDSCAPE AND SITE

Growing interest in site-specificity challenged early-nineteenth-century idealized conceptions of landscape. The former valued the particular and the unique, while the latter valued the general and repeatable.[20] A comparison of two parklike settings, one described by Olmsted, Sr., and the other by Cleveland, illuminates the distinction between the terms *landscape* and *site* for nineteenth-century landscape designers.[21] In his 1872 entry on public parks in a popular encyclopedia, Olmsted, Sr., traced their aesthetic and spatial origins to private English hunting parks that were managed, in large part, by deer grazing and eliminating the forest/meadow edge of its understory and shrub layer.[22] The park's spatial condition, then, was characterized by the meadow's ground plane slipping under the high woodland canopy. The manipulated forest edge appealed to Olmsted, Sr. It allowed the pastoral landscape of the meadow to appear both continuous, as the trees did not bound its surface, and mysterious, as its edges were not visible in the deep shadows under the canopy. Olmsted, Sr., valued this park scenery because he believed it aroused certain universal human emotions.[23] When this English park scenery was transposed to new locales such as North America, it became an idealized landscape type.

Writing in *Garden and Forest* (1890), Cleveland recounted a densely layered forest/meadow edge that couldn't be more different from that described by Olmsted.[24] The spatial edge Cleveland described was not based on an idealized type or a distant site, but the actual forest/meadow edges in the various regions in which he lived and worked. His preference for the richly layered ecotone of impenetrable perennials, shrubs, and small trees along the fringe of a forest was more than one cultivated by travel or regional identity, however. Cleveland's advocacy of the found site, his commitment to finding beauty in the actual site without abstraction, was gleaned from the ideas of Horacio Greenough and Ralph Waldo Emerson. These two critics shared a belief in the potential of American art forms not derivative of European models, but grounded in specific, not idealized, nature and in fitting responses to utility or function. Their writings appealed to Cleveland, who taught his readers and clients to see regional sites as worthy sources of landscape beauty and design form.[25]

Both Olmsted, Sr., and Cleveland believed certain landscapes engendered aesthetic experiences and restored the spirit as well as the body; but the actual landscapes they described are very different. Olmsted, Sr., idealized English landscapes with *a priori* formal relationships and transposed those scenes to new sites. Olmsted, Sr., relied on aesthetic theories imported from Europe to see and structure the landscape.[26] A plot was valued in relationship to the degree to which it possessed woods, meadows, and vales that approximated characteristics associated with idealized scenic tropes of the pastoral and picturesque. A design response revealed those latent characteristics in the actual through design tactics of amplification and subtraction or clearing. Cleveland valued found sites as indices of regional identity and American uniqueness. Relying more on Emerson and Greenough than on Gilpin, Price, and Ruskin, he appreciated sites for their idiosyncrasies, not their generalities. His design response was more about distilling or condensing a site's essence into design forms and spaces. This comparison underscores the fundamentally site-inflected and reception-focused bias of early modern American landscape theories. Landscapes meant something because of not only their appearance, but also the associations they aroused.

SITE READING STRATEGIES AND SITE DESIGN TACTICS

If site mattered, how did designers actually work on a site? For, unlike other landscape devotees, landscape architects were not simply connoisseurs or recorders of the landscape; they were simultaneously site readers and editors. The site's character was to be revealed through design. That editing—through amplification, subtraction, distillation, or compression—brought the found site's latent qualities and phenomena into clearer focus.[27] In addition to changing sites, landscape architects transposed sites.[28] They created designed landscape forms that evoked the memory of other culturally meaningful sites, such as distant prairies or fens. They abstracted the essential characteristic of other sites—in the form of a fragments or synecdoches—and transported them to new places.

Although the entirety of site approaches uncovered in the first century of American modern landscape architecture cannot be thoroughly examined in the confines of this essay, I have chosen a representative group of site-reading strategies and site-design tactics to discuss.[29] They are site as armature or framework; site as geomorphological figure; site as ecosystem or geological fragment; and site as temporal phenomenon, haecceity, and subjective experience. These lenses for site-reading and making assume that plots are not empty canvases, but full spaces, full of nature and history, whose latent forms and meanings can be surfaced, and made palpable, through design.[30]

Site as Armature or Framework

In 1849 Downing published an editorial in *The Horticulturist: Journal of Rural Art and Rural Taste* on the landscape beauty of new cemeteries that suggested how the existing site could be a framework upon which to build landscape art. He wrote, "The true secret of the attraction lies in the natural beauty of these sites, and in the tasteful and harmonious embellishment of these sites by art....Hence, to an inhabitant of the town, a visit to one of these spots has the united charm of nature and art,—the double wealth of rural and moral associations."[31] According to Downing, the site's natural beauty—in its landform, plant groupings, and varied spaces—was the framework or armature for the arrangement of the cemeteries' roads, walks, and crypts.

The idea that the site was not an empty canvas but an articulated field, or a textile with recognizable warp and woof, was a dominant site-reading in much of the early Calvert Vaux and Olmsted, Sr., practice. Their plan for Prospect Park is an excellent example of this site-reading strategy. Vaux and Olmsted, Sr., conceived of a sequence of pastoral meadows and lakes and picturesque wooded hills and vales connected by multiple circuits for promenading and driving in carriages through the urban park. But the arrangement of these aesthetic categories or idealized landscape types, the picturesque and the pastoral or beautiful, was site-inflected. The existing glacial landforms were read as an armature or framework for creating picturesque and beautiful scenery.[32]

As evident in their reports to the Brooklyn Park Commissioners, Vaux and Olmsted, Sr., understood that this landform armature contained latent qualities needing amplification and editing to reach the site's potential beauty, charm, and effect. They wrote, "A mere imitation of nature, however successful, is not art, and the purpose to imitate nature, or to produce an effect which shall seem to be natural and interesting, is not sufficient for the duty before us."[33] Later, Vaux and Olmsted, Sr., explained how they applied this design principle by magnifying and making "more distinct" the natural features, and by deepening and heightening existing depressions and hills.[34]

There were norms in picturesque and pastoral theory about the character and effect of its scenery, but nothing explicit about how those individual scenes were combined. Vaux and Olmsted, Sr., arranged spaces in relationship to the parcel's latent structure, not according to fixed compositional principles. The park's plan was based on the overlay of *idealized landscape types* transposed onto a particular landform armature. As evident in a diagram of the park plan inserted into an 1844 topographic map of Brooklyn, the resulting form was a composite of the general and the particular, idealized nature, and this specific site's topographic peculiarities.

One can find similar site sensibilities in other designers' works, such as Dumbarton Oaks in Washington, D.C. There, Beatrix Farrand overlaid a sequence of interdigitated terraced geometric rooms and sloping paths amidst planting drifts onto the ridges and swales of a Rock Creek Park tributary. For Farrand, this Piedmont topography was a framework for the plan and section of the terraced architectural gardens and the sloping wild gardens. Farrand explained this concept in a 1922 letter to her client: "The whole scheme for the north slopes of

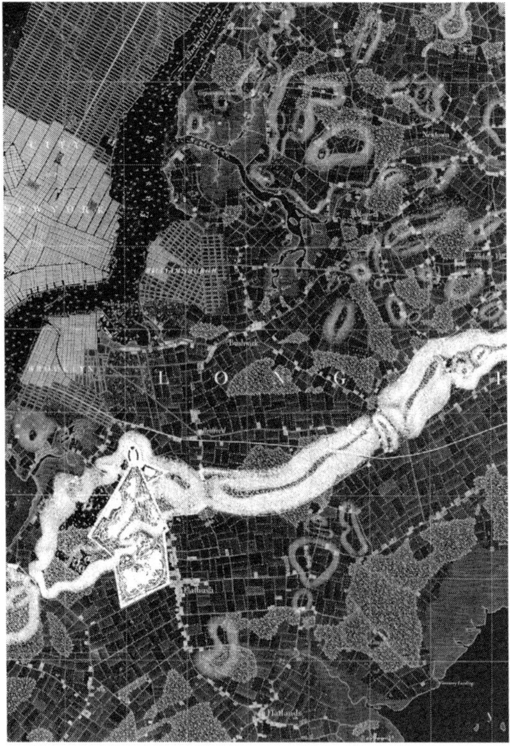

Figure 5.1. Context map. Olmsted, Sr., and Vaux's Prospect Park plan inserted into 1844 *Hassler Map of New York Bay and Harbour*, demonstrating the overlap of the park's picturesque areas with the topographic ridge running along the center of Brooklyn and Long Island.

the property should properly be studied from the ground itself rather from any plan, as the contours and expressions of the ground will control the plantations more strongly than any other feature."[35]

An interdigitated reading of the Dumbarton Oaks plan—ground as one part geometrical terrace and one part textured surface—counters the usual description of the plan as a transition from architecture to nature, from order to the wild. Rather there are two systems of order, two frameworks or armatures: one, the geometry of the house and the other, the geography of the site. These two fields of order intermingle, creating a complex tapestry of landscape form and experience that covers the parcel from wood to house.

Cleveland's town planning proposals contribute to this site-reading tradition. In *Landscape Architecture as Applied to the Wants of the West*, he proposed that forested ravines form a city park framework within and around which to arrange town streets and blocks.[36] He criticized the practice of plotting a town grid on flat land, siting the back of private lots along perimeter ravines, and relegating the steep wooded slopes to marginal roles in the city. Rather, he imagined the ravines as

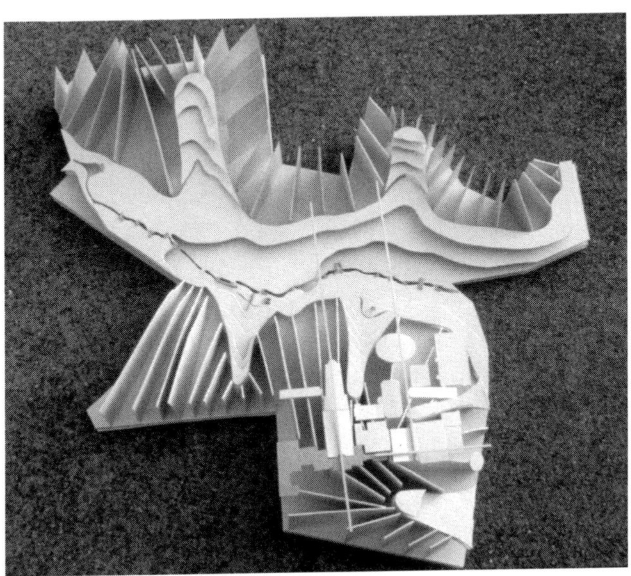

Figure 5.2. Analytical model. Farrand's Dumbarton Oaks garden depicting the interdigitation of two ordering frameworks—the geometry of the house and architectural gardens with the geography of the land and wild gardens.

town planning armatures, as central parks lined by public streets, as sources of civic identity. As in the work of Olmsted, Sr., Vaux, and Farrand, one discerns in Cleveland a design practice wherein the site is not circumstantial, but a topographic framework or scaffold for assembling designed landscape forms and spaces.

Figuring the Site

With increased knowledge of glacial processes came more refined lenses for reading topography as figure as well as surface framework. This was especially true in New England, where geologists Louis Agassiz and Nathaniel Shaler's scholarship on land formation was popularized in public lectures and magazines.[37] Through their work, one could read the land's surface as both a continuous undulating surface and an articulated field with thickened conditions, glaciated moments, or figures that could be named and delineated. Such ability to read the landscape's surface geologically influenced landscape architects such as Frederick Law Olmsted, Jr., who hired Shaler to teach courses in the Harvard landscape architecture curriculum.[38] Agassiz and Shaler's influence can be discerned in the geological references made by Olmsted, Jr., when describing the Wellesley College campus.

In 1902, Olmsted, Jr., advised President Caroline Hazard on campus expansion scenarios. His report began with a confession: "...for I must admit that the exceedingly intricate and complex topography and peculiarly scattered arrangement of buildings somewhat baffled me and that I came away with a less clear and comprehensive grasp of the whole situation than I could wish."[39] One imagines that, for this young designer who was then involved in the planning for Washington, D.C.'s monumental core, Wellesley College might have appeared disordered and informal. But, Olmsted, Jr., was fluent in multiple form languages, as his site description demonstrates:

> Wellesley College has in its grounds a peculiar endowment...the landscape beauty which often attaches itself to the type of glaciated topography there presented when it is fortunately accentuated by the distribution of trees. It is a landscape not merely beautiful, but with a marked individual character not represented so far as I know on the ground of any other college in the country....acre after acre

> it is being defaced and altered by man's occupation, until at last in its perfection it will be very rare indeed...And so this type of landscape with its peculiar kind of intricate beauty and significant expression of geological history must under ordinary occupancy be a vanishing type.[40]

Olmsted, Jr.'s letter described the various landforms on the campus and suggested how building construction could amplify the site's existing character and figure its topographic forms rather than erase them.[41] The 1910s Norembega Quad by Cram, Day, and Klauder and the 1921 Arthur Shurtleff (aka Shurcliff), Olmsted, Jr., and Cram campus master plan applied this site tactic. They both figured select geological formations through the siting of building clusters around specific topographic figures. Olmsted, Jr.'s site description illuminates how geological knowledge led to new ways of both reading and designing the site. It demonstrated that increased scientific knowledge about site reinforced and supplemented aesthetic preferences. Additionally, this case study reveals that complex, curvilinear, and irregular forms were not seen as informal counterpoints or foils to architectural forms and order. Rather, new hybrid orders of architectural geometry and site topography/geology were evident at multiple scales, as framework guidelines, master plans, site plans, and building massing.[42]

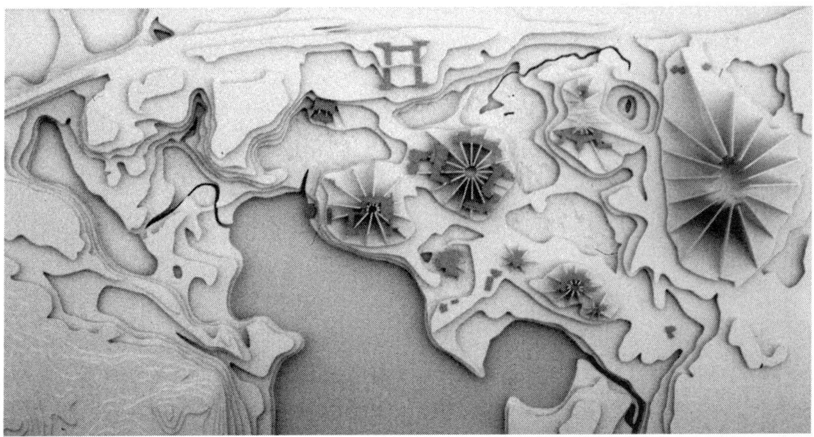

Figure 5.3. Analytical model. Wellesley College Campus, explaining how buildings figure the landform through placement, massing, and alignment.

Site Fragments

Olmsted, Jr., valued the site of Wellesley campus as an endangered, regional landscape type. Through preservation—paradoxically ensured through construction—its glaciated landforms could stand for a larger regional landscape that was encroached upon by suburbanization. This notion of one landscape element signifying the whole, or broader site, is a third site-reading strategy and site-making tactic, one that occurs when development threatens to erase regional sites. Utilizing a site fragment to refer to a distant whole was not a new idea in the nineteenth century.[43] What was different, however, were the ways that geological and ecological sciences altered and informed how a site fragment was found, defined, and valued, and then how that fragment was grafted onto a designed landscape. The impact of these sciences on the site vocabulary and meanings of landscape architecture can be elucidated by comparing sections of two parks: Central Park, by Vaux and Olmsted, Sr., and Columbus Park, Chicago, by Jens Jensen.

The primary public sequence into Central Park from the south through the Mall and Bethesda Terrace culminates in a vista across a lake to the most rustic place in the park, the Rambles. As one enters the upper terrace along the flanking stairs the close-up profile of a large rock outcrop looms in the foreground. The sequence transforms a circumstantial element into a significant figural event.[44] When the park was designed, the designers had access to geological cross-section maps of Manhattan which enabled them to expose rock through a process of subtraction to reveal even more of the site's deep structure.[45] Since the outcrop was by its very definition incomplete, a mere glimpse of the deep structure below, it was understood as a fragment of the larger site structure. Framing and foregrounding the outcrop also highlighted the striations of its surface, formed by glacial grinding. A touch of the sublime was injected into the landscape through both the outcrop's actual size and its grain, which registered the processes of its formation.[46] Appreciation of the rock fragment tapped into aesthetic (picturesque, pastoral, and sublime), as well as scientific categories. From the Bethesda Terrace, two site references were juxtaposed.[47] A foreground outcrop, a revelation of the site's actual subsurface geology, was juxtaposed with a transposed idealized landscape background.[48] A park visitor was transported and grounded at the same time.

Geological mapping enabled Vaux and Olmsted, Sr.'s regional references within Central Park (1857) through the device of the outcrop fragment. Fifty years later, plant ecology fieldwork provided Jensen an analogous opportunity at Columbus Park (1916). Fascinated with the regional landscape of his adopted home, Jens Jensen learned to read it from University of Chicago Henry Cowles, a scholar of plant communities.[49] Jensen read the Midwestern landscape as a mosaic of plant communities from which a designer could extract fragments to represent the whole.[50] Within Columbus Park, Jensen assembled a prairie landscape mosaic of meadow, woodland edge, and prairie river, each part of which was distilled into its essence and conveyed in fragmentary form.[51] Distillation and fragmentation of site types resisted and acknowledged the scale of the transposed prairie, a vastness threatened by the spread of cities and industrial agriculture.[52]

In Jensen's design, the wooded rise in the northeast corner of the park was the source of two springs and a rill that flowed into a constructed prairie river recalling the slow-moving waterways that meandered through gently sloping prairie meadows while cutting deep into their limestone substrata.[53] The siting of this river fragment provides clues to Jensen's site-reading and site-making design strategy. From this west-facing bluff, park visitors would look to the horizontal expanse of a central prairie meadow illuminated by the setting sun. This western prospect, framed by woods with a detailed foreground of wetland grasses and perennials, was a key component of many of Jensen's landscapes. For him, it captured the repetition of the horizontal line and the vastness of the sky that characterized the Midwestern American landscape.[54]

Jensen's commitment to creating a design practice that evoked, distilled, and compressed regional site qualities through an array of plant communities and habitats was not unique. Similar positions were taken by others, such as Wilhelm Miller in *The Prairie Spirit in Landscape Gardening* (1915), Frank Waugh in *The Natural Style in Landscape Gardening* (1917), and O. C. Simonds in *Landscape Gardening* (1920); Elsa Rehmann and Edith Roberts in *American Plants for American Gardens* (1929); and Marjorie Cautley in "Planting at Radburn" (1930). Their ecological knowledge allowed them to see a mosaic of sites within the region. These plant communities and their habitats were categorized into types that could be distilled, compressed, and

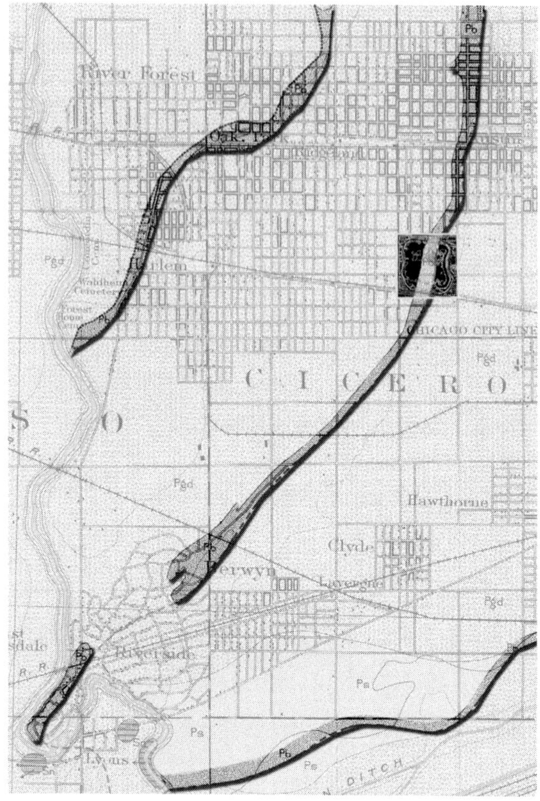

Figure 5.4. Context map. Jensen's Columbus Park plan inserted into geology map of Chicago, demonstrating the location of the beach ridge along which the prairie river and eastern terrace were constructed. (Arial Geology Map, Illinois Riverside Quadrangle, April 1902, *Geologic Atlas of the United States*. Department of Interior. U.S. Geologic Survey. Chicago folio #81, 1894. Scale 1:62,500.)

fragmented through design. In categorizing plant communities by site types, these publications translated scientific theories into site practices applicable to the scale of gardens and parks.[55]

Site as Haecceity or Phenomenal, Temporal Experience

Site as framework, site as figure, and site as fragment: each of these design strategies attends to the physical characteristics of a site. What about other aspects, such as the effect of early morning light on undulating surfaces? Or consideration for the emergence of a wildflower color-field that quickly disappears into the background of a meadow? These temporal moments, episodic contrasts, or *haecceities*[56]—individual, singular events that intersect with the places and things where they occur—are often site-specific. Two identically shaped and dimensioned spaces, built in different regions, have very different qualities given temperature, wind, light, and resultant microclimates. The importance of these nonphysical, phenomenal characteristics in the landscape has always been noticed. How could they be ignored?[57] Capturing, distilling, and condensing a site's temporal qualities is another way that site-readings lead to site-makings.

Throughout *Siftings* (1939), Jensen wrote eloquently about the nonvisual experience of the Midwestern landscape. One passage recounted a haecceity at his home.

> It was early morning when he called me to the open door....There was a peculiar light over this little sun opening, caused by the reflection of the sunrise. The clearing was bordered by a simple composition of hardwoods with a few hawthorns, crab-apples, and gray dogwood scattered on the edge. The light had added an enchantment to this simple composition....Many years have gone by since then, many mornings and many evenings, and I have watched the clearing. I have seen it on cloudy days and in full sunlight, in the starry evenings and on dark nights and moonlight nights, but I have never seen it the same.[58]

Columbus Park's bluff commanded a prospect of the big western sky. Such symbolic, phenomenal events were organizing tools in Jensen's residential gardens as well as his public parks. Significant rooms, activities, and spaces oriented toward a sunset, a sunrise, or a moonrise. In a 1930 interview, Jensen relayed that these phenomena were as much the "raw materials of the garden" as topography and vegetation.[59] When Jensen planted red maples and sumac between a terrace and the setting sun to capture the intense glow of their back-lit autumn leaves, or noted the deep shadows cast by a grove of red cedars in moonlight, he was reading and making sites.[60] Unable to recreate the physical scale of a prairie meadow, Jensen created a language of fragments and phenomena as a means to "portray its soul."[61] Granted, Jensen's view west should be appreciated for its cultural meanings as well as its formal and phenomenal qualities. The western sky and prairie were symbols of regional identity and indicators of national expansion. Again, site meanings and matters intermingle cultural, historical, and ecological references. Subjective and experienced mix with the scientific and observed.

Jensen's built work and writings are, perhaps, the best early-twentieth-century example of a site practice wherein phenomenal, temporal moments are consistently distilled into significant landscape places and experiences.[62] His work demonstrates spatial strategies that are in the service of manifesting time.[63] Once again, considering the designed landscape through the lens of site-reading and site-responding practices is a more effective mechanism for surfacing richer languages of landscape form and space than the terms *formal* and *informal*. Through the distillation and condensation of a site's ephemeral phenomena, landscape architects expand sit-reading strategies from the formal to the experiential, away from the landscape object to the landscape subject, expanding the spatial to include the temporal. It is perhaps not until works such as Sea Ranch by Lawrence Halprin, Robert Irwin's site-specific art, and Michael Van Valkenburgh's gardens in the latter half of the twentieth century, that this type of designed landscape as site-reading reemerges in such a powerful, yet subtle form.

Generalizations about Late-Nineteenth-Century to Early-Twentieth-Century Site-Reading Practices

Although the site-reading practices outlined here are not exhaustive, they do suggest that reading and altering sites were central issues for landscape architects during the period of intense modernization of the American landscape. Individual attitudes varied about how much of a site should be edited or altered, but one can discern a site-inflected bias in the most prominent modern landscape practitioners. These individuals were knowledgeable of their collective identity as a discipline that re-presented site through design. They made this identity contemporary through their translation of the writings about art and the found landscape by Gilpin, Ruskin, Durand, Greenough, and Emerson. They enriched the meaning of their designed landscapes by intermingling these aesthetic codes with new scientific theories for reading sites, such as glaciation and plant ecology, which appealed to societies seeking cultural forms that reinforced desires for unique regional and national identity. These lenses allow site meaning to be created as much through the enactment of social rituals, or the experience of temporal moments within them, as in design forms themselves. In other words, these modern, designed landscapes were sites of immersion and subjectivity. They required reciprocity between a viewer's experience and the apprehension of their artfulness. As these strategies demonstrate, unlike other fine art disciplines, the art of landscape design did not reside solely in the object; this characteristic was a source of disciplinary uniqueness, and an obstacle to the recognition of the discipline's formal invention and compositional codes. I believe this, among other factors, marginalized landscape architecture during the second half-century of its existence as a profession in the United States.

TWENTIETH-CENTURY CHALLENGES AND CHANGES: FROM SITE PRACTICES TO STYLISTIC CHOICES

Despite the varied site-based design practices that flourished during the late nineteenth and early twentieth centuries, written criticism often described the landscape through reductive stylistic codes. Throughout the 1890s, essays in *Garden and Forest* advocated for more complex thinking about the aesthetic debates concerning the "best style" of garden and landscape design. Rejecting the simplification of design to a choice between formal and informal, writers from editor Henry Stiles to Charles Eliot, Jr., presented alternative terms for describing landscape forms and spaces. In fact, after reading the articles and reports written by designers, in contrast to historians' writing about the period, one realizes that, for American landscape architects, the terms *formal* or *informal* were not the dominant categories for describing design landscapes before the 1890s.[64] Site concerns such as how to interpret, edit, amplify, or transpose sites were more pressing design concerns than were issues of style.

Still, outside the readership of this small, but influential magazine, the audience for landscape appreciation was changing. Influential books such as Reginald Blomfield's *The Formal Garden in England* (1892), a treatise on the garden as an outdoor room predicated on the plan geometry of architecture, reduced landscape design to one of two styles: geometric or formless. It is not until the so-called formal–informal or architectural garden–wild garden debates between William Robinson and Reginald Blomfield during the 1890s that style became such a highly charged landscape design issue, wrapped up as it was in both matters of nationalism and professionalism. These debates, carried out in books and journal articles, exemplify a shift in aesthetic preferences, but they were not solely responsible for the turn of events. As landscape criticism and garden history became more limited by the formal and informal nomenclature, site-inflected works were less likely to be seen and appreciated. Concurrently, landscape architecture as a discipline was viewed as less of a modern design practice. For those versed in visual arts vocabularies, complex, fragmented, overlaid forms and figures resulting from the intermingling of the natural sciences such as ecology and geology with art were construed as irregular, informal, and inconsequential. Arrangements resulting from reading and interpreting site clues through editing, amplifying, distilling, and condensing were rendered invisible, arbitrary, and lacking by other artists, designers, and some of the public. Style matters replaced site matters.[65]

Site practices were also limited by influential exhibitions and publications associated with changing architectural trends. When Henry Russell Hitchcock and Philip Johnson's *The International Style* (1932) took up the issue of site, it reduced landscape design to less than a choice of style:

> Natural surroundings are at once a contrast and a background emphasizing the artificial values created by architects. Choice of site, and the arrangement of buildings upon the site: these are the prime problems of the international style in relation to natural surroundings. As far as possible the original beauties of the site should be preserved. Mere open spaces are not enough for repose; something of the ease and grace of untouched nature is needed as well.[66]

This extraordinarily influential book, more manifesto than catalog, reduced site-reading and editing to site selection, nature preservation, and functional site planning. Site was in service of architecture.[67]

TWENTIETH-CENTURY LANDSCAPE ARCHITECTURAL MODERNISM AND SITE THEORIES

One treatise associated with mid-twentieth-century landscape architectural modernism, Garrett Eckbo's *Landscape for Living* (1950), responded directly to the marginalization of landscape architecture implicit in contemporary architectural theories. His book connected site practices directly to architectural practice, and in doing so repositioned landscape architecture in a collaborative role with architecture. For Eckbo, the site did not exist prior to human occupation and need. Rather, "...the site only exists, in its visual and spatial relation to people, through the introduction of the building which establishes a permanent relation between people and site. The building and site are one in fact and in use."[68] Eckbo's site theories were quite different from nineteenth-century landscape architectural writings that often emphasized the differences, not the connections, between architectural and landscape design.

Eckbo suggested that site strategies connected buildings and their inhabitants to nature. He made a profound and prescient criticism of contemporary architectural practices: that they often preclude this connective or mediating act by reducing the parcel to a visual landscape, a detached, albeit pleasant scene. Eckbo contextualized his arguments with a reference to a James Marston Fitch article:

> The Architectural Forum in November 1948 gives us perhaps the most recent summary of advanced architectural thinking on the esthetics of a building technology which, while it increasingly opens up the building to the landscape with the open structure and the glass wall, at the same time seems to increase the gap between man and nature by its increasingly precise and complete control of climate and habitat indoors. Never before in history has there been such a contrast between this potentially absolute control over interior climate, and the potentially complete transparency of glass walls and doors separating indoors from outdoors.[69]

Eckbo redefined landscape architecture as site-space design or land-and-building design, a mediating practice between architecture and nature. Instead of reducing the outdoors to an image framed through a ceiling-to-floor picture window, he advocated for indoor-outdoor spaces that created a site. His site-space strategy was primarily a means to connect architecture to its place, not so much a reading of place as a vehicle for the generating design forms or experiences.

In *Landscape for Living*, the term *site planning* enters into our site discourse.[70] Unlike the reductive and instrumental functionalist associations that this term has today, for Eckbo, site planning would overcome the divide between engineering, architecture, and landscape architecture.

> We are on the threshold of realizing that our concepts of architecture (including creative engineering) and of landscape design (or landscape architecture) are in reality two halves, or two sides, of a greater art. This is, or will be, site-space organization, of spatial continuity at the truly functional scale of site, neighborhood, and community....The bridge from the three formally separated spatial arts that exist, to the expanded concept of site-space form which is implicit in our thinking, is site planning as it is beginning to be understood today.[71]

Eckbo believed that space relations were the medium that connected the lived experience and the physical form of indoors and outdoors. Despite passages about the ground, plants, rock, and water, it is apparent that Eckbo's site language was primarily spatial. Eckbo's site vocabularies, like those of his predecessors, were inflected by the ways that the land was described in related disciplines. Geological and ecological vocabularies evident in earlier site-readings were replaced in Eckbo's text with a spatial vocabulary that entered into architecture and landscape architecture discourse through German art-historical writings and then entered mainstream discussions of these design fields after the 1920s.[72]

Site-space planning, while nominally connected to the site-as-framework strategy, differed in one key aspect from pre–World War II site practices. Eckbo's site-space planning surfaced during a period when multidisciplinary design practices—such as the Architects Collaborative: Skidmore Owings and Merrill; Perkins and Will; EDAW; and Sasaki Associates—increasingly tackled large, complex suburban housing, commercial headquarters, and shopping centers.[73] Site-space planning created a common vocabulary for such hybrid practices. It attempted to reduce, not reinforce, distinctions between the two design professions. In doing so, it substituted a temporal, geological, and ecological site framework with a spatial, environmental, and functional one. Later books, such as John Simonds' *Landscape Architecture* (1961) and Kevin Lynch's *Site Planning* (1962) extend this functional and structural sense of site planning. And while both Simonds and Lynch also address more artistic and intuitive site tactics, such as "reading and amplifying the site" and "this unsystematic, almost unconscious, reconnaissance," they have been primarily remembered for their clear, rational approaches to problem solving, site analysis, and site planning.[74]

FRAMEWORKS, FIGURES, FRAGMENTS, PHENOMENA, AND THE RECOGNITION OF MODERN AND POSTMODERN ART

The vocabulary and criteria of architecture were not the only obstacles to recognizing site practices as artistic and design activities. For, unlike the nineteenth century—when landscape and site issues were central to artistic production—twentieth-century art criticism and production placed less value on site and the particular. Instead, a range of other concerns, such as abstraction and invention, the autonomy of the art object, mechanistic and technological metaphors, and standardization and mass production, served to marginalize site practices as nostalgic or instrumental. By the mid-twentieth century, an emphasis on site as a marked canvas no longer positioned landscape architecture as a new and promising modern art practice. Whether construed as overly nostalgic or merely analytical, site concerns no longer resonated as strongly as the subject matter of art. Within this context, as landscape architectural theory such as Ian McHarg's *Design with Nature* (1969) and Lawrence Halprin's *RSVP Cycles* (1969) reasserted the dynamic, fluctuating characteristics of site relative to new ecological thought, landscape architecture was increasingly located outside the boundaries of art. Site practices favored systems and fields over objects, engaged experience over detached contemplation, embeddedness versus boundedness.

Site concerns challenged the very definition of abstract modern art. Building a conceptual strategy on a found condition weakened the designer's role as a creative genius, an individual with a unique, idiosyncratic voice. The use of site materials to build a site work on-site versus in a representation one step removed, such as a painting or photograph, proved problematic for landscape architecture's recognition as art. Since Quatremère de Quincy, J. C. Loudon, and Mariana Van Rensselaer, critics have noted the difficulty of recognizing the designed landscape as art given that its medium, subject, and canvas are so intertwined.[75] Yet, more recent scholars, such as Rosalind Krauss, Mara Miller, Kim Michasiw, and Miwon Kwon, have suggested art critics' and historians' biases hampered not only the recognition of landscape design, criticism, and history, but the history of art itself.

Object-biased modern art and design criticism marginalized site practices from the early 1900s until the 1960s, when artists began moving out of the gallery, working in site materials, and creating embedded works that did not fit the criteria of modern art.[76] Yet, these individuals called themselves and their work art. Eventually critics adapted to include these site works, and when they did, many of the criteria by which landscape architecture had been denied the status of art were called into question. When the autonomy of the art or designed object was no longer considered one of the major criteria for artistic appreciation, site-based practices flourished (and vice versa). Given the ambiguous condition that early modern site works found themselves in—of being neither hierarchical figure nor simply existing ground, but a kind of figured ground, or edited/amplified ground—the lukewarm reception bestowed upon landscape design by the fine-arts gatekeepers is not surprising.[77] As Miwon Kwon has argued, postmodern site works challenged the objecthood of modern aesthetic theory and criticism: autonomy, self-referentiality, transportability, and placelessness.[78]

The centrality of these issues to a postmodern anti-aesthetic suggests that this essay is more than a historical recovery of site practices. It is a reaction against a limited perspective of what was construed to be mainstream modernity, and a call for a new history of modern art, architecture, and landscape architecture. Reframing the history of the modern designed landscape through the lens of site provides perspective on the influential and widespread theories of site specificity in late-twentieth-century art, landscape architecture, and architecture.

BEYOND SITE CITATIONS

This essay represents the beginning of a larger enterprise. We need a more complete account of site in twentieth-century design texts of all kinds: articles, reports, and books. We look for more landscape histories that include descriptions and analyses of the actual sites where construction occurred, as well as the strategies that different designers invented to read and alter those sites. Such stories can underscore the multivalent lenses through which site was found, represented, construed, and constructed. They can uncover the order and intention behind the seemingly contingent and fragmentary forms previously deemed merely informal, open, natural, or soft. This rethinking of the relationship of figure to field, thing to *this-ness*, object to void, building to landscape, and form to formlessness, provides a counterpoint to the impoverished narratives of landscape architecture that began in the latter part of the nineteenth century and continue, to some degree, today.[79] Such endeavors will alter how we view the past and present, for they can enrich contemporary site-based practices by more firmly grounding ecological and scientific analytical methods within a cultural and historical dimension.

During the last quarter-century, diverse groups of artists and designers have gathered around site practices. The very issue that defined landscape architecture as a separate design discipline, and later estranged it from the fine and modern arts, is now central to contemporary discourse. We might well ask, why is this so? How long will it last? As is evident in the texts discussed here, the history of site practices has ebbed and flowed. I would suggest that there is a reason for this, beyond the vagaries of stylistic preferences and professional differences. Site practices ebb and flow because of the reciprocity between the milieu and conceptions of the relationship of humanity to the natural world, between the designed landscape and the reception of the work by others. It is not a coincidence that a profession committed to site-reading and editing emerged within an urbanizing social formation when its audience understood that certain sites were indices of regional identity, and that art, history, and science were intermingled in aesthetic appreciation of landscapes. Similarly, it is not a coincidence that the recent interest in site practices parallel public interest in environmentalism and sustainability and concern about the numbing homogeneity inherent in standard development practices.

Despite this revival of site practices, it is surprising how professionally compartmentalized they remain. Landscape architects read and write sites anew, hybridizing ecological processes with human experiences on marginal urban lands. They combine biofiltration strips with parking surfaces, producing new human/nonhuman habitats; apply bioremediation and phytoremediation to industrial landscapes, creating temporary and transitional landscapes that allow neighbors to witness site cleansing; and program urban renewal's infrastructural gashes, its vague terrain, with the stuff of everyday life. Sites permeate architects' thinking and making of buildings as well. But too often their concerns begin where the landscape architects' end. They apply green technologies to roofs and walls, transforming these water- and air-repelling surfaces into porous membranes that filter, cleanse, and store wild energies. They refer to site forms and operations, often made visible through digital media, to imagine new morphologies of space and structure. Site frameworks, fields, figures, and processes have dematerialized the very divide that Eckbo found in Fitch's 1948 article. The transparent curtain wall's "increasingly precise and complete control of climate and habitat indoors" has been replaced by a thickened zone of air and moisture exchange that responds to, and harnesses, the fluctuations between inside and outside. It has been transgressed by folded surfaces that defy emphatic boundary-making between in and out. Contemporary buildings as well as designed landscapes are site-full.[80]

So, if the boundaries between shelter and site have been renegotiated, and if the boundaries between designed landscapes and sites have been reconceptualized, why are the boundaries between architecture and landscape architecture still so parochially defined? And won't this DMZ of professional colonization and appropriation—without acknowledgement or collaboration—thwart the potential of site-based practices, not to mention the reception of those practices by a public that lives across and between inside and outside? Could Eckbo's 1950s conception of architecture and landscape architecture as "two halves, or two sides, of a greater art" suggest a bridge between?[81] What would it mean to practice site-space design, or land-building design, that did not limit site readings to generative strategies for designing landscape forms, processes, and spaces, or technical detailing of the two to five feet of space and (infra)structure between interior and exterior?

As we chronicle, and at times even celebrate, the recovery of historic and contemporary site practices in late-twentieth- and early-twenty-first-century design culture, we might probe deeper and consider unraveled paths such as that sketched out by Eckbo. And we might ponder how it is that we have come to expect so little from our languages of landscape description and designed landscape creation, especially from a prior generation of designers such as Downing, Olmsted, Sr., Vaux, Cleveland, Eliot, Olmsted, Jr., Farrand, and Jensen, who fought so hard to craft a new discipline a century and more ago. We might consider how those low expectations of formal and informal, soft and open, green and good, have contributed to the dumbing-down and sitelessness of both landscape history and much contemporary landscape design practice. And we might ask why a current generation of designers that has embraced site systems as analogs for architectural thinking, that has moved beyond formalism and object making in so many other areas of cultural discourse, and that has reveled in the hybrid operations and processes of eco-technological processes, continues to expect so little of the actual designed and inhabited site space between their (formless) building and the larger territory?

My inquiry focuses on past site practices, but it invites interrogation of our contemporary condition. Sites are found as well as invented. New directions for site practice might look less at new tools for how to read sites, and more at finding spaces within which to imagine sites. For those spaces might be as much between disciplines as they are between surfaces, membranes, and operations.

Notes

1. See Joan Nassauer, "Ecological Science and Landscape Design," in *Ecology and Design. Frameworks for Learning*, eds. Bart Johnson and Kristina Hill (Washington, D.C.: Island Press, 2002), 219, for a discussion of this shift. For a contemporary account that demonstrates the importance of mapping as an act of interpretation, versus analysis, see James Corner, "The Agency of Mapping: Speculation, Critique, and Invention," in *Mappings*, ed. Denis Cosgrove (London: Reaktion Books, 1999), 213–252.
2. The best, and most recent, example of this is John Dixon Hunt, *Greater Perfections. The Practice of Garden Theory* (Philadelphia: University of Pennsylvania Press, 2000). See Thierry Mariage, *The World of LeNotre* (Philadelphia: University of Pennsylvania Press, 1999), 53, regarding Boyceau and site.

3. I owe considerable thanks to Michel Conan, director of landscape studies at Dumbarton Oaks, for his questions regarding this topic during my 1999 Dumbarton Oaks Fellowship. They prompted me to initiate the research leading to this article and refining and revising the scope of my book manuscript.
4. Augustin Berque notes the irony that the concept of *landscape*, itself the product of modernity, "disappeared from avant-garde art early in the twentieth century." Augustin Berque, "Beyond the Modern Landscape," *AA Files* 25 (Summer 1993): 33.
5. A. J. Downing, "A Few Hints on Landscape Gardening," *The Horticulturist. Journal of Rural Art and Rural Taste.* (November 1851), editorial reprinted in *Rural Essays*, ed. George William Curtis (New York: Leavitt and Allen, 1858): 122.
6. Joachim Wolscke-Bulmahn and Jack Becker, *American Garden Literature in the Dumbarton Oaks Collection* (Washington, D.C.: Dumbarton Oaks and Trustees for Harvard University, 1998), 93. For greater discussion of how Downing translated English design theory for an American audience and context, see Judith K. Major, *To Live in the New World* (Cambridge: MIT Press, 1997).
7. H. W. S. Cleveland, *Landscape Architecture as Applied to the Wants of the West* (Chicago: Jansen, McClurg and Co., 1873).
8 Wilhelm Miller, *The Prairie Spirit in Landscape Gardening* (Urbana: University of Illinois, 1915).
9. Edith Roberts and Elsa Rehmann, *American Plants for American Gardens. Plant Ecology—the Study of Plants in Relation to Their Environment* (New York: MacMillan, 1929).
10. For a definition of transposed sites, see Mirka Benes, "Pastoralism in the Roman Baroque Villa and in Claude Lorrain," in *Villas and Gardens in Early Modern Italy and France*, eds. Mirka Benes and Dianne Harris (Cambridge: Cambridge University Press, 2001), 103.
11. John Ruskin, *Modern Painters* (vol. I, pp. 33, 36), cited in Anne Helmrich's "Representing Nature: Ideology, Art and Science in William Robinson's Wild Garden," in *Nature and Ideology. Natural Garden Design in the Twentieth Century*, ed. Joachim Wolschke-Bulmahn (Washington, D.C.: Dumbarton Oaks, 1997), 97. For an account of Ruskin's landscape painting criteria and criticism, see John Dixon Hunt, "Ruskin, Turnerian Topography, and Genius Loci," *Gardens and the Picturesque* (Cambridge: MIT Press, 1992), 215–239.
12. Asher Durand, "Letters on Landscape Painting," *The Crayon* 1:1 (January 3, 1855): 2.
13. See Dora Wiebeson, *The Picturesque Garden in France* (Princeton: Princeton University Press, 1978), as a model for understanding the picturesque as not a national style, but an aesthetic category that circulated from site to site, taking on different forms and meanings in different conditions. See also my 1992 essay, "Situating Modern Landscape Architecture," in *Theory in Landscape Architecture*, ed. Simon Swaffield (Philadelphia: University of Pennsylvania Press, 2002), 21–31.
14. Ralph Waldo Emerson, "The Young American," *Nature. Addresses and Lectures* (Boston: Houghton Mifflin, 1903), 367, 369. This lecture was given in Boston and published in *Dial* (April 1844). See Daniel Nadenicek, "Emer-

son's Aesthetic and Natural Design: A Theoretical Foundation for the Work of Horace William Shaler Cleveland," in Wolschke-Bulmahn, *Nature and Ideology* (1997), 58–80.

15. Ruskin's writings were popularized in American art circles through their publication in *The Crayon*. Laura Wood Roper notes that Olmsted, Sr., read Ruskin for the first time in the mid-1840s, a decade before his first landscape design project, Central Park. Roper, *FLO. A Biography of Frederick Law Olmsted* (Baltimore: Johns Hopkins, 1973), 40.
16. Downing writes of the aesthetic quality of the undulating surface of the earth. See A. J. Downing, "The Beautiful in the Ground," *The Horticulturist* (March 1852), reprinted in *Rural Essays* (1858), ed. George William Curtis, 106–109.
17. For an account of how the "popularity of geology" informed the works of six American painters, see Rebecca Bedell, *The Anatomy of Nature. Geology and American Landscape Painting* (Princeton: Princeton University Press, 2001), 150. Landscape appreciation and geology seem connected for a few more decades, as evidenced in books such as Edward Everett Hale's *Picturesque and Architectural New England. Picturesque Massachusetts*, vol. 2 (Boston: D.H. Hurd and Co., 1899), which is replete with geological explanations of scenic New England terrain.
18. The word *ecology* (*oecologie*) was coined by German scientist Ernst Haeckel in 1866. For more on the history of ecology, see Donald Worster, *Nature's Economy. A History of Ecological Ideas* (New York: Cambridge University Press, 1977).
19. See Henry Cowles, "The Ecological Relations of the Vegetation on the Sand Dunes of Lake Michigan" (1899), as well as Frederick Clements, "Plant Succession" (1916) and "Nature and Structure of the Climax" (1936) in Leslie A. Real and James H. Brown, *Fundamentals of Ecology. Classic Papers with Commentaries* (Chicago: Chicago University Press, 1991).
20. This tension between landscape and site is intrinsic to an understanding of the Picturesque debates. Recent critics have argued that it is also key to understanding the relationship between copies and originals and, in my reading, the difficulties in recognizing landscape practices as modern art. See Rosalind Krauss, "The Originality of the Avant-Garde," in *The Originality of the Avant-Garde and Other Modernist Myths* (Cambridge: MIT Press, 1985), 151–172; and Kim Ian Michasiw, "Nine Revisionist Theses on the Picturesque," *Representations* 38 (Spring 1992): 76–100.
21. See Carol J. Burns, "On Site," in *Drawing/Building/Text*, ed. Andrea Kahn (New York: Princeton Architectural Press, 1991), 148–149. See J. B. Jackson, "The Word Itself," in his *Discovering the Vernacular Landscape* (New Haven: Yale University Press, 1984), 1–8.
22. Frederick Law Olmsted, "Parks," in *The New American Cyclopedia. A Popular Dictionary of General Knowledge*, eds. George Ripley and Charles A. Dana (New York: D. Appleton, 1872), 768–775.
23. For example, see Charles E. Beveridge, "The Art of Landscape Design" in his *Frederick Law Olmsted. Designing the American Landscape* (New York: Rizzoli, 1995), 32–44.

24. H. W. S. Cleveland, "Shrubs on Tree Borders," *Garden and Forest* 3 (September 17, 1890): 459. For a discussion of the historical significance of this magazine, see Ethan Carr, "*Garden and Forest* and Landscape Art," *Arnoldia* 60:3 (2000): 4–7.
25. For details on Cleveland's relationship with Greenough and Emerson, see Nadenicek, "Emerson's Aesthetic and Natural Design" (1997); as well as Lance Neckar, "Fast-Tracking Culture and Landscape: Horace William Shaler Cleveland and the Garden in the Midwest," in *Regional Garden Design in the United States*, eds. Therese O'Malley and Marc Treib (Washington, D.C.: Dumbarton Oaks, 1995).
26. Olmsted, Sr., scholar Charles Beveridge similarly argues that Olmsted, Sr., was not a regionalist. Charles E. Beveridge, "Regionalism in Frederick Law Olmsted's Social Thought and Landscape Design Practice," in *Regional Garden Design,* eds. O'Malley and Treib (1995), 241.
27. In *The Languages of Landscape* (University Park: Penn State University Press, 1997), 4, Mark Roskill discusses how landscape paintings convey meaning via distillation and compression.
28. Benes and Harris, *Villas and Gardens* (2001), 103.
29. I am bracketing the modern landscape period in America from the 1840s, and the publication of A. J. Downing's *Treatise on the Theory and Practice of Landscape Gardening* to the 1969 publication of McHarg's *Design with Nature*; A. J. Downing, *Treatise on the Theory and Practice of Landscape Gardening* (New York and London: Wiley and Putnam; Boston: C. C. Little & Co., 1841). Ian McHarg, *Design with Nature* (New York: Published for the American Museum of Natural History by the Natural History Press, 1969); Granted, Downing's is not the first American book to examine topics of interest to landscape gardening. But, as Wolschke-Bulmahn asserts, "It was the first book devoted entirely to landscape gardening in the United States and probably the most influential treatise on the subject." Wolschke-Bulmahn and Becker, *American Garden Literature* (1998), 95. McHarg's manifesto simultaneously exemplifies the modern mastery of nature through a rational method of site analysis and acts as a catalyst for the next generation of postmodern landscape practitioners and theorists.
30. For an examination of the ways that natural processes and social routines are inscribed in space, see Henri Lefebvre, *The Production of Space* (Cambridge: Cambridge University Press, 1991 translation), especially Chapter 2, "Social Space," 117.
31. A. J. Downing, "Public Cemeteries and Public Gardens" in *The Horticulturist* 4:1 (July 1849): 1, 10.
32. This sense of site as armature draws on the OED definition of site as "a framework of timber for forming the foundation or basis for a piece of scaffolding." *Oxford English Dictionary*, online edition (Oxford University Press, 2001), *site*, definition 4.
33. "Preliminary Report to the Commissioners for Laying out a Park in Brooklyn, New York: Being a Consideration of Circumstances of Site and Other Conditions Affecting the Design of Public Pleasure Grounds" (January 24, 1866), in *The Papers of Frederick Law Olmsted. Supplemental Series, Volume I, Writings on Public Parks, Parkways, and Park Systems,* eds. Charles

E. Beveridge and Carolyn Hoffmann (Baltimore: Johns Hopkins Press, 1997), 89–90.

34. "Report of the Landscape Architects and Superintendents to the Brooklyn Park Commissioners" (January 1871), in *The Papers of Frederick Law Olmsted, Volume VI, The Years of Olmsted, Vaux, and Co 1865–1874,* eds. David Schuyler and Jane Turner Censer (Baltimore: Johns Hopkins Press, 1992), 401.
35. Correspondence from Beatrix Farrand to Mrs. Robert Bliss, "The Oaks" (June 24–25, 1922). See Maureen Joseph, Kay Fanning, and Mark Davison, *Cultural Landscape Report Dumbarton Oaks Park, Rocke Creek Park* (Washington, D.C.: National Park Service Cultural Landscape Program, 2000), 98 and footnote 262. Farrand's varied influences included Charles Sprague Sargeant, Edith Wharton, Gertrude Jekyll, and Thomas Mawson; each of them reinforced her site sensibilities.
36. Cleveland, *Landscape Architecture* (1873), 54–56.
37. Both Louis Agassiz and Nathaniel Shaler wrote for *The Atlantic.* For an account of Agassiz's effect on regional landscape painting, see Bedell, *The Anatomy of Nature* (2001), 118.
38. Nathaniel Shaler, Harvard professor of geology, taught a required course in the first professional landscape architecture curriculum in the United States. Shaler's article, "Landscape as a Means to Culture," *The Atlantic Monthly* 82 (1898), 777–785, calls for a new academic discipline focused on landscape appreciation from an aesthetic and cultural perspective. One can see the genesis of a landscape architecture curriculum in this writing. See Melanie Simo, *The Coalescing of Different Forces and Ideas. A History of Landscape Architecture at Harvard 1900–1999* (Cambridge: Harvard University Graduate School of Design, 2000).
39. Letter from Frederick Law Olmsted, Jr., to Miss Caroline Hazard (March 24, 1902), 1. Copy in Wellesley College Archives. Original in Library of Congress: Olmsted Associates Archives: Series B: Job Files. Job File #250: Wellesley College: Correspondence (February 28–November 13, 1902).
40. Ibid., 1–2.
41. Ibid., 3, 8.
42. My research on Wellesley College campus is published in Michael Van Valkenburgh Associates, *Wellesley College Landscape Master Plan* (1999). Jean Glasscock, *Wellesley College 1875–1975. A Century of Women* (Wellesley: Wellesley College, 1975); and Peter Fergusson, James O'Gorman, and John Rhodes, *The Landscape and Architecture of Wellesley College* (Wellesley: Wellesley College, 2000) are excellent histories of this college campus.
43. See Benes and Harris, *Villas and Gardens* (2001); and Hunt, *Greater Perfections* (2000) for histories of such garden and landscape designs in nineteenth-century societies.
44. These large, rocky masses that heave out of the grassy meadows and line the entrance drive were noted in 1852 by a group evaluating the site's future potential as a park: "There is no section on our island...so diversified in surface, abounding so much in hill and dale, and intersected by so many natural streams...The great and many points abrupt, difference of level of the surface, and the projecting points of rock, render these grounds peculiarly

adapted to the construction of the most beautiful and varied roads." Elizabeth Barlow, *The Central Park Book* (New York: Central Park Task Force, 1977), 52.

45. A copy of the geological cross-section was published in the 1861 Central Park Annual Report (Washington, D.C.: Dumbarton Oaks Landscape Studies Rare Book Collection).
46. See Bedell, *The Anatomy of Nature* (2001), 121, for similar analysis of Haseltine's Nahant rock outcrop paintings. "These forces of rock formation—volcanic heavings and glacial action—that Haseltine's contemporaries apprehended in his pictures lend a sublime edge to taut canvases."
47. Ibid., 102.
48. John Ruskin, *Modern Painters* (New York: Wiley and Halsted, 1856), 419, advised painters to include foreground details "which appear peculiar to the place."
49. Worster, *Nature's Economy* (1977), Chapter 11, "Clements and the Climax Community," describes the intellectual contributions of Frederick Clements and Henry Cowles to ecological theory. The Library of Congress "American Memory" Website has an informative account of Cowles's role within the community of ecological scholars. http://memory.loc.gov/ammem/award97/icuhtml/aespsp.html
50. In 1915, Wilhelm Miller published a manifesto on this regional landscape design movement, in the unlikely guise of Illinois Cooperative Extension Circular #184, entitled *The Prairie Spirit in Landscape Gardening*. Wilhelm Miller, *The Prairie Spirit in Landscape Gardening* (Reprint, Amherst: University of Massachusetts Press, 2002).
51. I am indebted to Breck Gastinger, M. Arch. student, for his research on Columbus Park for a course I teach, LAR 514: Theories of Modern Landscape Architecture (2001).
52. As Christopher Vernon has written, the native landscape that was the source for this Prairie Spirit was "...the actual and remembered grove and prairie checkerboard of the native landscape of the Midwest." Vernon's use of the term *checkerboard* refers, of course, to the impact of the Land Ordinance Grid on the American Midwestern and Western land uses and land forms. Christopher Vernon, "Wilhelm Miller and the Prairie Spirit," in *Regional Garden Design*, eds. O'Malley and Treib (1995), 273.
53. Robert Grese, *Jens Jensen. Maker of Natural Parks and Gardens* (Baltimore: Johns Hopkins Press, 1992), 80–82.
54. Jens Jensen, *Siftings* (Chicago: Ralph Fletcher Seymour, 1939), 80–84. See also Grese, *Jens Jensen* (1992). As Wilhelm Miller wrote, "The prairie horizon has been called 'the strongest line in the western hemisphere'...the prairie is the most characteristic scenery over the American continent...the essence of the prairie's beauty lies in all these horizontal lines, no two of which are at the same elevation, but all of which repeat in soft and gentle ways the great story of the horizon." Wilhelm Miller, *The Prairie Spirit* (1915), 19.
55. Marjorie Cautley, "Planting at Radburn," *Landscape Architecture* 21:1 (October 1930): 23–29; Frank A. Waugh, *The Natural Style in Landscape Gardening* (Boston: Richard G. Badger, 1917), 51–73; O. C. Simonds, *Land-*

scape Gardening (New York: MacMillan, 1920); Roberts and Rehmann, *American Plants for American Gardens* (1929).

56. See Giles Deleuze and Felix Guattari, *A Thousand Plateaus. Capitalism and Schizophrenia* (Minneapolis: University of Minnesota Press, 1987), 263, for discussion of haecceities. For a discussion of episodic contrasts and temporal moments, see Kevin Lynch, *What Time Is this Place?* (Cambridge: MIT Press, 1972), 173 ff.
57. One of the first landscape design treatises to discuss the changing seasonal effects, such as light, shadow, and atmosphere, as sources of aesthetic delight was Thomas Whately's *Observations on Modern Landscape Gardening* (London: T. Payne, 1770). This fourth design strategy builds on the sensibility found in Whately.
58. Jensen, *Siftings* (1939), 61.
59. "Jensen's raw materials of the garden...'the contours of the earth, the vegetation that covers it, the changing seasons, the rays of the setting sun and the afterglow, and the light of the moon.'" Robert Grese, "The Prairie Gardens of O. C. Simonds and Jens Jensen," in *Regional Garden Design,* eds. O'Malley and Treib (1995), 14. Grese quotes an article by Jensen and Eskil, "Natural Gardens," *The Saturday Evening Post* 202:36 (March 8, 1930).
60. Jensen, *Siftings* (1939), 44, 40, 49. Given Jensen's interest in these ephemeral landscape qualities, it is not surprising that he admired the paintings of George Innes, who donated a number of his works to the Chicago Art Institute.
61. Grese, "The Prairie Gardens," *Regional Garden Design*, eds. O'Malley and Treib (1995), 118. Again, Grese, quoting Jensen and Eskil, 169.
62. But he was not alone. He and others such as Beatrix Farrand, were working within earlier design traditions of the wild garden, defined by William Robinson in the 1870s, as well as within the landscape garden design discourse begun in eighteenth-century England. Both these traditions celebrated the unique medium of the landscape—its dynamic, temporal qualities—as an agent of subjective experience.
63. See Mara Miller, *The Garden as an Art* (Albany: SUNY Press, 1993), for a philosophical account of how temporality accounts for landscape design's distinction from architecture.
64. Here, I disagree with John Dixon Hunt's assessment that, "In garden writing generally, the nineteenth century was interpreted as a debate between 'formal' and 'informal,' undistracted by any understand about other ideas of the garden." Hunt, *Greater Perfections* (2000), 212.
65. That these debates were occurring during the same decade that the first university degree program in landscape architecture was created at Harvard and a national professional organization for landscape architects, the American Society of Landscape Architects (ASLA), was founded is curious and worthy of interrogation. See Henry V. Hubbard and Theodora Kimball, *An Introduction to the Study of Landscape Design* (Reprint, New York: MacMillan Co., 1935), 32–34, for a Harvard landscape architecture professor's account of formal and informal garden and landscape designs: "It is so evident that the negative term informal is so general that it is of very little value in nam-

ing a style, and should certainly not be used as the designation of the principle of organization of naturalistic design."

66. Henry Russell Hitchcock and Philip Johnson, *The International Style* (New York: W.W. Norton, 1966), 76–77.
67. Although significant, *The International Style* was only one of many architectural texts that address site. For another exhibition catalog, see *Contemporary Landscape Architecture and Its Sources* (San Francisco: San Francisco Museum of Modern Art, 1937), especially essays by Henry Russell Hitchcock and Richard Neutra. For an example of recent scholarship that examines the site concerns of several modern architects, see David Leatherbarrow, *Uncommon Ground. Architecture, Technology, and Topograph*y (Cambridge: MIT Press, 2000).
68. Garrett Eckbo, *Landscape for Living* (New York: Dodge, 1950), 238.
69. Ibid., 37. This passage resonates with late-twentieth-century critiques of the visual biases of landscape by Beatrice Colomina, James Corner, Denis Cosgrove, and Gina Crandell.
70. More research is necessary to ascertain where and how Eckbo adopted this term. Concurrent with the book's publication, landscape architect Hideo Sasaki worked in the site planning division within the multi-disciplinary architecture firm, Skidmore Owings Merrill (SOM), so one can surmise the term was in common use by the mid 1940s. Peter Walker and Melanie Simo, *Invisible Gardens* (Cambridge: MIT Press, 1994), 225.
71. Eckbo, *Landscape for* Living (1950), 234, 236.
72. An early-twentieth-century writing about space as a landscape is Charles Downing Lay, "Space Composition in Landscape Design," *Landscape Architecture* 8:2 (January 1918), 77–86. See Peter Collins "New Concepts of Space," in his *Changing Ideals in Modern Architecture*: *1750–1950* (Kingston: McGill-Queens University Press, 1984), 42–60, 285–294.
73. Sasaki opened his office in 1953, according to Walker and Simo, *Invisible Gardens* (1994), 224.
74. John Simonds, *Landscape Architecture. The Shaping of Man's Natural Environment* (New York: Dodge, 1961) 47–48, 56; and Kevin Lynch, *Site Planning* (Cambridge: MIT Press, 1962), 62.
75. See Melanie Simo, *Loudon and the Landscape* (New Haven: Yale University Press, 1988); and Mrs. Schuyler (Mariana) Van Rensselaer, *Art Out-of-Doors. Hints on Good Taste in Gardening* (New York: Charles Scribner's Sons, 1893), 4–8.
76. For a sense of the critics' responses to this new art, see Michael Fried, "Art and Objecthood," *Art Forum* (June 1967): 12–23; and Jack Burnham, "Systems Esthetic," *Art Forum* (September 1968): 144–156.
77. See Miller, *The Garden as an Art* (1993) for an account of how shifts in art practices over the last quarter-century have altered the reception of the garden and designed landscapes within aesthetic theory.
78. See Miller, *The Garden as an Art* (1993); and Miwon Kwon, "One Place after Another: Notes on Site-Specificity," *October* 80 (Spring 1997): 85–110.

79. Haecceitas/this-ness, see John Dixon Hunt, "Ruskin, Turnerian Topography, and Genius Loci," *Gardens and the Picturesque* (Cambridge: MIT, 1992), 218.
80. Eckbo, *Landscape for Living* (1950), 37.
81. Ibid., 234, 236.

Zurichhorn Park, Zurich, Switzerland.

6

Shifting Sites

Kristina Hill

Over the last several decades, the evolving notion of the natural world as a dynamic ecosystem has slowly but radically altered the ways ecologists talk about the patterns and dynamics of a site. Many of these changes in theory have led to shifts in the natural sciences as dramatic as transitions initiated by the Modern Movement in design. In short, a wholesale reevaluation of boundaries and predictability has occurred, posing special challenges for professions that propose site designs.

Indeed, recent work in the ecological sciences seeks to envision landscapes as composed of shifting nodes of interaction, driven by dynamic temporal relationships rather than deterministic trends. This tendency to describe trends as nondeterministic has altered the scope and type of the predictions that these scientists seek to make. A nonequilibrium view of natural processes has literally changed the way scientists think about the nature of nature; they now frequently see change as probabilistic and multidirectional, rather than as a progressive march toward clear endpoints. To the extent that the new ontological assumptions of ecology will be or have already been adopted by other disciplines and in popular culture, scientists and designers will increasingly meet on a different intellectual basis than in the recent past, particularly the last fifty years. As new paradigms develop and preconceived boundaries dissolve, fields such as design and science may find themselves in an altered relationship, making this a critical time for those fields to take a fresh look at each other.

Mapping disciplines such as geology and geography, among others, typically define sites as places bounded by some degree of internal homogeneity. This definition implies that sites exist as a function of our human ability to perceive and reify contrasts and similarities in the features around us, such as topographic landforms, subsurface geology, typical associations of plants, or typical patterns of human use. The combination of perceptions and preconceptions that construct the "sites" of science, like any cultural tool, both derive from and influence how we see and experience the world around and within us. Science and its theories function as lenses that influence perceptions and preconceptions, just as art does—although the methods of the arts and sciences stem from very different epistemological origins. Not surprisingly then, the new scientific assumptions of the past thirty to fifty years have been associated with broader cultural trends; scientists' interest in ecological diversity, for example, parallels a broader social and political concern for human diversity. Theoretical metaphors can cross disciplinary boundaries and inform an emergent *zeitgeist*, perhaps becoming even more influential as we begin to take them for granted.[1]

A new understanding of place has emerged over the last few decades, as have the new ontological assumptions underlying what some scientists call the *nonequilibrium paradigm* in ecology. These two notions, of place and of the nonequilibrium ecological paradigm, might seem unrelated to my colleagues in the sciences. But there are good reasons why both designers and scientists should reflect on them now, as a pair. As shifts occur in significant elements of the theoretical framework of ecology, new metaphors will emerge that affect designers' conceptions of place. Like any successful metaphor, these will probably not be perceived as abstractions for long. Successful metaphors are rapidly reified, treated as an acceptable substitute for reality. The central problem of reification, however, is that it encourages the formation of dogmatic preconceptions, closing the window of critical self-reflection that might open up briefly as intellectual eras begin and end. Dogmatic preconceptions have historically posed obstacles to understanding the world from new points of view, preventing all but a few thinkers from remaining open to new insights. The first argument for considering the idea of place, which by definition has implied fixity,[2] in juxtaposition to the idea of a world constantly in flux takes advantage of an opportunity to "look" simultaneously backward at past thinking and forward to what may be the future of landscape theory.

The second reason to reflect on place and dynamics is that representing the nature of sites poses the substantial challenge of integrating diverse scientific knowledge and methods, and relating them to proposals for human intervention. On a ridge in the Brazilian rainforest, a botanist may meet a climatologist sharing tea with a population ecologist. All three could be standing by the trail as a group of planners and designers walks by, intent on altering the urbanization patterns that affect the rainforest. When the futures of particular places are at stake, scientists from different disciplines often find themselves working from different assumptions that arise from their disciplinary training. The much larger epistemological gulf between science and design makes it difficult for human cultures to intervene in the spatial patterns of landscapes on the basis of scientific knowledge. Confusing gaps can appear to open up in expert understanding at the precise moment when coherent strategies are needed to respond to change.

Third, sites evoke palpable tension between general cultural aspirations, which may convey a sense of shared meaning to a broad audience (such as owning a home), and the conclusions of specialized researchers and practitioners (that single-family neighborhoods take up too much land, displacing other species). Consider the design of a large urban park: should the design maximize regional biodiversity among native (nonhuman) species? Should it entertain large numbers of people who can afford to pay for such entertainments, and thereby generate revenue? Should it memorialize its history or surroundings? Sites are where the future of landscapes—as seas of detached housing, or as parks that support regional biodiversity—first becomes recognizable as potential outcomes. Even the most widespread expressions of cultural aspirations began in specific places. Sites allow us to preview what may become the standards of the future.

For all three of these reasons, sites have been and continue to be flashpoints in the theories of both science and design.

THE NATURE OF A BOUNDED PLACE

My purpose in this chapter is first to review the major theoretical shifts in ecology over the past several decades, with attention to their roots in earlier ideas about landscapes and the biophysical changes that occur in them over time. In addition, I will try to demonstrate that the history of these ideas provides an essential intellectual point of view for contemporary designers and for design writing dealing with the concept of a bounded place and its nature.

Over the past thirty to fifty years, theories in the science of ecology have been reconsidered in at least three major areas: first, with regard to whether local ecosystems can be considered "closed" to larger-scale flows of materials and energy or whether the influences of these larger flows should be considered integral to local systems (I will refer to this as the spatial scale paradigm shift); second, in the degree to which local and regional history influences contemporary ecosystem dynamics (i.e., the temporal scale shift); and third, in the explicit consideration of physical landscape patterns as an important component of ecosystem functioning (i.e., the pattern shift).[3] These developments have broad implications for ecologists who now think differently about relationships between local observations and events (or local spatial arrangements) and relationships that are neither local nor recent. Simply put, ecological scientists have replaced their expectations for determinism and predictability with expectations of greater complexity in ecosystem behavior.[4] Although this has sometimes resulted in a reduced willingness among scientists to predict the specific outcomes of dynamic processes, it has also led to an increased ability to understand fluctuating human economies as components of ecosystems.[5] Moreover, these new expectations acknowledge the enormous potential influence of temporal processes without requiring them to produce deterministic unidirectional trends, as was typical in the ecological sciences only a few decades ago.[6]

What all these theoretical shifts in the sciences might mean for design theory remains an open question. At the very least, collaborations between designers and scientists will occur on a renewed basis as new metaphors are sought and accepted as the basis for the development of theory. The risk, of course, remains that new metaphors will simply become reified, replacing abstractions that were once accepted as "reality" with new assumptions that leave people equally blind to cross-disciplinary reasoning. To prevent the loss of this opportunity for creative juxtapositions in theory—to keep new metaphors from simply becoming new dogma—the interplay of metaphors that previously shaped perceptions of nature and place must be better understood.

THE SPATIAL SCALE SHIFT: ORGANISM VERSUS SYSTEM, BOUNDARY VERSUS NODE

Cognitive research has shown that metaphors are fundamental to human thinking in everyday situations, as well as in formal theory building.[7] These abstractions appear to be vital to the human ability to form meaningful expectations about relationships and patterns. Metaphors do not exist in a vacuum, of course, but in the richly physical world of embodied experience. Research on human languages, and on cognition, has shown that lived experience affects the fundamental categories people use to describe the world.[8]

For example, the experience of living in a body that appears to be separated from its surroundings by a skin has been very influential in the development of metaphors about the nature of biological relationships.[9] Scientists have used two dominant metaphors to describe these relationships. The first refers to them as forming a "super-organism," as if the interactions among species can be compared to the interactions among individual organs within a body; the second describes them as a system of energy flows and exchanges, as if they are comparable to the mechanical and electrical systems designed by humans. Each metaphor has implications for how a scientist might make sense of new observations obtained in the field, and each influences the hypotheses that are used to express new expectations. Indeed, the competition between these two metaphors has dominated a significant portion of the debate in ecological theory over the last few decades. As ecology enters an era in which the "system" metaphor seems to have won the competition, I argue that the origin of this theoretical debate lies in the human experience of embodiment, and that this origin has also been significant for the development of theories that describe the ecology of sites.

Proposals by nineteenth- and early-twentieth-century biologists that "communities" of plants and animals could be identified by their close interrelationships, and further, that these communities behaved like a kind of super-organism, emphasized physical and biological boundaries observed between groups of organisms. They extended the metaphor of embodiment to groups of interacting species, proposing a sort of conceptual "skin" that united some species in closer relationships, dividing them from others. Nineteenth-century botanists actually classified plant associations using nomenclature that previously had been reserved for individual species, as if the group of plants functioned as a super-organism that existed at a different spatial scale.[10] The notion of an "oak-hickory forest type," for example, referred to the association of oak and hickory trees as if it was a necessary evolutionary relationship that occurred within a particular set of climate and soil conditions. At a scale larger than the human body, ecological theory used the metaphor of the organism to demarcate a complete set of what were then considered necessary functional relationships. In a sense, a holistic (organismal) bias affected the way scientists and designers talked about geographic associations among plant species.

At a scale smaller than the human body, nineteenth-century biologists identified other functional units: for example, bacteria, the necessary but invisible foundation of the germ theory of disease.[11] A hierarchy of organisms began to seem like a reality, some of which were tiny and invisible, and some of which were made up of multiple species in necessary relationships. As a result, theories that described natural processes as acting independently on individual species seemed to be missing the big picture; the idea that relationships among many species were real and necessary became pervasive, and theories were proposed that described nested hierarchical relationships between individual species and their community-level super-organisms.

A competing theory that plant species responded individualistically to environmental gradients was published in the 1920s by Henry Gleason and was promptly rejected without significant debate.[12] It resurfaced in the works of Robert Whittaker and Margaret Davis during the 1940s and 1950s,[13] although the notion that fixed plant associations were a necessary condition was so dominant that his dissent appears to have cost Whittaker his first teaching job.[14] Davis tested the idea that plant communities migrated as a cohesive group during periods of climate change, using the laborious methods of pollen analysis on soil cores from bogs that originated shortly after glaciers melted across the northern Midwest. She found that plant species returned to formerly ice-covered regions as individuals, not as intact communities. As the theoretical hegemony of the super-organism metaphor began to unravel, researchers rediscovered the work of others who had advocated using the notion of a dynamic system to describe ecological relationships even earlier than Whittaker and Davis, such as Henry Cowles.[15]

Well before ecologists widely adopted the system metaphor to describe biological relationships in the 1950s, the geologist-turned-botanist Henry Cowles was studying the relationship between the spatial and temporal dynamics of windblown sand dunes and the development of vegetation patterns on the moving dunes. Cowles developed the first theory of dynamic plant succession, in which plants interacted with a constantly changing environment, between 1898 and 1911.[16] Geological theory had already wrestled with defining the

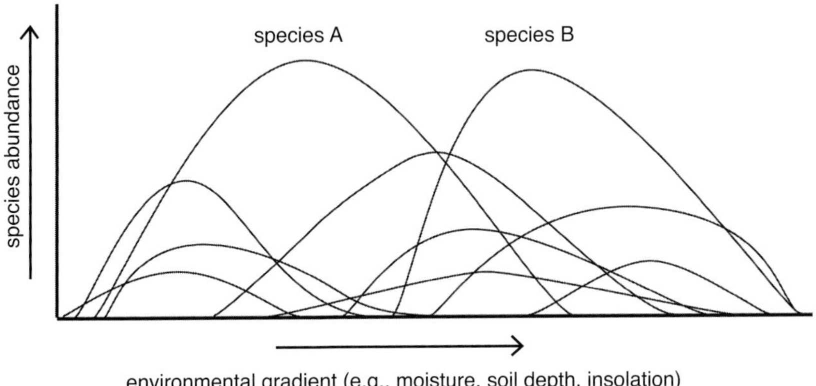

Figure 6.1. A generalized model of the abundance of species along an environmental gradient. Each species is represented using a curve of abundance. The dominant species (A and B) are not necessarily associated with any of the less abundant species, although they might appear to be if one examined the distributions of only a few less-abundant species. If species A and B are physically large in comparison to the less abundant species, it might seem to human eyes that two distinct vegetation "types" exist. Studies have shown, however, that each plant species is more likely to respond to changing conditions on such a gradient in an individualist manner.

nature of time, describing processes such as glaciation as recurring cycles that produced different regional landscape mosaics depending on the depth of ice and the directions of its flow. The very idea of naming something that took thousands of years to move a "flow" required an audacious act of imagination; sand dune movements were instantaneous in comparison. Two early animal ecologists who worked with Cowles at the University of Chicago carried his idea that living things constantly interact with a dynamic world into the "other half" of the biological sciences, creating a crossover of theories into animal ecology that anticipated contemporary ecological thinking by some sixty years.[17] The multidisciplinary context of Henry Cowles's work and that of his colleagues in animal ecology seems to have provided them with greater flexibility in conceiving dynamic relationships between landscapes and a wide range of biological organisms, including both plants and animals.[18]

This example of evolving ecological theory shows, first, the tendency for humans to extend the metaphor of the organism to relationships among species, and even to landscapes themselves. I argue that this occurred as a projection of the human experience of embodiment, which influenced the development of a dominant metaphor in ecological theory. Second, this example stresses that an interdisciplinary context, such as the intellectual environment created by Henry Cowles and his colleagues, can offer significant opportunities for theoretical crossovers to occur between fields. The stultifying effects of reification, in which metaphor becomes dogma, are also evident in this example of changing theories.

As the metaphor of a mechanical or electrical system became more common in ecological theory, the significance of organisms and species was increasingly described through maps of the energy flows or exchanges in which they were seen to participate.[19] Boundaries between these systems of flows were described more abstractly, on the basis of the amounts of energy exchanged rather than the physical co-occurrence of different species. The idea of the site as a distinct, bounded space in a landscape became less relevant to this system-based concept of biological relationships, because these energy flow systems were generally described in terms of graph theory, without using geographic dimensions. Instead, the system metaphor suggests that nodes exist where more numerous interactions occur. In ecosystem ecology, sites can be thought of as nodes of interaction: a conceptual shift that places emphasis on the processes of exchange and flow, rather than the geography of bounded spaces.

The attempt to conceive of human settlements as comprised of systems of flows has a significant intellectual history. Patrick Geddes, another multidisciplinary thinker from the same era as Cowles, helped call attention to energy flows and dynamic systems in his studies on cities and towns as human habitat. Geddes, formally trained as a botanist in Scotland during the late-nineteenth century, wrote and worked as a professional urban planner in the early-twentieth century. In 1884 he wrote about the need to conceive of human societies as energy systems;[20] later, he described cities in terms of both their biological and social energy flows.[21] When Jane Jacobs took up the subject of cities in 1961, she echoed some of Geddes's thoughts. Her emphasis on cities as systems, and her argument that they be conceived as problems of organized complexity,[22] raised an epistemological issue that ecologists took up in the 1970s when they considered why the organism metaphor persisted in ecological theory.[23] The crossover of theories between urban design and ecology over the last century that has emphasized energy flow and system dynamics strongly suggests that the evolution of thinking in ecology and the other environmental sciences did not occur in isolation, but rather that similar developments were taking place in different fields at approximately the same time.[24]

Some proponents of the system metaphor in ecology over the past several decades maintained a kind of conceptual ambivalence about the importance of boundary concepts in describing biological relationships. Eugene Odum returned to the metaphor of the super-organism in his later writing, despite the fact that he was a prominent popularizer of the ecosystem concept.[25] G. M. Weinberg has described the recurrence of this metaphor as an epistemological problem related to the representation of complexity.[26] I argue that this metaphor persists because of our tendency to conceive of our own bodies as a strictly bounded "interior space," in spite of epidemiological evidence to the contrary, and to project that concept onto other biological relationships.[27]

Like ecologists, contemporary biological scientists who study human bodies have also reconsidered the classical notions of boundaries. The human skin that was once considered a significant boundary no longer appears to be so discrete. The work of Sandra Steingraber, an ecologist who has written about cancer and the environment, provides a case in point.[28] Her reconsideration of the human boundary with landscape has been both poetic and radical. Steingraber suggests that humans actually incorporate into their bodies the molecules of landscapes where their food is grown; she argues that Americans have all become the embodiment of the Midwestern prairie, given the amount of corn syrup consumed (an ingredient of common prepared foods that originates in that region). Steingraber has applied ecological thinking to study the strength of interactions between body and landscape in contemporary American culture; she has found that the boundary between geographic sites and the internal functions of the human body is in many ways an insignificant fiction. The body, much like what was once conceived as a geographically discrete site, genuinely seems to function as a node in a system rather than a distinct entity. As the new ecological paradigms have suggested, when spatial scales of perception shift, boundaries in the mosaic—like those at a single site—realign or disappear.

The notion that humans are somehow separate from the flows of energy and organisms that define ecological systems is one of the most thoroughly reified metaphors in popular culture and has influenced the kinds of research undertaken in ecological science.[29] Boundaries appear to have been a critical component of representations of the world that use the metaphor of the organism to describe relationships among multiple species and physical processes. Humans seem to frequently project the notion of "skins" onto observations of phenomena, including landscape sites and ecological communities of species. Yet extensive evidence shows that the human body is permeable to many kinds of flows—of energy, materials, and organisms that can both support health and cause disease. If scientists and others were to completely embrace the notion of the ecosystem, the skin of the body would be no more important to our descriptions of life than the geographic accidents that define a site in an ecosystem made up of energy exchanges. I find this interesting to note, particularly because theorists in the ecological sciences still seem to struggle with describing the role of humans in ecosystems. If theorists followed the logic of the system metaphor to its full extent, human bodies (like geographic sites) would be treated as nodes in energy flow systems.[30] My own observation is that we humans typically find it too difficult to suspend the feeling that, because we have skins, we are separate from the flows all around us. Yet a system-based description of biological relationships demands an end to the persistent emphasis on the skin as a boundary, to a very great extent, just as it calls on theories of landscape to represent sites as nodes of interaction rather than bounded places.

If the related notions of bounded sites and bounded bodies ceased to function as useful concepts because of a theoretical emphasis on the open nature of systems in space, then new conceptions of demarcation in space would be more dependent on the density (and intensity) of biological interactions that occur over time. Adopting that basis for demarcation and delineation would require a major shift in thinking for design theorists, who have relied heavily on geographic dimensions as their primary means of recognizing and reproducing important relationships. Ecological theorists have confronted this problem already, and some of the responses they have proposed follow.

THE TEMPORAL SHIFT: CYCLES, RATES OF CHANGE, AND THE ROLE OF HISTORY

For students of human culture, the relevance of historical events to contemporary patterns of human settlement and human interactions might seem self-evident. But ecological science has not always recognized changes in temporal patterns as significant to the development of explanatory theory. In part, this is because the natural sciences have been influenced by the ontological assumptions inherent in the Law of Uniformitarianism as proposed in the science of geology.[31] This law simply states that geological processes operating today, such as weathering and soil formation, also operated in the past. It was used to establish stable theoretical ground on which to develop hypotheses about the processes that might have formed geologic landforms over millions of years. It also allowed scientists to calculate, for instance, how long it might take for water flows to carve out a canyon based on current measurements of flow and erosion rates. The assumption that processes observable today also operated in the past was very important to the development of scientific theory in the eighteenth and nineteenth centuries, in both biology and geology, in part because it placed new significance on the ability of tests and observations carried out in the present to help explain the past and predict the future.

To the extent that ecological theories emulated the theories of other sciences, such as chemistry or physics, historical studies were sometimes described pejoratively as "just descriptive," that is, primarily useful to describe sequences of past events. The quest to identify generalizations about system behavior was seen as more important in that it would allow scientists to predict future trends or events. But in the 1970s, as ecologists began to reconsider the nature of biological systems, they found increasing evidence that deterministic equilibrium-based concepts of ecosystem functioning were insufficient to explain observed energy inputs and losses.[32] New evidence suggested that ecosystems were in fact "open systems"; they functioned in less predictable ways than had previously been thought, leaking energy and sometimes even materials. The ecologist Steward Pickett has referred to this insight as the nonequilibrium paradigm in ecology.[33] In practical terms, this paradigm implies that the goal of predictability in ecosystem dynamics over time is probably not achievable—at least not as often as earlier ecologists might have hoped. Any predictions would be more probabilistic than deterministic, requiring ecologists to comprehend probability theory as a basis for describing system behavior through observable phenomena. It has also become clear, via a network of U.S. ecological research sites as well as long-term ecological research in other countries, that ecosystem events can produce an enduring temporal legacy. Events that occurred three hundred years ago, for example, can exert significant influence on the contemporary distribution and abundance of plants and animals.

As a case in point, researchers at the Harvard Forest Long-Term Ecological Research (LTER) site in Massachusetts have found that the loss of topsoil from the eighteenth-century clearing of forests for colonial agriculture influenced the mix of tree species that recolonized those landscapes during the nineteenth century, when agriculture was largely abandoned. Most original old-growth forest species returned, but not in their original proportions. Some, like the American chestnut, returned but were subject to new disease pathogens that prevented them from maturing into adult trees. Research at the Harvard Forest LTER site provided evidence for connections that environmental historians like William Cronon and Carolyn Merchant have drawn between socioeconomic trends and environmental change in New England, linking ecological dynamics not only to future ecological states but also to future social conditions and trends.[34] This type of research is part of a widespread reconsideration of the role of humans in ecosystems. Ecologists now try to write as if human habitat alterations are an integral process in ecosystems, effecting both disturbance and regeneration. The challenge of this theoretical shift is that it requires ecologists to treat human activities as similar to other "natural" disturbance processes, such as windstorms, insect population booms, and fires.[35] Just as theorists have found it difficult to abandon the notion of human bodies as separate from their environments, it is conceptually and culturally difficult to abandon the idea that human actions are fundamentally different from nonhuman processes.

Recent investigations at this, and other, long-term ecological research centers have tried to tease apart the relative importance of human and natural disturbances as shapers of ecosystem states, a difficult intellectual task in a field that has only recently included humans as significant organisms for study. Although sites are now seen as parts of larger mosaics of vegetation and topography that transform over time, to date no clear or consistent lens has developed through which to study humans and their influences on these landscapes. Steward Pickett and his colleagues at the Baltimore urban LTER site have published a couple of new models seeking to encapsulate what they have learned about the ecology of urban ecosystems, most recently summarizing their insights in terms of the metaphor of "cities of resilience."[36] Noting that their chosen metaphor of resilience intentionally emphasizes dynamic change over time, Pickett and his colleagues stress that the meaning of resilience, as an ecological concept, has been modified over the past thirty years as the nonequilibrium paradigm has come to dominate the discourse of ecological science. In their description of this paradigm, "resilience is the ability of a system to adapt and adjust to changing internal or external processes…The emphasis is not on reaching or maintaining a certain end point or terminal condition, but on staying 'in the game.'"[37]

This notion of nonequilibrium dynamics holds that a stable state does not exist in living systems and, instead, that a "meta-stable" set of conditions constantly disappears and reappears. The nonequilibrium view of ecology has very significant implications for the idea of sustainability in both human and nonhuman environments. In this new paradigm, sustaining a particular set of conditions is less meaningful than adapting to a fluctuating set of contextual variables. Attempts to hold systemwide conditions constant in a complex set of interacting variables are unlikely to succeed, if not impossible. The relaxation of boundary concepts in ecosystems makes constancy even more unlikely, since these systems are now understood to be more heavily influenced by processes that occur at spatial and temporal scales both much larger (e.g., global climate change) and much smaller (e.g., the evolution of disease-causing organisms over very short lifespans). As a corollary to the relaxation of spatial boundaries, the boundaries of temporal states are also less likely to be discrete in this new theoretical paradigm.

This temporal shift in ecological theory has important implications for designers' conceptions of bounded geographic sites. In the new metaphor of open systems with no steady states, bounded places must be seen as part of a changing context in which trends cannot be exactly predicted, and surprises should be expected. The arrival of a new invasive plant species, for example, could completely alter the successional trajectory of a landscape over a period of a decade or less. In short, contemporary ecological theory does not see sites as the fundamental unit of prediction for future states of nature; instead, it must consider systems that exist at both larger and smaller scales than the site. These systems are seen as the source of future influences that may affect the site more than its local flora or its local geomorphology and drainage patterns.

In the past, many designers in ecological planning and design sought to conserve the biological resources of a site by "defending" it against external influences—essentially treating valuable sites as fortresses to be walled off and protected from the influences of a hostile matrix. But the nonequilibrium paradigm of ecology implies that those sites should be treated as if they were desirable sandbars in a shifting, flowing river. Preserving the sandbar would require the designer to let the river continue to flow; on the other hand, a designer might consider altering the watershed of the river to influence flood levels and flooding frequency. Building a levee around the sandbar would make no sense at all; this would only cut the sandbar off from its source of renewal and sever its relationships to the dynamic context that provides its identity and supply of material over time. As designers take in the new paradigms of ecology, they must grapple with the disappearance of fixed boundaries, a much greater emphasis on the

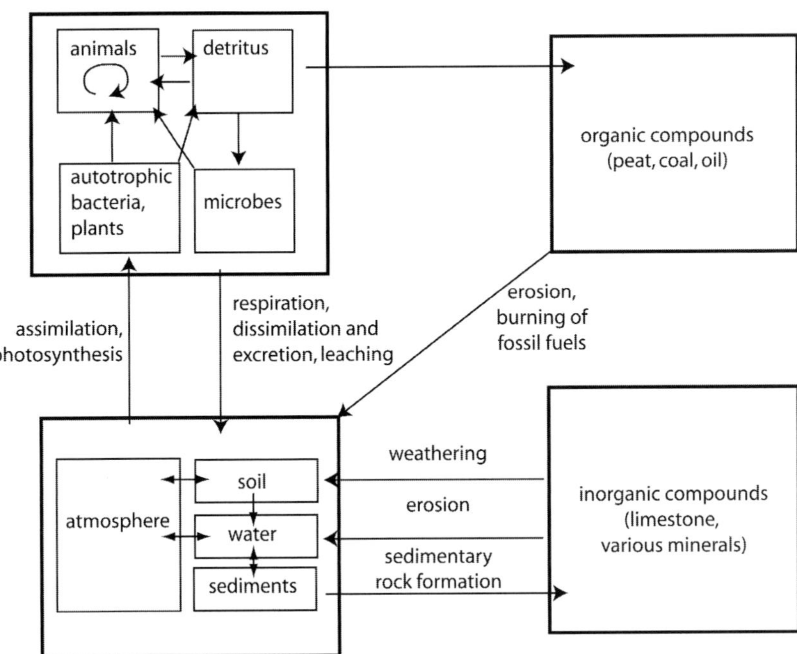

Figure 6.2. A generalized model of an ecosystem, showing the different compartments that are used to represent relationships within the system. These boundaries are typically conceptual, rather than geographic. (Adapted from Ricklefs, 1990.)

use of temporary spatial features, and the critical significance of processes that create flows in the matrix (or "background") of the landscapes in which they work.

This redefinition of the site would allow designers to continue to treat boundaries as significant cultural features, but it would prevent designers from engaging in a wholesale reification of those cultural boundaries through design inspirations and interventions. My larger point here is that boundaries should not be treated as real biophysical phenomena, but rather, be stretched, shrunken, and re-envisioned across multiple landscape scales. Designers must come to treat these edge zones as dynamic, like weather patterns, and not as artifacts that deserve permanent memorialization simply because they once existed. In cultural terms, sites are best understood as shape-shifters, and boundaries as tricksters that teach us that what we see in a moment of time is not necessarily what matters most to the river of time.

THE SPATIAL PATTERN SHIFT: LANDSCAPES AS DYNAMIC MOSAICS

The development of the theoretical perspective of landscape ecology—the third and final major development in ecological theory that I present here—in ecological theory is significant in providing a language for the integration of spatial and temporal patterns, reconnecting the abstract graphs of ecosystem studies to the Cartesian dimensions of geography. By defining landscape ecology as the study of flows of organisms, energy, and materials through space, ecological theorists created a new conceptual bridge that can connect the contemporary paradigms of ecology to the theoretical and practical concerns of landscape architecture.

The metaphor that currently dominates landscape ecological conceptualizations of landscapes is the "shifting mosaic," a pattern that consists of sporadic, repeated emergences and disappearances of different ecosystem types (vegetation or hydrologic features like wetlands, for example). Landscape ecologist Richard Forman has explained this metaphor by asking people to imagine looking down from an airplane at a major city at night and perceiving the illusion of continuous light even though many of the individual lights are in fact switching on and off at the spatial scale of individual windows and individual sites.[38] This conceptualization of dynamics within a spatial framework suggests that component sites or elements may appear and disappear from a resilient overall form. It allows ecologists to consider the nonequilibrium notion that local sites may change while a larger landscape retains its overall functionality—if, in the aggregate, those local changes do not fundamentally alter functions or patterns of distribution at broader spatial scales.

Building upon the nonequilibrium paradigm of recent ecological theory, the metaphor of a shifting mosaic relies on a probabilistic conceptualization of change. It would, for example, be impossible to know for certain which light in a city would be the next to go off or on. But a reasonable probability could be established based on a record of many such events. Over time, landscape patterns can appear and disappear locally yet still support the dispersal and reproductive success of animals or plants, provided that the overall mosaic pattern continues to offer shelter from predators, an appropriate degree of connectivity for movement, access to reproductive sites, and access to mates, pollinators, and so forth.[39]

Understanding sites as components of a probabilistic landscape mosaic requires that the significance of spatial and temporal patterns be evaluated on a species-by-species basis. The truism that "there is no habitat without specific species" applies. For example, a meadow mowed in spring, when juvenile mice are dispersing in search of new territory, may expose large numbers of these young animals to high mortality rates if they are clearly visible to hawks in the absence of tall grasses. On the other hand, an insect that lays eggs in the meadow may find its population maintained if the meadow is not mown until summer, after its eggs have hatched and the insects have developed wings to fly away. Timing is critical in the mosaic, in general. At specific sites, for specific organisms, it means life and death.[40]

The different ecosystems within this mosaic are often described as interspersed in a range of "grain sizes" (usually a reference to typical patch sizes) from coarse to fine grained. They may also exist in dendritic patterns, grids, or ladders. An almost infinite number of descriptive metaphors for observable spatial patterns could be applied at different geographic scales.[41] The significance of these patterns for specific species varies. Flight alone provides much of the mobility birds need to travel from one suitable habitat patch to another; insects, however, might follow particular zones of consistently high air temperature to gain the benefits of updrafts, or might follow a line of flowering plants, or might simply drift downwind. The value of different kinds of connectivity within the shifting mosaic is, again, almost a species-by-species question. Some species can be treated as similar if grouped by characteristics such as mobility or vulnerability to predators, but overall, to anticipate the effects of pattern dynamics on species abundance and geographic distribution can only produce maps of probabilistic likelihood. The actual patterns that might occur could be quite different from those that were expected. Resilience may be more likely if redundant ecological systems are designed that provide a functional backup when surprises do occur.

The question of boundaries is very significant in landscape ecology, since they must be described in terms that are appropriate to the size and behavior of individual species to have meaningful biological implications. Many landscape boundaries can act as metaphorical filters, barriers, and conduits, depending on the specific mobility and body size (or seed size) of organisms. The key requirement here is that designers and ecologists must not represent boundaries that operate only at the scale of human bodies and mobility, but instead try to understand the implications of embodiment for the dispersal ability of other forms of life. On the same physical site, the landscape a beetle encounters may be very different from the barriers and conduits perceived by a snake, a bird, or an airborne seed. In this multispecies sense, a very large variety of landscape patterns are contained within a single discrete site. The multiplicity of perspectives that must be understood in order to capture even an approximate picture of ecological functions can be daunting, resulting in a kind of ecological postmodern view comprised of petite narratives, in the sense of Jean-Francois Lyotard.[42] This enormous complexity and variety can be organized only by using some form of approximate reasoning that finds similarities among the morphological characteristics and life history traits of many species.

In the 1980s, Christine Schonewald-Cox and J. Bayless presented a typology of boundaries that summarized the different kinds of edge experiences organisms might perceive, focused in particular on the perceptual responses of large mammals.[43] In this work, Schonewald-Cox and Bayless considered a single patch protected as part of a biological reserve. They noted that some edges had been "generated" because of restrictions on human uses, and others had been made more discrete by the imposition of a reserve boundary in a forested area, allowing timber harvests on one side and not the other. Schonewald-Cox and Bayless's work emphasized the need to describe boundaries to understand their effects on the flows of organisms, energy, and materials that occur in ecosystems. In particular, their efforts to map and describe the different edge conditions that occur along the boundaries of protected landscapes have drawn attention to the need for edges to be designed to protect the vulnerable interiors of unusual landscapes. This point of view has allowed landscape ecologists to combine the notions of the "skin" and the system, but without requiring them to reintroduce the organism metaphor. Instead, ecologists like Richard Forman have used the membrane of a single biological cell as a metaphor for how the edge of a patch affects its role in a larger ecosystem.[44]

Digital mapping techniques developed over the past fifteen years allow researchers and designers to represent abstract environmental gradients as landforms using variable surfaces. Mapping the magnitude of these variables across a Cartesian grid has expanded the options for visualizing the mosaic in landscape ecology, transforming it into a sea with dynamic crests and troughs. Imagining the paths an organism might choose within this multidimensional landscape and modeling the implications of these choices allows the movements of birds, beetles, and other organisms to be represented more like the movements of wind and weather, and less like chess pieces on a simplified playing board. Instead of representing a patchwork of contrasting types, this technology allows a landscape to be mapped as a three-dimensional

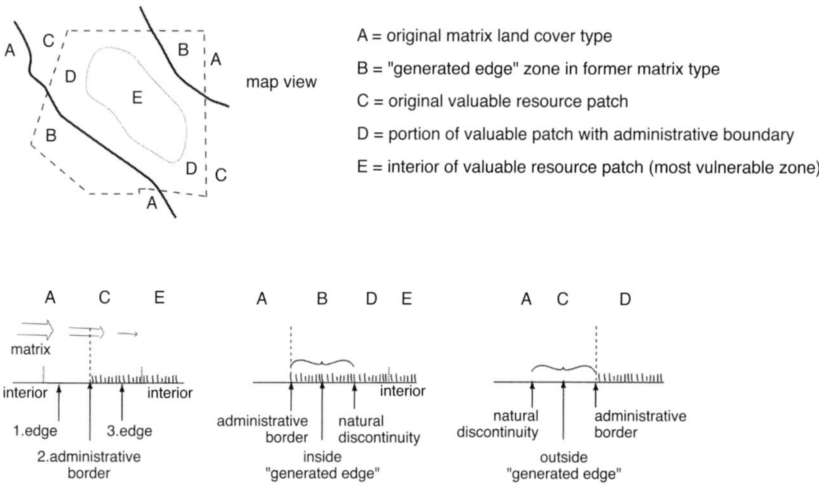

Figure 6.3. A boundary model of patch–edge–matrix relationships, emphasizing the effects of legal or administrative boundaries on the ability of a patch of some valuable resource to persist in a matrix dominated by a different land cover type. The influence of the matrix decreases beyond the edge zone of the valuable resource patch. Placing the administrative boundary outside the original patch allows a "generated edge" to form, which can provide some protection from the influences of the matrix within the interior of the patch. (Section drawings adapted from Schonewald-Cox and Bayless, 1986.)

surface formed by any continuous variable, such as moisture levels, temperature, or an index of hostility to a particular species.

As a final example of the changes in scientific theory that could affect contemporary design theories about sites, I would like to briefly refer to the sweeping theoretical transformations that have occurred in geology. Geology is especially significant to site description, which, over the past century, often began by describing the very large-scale processes of geology and geomorphology as a way to construct a meaningful history of larger-scale processes that affect a local area. But like ecology, the last thirty years have introduced an entirely new theoretical process paradigm to the geological sciences. This new paradigm is also relevant because, unlike the ecological theories I have described thus far, it is a generative theory—by which I mean that it uses underlying thermodynamic processes to explain why large-scale geologic processes occur.

In geology, theories describing the interactions between time and place have changed radically since the 1970s. Simply put, in that decade geologists were first able to provide compelling evidence that the mosaic of large-scale landforms on the surface of the earth is continually created and recreated by the dynamics of plate tectonics. The observation that plate tectonics appear to be driven by thermodynamics—the loss of heat energy in convection currents that circulate between the earth's surface and its core—suggests that there may someday be opportunities to describe ecological dynamics in terms of their origins or, at least, in terms of a set of simpler "driving" patterns.[45]

FLASHPOINTS

This essay presents a transitional moment in ecological theory. Tracing recent developments using three categories (spatial scale shifts, temporal scale shifts, and the shift to seeing landscapes as dynamic mosaics that conceptually integrate spatial and temporal dynamics), it occurs to me that the complexity of the topic derives in part from my conscious effort to reveal changing conceptual frameworks by alternately thinking through both old and the new conceptual lenses. Future designers will doubtless find it easier to pick up the current ecological theories and run with them without looking back. But my intent, to try to hold a window open between the new and old theories of ecology, encourages critical reflection on the theories themselves and the interplay of the metaphors used to conceive them. It will be harder to understand the cultural context of twentieth-century design after this window closes on the past. That is why I have argued that a historical perspective on ecological theory might allow us to see simultaneously where we've been and where we're going in the development of theories about the relationship between site and design.

The reconceptualization of boundaries associated with the spatial scale shift I described here will probably be a key influence on future design thinking. As sites were once described by ecologists using the metaphor of organisms, I expect that future designers will see organisms more clearly as sites—as nodes in a network of flows that penetrate permeable skins (human skins, animal skins, plant skins, even soil "skins"). Body and site overlap; as Sandra Steingraber has implied, we are the prairie from which we eat. The comforting illusion that our bodies can remain separate from their ecological surroundings cannot be sustained, nor can the idea that relationships with landscapes are unidirectional—that they may be described solely by what we do to the landscape, without accounting for the effects of landscape on and in our bodies. Similarly, the consequences of our actions for other forms of life may affect us as well, as an increasing body of ecological and epidemiological evidence suggests.[46]

The three conceptual categories of theoretical change described here could also function as tools that allow historians and theorists to track the ways in which the approaches taken by designers reflect a new intellectual milieu. A dynamic and perhaps more kinesthetic aesthetic is clearly in the process of developing, in a slightly delayed response to the evolution of nonequilibrium views of the world. Sites play a critical role in the development of this aesthetic, because sites are where the sciences and the humanities meet. The trick lies in remembering that the representation of sites in the theory of different fields has been changing, and that these changes are significant to design.

As designers participating in a contemporary intellectual milieu, we can no longer see sites as evidence of equilibrium states. Sites are not what we humans once thought they were, and probably are also not what we will come to think they are. Sites matter precisely because it is in place that we can prop the windows open on the past and be specific about what is known and how. At the same time, sites allow us to gain insights about the ways things are changing in both the world and our own theories by allowing us to examine the nature of those theories in relation to human experience. The comparison of theories as they change over time, in relation to social and cultural contexts, provides an intellectual device that can act as a periscope, allowing us to peer out over the reifications that might otherwise limit our capacity for insight. For designers, a more specific knowledge of the major recent shifts in ecological theory can act as just such a device, allowing us to prop theoretical windows open on the past and the future at the same time.

Notes

1. As another example, see R. Rozzi, E. Hargrove, J. Armesto, S. Pickett, and J. Silander, "'Natural Drift' as a Post-modern Evolutionary Metaphor," *Revista Chilena de Historia Natural* 71 (1998): 5–17; and also, see K. Hill et al., "In Expectation of Relationships: Centering Theories around Ecological Understanding," in *Ecology and Design*, ed. B. Johnson and K. Hill (Washington, D.C.: Island Press, 2002), 271–303.
2. *Place* is defined as a "particular part of space, of defined or undefined extent, but of definite situation," in the *Oxford English Dictionary* [electronic resource] (Oxford, England: Oxford University Press, 2000).
3. For a more extensive discussion of these changes in theory from an ecological perspective, see R. Pulliam and B. Johnson, "Ecology's New Paradigm: What Does It Offer Designers and Planners?" in *Ecology and Design*, ed. B. Johnson and K. Hill (Washington, D.C.: Island Press, 2002), 51–84.
4. See for example, T. Allen and T. Starr, *Hierarchy: Perspectives for Ecological Complexity (*Chicago: University of Chicago Press, 1988).
5. See for example, R. Costanza, *An Introduction to Ecological Economics* (Boca Raton, FL: St. Lucie Press, 1997).
6. M. Barbour, J. Burk, and W. Pitts, *Terrestrial Plant Ecology* (Amsterdam: Benjamin Cummings Publishing Co., 1987).
7. See G. Lakoff and M. Johnson, *Metaphors We Live By* (Chicago: University of Chicago Press, 1990); E. Keller, *Secrets of Life, Secrets of Death: Essays on Language, Gender, and Science* (London: Routledge, 1992).
8. F. Varela, E. Thompson, and E. Rosch, *The Embodied Mind: Cognitive Science and Human Experience* (Cambridge: MIT Press, 1991).
9. G. Lakoff, *Women, Fire, and Dangerous Things: What Categories Reveal about the Mind* (Chicago: University of Chicago Press, 1987).
10. M. Barbour, J. Burk, and W. Pitts, *Terrestrial Plant Ecology* (Amsterdam: Benjamin Cummings Publishing Co., 1987), 20.

11. As an example of how the discovery of microscopic pathogens changed biological science and medical practice, see M. Worboys, *Spreading Germs: Diseases, Theories, and Medical Practice in Britain*, 1865–1900 (New York: Cambridge University Press, 2000).
12. H. Gleason, "The Individualistic Concept of the Plant Association," *Bulletin of the Torrey Botanical Club* 53 (1926): 1–20.
13. R. Whittaker, "A Consideration of Climax Theory: The Climax as a Population and Pattern," *Ecological Monographs* 32 (1953): 41–78; and M. Davis, "Phytogeography and Palynology of the Northeastern United States," in ed. H. E. Wright, Jr., and D. G. Frey, *Quaternary of the United States* (Princeton: Princeton University Press, 1965), 377–401.
14. M. Barbour, J. Burk, and W. Pitts, *Terrestrial Plant Ecology* (Amsterdam: Benjamin Cummings Publishing Co., 1987), 22.
15. H. Cowles, "The Causes of Vegetative Cycles," *Botanical Gazette* 51 (1911): 161–183.
16. M. Barbour, J. Burk, and W. Pitts, *Terrestrial Plant Ecology* (Amsterdam: Benjamin Cummings Publishing Co., 1987).
17. Ibid.
18. It is interesting to note that Ian McHarg used Cowles's example of sand dune–vegetation relationships in his influential book, *Design with Nature* (Garden City: Doubleday, 1969). This usage suggests that Cowles's work created a persistent example of landscape and biological interactions that crossed disciplinary boundaries and affected the way that generations of designers were introduced to the idea of the ecosystem.
19. One of Cowles's students, Edgar Transeau, produced one of the first known energy studies in ecology when he described the energy budget of a cornfield in 1926; Arthur Tansley coined the term *ecosystem* in 1935; Odum popularized it in the United States in the 1950s. For more information on the history of these ideas, see R. Ricklefs, *Ecology* (New York: W.H. Freeman, 1990).
20. The talk was titled, "An Analysis of the Principles of Economics," and was presented to the Royal Society of Edinburgh in 1884. See M. Stalley, *Patrick Geddes: Spokesman for Man and the Environment* (New Brunswick, NJ: Rutgers University Press, 1972), 17.
21. P. Geddes, *Cities in Evolution*, edited by the Outlook Tower Association, Edinburgh, and the Association for Planning and Regional Reconstruction, London (New York: Oxford University Press, 1950).
22. J. Jacobs, *The Death and Life of Great American Cities* (New York: Random House, 1961).
23. G.M. Weinberg, *An Introduction to General Systems Thinking* (New York: Wiley, 1975).
24. K. Hill et al., "In Expectation of Relationships," in *Ecology and Design*, ed. B. Johnson and K. Hill (Washington, D.C.: Island Press, 2002), 271–303.
25. An in-depth discussion of the continuing interplay between these metaphors can be found in R. Ricklefs, *Ecology* (New York: W.H. Freeman, 1990).

26. G.M. Weinberg, *An Introduction to General Systems Thinking* (New York: Wiley, 1975). Note the connection to similar ideas expressed by Jane Jacobs about cities, epistemology, and complexity in the final chapter of *The Death and Life of Great American Cities* (New York: Random House, 1961).
27. The Gaia hypothesis, named after a Greek goddess, could be seen as a contemporary example of this tendency in its source of metaphors. See J. Lovelock and L. Margulis, "An Atmospheric Homeostasis by and for the Biosphere: The Gaia Hypothesis," *Tellus* 26 (1974): 1–10; see also similar examples of uses of metaphors in *Metaphors We Live By,* by G. Lakoff and M. Johnson (Chicago: University of Chicago Press, 1980).
28. S. Steingraber, *Living Downstream: An Ecologist Looks at Cancer and the Environment* (New York: Addison-Wesley, 1997).
29. Even a cursory review of the ecological literature reveals that most research has been done in ecosystems in which humans are not the dominant species, and humans are often not mentioned as an important biological entity in those systems. The absence of studies related to human health in ecology is also significant, in that it shows that the idea of flows in an ecosystem has rarely been extended to include flows across the boundaries of the human body.
30. The Czech playwright and politician Vaclav Havel described a human being as just a particularly busy intersection of molecules in *Vaclav Havel, or Living in Truth* (London: Faber and Faber, 1987). I argue that the unexamined belief among many researchers that only humans have an emotional life and the ability to reason underlies the treatment of humans as primarily moral actors in ecological studies, rather than biological entities.
31. This doctrine was proposed in 1832 by William Whewell, a geologist at the University of Cambridge, and was based on the earlier ideas of James Hutton. Hutton claimed in 1785 that historical processes could be used to explain geological patterns. Uniformitarianism, with its contention that contemporary processes could be used as models for understanding geological change in the past, was proposed during a time when most geologists still ascribed to the doctrine of catastrophism, in which the earth was seen to have been formed primarily by very unusual historical events.
32. G. Likens and H. Bormann, *Biogeochemistry of a Forested Ecosystem* (New York: Springer-Verlag, 1995).
33. S. Pickett, M. Cadenasso, and J. Grove, "Resilient Cities: Meaning, Models, and Metaphor for Integrating the Ecological, Socio-Economic, and Planning Realms," *Landscape and Urban Planning* 69(4), (October 2004): 369–384.
34. W. Cronon, *Changes in the Land: Indians, Colonists, and the Ecology of New England* (New York: Hill and Wang, 1983); C. Merchant, *Ecological Revolutions: Nature, Gender, and Science in New England* (Chapel Hill, NC: University of Chapel Hill Press, 1989).
35. M. McDonnell and S. Pickett, eds., *Humans as Components of Ecosystems: The Ecology of Subtle Human Effects and Populated Areas* (Berlin: Springer-Verlag, 1993).
36. S. Pickett, M. Cadenasso, and J. Grove, "Resilient Cities."
37. Ibid.

38. R. Forman and M. Godron, *Landscape Ecology* (New York: Wiley, 1986); R. Forman, *Land Mosaics: The Ecology of Landscapes and Regions* (Cambridge: Cambridge University Press, 1995).
39. M. Turner, R. Gardner, and R. O'Neill, *Landscape Ecology in Theory and Practice: Pattern and Process* (New York: Springer-Verlag, 2001).
40. See for example, J. Luey and I. Adelman, "Downstream Natural Areas as Refuges for Fish in Drainage Development Watersheds," *Transactions of the American Fisheries Society* 109 (1980): 332–335; W. Laurance, "Ecological Correlates of Extinction Proneness in Australian Tropical Rainforest Mammals," *Conservation Biology* 5 (1991): 79–89.
41. R. Forman, "The Role of Spatial Configuration in Environmental Sustainability," in ed. I. Zonneveld and R. Forman, *Changing Landscapes* (New York: Springer-Verlag, 1990).
42. J.F. Lyotard, *La condition postmoderne: Rapport sur le savoir* (Paris: Minuit, 1979); for a more in-depth discussion of Lyotard in relation to scientific narratives, see K. Hill, "Visions of Sustainability," in J. Benson and M. Roe, *Landscape and Sustainability* (London: Spon Press, 2000).
43. C. Schonewald-Cox and J. Bayless, "The Boundary Model: A Geographic Analysis of Design and Conservation of Nature Reserves," *Biological Conservation* 38 (1986): 305–322.
44. R. Forman, *Land Mosaics: The Ecology of Landscapes and Regions* (Cambridge: Cambridge University Press, 1995).
45. Ibid. Forman suggests the beginnings of such a thermodynamic landscape ecological theory.
46. See F. Grifo and J. Rosenthal, eds., *Biodiversity and Human Health* (Washington, D.C.: Island Press, 1997); S. Steingraber and K. Hill, "Human Health and Design: An Essay in Two Parts," in *Ecology and Design*, ed. B. Johnson and K. Hill (Washington, D.C.: Island Press, 2002); and also, K. Hill, "Urban Design and Biodiversity," in *CASE: Downsview Park Toronto*, ed. J. Czerniak (New York: Prestel Publishers, 2001).

James Stirling, Staatsgalerie, Stuttgart, Germany.

7

Contested Contexts

Sandy Isenstadt

> I discovered context six months ago.[1]
>
> **Bernard Tschumi, April 14, 2003**

Context is one of the concentric rings of circumstance comprising our understanding of site: from lot to plot, from neighborhood to region, from locality to landscape to climate. It implies the whole set of conditions from which an architect will construct an idea of site suitable to a specific scheme, and will include the technologies used to shape the site, such as infrastructure and earth-moving machinery, as well as technologies of seeing that mediate any conception of what is unique and local at a site with images from other places. The concept of context is hard to pin down because it always points to surrounding circumstances; context is the crucible in which buildings happen. Complicating this, *context* is at once a general and a specialized, disciplinary term. The same word appears prominently in two dissimilar realms: a common, casual usage where it can signify a set of immediate general conditions that help situate meaning, and a narrower professional field, where it evokes both current debate and a history still fresh from the 1970s. But, insofar as architecture is part of everyday life, these usages blend. Thus, as a factor in the understanding of site, context emerges from multiple perspectives, not just disciplinary ones, and is reordered routinely by mostly uninvestigated conceptual mechanisms.[2]

Important questions remain even if context is restricted to refer only to physical fabric. How far does context go? To adjacent buildings? To the monument down the street? To forms common to the region but absent at the site? Is the existing context even worth consideration? (Raising this question today in commercial-strip America invokes decades-old debates that have hardly been resolved.) Which aspects of context have relevance when scale or materials or use of a new building are unprecedented at a particular location? Which aspects matter most when the context is conceived as an undifferentiated background for a new, figural design? Also, context does not stand still: it changes, from day to day or decade to decade, in cycles and cataclysmically. Physical context is as much a question of *when* as *where*, as Kevin Lynch detailed in his 1972 book, *What Time Is This Place?* Further, placing an emphasis on context in a new design is tantamount to making the background foreground; it reverses the customary view of the architect's role in the creation of form. Although made up of buildings, context represents the generation of form as dictated by elements outside the process of design as it is often understood, having to do with neither function nor spatial concept.

Because context can refer just as easily to surrounding fabric as to widespread attitudes, or even to debates regarding physical fabric, the same term ranges in meaning from built form to implied meaning to underlying ideology. Architects, critics, historians, preservationists, and casual observers all may use the same word but to differing ends, their common vocalization veiling often opposed intentions. Like a single magnet with two poles, context invisibly sets up an ideational field and so attracts antagonists. However, greater precision in speech will not improve communication since the basis for the term's disciplinary specialization is not its specificity but, rather, its flexibility. As often as not, an architect's description of an existing context will soon underpin a subsequent series of decisions to intervene in that context. A characterization of context smuggles into the design process a set of confirming values camouflaged as a description of existing conditions and observed facts; the details of any description of context will usually indicate whether the speaker aims to respect or reject it. Dressed as an inventory of what is here now, the architect's analysis of context is often a preliminary step in the struggle for what will come next.

While context, the product of countless uncoordinated decisions, continues to metamorphose regardless of anyone's intention or interpretation, the issue of context has today become contentious. In the summer of 2001, for example, architectural journalist Herbert Muschamp bemoaned in the *New York Times* the latest surrender to context, the excuse given during the review of submissions to redevelop the Con Edison site in Manhattan for favoring corporate architects over innovative, but edgy, designers. Context, he wrote, "...the idea that new buildings should fit in with their surroundings rather than add to them, has led our architecture into the deadest of dead ends." Too much, or too literal a respect for context has led to a crisis in the creation of form.[3] In Muschamp's case, context refers to contemporary consumer culture. The apartment building he lives in, he explains, is red brick, like the one it shadows, but, he says, it "...has nothing to do with the context of New York....It exists in the context of matched towels, bath mats and toilet bowl covers....It exists in the context of suburbia." In response to Muschamp, Douglas Kelbaugh, Dean of the College of Architecture and Urban Planning at the University of Michigan, wrote *The New York Times* saying that too much emphasis is currently placed on innovation, which might make for good individual buildings, but creates discord at an urban scale: "Don't make excitement for its own sake habitual, mandatory or, worse yet, a style. I realize it may make less-exciting copy, but we need to hear about aesthetically compelling buildings that also function well, fit in well and age well." Kelbaugh understands that his position may be criticized for constraining expression, and so adds, "Contextualism need not stifle invention or creativity." He admits, however, that it often does.[4]

This essay asks in particular how the very idea of context—specifically, existing built fabric, to keep the discussion tractable—has come, even for its advocates, to stand for what is responsible but dull, for an architecture at once observant and obsequious.

CONTEXT COMES

Although clearly subject to various interpretations, context is a crucial concept for architecture. Despite its amorphousness, it must be addressed as part of the very fabric of architecture. The word intensifies the act of joining, with *con* meaning together, and *text*, from the Latin *texere*, meaning to join, or weave. The Indo-European root *teks* also means to weave, as in wicker, or to make wattle, for wattle-and-daub structures. The person who makes wattle is called the *tekson*, or *tekton* in Greek, from which we get *tectonic*, and the master of all things tectonic is the *arch-tekton*, or *architect*. In addition, context takes its place in a spectrum of terms concerned with perception of place and the creation of placefulness. Curiously, despite being central to the making of architecture, context has not been much invoked in architectural theory. Vitruvius hinted at it in regard to climate and orientation, but his building types—villas and temples—were their own centers of gravity, while later theories of proportion related formal elements within a composition, rarely outside it. In the twentieth century an outright dismissal of context was preceded by nearly two centuries of Beaux-Arts design problems, which rarely indicated actual sites. As a defining issue for architecture, context, it turns out, appears only recently—during the 1950s and 1960s. After being irrelevant as an issue for most of architectural history, context came suddenly to occupy a prominent place in architectural discourse, becoming a historical problem for architecture in response to the collapse of a more or less coherent program of modernism. The issue of context arises as a consequence of the critique of modern architecture.

In their rush toward a better society, existing built fabric often stood in the way of modern architects. In its more polemic formulations, modernism scorned traditional cities and contemporary architecture for lagging behind advances in material culture. For Le Corbusier, ancient architecture was admirable because it had made the most of the constructive means of its time. Practitioners of his own day, however, ignored the possibilities of new building techniques or, worse, used them as an armature upon which to prink a building with the ornamental regalia of another era. In contrast, a modernist such as Le Corbusier insisted that architecture emerge from the tools of its own time. Thus, some of modernism's most memorable moments are captured and appear in projects that gain visionary thrust in equal measure from an innovative formal proposal and a demolition plan. The Radiant City, for example, astonishes as much for its effortless sweep across Paris as for its array of point towers in a park. The plan was drawn on a *tabula rasa*: not a clean slate but, more literally, a slate that has been erased. Not shaped by the irrelevant surrounding fabric, modernist works issued from internal matters such as structure and program. They needed free space around them; existing physical context was seen as a kind of confinement. The belief that modern space was hemmed in by neighbors can be tracked from early modernists such as Le Corbusier, and his idea that form arises from the plan, to van Doesburg's notion of modernism as "an all-sided development in space and time," through later characterizations made by historians, like the four-sided expansion of modernism that Lewis Mumford contrasted with a Georgian "architecture of fronts," or in accordance with what Colin Rowe called modernism's "peripheric principle," or what Vincent Scully traced as a "new sense of open space."[5] This is a partial view, to be sure. Many modern buildings respected their surroundings; they might be hard-edged but they were not necessarily hostile, an attitude evident, for example, in projects by Loos, Berlage, Asplund, and others. Further, disregard of existing fabric is hardly unique to modernism. Well before Haussmann ventilated Paris, Renaissance architects flattened districts for the sake of order and open space. Existing physical fabric, overflowing with happenstance, has always conflicted with ideal forms. Nonetheless, twentieth-century architectural modernism continued this usually hopeful, always rationalizing impulse with gusto—and industrial equipment.

Modernism was not immune to thinking about context, of course. Historic city centers came up for discussion at CIAM in 1945 and then again in 1951. In 1945, while Europeans quickly set about rebuilding districts demolished by war, Camillo Sitte's defense of urban fabric was first translated into English; in 1950 Robert Venturi was already exploring a wider range of possibilities for surrounding structures in his master's thesis, "Context in Architectural Composition;" Paul Rudolph drew inspiration from the Gothic setting of Wellesley College for his Jewett Center; defenders of Eero Saarinen's bulky American Embassy in London, built in 1956, argued that it repeated the scale and proportion of the Georgian architecture of Grosvenor Square; while Ernesto Rogers, designer in 1958 of Milan's Torre Velasca, began to speak about the importance of *ambiente* in the mid-1950s, partly in response to Frank Lloyd Wright's proposed Masieri Memorial in Venice. By 1961 Nikolaus Pevsner noted no fewer than eighteen historicist impulses in modern architecture, many due to an architect's response to context. At that time, however, and for a polemicist like Pevsner, deference to surrounding historical context was "alarming" and "one of the least attractive developments of recent architecture." Whereas for Pevsner modernism represented the triumph of functional thought, the new emphasis on a building's exterior, its public face, smothered invention with the piffle of precedent. He labeled the first historicist tendency "Neo-Accommodating" and defined it as friendly and fitting in. The long-term trend would be a dead end, he wrote, because historicism, whatever motivated it, required a "belief in the power of history to such a degree as to choke original action."[6] When historical context becomes a building's content, Pevsner argued, innovation dries up.

But after nearly two decades of modernist urbanism, many writers wondered whether there might not be an alternative point of view lodged in the parcels of existing structures that had yet to be bulldozed. In 1960, for instance, Kevin Lynch had turned from the monumental blueprints of architects to the mental maps of taxi drivers, while Jane Jacobs made minute observations of her Hudson Street and the way social relations were embedded in physical fabric. "The City in History," a conference sponsored in 1961 by the Joint Center for Urban Studies of the Massachusetts Institute of Technology and Harvard University, attempted to redress the lack of historical attention to the forces of modernization in the growth of Western cities. The same year, *Daedalus* published a special issue on metropolitan sprawl and the chances of downtown revivals. The Joint Center also sponsored Bernard Frieden's advocacy of an incremental approach to rebuilding cities, described in his 1964 book, *The Future of Old Neighborhoods*. As a consequence, urban design was given a new sense of urgency, with programs such as those of Cornell, Washington University, Columbia, and Harvard first established in the early 1960s. In Italy, Aldo Rossi and Vittorio Gregotti had begun developing morphological approaches to the study of existing urban form while the multiterritorial Christian Norberg-Schulz revived the Picturesque-era term *genius loci* to emphasize the character of an existing place.

Most significant, certainly in the American setting, was the preservation movement, which quickly and forcefully drew attention to the neglected condition of urban physical fabric. Stunned by the demolition of New York's Penn Station in 1963, and outraged at the willful destruction of civic treasures for short-term profits and machine-age rhetoric, a coalition of citizens banded together to promote federal laws to protect existing context. Passing the Historic Preservation Act three years later, Congress was explicit about the need to shelter the nation's built heritage from postwar development, which was typically, if loosely, modernist. Advocates of modernism were, in fact, quick to endorse a preservationist agenda. In the 1960s, James Marston Fitch, for example, turned his earlier zeal for modernism to fervid support of preservation; he became one of the movement's galvanizing figures and a leading educator as he worked for years to establish the degree program in historic preservation at Columbia University. When, in 1966, Robert Venturi famously addressed the ambiguities of context, citing T. S. Eliot's essay, "Tradition and the Individual Talent," on the problem of mediating "the pastness of the past" alongside the presence of the past, the modernist remedy for the urban ailment had, in the eyes of many critics, become more debilitating than the disease of tradition it had set out to cure.[7]

Physical context received its most sustained engagement at this point with the teaching and writing of Colin Rowe. Immediately upon arriving at Cornell University in 1964, Rowe began teaching some of the first urban design studios in the nation. Stylistically open-minded, he seemed less interested in the results of student projects than in their method, which for Rowe began with the existing urban fabric. Engagement with context produced new forms or, more precisely, new configurations of older forms. His theories of urban design were later designated *contextualism* and summed up definitively in *Collage City*, co-authored with Fred Koetter and published in 1978, though written years earlier. Modernism had its virtues, the authors wrote in *Collage City*, but it was not "responsive to circumstance," it required a clean slate upon which to write the rationalized forms of social utopia. Modernism had managed in its time to join scientism to humanism, a simultaneous concern both for empirical technique and poetic inspiration, but the collapse of modernism revealed how incompatible these goals had been from the start. Worse, modernism had degraded into its components, its empiricism having collapsed into romantic but directionless affection for the accidental, most evident in townscape studies such of those of Gordon Cullen, while, on the other hand, its utopian poetry had evaporated into idealizing schemes such as those of Superstudio or Disneyworld. But, Rowe and Koetter affirmed, "only the middleground of an argument is of use," and so prepared to lay out an "alert and workable *détente*" between existing and new form. Whereas Superstudio and Disney were fragmentary urbanisms based on either prophecy or memory, theirs would be a complete urbanism of prophecy *and* memory; visionary form embodied human hope but it relied upon the common heritage and sense of community that underpins communication. The new, they wrote, in all its power and promise, must relate "to the known, perhaps mundane and, necessarily, memory-laden context from which it emerges."[8] The authors proposed to mediate the repressive mechanisms of existing relations of power, as embodied in physical fabric, with the ambition of a social vision, whose redemptive power lay precisely in its remaining potential. Collage was the specific compositional technique they proposed to impart both aesthetic authority and historical inevitability to the weaving of old and new.

The genius of their working method of figure–ground studies was its suitability to both evaluate and intervene in context. Traditional planning was characterized by a pattern of figural space against background buildings, whereas modern planning relied on figural buildings on a spatial field. Since figure and ground are reciprocal, the traditional city was on equal terms with the modern city. The methodological symmetry between analysis and design guaranteed conceptual congruence even when old and new were visually dissimilar. Contextualism did not repeat context so much as register changes in context. A contextualist project would become an index of accommodations to context, in contrast to modern insensitivity to circumstances such as orientation or entry, external vectors that were overwhelmed by the outward expansion of modern space. In short, overturning the coin of modernist planning meant having two sides, not one or the other. Contextualism proposed a process to mediate between inevitable change and existing conditions.

Heterogeneity was a broadly shared interest in the 1960s, extending well beyond architectural and urban design circles. The Civil Rights Movement in the United States, along with studies of urban ethnicities that would not blend, such as Nathan Glazer and Daniel P. Moynihan's *Beyond the Melting Pot*, from 1963, called greater attention to recalcitrant demographics that suburban idealizations had managed to pave over in the previous decade.[9] Sixties-era social movements showed that the nation's institutions were anything but a neutral context for minority participation. Environmentalists argued that the earth was no longer a passive backdrop for modern science but an active and increasingly disenchanted partner. Echoes of context fighting back can even be seen in Frank Herbert's science fiction classic, *Dune*, from 1965, a harbinger of the ecology movement, in which society must be reorganized in response to an environment that has ceased to be accommodating, and context, to invert Pevsner, had become "neo-hostile." In art, earthworks and site-specific projects turned context *into* content, by drawing the setting into the active creation of aesthetic experience. Robert Smithson's *Spiral Jetty*, for instance, from 1970, created a striking figure by redefining existing relations between land and water at the Great Salt Lake. His *Partially Buried Woodshed*, in Kent State, Ohio, also from 1970, made the formerly neutral ground an active compositional element. Conceptual artist Hans Haacke, in his installation *Shapolsky et al. Manhattan Real Estate Holdings*, from 1971, showed how the very production of art relied on an institutional context to neutralize all but the aesthetic connotations of a work. Even within the academy, structuralism, for instance, and later poststructuralism, led to the recognition that meaning was never contained by a single term but emerged only in relation to other terms, to a linguistic and behavioral context. Meaning could be gathered only in the larger field of signification, never from a single instance of it. To whatever extent Venturi was influenced by structuralism, his model of architectural communication was based on a sender *and* a receiver, who might not get the message if its terms were without precedent. The fact that meaning and communication were contingent on context was hard to avoid. For their part, Rowe and Koetter concurred, suggesting that acquiescence to the rape of the city, the Futurist celebration of the *force majeure*, was no longer intellectually viable nor was it morally acceptable.[10]

In short, by the 1970s it was commonly agreed that modernism had collapsed under the weight of its own idealism and that context, enumerable and specific, was one of the most promising "new directions in architecture," as the title of the Braziller series then had it.[11] Brent Brolin's 1976 *The Failure of Modern Architecture* is representative; it concludes its belated exposé of modernist myopia with the rediscovery of tradition and a new effort to "reinforce rather than undermine the character of neighborhoods and cities." Existing fabric, said Brolin, "is not historical refuse," but "an asset that should be used as a bridge to the future."[12] The past was no longer passé, as some of the most talked-about work of the late 1970s rendered tradition progressive. Indeed, *context*, rather than *history*, is the more persistent, if more submerged, term in debates regarding the autonomy and continued vitality of architectural practice after modernism. Following from Aldo Rossi's 1966 *Architecture of the City*, published in English in 1972, recognition of the integrity of existing urban fabric was transmuted into a notion of typological history, the deep geometric memory of a culture to which the architect has special access. History thus refers to an internal context, which the architect brings to a project based on program and type and smuggles in beneath the client's nose under the name of precedent. With history, precedent eclipses existing context as the primary point of reference, keeping the problem within architectural categories and reestablishing the modernist notion that an art should develop from its own inner logic. *History* means the history of architecture, which replaces a context given by the site with a context hidden in the problem, a context that is up to the architect to uncover, for typology is disciplinary knowledge. History, in short, trades the constraints of an immediate spatial context for the adaptive possibilities of disciplinary contexts, making room for an architect's individual expression and reasserting the profession's autonomous knowledge of form.[13] Context, in contrast, devours autonomy.

In retrospect, 1978 presents a watershed for the issue of context. That year, in addition to Rowe and Koetter's *Collage City*, Leon Krier and Maurice Culot published their essay, "The Only Path for Architecture," declaring that modernism had been an historical misstep of enormous proportion; a delusion that, somehow, took root. Cutting through traditional cities, letting blood and space from the network of street and square, modernism nearly wiped out civilized society, and the time had come to reknit in sympathetic forms what remained of the traditional city. Also that year, Rem Koolhaas published *Delirious New York*, which argued that heroic figures of modernism never really understood what modern was. Koolhaas presented Le Corbusier as unable to see during his famous visit to New York City that modernity's monuments were everywhere in Manhattan and only weak vision would require a plinth to make them better appear. Its modernity lay in its affirmative context, a setting so hungry for invention it absorbed change like a sponge. Koolhaas called his book a "retroactive" manifesto, written not on a blank slate but discovered within an existing order.[14] Even Peter Eisenman, whose earlier projects concentrated on the autonomous generation of form, to the exclusion of all else, in 1978 produced the Cannaregio project, his first work to engage in a sustained manner with an existing site. Perhaps most important, 1978 was the culminating year of the preservation movement in the United States, when the Supreme Court handed down its decision upholding the New York City Landmarks Law, established the decade before to protect "existing urban fabric."[15] As unlike as these instances are from one another—emerging from inimitable personalities working in different nations with distinct media on singular problems seen through varying historical perspectives, and soon to lead in divergent directions—each endows an existing urban fabric with unique and formally generative properties. As it turned out, 1978 was a bad year for modernism but a good year for context, as architects began to discover how expedient and ductile context could be.[16]

Roma Interrotta, also from 1978, is paradigmatic in this regard: it reveals consensus regarding the issue of context but it also makes plain some of the issue's internal fissures, fault lines that would soon split any confidence connected with context into stylistic factions. Art

Figure 7.1. Venturi and Rauch, Roma Interrotta, Competition Entry.

historian and conservator Guilio Argan, then mayor of Rome, invited twelve internationally recognized architects to imaginatively complete that city, which, he said, had been "interrupted" in its development. Colin Rowe's contribution drew from his own theories of contextualism, which took Rome's built context as a series of formal cues for the generation of new form. His design was conceived as an intervention into a specific context, which was then redefined by his intervention. Robert Venturi was also invited, but his submission included the marquis from a casino, implying that present-day Rome had as much to do with Caesar's Palace in Las Vegas as with Caesar himself. Venturi took a more cultural approach to context, in contrast with Rowe's concentration on physical context. At the same time, however, less conspicuously and without much explanation, Rowe had included fragments of Rockefeller Center in his scheme. Unparalleled in both the temporal scope and continuity of physical fabric, from antiquity to modernity, Rome was somehow not sufficient an impetus for new form without the leavening of invention. Formal resonance was the low threshold that, as it turns out, contextualism required to link Rome with Rockefeller Center.

CONTEXT CONFOUNDED

Thomas Schumacher, as early as 1971, had already observed that contextualism tended toward a "formal 'shorthand.'"[17] It was committed to geometry and so became, at points, a useful but often reductive exercise. Although a studied engagement, contextualism approached existing context through its own formal preoccupations and thus obscured the developmental dimensions of physical context, its ability to corporealize social history. For the contextualist designer, urban form could become a treasure chest of geometric possibilities, all equally within reach despite origins centuries apart. The formal predilections of architects can transform the typical temporal diversity of urban context into a return to history that is nonetheless ahistorical. Although O. M. Ungers was often at odds with Rowe while they taught at Cornell, their work shares this interest in establishing a formally generative method. Both distill formal complexity to geometric essence, yielding a desktop set of operations and prototypes, a kind of shape grammar. The power and the peril of such an approach reside precisely in its mechanical appeal, like limiting design to the predefined commands in CAD (computer-aided design) programs then under development. When used in combination, geometric operations such as "stretch," "mirror," and "rotate" can generate any form, posing no real limits to formal invention; but whether their formidable generative power, coupled with their seeming simplicity, tempt the designer toward a self-limiting practice, remains open to question. Ungers's students have even joked that his "dogmatic application" of a square module is due to an ancient demon that snarls when it sees a line start to curve, with the resulting designs best suited for little Lego men.[18] A commitment to rationalized technique, in other words, rests on the most irrational of foundations. Further, such formalisms risk incurring the charge leveled at modernism: that it facilitated an overly rational-

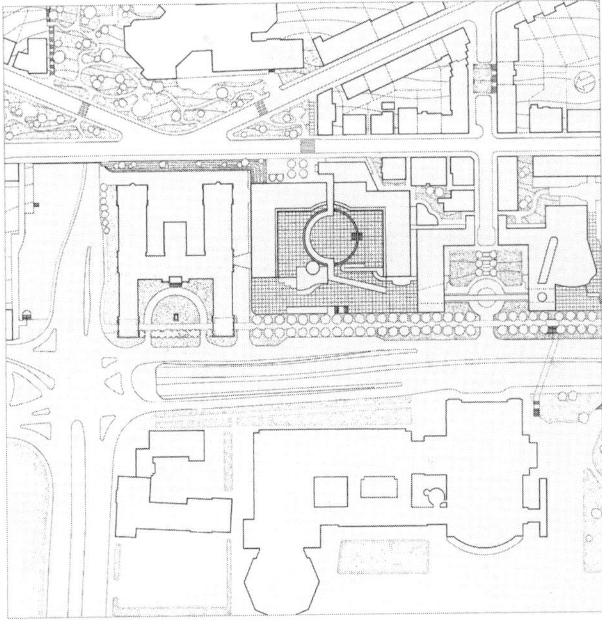

Figure 7.2. James Stirling, Staatsgalerie, Stuttgart, Germany, beginning 1977. Site Plan. Stirling worked historical and typological references together at the Staatsgalerie with the surrounding context by incrementalizing elements (the neighboring gallery's massing and scale; fragments both of classical and high-tech architecture; Schinkel's plan for the Altes Museum) and juxtaposing them without then trying to blend them either with each other or with the larger site. Pieces of the building are proximate but remain distinct, related but not subservient.

ized and technocratic society, rather than fulfilling its promise to lead to a more authentic human experience.

With the issue of physical context so conspicuously promiscuous and, of course, ultimately ineffectual in generating new form when isolated from other factors of design, confidence in existing context as a touchstone for design began to erode. But it had become too important an issue to ignore altogether. By the early 1980s, a number of architects may be seen measuring how far from an existing context they might make their stand. If one could no longer ignore context, neither need one kowtow to it. Many maintained an arms-length relationship to built context, publicly declaring commitment to it, while renouncing it to their muse. Indeed, at this point something about surrounding physical fabric seems to become inimical to great architecture. Writing in 1986 on the proposed Guggenheim addition by Gwathmey Siegel, Michael Sorkin suggested that the former consensus on the value of context had unwittingly fueled an unprincipled pluralism. Thinking about context led architects to imagine they could enter the spirit of someone else's design work, encouraging what Sorkin called "the ethics of occasion," an architecture with the conscience of a chameleon.[19]

Figure 7.3. Observatory Hill Dining Hall Additions, University of Virginia, Charlottesville, VA, 1984. Robert A. M. Stern Architects. Bridging the existing, ungainly facilities with the demanding context of Jefferson's architecture, Robert Stern's design is itself bridgelike, with strong horizontal banding and a long loggia level span. At first glance simply a comfortable contextual fit, the project, with its glazed walls and interior hall first stretched taut and then plucked high into several pyramids, reads as much as a modernist revision of the pavilions along the university's main lawn as it does deference to context.

Postmodernists, for instance, were quick to point to their sensitivity to context as reason for their aesthetic innovations, and the best postmodern work, of course, did not just tattoo itself with tokens of surrounding fabric but aimed to make memorable spaces. It worried about craftsmanship and siting, not just fitting in. But much postmodernist work was not really about a surrounding physical context at all. Rather than a reworking of proximate form, it was more a composition with historical motifs. Similarities were serendipitous rather than studied. Without growing from structure or function, classical motifs referred to a generalized classicism, an architecture that represented Architecture rather than related to the specifics of a particular place.[20] As often as not in postmodernist work, echoes of existing context were allusions to the profession's internal history as a discipline, rather than attempts to enrich and thicken the sense of time embedded in any particular context. If modernism was motivated by an idea of *zeitgeist*, an architecture of its time, then postmodernism was an architecture of its past; neither was an architecture "of its place."[21] Further, postmodernism's highest theoretical mode is irony, which involves a deliberate distancing of an apparent form from an intended meaning.

Postmodernists, in other words, turn to place with tongue in cheek, as Venturi's *Roma Interrotta* entry bears out. Even when postmodernism borrowed from surroundings, it did not always pay back the debt. Themeatizing context could lead to self-reflection and a sharpened awareness of contingency, the historical debt owed by the present to the past. But, bridging the gap with an older way of building sometimes blurred differences; it hid discrepancies that generate a sense of passing time. If physical context embodies a narrative or temporal dimension, then postmodernism risks clipping context to a sound bite, or rather, a site bite. If anything, postmodernism's at-times untenable kitsch gave fuel to a reactive search for authenticity, equally untenable but commonplace nonetheless.

Other aesthetic trends of the 1980s connected to the issue of context but, at the same time, were careful to maintain their distance. Deconstructivism questioned long-standing architectural virtues—firmness for instance—aiming to show not merely that structure is provisional despite its display of permanence, but that the very idea of structure requires silencing the unstable. However unbalanced visually, Deconstructivist work contributed to architectural knowledge by discovering how the field's foundational metaphors required a series of otherwise unspoken value judgments. Context, in a deconstructivist mode, affirms with familiar forms common and sometimes invisibly insidious values; context foregoes new knowledge in exchange for comfortable numbness. In his 1988 essay on the Deconstructivist show at the Museum of Modern Art, Mark Wigley argued that the exhibited work was fully engaged with its various contexts, not to reaffirm convention, but to disclose how architectural affirmation operates, precisely by exposing what was subterranean and strange within the familiar context. As Wigley put it, "contextualism has been used as an excuse for mediocrity, for a dumb servility to the familiar," "dumb" suggesting here not "brainless" but "without voice" to either clarify or ask questions.[22] In Frank Gehry's house in Santa Monica, dating from 1978 and exhibited in the Deconstructivist show, the existing building is not only *not* erased, it is thematized. Punctured and punctuated, the existing house makes the new space, rather than being made an appendage to it. The old actively creates the new. The disruption looks at first like disrespect, but becomes instead a kind of riff on existing fabric, showing how much life was left in the old house, which not even the most adoring observer of context had noticed before. Rather than having the new stand against an old background, Gehry gave the gap between the two a spatial figure. In a sense, distance from context is Gehry's subject, measured and made present in his design.

To summarize, since the late 1970s architects working in a wide range of aesthetic modes and focused on divergent matters registered some concern for context, whether or not they respected, rejected, or inverted it in the end. For critics, a concern for context had become so naturalized in practice as to be almost invisible. In 1982, architectural historian and critic William Curtis described "an obsession with streetscapes at the expense of individual buildings," clearly evident in the mid-1970s urban morphologies of Leon and Robert Krier.[23] A 1986 article from *Inland Architect* began, "To call oneself a contextual designer is the most characteristic statement of architectural faith, ideology, and commitment made today." Several years later, in 1992, an issue of *Lotus* started off, "Contextualism has become such a widespread attitude as to have a practical effect on the greater part of contemporary architecture."[24]

For some, deference to context came to appear as a kind of salvation for contemporary architecture. Writing in 1994 in *Progressive Architecture*, Thomas Fisher described present-day pluralism as a sign that various values are rising in importance. Signature styles that transcend program and place are artifacts of modern practice, Fisher explained, but come to be replaced by greater attention to "the content, context, climate, and culture of a place." What appeared to be a professional lack of direction turned out to be a new kind of responsiveness to place, what Fisher called "architecture after style." The undermining of autonomy is a healthy condition, he said. John Morris Dixon, editor of *PA*, agreed. Dixon saw diminished autonomy in the design process as ultimately beneficial, even for monumental projects, in which architects had been traditionally the most free. He wrote,

Figure 7.4. Gehry House, Santa Monica, CA, Frank Gehry, 1978.

"As ever our monumental projects become increasingly intertwined with their settings, architects should accept the shared decision making that they represent."[25]

However positive the development, though, such views imply the sense that close attention to context precludes the making of great architecture. Thus, at the same moment some architects and critics embrace the concern for context, others reject it directly, as if the rejection of surrounding fabric were somehow the necessary first step toward architectural invention. Rem Koolhaas, for instance, said that his design for La Villette aimed to produce new "fields" of social encounter, incongruous juxtapositions of function, which would open up a kind of individual freedom precisely by their refusal of existing cultural forms. The final theorem of his squib on "Bigness" was "independence of context"; in regard to his 1989 competition entry for the French National Library, Koolhaas, writing in the most internalized of all genres—the diary—said, "But can such a container still have a relationship with the city? Should it? Is it important? Or is 'fuck context' becoming the theme? Beginning to note signs of conviction."[26] Or, as an article in *Progressive Architecture* put it more delicately in regard to a beautiful but unwarranted monumentality on the part of several architects, including Koolhaas: "Forget context."[27] Too much respect for context, as both Muschamp and Kelbaugh seem to agree, places limits on artistic expression, as if a blank canvas might insist that anything pictured upon it must reproduce its own proportions.

At root is a common view of the creativity driving artistic practice. Although nearly two centuries have passed since Byron set the standard, the true artist is still an individual innovator, feeding on insights, not catalogs, limits, or rules. Creativity cracks open old habits; making breaks with convention seem a necessary and intoxicating first step toward new work. The true artist, in short, is autonomous: unwilling, perhaps even unable, to collaborate with other artists, cautious clients, or, by extension, adjacent buildings. Beyond the individual artist, creativity turns on the question of whether authentic creative acts are still possible in contemporary society; context has been described less as a neutral backdrop than as the very infrastructure of existing authority and relations of power. Suggesting, as Venturi did, that existing context is "almost alright" is akin to approving of everything from bad taste to social injustice. In the culture industry described by Adorno

Figure 7.5. Vietnam Veterans Memorial, Washington, D.C., Maya Lin, 1982. Maya Lin's design for the Vietnam Veterans Memorial is rigorously generated from its imposing context, although Lin's respect for context appears at first glance to be disrespect, as many critics at first complained. Where other objects on the National Mall are white, the Memorial is black; where others go up, it goes down; where others are certain and assuring, it is ambiguous, disquieting. Although it looks like nothing else on the Mall, the design visibly engages its surroundings' physical context because its inversions are so precisely calculated, its respect for prominent local features, like axial relations, are respected but rewritten in a minor key.

and Horkheimer, spontaneity is calculated and individuality mass produced so that submission to consumer capitalism feels like an emancipatory freedom to choose. In this view, to be contextual entails more than simply agreeing to formal limits; it means complying with a society that puts up with the junk it puts up. At the social level, resisting context becomes a political act; context is the substance against which a negative dialectic pushes in pursuit of a more just society.

An example of this position appeared in the June 2001, issue of *Architecture* magazine. Deborah Berke's renovation and addition to an existing building in New Haven, a modest and by all accounts unambitious building, is rendered subtly demoralizing in a commentary by K. Michael Hays. Hays brings the deadweight of contemporary consumer culture to bear on a deliberately ordinary building. His charge is less about the building itself than the diminished expectations of everyday architecture that surround it—a veil, he implies, that let one more confirmation of the culture of affirmation slip in, while our critical radar was locked on more explicit threats. Precisely because it seeks an intellectual reflexivity absent elsewhere, critical theory has to be suspicious of an outspokenly unassuming project like everyday architecture, whose ambition shows up in its humility and the decision to forgo a wholesale socially transformative practice for retail accommodations to everyday life.[28]

The conflict between creativity and context hints at a current moral dilemma between goodness and freedom. To be good is to act on behalf of others—selflessly—to make the world a better place. This involves knowing the needs of neighbors in some detail. To be free, on the other hand, means to choose one's own path, regardless of others. Being free involves turning inward, rather than outward. "Good" architecture comes from culture and accommodates it; it looks to context for rules to live by. Rules are anathema to a "free" architecture, which must follow its own sometimes naughty behavior to a truth so dense it bends current culture toward itself, a view of artistic practice that does not imitate life so much as it transforms life. As opposed to the experiments of an unfettered imagination, context is part of the public realm; it works like Freud's reality principle, in which reality is constructed from constant comparisons between one's own behavior and the responses of others. To subscribe to social reality means to some degree to conform to its precepts, so that the architecture of selfhood is built up from the countless do's and don'ts of others, like so many bricks in a wall. Thus, calls to context sound like the therapist's voice, acknowledging past trauma but urging us to find some compromise between desire and reality, talking us down gently from the heady but dangerous ledge of delirium. The issue of context sets up a contest between memory and speculation, between an architecture that either reinforces old habits or scans for future directions.

CONCLUSION

Around 1978, context was an issue taken up by a wide range of practitioners and critics. Design attention given to a building's context was, if not exactly progressive, at least not antagonistic to the possibility of architectural creation. That context became an issue in the first place attested to a field—a domain already cultivated, offering both structure and opportunity and resting on a deep history—that lay beyond the rubble of modernist ideals. Today, the issue of context inflames passions in two separate camps. What has changed less than the value placed by architectural discourse on paying attention to existing physical fabric, is context itself. Once a potential answer for almost all designers, it has calcified as a mandate for some and a vacuum for others, an issue that either confirms the continuity of society itself or siphons off personal expression and so hobbles the forward march of formal invention.

In this sense, the question of context is kin to that of style, which loomed large in the nineteenth century as a result of published accounts of archaeological discoveries and the cult of ruins. At that time, architects were positively obsessed with the issue of style, although their fluid movement between styles hints at a certain lack of commitment as well. Style, then and now, was a fossil of invention; it implied a deadening of design inquiry. Part of modernism's disciplinary success was that its reconfiguration of design values and process displaced previous generations' preoccupations. Modernism transcended style in its own accounts; to its critics it merely produced an airless version of style. But whether transcendent or indulgent, modernism's collapse, as outlined in the preceding pages, revealed that style, like context, was really an attitude toward history; at different points both terms described a legitimate foundation for subsequent change as well as a force running counter either to progress or authenticity.

That the issue of context is as much about history as about adjacency helps explain why it appears subject to greater debate in the United States than in Europe. Whereas the United States faced its preservation issues in the mid-1960s, European countries had rebuilt quickly some twenty years earlier, in the aftermath of World War II, without protracted debate. Several American modernists took sober note of the opportunities opened up for new architecture in Europe by wartime bombings, and worried that the built fabric of the prewar period would grow back over blasted blocks before modern architecture could take root.[29] But European cities not only had scope and depth of historic fabric, they also lacked the cycles of "creative destruction" typical of American development practice. Cities such as Cologne rebuilt not just a lost monument like Penn Station, but an entire historic core. The historic fabric was still fresh in cultural habits and its reconstruction was feasible even with the depleted resources available in the years immediately following the war; indeed, with industrial capacity diminished, rebuilding the past made sense in terms of the modernist mandate to match architecture with the state of contemporary production. With history woven at various levels in the built fabric of many European cities, working with the past has not seemed to pose much of a barrier to design, as suggested by architects as diverse as Jørn Utzon or Carlo Scarpa, who was active in restoration efforts immediately following the war and whose later unprecedented formal inventions began, precisely, with precedent. Such figures have in recent years been understood as "critical regionalists," a rubric that appropriates their work for an ongoing history of modernism, as a means of assimilating modernism to a generalized notion of place, rather than allowing that they work in dialogue with existing contexts. With *Roma Interrotta*, Argan had simply touched upon a professional issue of much popular interest in Rome, a place where the richness of the present *is* architectural history. Further, the issue of context arose in the United States just at the moment that architectural theory also blossomed, in part, as Michael Hays describes it, as a result of the perceived illegitimacy of spontaneous cultural production. The incipient issue of context was thus caught up implicitly as part of the bourgeoisie's reproduction of itself.[30]

In the United States today, taking up the issue of context implies a formal profile, directing attention to the past by directing it toward existing surroundings, especially in comparison with *site*, a more general term without a specific formal trajectory. Architecture needs a more robust or at least a bidirectional notion of context; it requires a wider range of relations to context than the dichotomy between responsible, good architecture and freely expressive architecture—a dichotomy that serves only a few outspoken ideologues. When compared with other terms architects use to conjure ideas of the local and specific—like *place* or *position*, or *spot* or *station*, or even *frame* or *land*, as well as *site*—it becomes apparent that *context* is the only one that is not also a verb. It links to matter and fixed form, but not to action. To site a building takes geometric account of existing conditions such as exposure to weather, relation to services, distribution of public and private spaces in relation to patterns of surrounding access, and so on. "To site" is to relate what will be to what currently is, without, however, setting any limits on formal invention. The action of siting is not hampered by any mandate regarding how it will occur, neither in regard to the order in which aspects are considered, how seriously they will be taken, nor what will delimit the forms finally generated. Also, a building's siting has little effect upon the weather it responds to, in contrast to context, which is always affected by new construction. Similarly, "to place" something betokens an intervention in the physical world, an action that will result in a new and specific configuration of spaces, at the same time without determining those specifics. To place a person is to recall clearly, to put someone in their proper order in memory; "to place" insists on moving from the general to the specific, to narrow down options to a single choice. Design is like this, narrowing from the field of possibility to unique and particular form. Conversely, "to space" means to set up an interval, an emptiness between actions or things that then becomes integrated in a larger rhythm. *Contextualize* is a verb, of course, but it means relating something to a larger setting, so the direction of energy is, as expected, one way, toward an accounting of specific features in relation to an existing context. In the case of a building, "to contextualize" implies a set of responses to a given context that will be visible in the new design. The issue of context, as described in this essay, addresses the new in terms of the existing. What, then, is the term for thinking through existing fabric, the sphere of the present, in terms of what is to come? And what storm—Walter Benjamin called it progress—continues to propel us away from visible context toward a future we can never see?

Notes

1. Bernard Tschumi, "24/7," public lecture at the Yale School of Architecture, New Haven, CT. April 14, 2003.
2. Carol J. Burns details many of these connections in her essay, "On Site: Architectural Preoccupations," in Andrea Kahn, ed., *Drawing/Building/Text* (New York: Princeton Architectural Press, 1991), 158.
3. Herbert Muschamp, "Measuring Buildings without a Yardstick," *New York Times* (July 22, 2001): Sect. 2, p. 30.
4. Douglas Kelbaugh, "Attention Getting," letter to the *New York Times* (August 12, 2001): Sect. 2, p. 4, c. 5. Compare also Witold Rybczynski's contrast of "show-dog architecture" with the "devaluing of context," which he dubs "The Bilbao Effect," *Atlantic Monthly* (September 2002): 138–142.
5. Colin Rowe, "Neo-'Classicism' and Modern Architecture I" and "Neo-'Classicism' and Modern Architecture II," [1956–1957], in his *The Mathematics of the Ideal Villa* (Cambridge: MIT Press, 1976), 127–130, 143–144; Vincent Scully, *The Shingle Style: Architectural Theory and Design from Richardson to the Origins of Wright* (New Haven: Yale University Press, 1955); Theo van Doesburg, "Towards a Plastic Architecture," in Ulrich Conrads, ed., *Programs and Manifestoes on 20th-Century Architecture* (Cambridge: MIT Press, 1975), 78–80; Lewis Mumford, *The Culture of Cities* (New York: Harcourt, Brace and Co., 1938), 136. To take a single example, Katherine Fischer points out that Le Corbusier's Purist art loses its "referential scale" by denying "environmental context." See Fischer, *Oppositions* 15:16 (Spring 1979): 157. Even Frank Lloyd Wright, typically sensitive to context, conceived it as devoid of other architecture. See, for example, "The Character of the Site Is the Beginning of Architecture," in *House Beautiful* (November 1955). More recently, but similarly, Kenneth Frampton, in Frederic Jameson's reading at least, considers context in terms of a vertical poetics of earth and sky architecture-links rather than horizontal connections to neighbors, an attitude Jameson labels Frampton's "telluric" position in his *Seeds of Time* (New York: Columbia University Press, 1994), 198–199. Jameson is saying that Frampton's is a modernism by other means.
6. Nikolaus Pevsner, "The Return of Historicism," *Journal of the Royal Institute of British Architects* 3:68 (1961). See also Manfredo Tafuri, "Modern Architecture and the Eclipse of History" in his *Theories and History of Architecture* (New York: Harper & Row, 1980).
7. Kevin Lynch, *The Image of the City* (Cambridge: MIT Press, 1960); Jane Jacobs, *The Death and Life of Great American Cities* (New York: Random House, 1961); Aldo Rossi, *The Architecture of the City* [Padua: 1966] (Cambridge: MIT Press, 1982); Vittorio Gregotti, *Il Territorio dell' Architettura* (Milan: Feltrinelli, 1966). Adrian Forty discusses Rogers and other Italian architects, pointing out the inadequacy of translating the Italian term *ambiente* to mean context, rather than the more likely *contesto*, "Context," in his *Words and Buildings: A Vocabulary of Modern Architecture* (New York: Thames & Hudson, 2000), 132–135. See also Bruno Zevi's article in *L'Architettura* (September 1956).

8. Colin Rowe and Fred Koetter, *Collage City* (Cambridge: MIT Press, 1978), 49. See also Christian F. Otto, "Orientation and Invention: History of Architecture at Cornell," in Gwendolyn Wright and Janet Park, eds., *The History of History in American Schools of Architecture, 1865–1975* (New York: Buell Center, 1990); Alexander Caragonne, *Texas Rangers: Notes from an Architectural Underground* (Cambridge: MIT Press, 1995); and the articles on Rowe in the special issue of *ANY: Architecture New York* 7:8 (1994).
9. Nathan Glazer and Daniel Patrick Moynihan, *Beyond the Melting Pot: the Negroes, Puerto Ricans, Jews, Italians, and Irish of New York City* (Cambridge: MIT Press, 1963).
10. Rowe and Koetter, 8.
11. Between 1968 and 1969 the publisher G. Braziller brought out five volumes under the series title *New Directions in Architecture*. The five—*New Directions in African Architecture, New Directions in British Architecture, New Directions in Italian Architecture, New Directions in Japanese Architecture,* and *New Directions in Latin American Architecture*—were separately authored, but followed a common format.
12. Brent Brolin, *The Failure of Modern Architecture* (New York: Van Nostrand Reinhold, 1976), 123; and see also his following book, *Architecture in Context: Fitting New Buildings with Old* (New York: Van Nostrand Reinhold, 1980).
13. This clarifies the source of critical responses to Rossi's architecture, for instance. To Rossi, the city was a site for historical speculation, a study of urban form divorced from urban function in an effort to describe a culture's geometrical unconscious, which helps explain why his school designs have been criticized for looking more like crematoria or panopticon prisons than schools. Discussed in Forty, op. cit.
14. Rem Koolhaas, *Delirious New York: A Retroactive Manifesto for Manhattan* (New York: Oxford University Press, 1978).
15. Maurice Culot and Leon Krier, "The Only Path for Architecture," *Oppositions*, 14 (Fall 1978): 39–53; Rowe and Koetter, op. cit.
16. Other examples of an architectural interest in context may be found in contemporaneous work of Christopher Alexander, Oscar Newman, Amos Rapoport, and Joseph Rykwert.
17. Regarding contextualism, Schumacher writes, "the primary intention has been to create a formal 'shorthand' which explains site pressures to an imaginary project architect," in his "Contextualism: Urban Ideals and Deformations," *Casabella* 35:359–360 (December 1971): 78–86. On figure–ground studies as "the key to the contextualist approach to urban space," see Graham Shane, "Contextualism," *Architectural Design* (November 1976). For a contrary view, see George Baird, "Oppositions in the Thought of Colin Rowe," *Assemblage* 33 (1997).
18. Niklas Maak, "Ungers' Not," *Frankfurter Allgemeine Sonntagszeitung*, (October 28, 2001): 28. My thanks to Wallis Miller for mentioning this article to me.
19. Michael Sorkin, "Leaving Wright Enough Alone" [1986] in his *Exquisite Corpse* (New York: Verso, 1991), 148; cited in Forty, op. cit.

20. This is Alan Colquhoun's argument in his essay, "From Bricolage to Myth, or How to Put Humpty-Dumpty Together Again," *Oppositions* 12 (Spring 1978).
21. I owe this terse formulation to Andrea Kahn.
22. Mark Wigley and Philip Johnson, *Deconstructivist Architecture: The Museum of Modern Art, New York* (Boston: Little, Brown, 1988). Similarly, Hitchcock contrasted "assurance," "uneventfulness," and "excessive familiarity" of conventional forms with a modernist spirit of inquiry in his responsible but dismissive inclusion of the ponderously labeled "Architecture Called Traditional in the Twentieth Century," in Henry Russell Hitchcock, *Architecture: Nineteenth and Twentieth Centuries* [1958] (New York: Penguin Books, 1977), 531.
23. William Curtis, *Modern Architecture* (Englewood Cliffs, NJ: Prentice-Hall, 1982), 382.
24. Wojciech Lesnikowski, "Contextualism Today," *Inland Architect* 30:6 (November–December 1986); "Contextualism?" *Lotus International* 74 (1992): 109.
25. Thomas Fisher, "Escape from Style," *Progressive Architecture* 75:9 (September 1994): 59; John Morris Dixon, "Monumental Buildings in Context," *Progressive Architecture* 74:6 (June 1993): 7.
26. In Office for Metropolitan Architecture, Rem Koolhaas and Bruce Mau, *Small, Medium, Large, Extra-Large* (Rotterdam, Netherlands: 010 Publishers; New York: Monacelli Press, 1995), 640. Cited in Forty, op. cit. "Bigness" and context are discussed on pp. 502, 514–515.
27. Steven Litt, "Monolithic Architecture's Mysterious Rationale," *Progressive Architecture* 76:12 (December 1995): 41. For his part, Steven Hurtt, who had earlier studied with Colin Rowe, the idea that new designs might to a great extent be generated by a series of responses to context, argued that contextualism simply never took root in the first place. For proof, one needed only observe contemporary teaching in schools of architecture, where high modernist ideals remained supreme, still focused on the utopian horizon rather than the building next door. See Steven Hurtt, "Contextualism of Paradigms, Politics and Poetry: A Rebuttal of Wojciech Lesnikowski's Series on Contextualism," *Inland Architect* 31:5 (September–October 1987): 66–75.
28. K. Michael Hays, Julie Iovine, and Gwendolyn Wright, "Exceptionally Ordinary: Yale University School of Art and New Theater," *Architecture* 90:6 (June 2001): 90–101. Hays prepared the ground for his critique in his essay, "Critical Architecture: Between Culture and Form" *Perspecta*, 21 (1984): 14–29—where a critical practice is located between complete autonomy and complete surrender to "the self-confirming, conciliatory operations of a dominant culture." The position was outlined by Clement Greenberg in 1939: artists turn toward matters internal to medium and craft as means of repudiating the existing social order. Manfredo Tafuri's "L'architecture dans le boudoir: The Language of Criticism and the Criticism of Language" *Oppositions* 3 (May 1974): 37–62, follows a similar logic but subsumes social critique to stealth aesthetic pleasure. Later writers such as Dwight MacDonald, Greenberg's interlocutor for this essay, would say that kitsch became

entrenched with "midcult" populisms of the 1960s and 1970s, which would probably include the various returns to context. See Clement Greenberg, "Avant-Garde and Kitsch," *Partisan Review* 6:5 (Fall 1939): 34–49.

29. See, for one example, Richard Neutra, *Survival through Design* (New York: Oxford University Press, 1954), 6.
30. K. Michael Hays, "Introduction," in his *Architecture Theory since 1968* (Cambridge: MIT Press, 1998), ix.

Le Corbusier, La Roche Gallery, Maisons La Roche-Jeanneret, Paris, France.

8

The Suppressed Site: Revealing the Influence of Site on Two Purist Works

Wendy Redfield

THE IDEAL SITE AS SUPPRESSED SITE

> Proceeding in the manner of an investigator in his laboratory, I have avoided all special cases, and all that may be accidental, and I have assumed an ideal site to begin with.[1]
>
> **Charles-Édouard Jeanneret, *Urbanisme***

Many of the works of great modern architects show a tremendous awareness of local conditions and a care for siting in the design process. Yet the portrayal of these works as "siteless" objects or universal propositions by historians as well as designers themselves has obscured this fact. The quotation above—intended by Le Corbusier to qualify and frame the theoretical proposal, "Une Ville Contemporaine pour 3 Millions d'Habitants"—succinctly epitomizes an inherent bias against site in the ideological foundations of modern architecture. To "assume an ideal site" clearly removes site matters from the design process; it negates the meaning of site as a particular location. The decision to "avoid all special cases" suspends the consideration of site until after the architectural construct has become virtually manifest.

This approach places emphasis on idealized, abstract composition as the primary design vehicle that is only later accommodated to specific circumstance. In the words of Reyner Banham, Le Corbusier "elaborates first a *solution-type*, in the abstract, its real life application can wait."[2] Another foundational premise of modernism, equally antagonistic to serious site theorizing, is the goal of proposing universal strategies in place of local or regionally developed traditions. From De Stijl to Futurism, the rhetoric of the early-twentieth-century manifestos that provided the theoretical basis for modernism and characterized the subsequent analysis of its works is pervaded by a tendency to favor the universal and the abstract over local variation and specificity.[3]

As a result, a significant disconnection exists between the received understanding (and influence) of many modern works as established by mainstream histories and their full value and meaning. Le Corbusier's houses and villas of the 1920s, comprising his so-called Purist phase, offer a pertinent example. A first-time visitor to these buildings situated in and around Paris is surprised by how skillfully they are woven into their complex, surrounding neighborhoods. Nothing prepares one for the adroitly choreographed connections made between these starkly modern buildings and their contexts, for, despite more than a half-century of scholarly examination of these works, the influence of site has been largely suppressed or ignored. Even the physical surroundings of Le Corbusier's best-known projects of this period—Villas Savoye and Stein, and Maison Cook—have received little attention.[4] Since interest in Le Corbusier is hardly waning (judging from the recent spate of publications on the architect), there can be only one explanation for this omission: site has been thought to be irrelevant.

This assumption results in part from Le Corbusier's own publications of the period, which rarely addressed specific site conditions and their role in his design process.[5] During his early career, Le Corbusier was developing the formal language and theoretical priorities for his vision of the future of architecture. His Parisian houses, portrayed as prototypes for unlimited transposition and transformation, coincided with his prolific publication of manifestos in the journal *L'Esprit Nouveau* and his investigation of idealized (siteless) house and city typologies.[6] Intent on formulating essential principles and prototypical arrangements, Le Corbusier idealized the early Parisian houses. He published them carefully framed—cropped of idiosyncratic detail (Figure 8.1).[7]

To propose these buildings as universal types, any unique aspects imposed by the personality of clients or particular site conditions were expunged from published images. Clearly, Le Corbusier's attempt to universalize his work has a self-promotional aspect. Portrayed as uninformed by and unresponsive to their unique setting and program, projects are represented as potentially reproducible for an unlimited number of other clients, on an unlimited number of other sites (Figure 8.2). This prototypical cast applied to what were in fact highly customized projects is epitomized by a Le Corbusier sketch depicting multiple "Villa Savoyes" in a suburban, cul-de-sac arrangement.[8]

The apparent dismissal of context and site in the representation and reception of Le Corbusier's work can also be traced to a broader tradition stemming from Enlightenment-inspired Neoclassical and

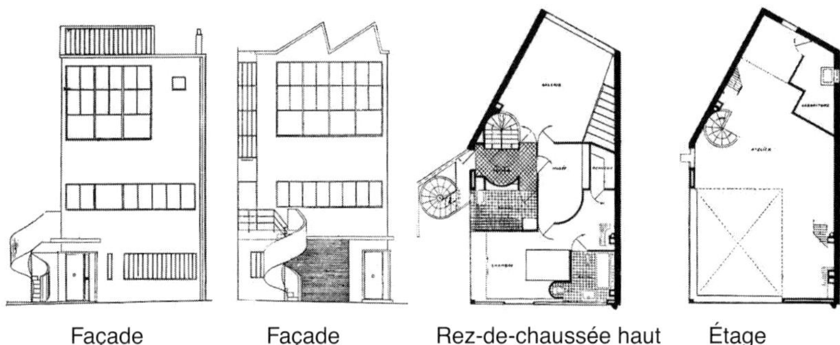

Figure 8.1. Plans and sections of Atelier Ozenfant from the *Oeuvre Complète*. The *Oeuvre Complète*—the authorized, but not (as it purports) comprehensive record of Le Corbusier's professional output—documents the houses of the 1920s in a deliberately objectified manner. Plan drawings float on the page, with no reference to even the most immediate site elements of sidewalk, street, and adjacent building; site plans are virtually nonexistent. Photographs emphasize interiors, carefully staged with only the barest of architect-selected furnishings. The few exterior photographs focus on the building alone, any hint of the surrounding site omitted wherever possible. Even the layout of the two façade drawings above (the north elevation on the left, the east on the right) doesn't allow one to understand the corner condition of the site. To properly relate the two façades to each other around the turn of the corner, they would need to be shown in reverse order—the east to the left of the north elevation.

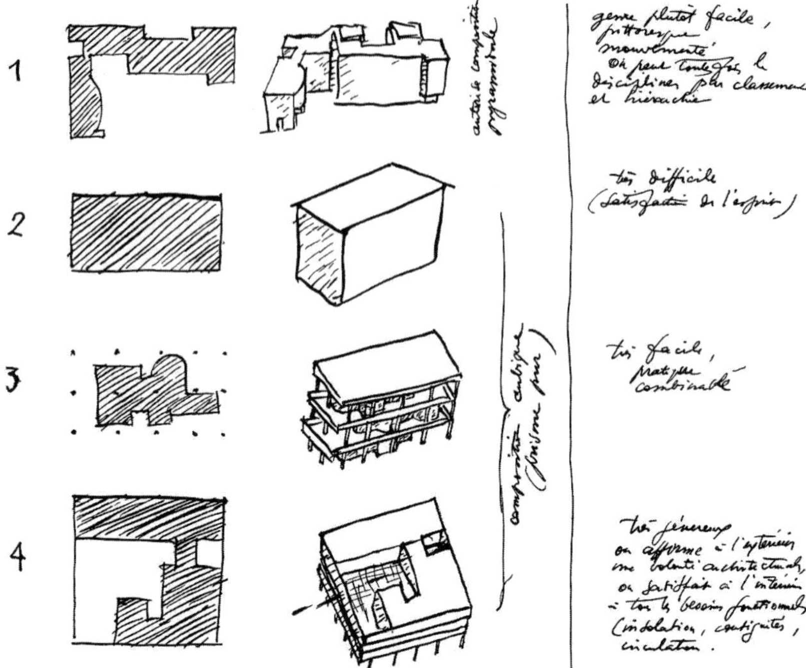

Les 4 compositions: 1) Exemple maison La Roche 2) Maison à Garches 3) Maison à Stuttgart 4) Villa Savole

Figure 8.2. "Les 4 Compositions." The *Oeuvre Complète* entry entitled "The Five Points of a New Architecture," is illustrated by a drawing captioned "Les 4 Compositions," which portrays Maison La Roche, Maison à Garches, Maison à Stuttgart, and Villa Savoye as freestanding composition types, labeled with verbal descriptions of their distinct formal characteristics and an assessment of their varying degrees of design difficulty. La Roche (in contrast to the others) derives its idiosyncratic, picturesque configuration from responses to a highly complex and dense urban site, though this is belied by the absence of any drawn or captioned site description. Again, the building floats in isolation, as if its particular location could (and should) be anywhere or everywhere.

visionary architecture. In this genre, ideal form linked inextricably to a "rational" language of pure Euclidian geometry assumes primary importance. Any forces that might taint or alter the ideal are regarded as secondary and regrettable. In the dominant, received strain of the Beaux-Arts tradition, buildings were designed to retain their idealized compositional form even after being ascribed a specific site.

The Neoclassical plinth provided Beaux-Arts–trained designers one technique for staging the perfected architectural object on a *tabula rasa*, unhindered by the corrupt and varying ground; plinths deformed to the vagaries of the site so that buildings could retain their ideality.[9] This strategy of reestablishing and perfecting the ground plane as a prerequisite to architectural design prefigures and acts as corollary to Le Corbusier's use of *piloti* as an architectural device allowing freedom from topographic circumstance. The *rez de chaussée* understory of Le Corbusier's early buildings, propped on their thin *piloti*, acts as a spatial—or negative—plinth; it epitomizes the modernist restatement of Neoclassical poché *mass* as undifferentiated, homogenous, ever-flowing *space*. Both, however, are built on the same ideological foundations, and both express the same sentiment with respect to site: it does not matter.

In addition to this Enlightenment-based preference for idealized compositional arrangements that must be freed from the site's specificity, the revolutionary and utopian cast of early modern architecture emanating from the Futurists invested "the new" with intrinsic value; and the site, because it always contains the traces of its social and natural histories, can never be new. Its inherent inclusivity stands as testament to the organic cycles of growth and decay and change and accumulation that modern architecture—with its visions of a new age—sought to obliterate. In "Hapticity and Time: Notes on Fragile Architecture," Juhani Pallasmaa writes:

> In its quest for the perfectly articulated autonomous artifact, the main line of modernist architecture has preferred materials and surfaces that seek the effect of flatness, immaterial abstractness and timelessness....Abstraction and perfection transport us into the world of ideas, whereas matter, weathering and decay strengthen the experience of time, causality and reality....The architecture of the modern era aspires to evoke an air of ageless youth and of a perpetual present.[10]

Pullasmaa's argument regarding the atemporality of modern architecture finds a fitting corollary in the modernist suppression of site. The ideals Pullasmaa ascribes to modernist architecture that detach it from "time, causality and reality" also detach the architectural construct from its unique and specific place; modernist architecture prefers an "ideal site," which is to say, no site at all.

Moreover, the phenomenon of site suppression is not limited to the way Le Corbusier's work has been framed. It runs deeper; characterizing the nature of modern architectural historiography generally. By and large, historians have tended to overlook issues of site, showing little interest in the field, the urban ground, or the typical building. Rather, history has privileged the special contributions of "heroic" architects. Vernacular histories have only recently received any exposure.[11] Typical urban patterns and structure have also escaped notice, precisely because they are not exceptional conditions (Figure 8.3).

In the larger historiographic context that suppresses the ground in favor of the object, it is particularly revealing to observe the biases against addressing questions of site and urban typology written into the Corbusian literature. Projects such as Atelier Ozenfant, Maisons La Roche-Jeanneret, Maison Ternisien, and Maisons Lipchitz and Miestchanninof, among others, have extraordinarily rich and complex urban sites that inevitably exerted consequences on their designs. Yet if these sites get mentioned at all, they are usually referred to only as being too "tight," "awkward," or "cramped" to allow the full realization of a Purist architectural language; it is often implied that the projects were compromised by the limitations imposed by their sites.

Villa Savoye offers one notable exception. This project is often set forth as Le Corbusier's masterpiece of the period: his first opportunity to fully achieve his aesthetic aims, since its "open site" provided none of the limitations imposed by more densely inhabited plots. Notice, for example, Sigfried Giedion's cursory treatment of site by way of introducing the Villa Savoye: "Previously [to the Villa Savoye], Le Corbusier's houses had been built on rather cramped plots, in more or less close proximity to their neighbors. The site of the Savoye house, on the contrary, was completely isolated."[12] The implied suggestion is that, as a site characteristic, "isolated" is good and "cramped" is not.

At Villa Savoye, historic maps and aerial photographs reveal the creation of the site as an apt stage for the house: originally a wood, it becomes an agricultural field, and finally, under the architect's hand, a "clearing" in the midst of a newly planted grove of trees.[13] This type of site—the one recognized and appreciated by modern histories—is clearly subservient to and created for the enactment of an architectural

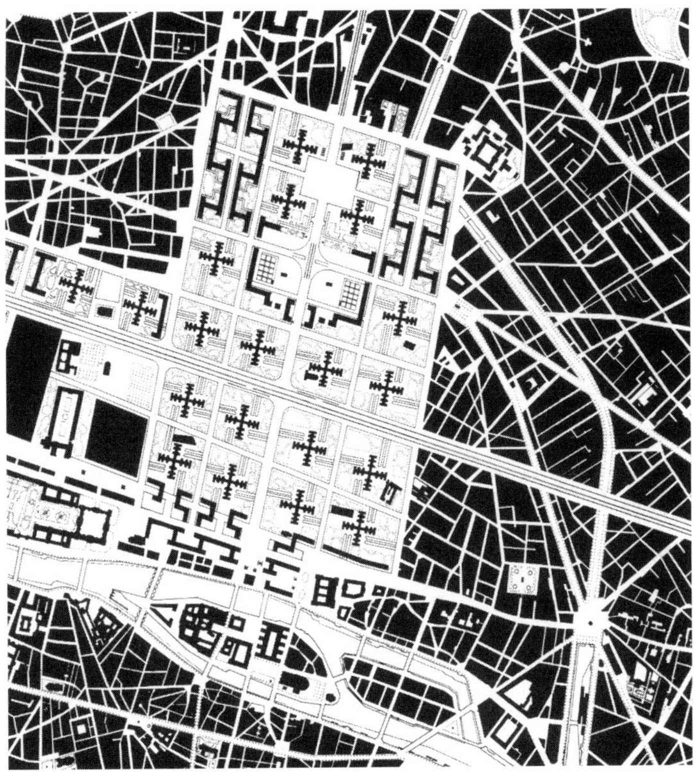

Figure 8.3. Le Corbusier's Plan Voisin with a portion of Paris razed and replaced with tower blocks. Le Corbusier's theories on the modern city further confound a thorough examination of his treatment of sites within the city of Paris, in particular. His idealized urban design proposals (which almost always involved razing large urban sectors—proto-urban renewal—and erecting tall discrete towers in open parklike terrain) suggest an incompatibility of Modern architecture and traditional urban structure. These projects have indelibly marked Le Corbusier as anti-urban—unconcerned with the complexity of accumulated conditions of the urban ground. The social and political context in which these projects were conceived is frequently overlooked. At the time the Plan Voisin was developed, tuberculosis ran rampant in Paris, and the only known cure was exposure to the sun. Le Corbusier observed the deleterious effects on health of the modern city and wanted to make unsentimental proposals to open up the city to his "sun, space, and green" as a remedy. In fact, the growing public sentiment to pursue the kind of urban clearing suggested in many of Le Corbusier's early proposals was stopped only by the timely development of an effective tuberculosis vaccine.

idea. In "Concluding with Landscapes," J. B. Jackson raises this issue of valuation of different site types by comparing the monumental, designed landscape associated with the Renaissance (which he labels "Landscape Two") to the vernacular one ("Landscape One"). He argues that designers and historians are very familiar with Landscape Two:

> Artists and architects and landscape designers spend much time studying it, and they copy it in their professional work; and all of us who write about it travel to Europe to see it at firsthand....Unlike Landscape One, which mixed all kinds of uses and spaces together, Landscape Two insists on spaces which are homogenous and devoted to a single purpose. [Landscape Two] makes a distinction between city and country, between forest and field, between public and private, rich and poor, work and play; it prefers the linear frontier between nations rather than the medieval patchwork of intermingled territories.[14]

Jackson identifies the modern bias—stemming from Renaissance ideals—against sites with complex, layered histories and the inclination toward newly recreated sites fashioned to a singular architectural purpose. The vital *received* urban site of Le Corbusier's Maisons La Roche-Jeanneret (and other works prior to Savoye) derives its complexity from mixed authorship. Such sites—resisting categorization—are unfamiliar and therefore unvalued. This leads to their suppression in publication and analysis, thereby reifying their unfamiliarity, and undervaluation. Could it be, in fact, that it is not the building itself, but Villa Savoye's site typology—site as constructed, neutral tableau—that has led the building again and again to be proclaimed in the history books the "masterpiece," the canonical example, of Le Corbusier's Purist phase?

Le Corbusier's propaganda proved extremely effective. With it, he managed to detach built works from their specific sites for the purpose of producing universalized, canonical images—apt illustrations of his stated aesthetic ideal.[15] However, looking more carefully, and with a broader lens, at Le Corbusier's early work—at what he did, not what he said—supplies evidence that a vital part of this history has been missed, that modern architecture has been at least partially misrepresented by dominant historical narratives. Efforts to understand Le Corbusier's "universal grammar of design" and to categorize his vast body of work (categorization is what history craves) has left a vital part of this history unwritten. Le Corbusier's Parisian houses of the 1920s display a powerful but unheralded view of modern architecture and the city—of the relationship between buildings and their sites—which provides a valuable counterpoint to his grand utopian schemes and written manifestoes of the same period. In these small but bold works, the architect demonstrated a radically modern architecture at ease in a traditional urban setting. He pursued an incremental urbanism in which repeatable building types adjust to changing times and conditions without negating or wholly replacing what came before. He introduced startlingly new forms into the urban fabric of Paris, creating an aggressive but fluent dialogue between old and new, building and urban structure, figure and field. In both spatial and temporal terms, these buildings are exceptional *and* they belong.

To make the case that the ideological framing of modernism has suppressed site as a matter for serious theorizing, it is necessary to demonstrate the site's relevance in the conception and design of modernist-built works. In other words, it is necessary to establish that there was in fact something to suppress. The section that follows aims to expose how the ideality of Le Corbusier's early works is reconciled and enlarged by the particularity of their physical, typological, and cultural contexts. Atelier Ozenfant (1922–1923) and Maisons La Roche-Jeanneret (1923–1925), two notable examples from Le Corbusier's Purist period, serve to demonstrate the various levels on which his houses engage their urban sites. In these buildings, Le Corbusier created formal responses to particular neighborhood patterns, alternately reinforcing and subverting them. He adapted traditional Parisian building typologies to particular site and program conditions. He unified the series of works with a consistent architectural language that transcends specific location but remains deeply rooted in the conceptual milieu of the avant-garde discourse of Paris at that time. These three categories of site influence—physical, typological, and cultural—together created a unique field of play: an environment of architectural possibilities which could not have emerged in quite the same way anywhere else, or at any other time. They are situational.

THE PHYSICAL SITE

Atelier Ozenfant and Maisons La Roche-Jeanneret engage their respective Parisian neighborhood locales in very different ways (Figure 8.4). On the cusp between two dissimilar urban conditions in a fairly jumbled sector, the Atelier Ozenfant assertively and explicitly engages its physical site. By contrast, the relationship of the Maisons La Roche-Jeanneret to their more uniform surroundings is stealthy, subversive, and opportunistic.

The Atelier Ozenfant—located in the 14th Arrondissement—has a highly visible profile and plays an important civic role belying its modest domestic program. The house sits on a pivotal threshold in this area marked by dramatic scalar, programmatic, and temporal oppositions. Le Corbusier responded to the site's embedded dialectics (institutional/domestic, monumental/diminutive, old/new) by devising subtle deflections and extensions that allow this small building to mediate between extremely divergent urban conditions along two distinct axes: one front to back, the other around the turn of a street corner.

The house/studio stands in a small, triangular-shaped block immediately north of the city's seventeenth-century fortifications (now replaced by the extensive grounds of the Cité Internationale Universitaire de Paris). Its neighborhood's small cluster of houses is sandwiched between two very large pieces of civic infrastructure: the Réservoir de Montsouris (across the Avenue Reille to the north) and the Hôpital Université de Paris (just to its south). The Parc de Montsouris, built between 1868 and 1878 on a former quarry, borders the neighborhood to the east.[16]

A site section taken longitudinally through the building reveals the startling transition in site circumstances from back to front (Figures 8.5 through 8.7). Cramped, dark, and compressed at the rear of its lot, the house appears to open telescopically toward the broad and comparatively unencumbered terrain of the Avenue Reille.[17] The studio—located at the northeast corner of the lot and facing both streets—thrusts visually out into the space of the large avenue. This important interior volume is almost fully exposed as the totemic figure on the exterior, with the rest of the house effectively serving as *poché* to frame this one pure space.

The Réservoir de Montsouris, though rarely if ever mentioned in analyses of the project, seems to have exerted a profound influence on its design. The interior studio space provides a view out and across the Avenue to the Réservoir's retaining wall beyond. The horizon from

Figure 8.4. View of building façades facing the Seine on Île St.-Louis, Paris. The urban field of Paris—the larger context for many of Le Corbusier's Purist works—is remarkably uniform, punctuated by the rare, outstanding exception: Eiffel's Tower, the Arc de Triomphe, Nôtre-Dame. Rules of urban building—not unlike expectations of social comportment—are clear and rarely broken. Buildings conform by law and convention to standard heights, widths, forms, and materials. City fabric is an assemblage of standard building types, interior plan arrangements, façade compositions, cornice heights, and fitments refined over centuries. Use of repetitive types and elements extends to the street furnishing, planting, ground surfacing, and lighting. Street proportions are maintained by consistent building setbacks, sidewalk dimensions, orientation, lot sizes, and configuration. Buildings and streets construct a uniform ground—a larger whole—where layered thresholds between public and private—shared and individual—choreograph and maintain a civic decorum. With the exception of important institutions, exterior expression suggests little about interior diversity. Behind the veneer of sameness, however, lies a variety of block and neighborhood types diverse in scale, program, and character. To varying degrees, Parisian neighborhoods derive their local character from the historic precincts on which they are built, the era of their construction, and their relative proximity to the city center, the Seine, or the original city fortifications.

Figure 8.5

Figure 8.6

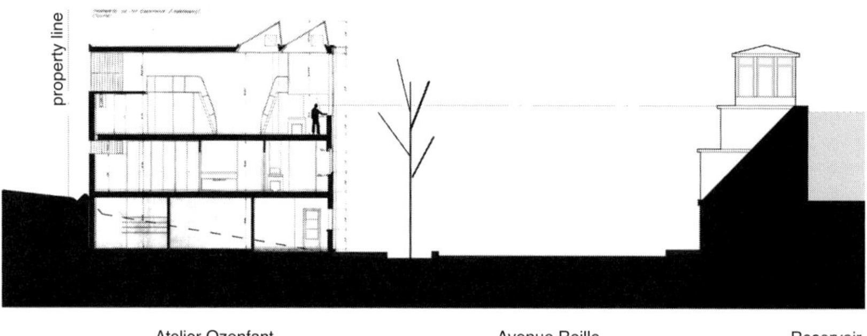

Figure 8.7

the studio level meticulously aligns with the top of the Réservoir wall, bringing the two—studio and réservoir—into a direct, even parallel relationship. With the oft-mentioned nautical fitments of the studio space (ship's ladder, etc.), one might even imagine "sailing" across the Avenue and onto the surface of the Réservoir.[18] In this tiny building, the studio space stands up to the monumental scale of the Avenue and the Réservoir beyond. Indeed, this transparent box of air and light is a fitting if diminutive corollary to the enormous box of water across

Figures 8.5 through 8.7. North-south site section of Atelier Ozenfant, facing west; photograph of reservoir towers; photograph of Atelier Ozenfant. The ground level of the lot sloped down almost a full story from the rear boundary to its Avenue Reille frontage. The original section drawing titled "Proprieté de M. Ozenfant (Montsouris). Coupe" (Le Corbusier Foundation document #7824), gives meticulous dimensions and detail, but only of the building envelope and its interior; the original ground line is not shown, nor any adjacent site conditions. The spatial (and roof) profile of the house, in contrast to the original ground line, slopes up, an effect created by the sectional opening of the double height studio beyond the mezzanine loft at the back and accentuated by the up-sloping profile of the sawtooth skylights facing north. The dark, contorted garage, gallery, and studio mezzanine hug the cramped back corner in service of the double height space in front. From the street, the studio proposes a modern, factory-aesthetic analog to the surveillance towers that punctuate the Réservoir's cornice at regular intervals. Similar in scale, material, and character, the Atelier lacks only their peaked roofs and decorative flourishes.

the street. In their shared geometric and elemental purity, each belongs equally to the civic realm of Paris.

As the Ozenfant house turns the corner from the Avenue Reille to the Rue du Square Montsouris, it acts as a gate to the small domestic island of artists' studios and houses huddled together in this otherwise fairly institutional sector of the city. Le Corbusier's management of this pivotal corner site makes a graceful transition from the large scale and monumental character of the Avenue to the small, largely pedestrian Rue du Square Montsouris. A site plan of the house reveals the architect's restrained but adroit resolution of this complex urban corner. Atelier Ozenfant sits assertively poised on the threshold between two entirely different spatial and urban conditions (Figure 8.8).

Each of the atelier's two primary bearing walls "belongs" to the adjacent street and respective family of party walls (Figure 8.9). Placed at the turning point of the two streets is a single, square corner column (see Figure 8.1). Belonging equally to the small street and the broad avenue, this third distinguishable structural element provides the centerline for a façade composition that, by wrapping around the corner, renders the overall building form coherent, resolved, and sculpturally autonomous. Ozenfant's upper-level, two-story studio window and its first-floor band window extend across both north and east façades, further easing the corner transition.

At the same time, a more dynamic compositional play "customizes" each face of the building to its primary street (see Figure 8.1). The

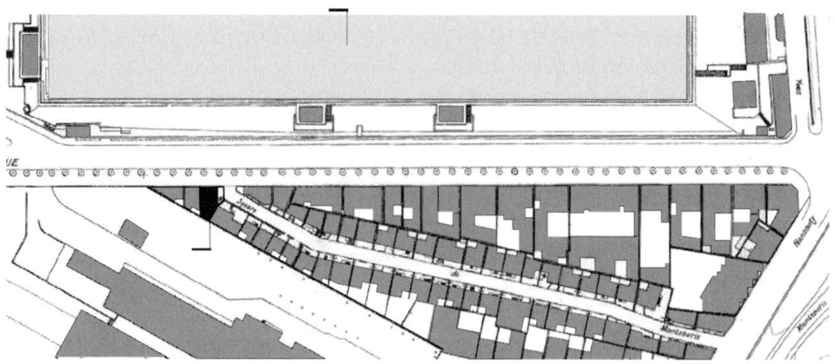

Figure 8.8. Site map of the Atelier Ozenfant. Avenue Reille, close to 60 feet wide, accommodates two lanes each of traffic and parking and an 18-foot-wide sidewalk (10 feet paved walking area, the rest for locust trees). Avenue Reille is bordered to the north by the three-story retaining wall enclosing the enormous Réservoir de Montsouris. The Rue du Square Montsouris is a mere 10 feet wide, cobblestoned and uneven, lined by the lushly fenced front-yard gardens of two- to three-story houses. In contrast to Avenue Reille, its 2-feet-wide sidewalks are barely navigable.

north façade is sheer and taut, stepping right up to the sidewalk's edge like its neighbors on the Avenue. With the exception of the slightly projecting ground floor lintel, it creates no spatial threshold with the street. On the right upper half of the façade, an opaque panel, punctured only by the tiny square window lighting the library loft, balances the brittle transparency of the large studio window. This loft provides an elevated view of the Réservoir, the water surface of which would be visible from this vantage point. A long, horizontal ground floor window that begins on the north façade is interrupted by entry doors and a garage opening, before it reaches the end of the east façade. At the roofline, original sawtooth skylights once modulated how the house met its two street conditions. Along the monumental avenue they increased the building's apparent height and scale, perceptually adding a fifth floor to match adjacent elevations. On the east façade the skylights appeared as mere projections from the roof plane, bringing the scale down to more closely match the smaller, lower buildings on the Rue du Square Montsouris.

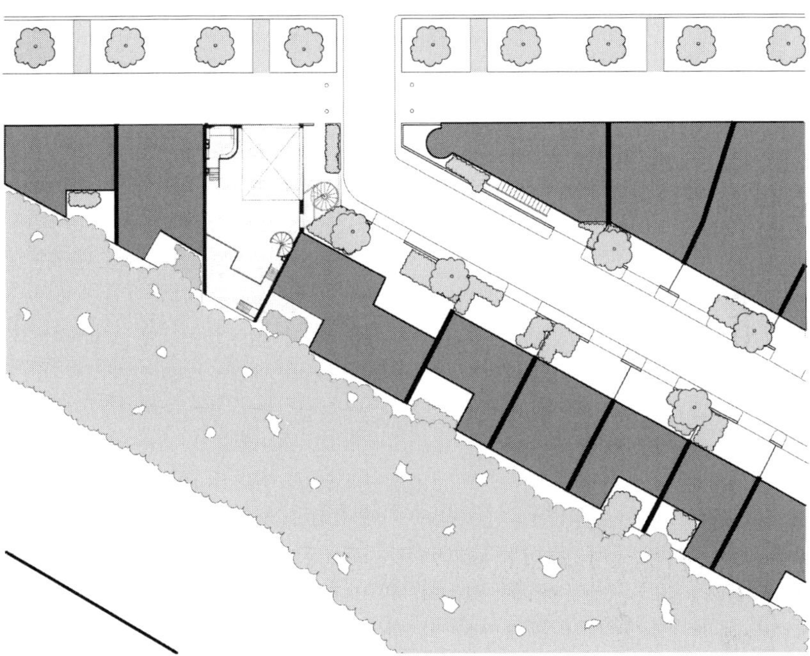

Figure 8.9. Site plan of the Atelier Ozenfant. The west party wall of Ozenfant lies perpendicular to Avenue Reille. The southeast party wall of the house deflects from the dominant geometry to run perpendicular to the Rue du Square Montsouris, a tiny street that slopes up and away from the Avenue at an angle. The varying geometry of Ozenfant's walls, as they respond to the site, results in the plan's odd, trapezoidal shape.

The most significant transformation around the corner involves Le Corbusier's creation of an entry court that gives depth to the east façade on Rue du Square Montsouris (see Figure 8.9). This face of the building recedes from the sidewalk by approximately 10 feet, contributing to a zone already existing in the overall pattern on this residential street; each house on the Rue du Square Montsouris has a small front-yard garden/driveway. Ozenfant's 10-foot zone accommodates a small, fence-enclosed entry court containing a planter and a voluptuously sculptural spiral stair (I will return to these later) leading to the primary entrance to the house on the first floor. Since the garage entry on the Rue du Square Montsouris has long been abandoned, the small court (with its original planter) has been overtaken by potted trees and flowers; it completes the lush character of this street, barely containing its bursting vegetation. The Ozenfant house reinforces its existing urban site conditions by integrating and resolving two divergent street typologies. The distinction between the large avenue and the smaller street addressed by Atelier Ozenfant registers succinctly in the building's two façades, and in the different spatial thresholds each creates to its respective street frontage.

If the Atelier Ozenfant's site strategy may be best characterized as assertively reinforcing existing urban orders, the Maisons La Roche-Jeanneret demonstrate an altogether different approach by quietly subverting and exploiting the dominant pattern of the surrounding neighborhood. In this project, Le Corbusier expanded his role as architect by acting as quasi-developer and realtor in the gradual acquisition of several distinct properties that ultimately comprised the La Roche-Jeanneret site. Located in the interior of a block in the fashionable residential Auteuil District of the 16th Arrondissement, this double residence was designed for Raoul La Roche, and Albert Jeanneret and his new wife Lotti Raaf.[19] Since Le Corbusier was instrumental in selecting and to some degree defining the extent of the building lot, this building's siting carries special significance in revealing the complex influences of site on his design thinking during this period.

In contrast to the Ozenfant house, which integrates and thus reinforces existing site conditions, the genius of the Maisons La Roche-Jeanneret siting lies in an inversion of the surrounding normative block pattern. By gradually acquiring lots to create an unorthodox and, in conventional real-estate terms, "undesirable" site, Le Corbusier reinvented a common service alley to create a monumental, frontal approach to the Maisons (Figure 8.10). The other houses on the typical block establish an uninterrupted perimeter façade along the narrow streets. Each house can be approached only obliquely (not frontally), and is inevitably seen as one of a series; private gardens

Figure 8.10. Site plan of the Maisons La Roche-Jeanneret. The Auteuil neighborhood, located on the western edge of Paris, is in an area bounded by the right bank of the Seine to the east, and the Bois de Boulogne to the west. Extremely uniform and almost entirely residential, its fabric comprises relatively homogenous materials and building types, consistent with the era of its development. All four streets bounding the block of the Maisons La Roche-Jeanneret are relatively small and, for the most part, of equivalent urban significance. In this neighborhood, blocks tend to be ringed with a uniform outer "wall" of houses; there are no front yards, stoops, or notable transitional elements elaborating a spatial threshold at the street. On the block's interior this uniformity and impenetrability is replaced by a mixture of varied building depths, small service buildings, and a residual but lush porosity created by backyard gardens and small access alleys.

extend inward behind this impenetrable layer. Maisons La Roche-Jeanneret, located at the east interior end of the block in a cul-de-sac, is surrounded by the lush vegetation of neighboring gardens. By cleverly appropriating the fence-enclosed rear gardens belonging to immediately adjacent properties, Le Corbusier creates a modest entry *allée*—reminiscent of the long, symmetrical entry lanes associated with classic villa siting. The approach to the house thus becomes a retreat from the dense urban surround: a journey into a quiet, verdant oasis.

The two parts of the house—an elevated gallery and a grounded side wing—further emphasize the monumentality of the approach. Le Corbusier treats the gallery—on axis with the long entry lane—as the sculptural face of the house, while the side wing operates as "street fabric." The gallery—preferred object and inaccessible destination—

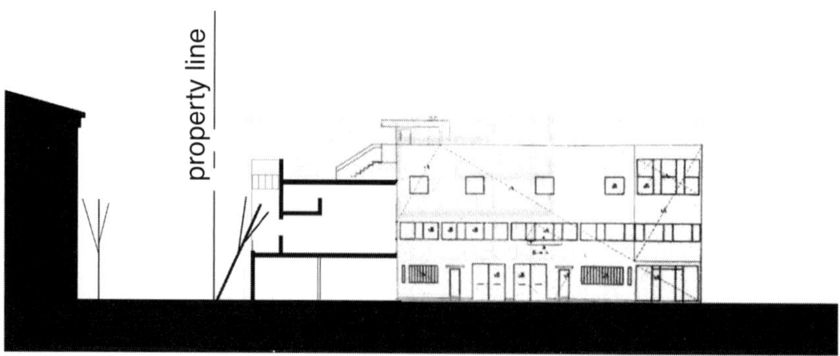

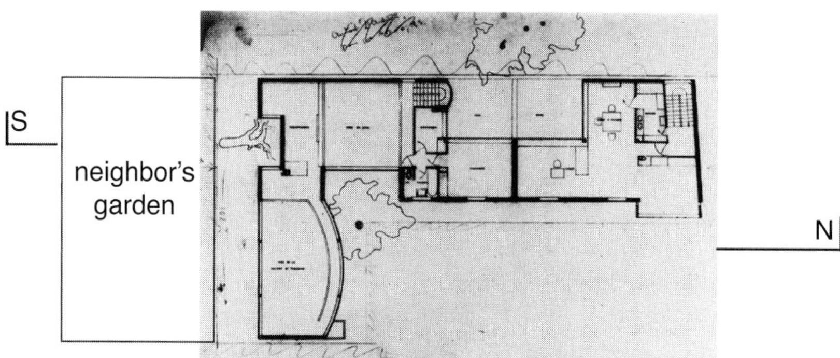

Figure 8.11. North–south site section of the Maisons La Roche-Jeanneret with First Floor Plan (for reference). The light court on the south façade began as an indentation for an existing acacia tree leaning well into M. La Roche's lot at the canopy level, but rooted on the property of M. Sorel, the rear neighbor. To accommodate the tree, a glazed indentation at the first floor above ground was originally designed as conical in shape—approximating the varying diameter of the acacia's canopy. In the built work it assumes an orthogonal form. On the ground floor, the glass in plane with the outer wall defies the rules of the *jours de souffrance* by facing directly onto the Sorel property. On the gallery level a recessed glass-lined balcony breaks the privacy laws in spirit, if not in fact. On the second level, at M. La Roche's library loft, the windows lie perpendicular to the exterior façade, providing ample (if legal) views of M. Sorel's garden.

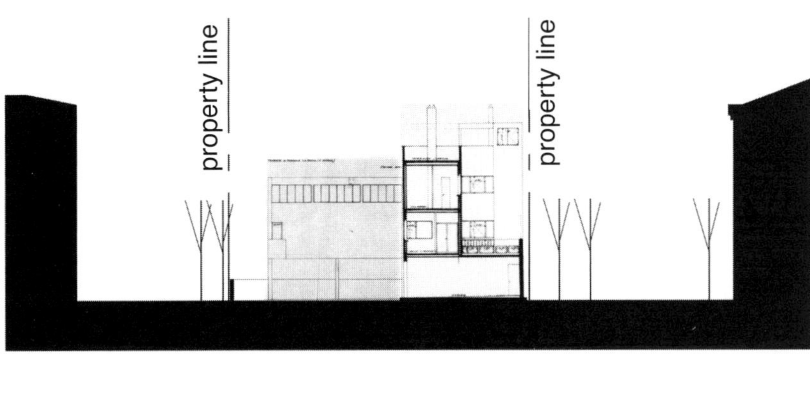

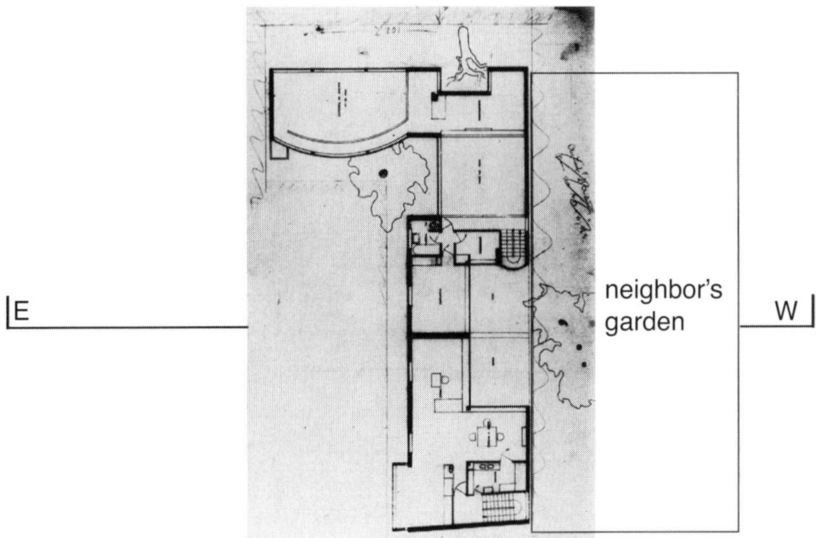

Figure 8.12. East–west site section of the Maisons La Roche-Jeanneret with First Floor Plan (for reference). The west light courts are situated over the back half of the ground floor twin garages, Mme. Raaf's studio, and the concierge kitchen of M. La Roche. Although labeled "terraces" on the plan, these exterior rooms clearly are not intended to be occupiable *toit jardins*. Rather, they allow light and air to penetrate the house from the rear. At the first-floor level, the neighbors appear to have prevailed: there are only small windows on the lateral walls of the court, and a high parapet in the plane of the exterior wall blocking views. On the upper two floors, however, the lining of the light court indentation is totally glazed, providing full access to light, air, and the occasional illicit view.

"floats" free of the ground and the rest of the building, whereas the side-house wing is workaday, compact, and efficient. This side wing is outfitted with curbs, drains, planters, entry steps, door mats, canopies, garage ramps, boot scrapes, and hose bibs—all compressed into a continuous, narrow, concrete threshold. The house has the tough, pragmatic look of an industrial building, regulating everything that enters and exits: people, water, cars, and utilities. Yet these prosaic acts of accommodation assume an impressive elegance. For all their simplicity, these humble elements are raised to the level of ritual. Compared to the monumentality and sculptural autonomy of the gallery's lifted curve, they speak poignantly of the imperfection and transience of daily life.

The unorthodox assemblage of partial lots comprising the site posed major challenges for the fenestration of the building. *Jours de souffrances*—French privacy laws—prohibited windows on exterior walls adjoining neighboring properties.[20] The embedded nature of this internalized site, virtually surrounded by neighboring properties, left only the east and north walls facing the entry lane available for openings. Since these were insufficient to supply adequate light and air to the building, Le Corbusier exercised great creativity and even a little deviousness to overcome the legal and physical limitations of this site.

He solved the problem by providing two light courts, excavated from the principal L-shaped building volume. The design of the first, on the south façade, accommodates an existing acacia tree (Figure 8.11). Extending the full height of the building, this court co-opts the neighbor's light, air, and greenery to enrich the La Roche residence. The second court, on the west façade, employs a similar strategy to illuminate and ventilate the La Roche dining and bedroom, as well as the entire Jeanneret-Raaf residence (Figure 8.12). Two conjoined roof terraces—one each for the La Roche and Jeanneret domains—cut halfway into the width of the residential wing, starting at the first-floor level. By covering nearly fifty percent of their overall floor areas with skylights, Le Corbusier illuminated the shadowy rooms on the ground floor below. By lining their walls—now recessed from the property line—with glazing, he provided light from the north, west, and south, and cross-ventilation to the upper floor of the La Roche and Jeanneret residences.

The combined effect of the light drawn in from the court excavations and the views offered by the *toit jardin* (covering the entire roof of both houses) extends the experiential landscape of the house well beyond its legal site boundaries. Perceptually trespassing the lot lines and built envelope, the building claims the neighbors' gardens and all else within the block as its domain.[21] The houses lining the outer edge of the block are effectively appropriated as a wall for the "villa precinct" within. The benefits of this siting strategy are immediately legible from the first view of the house at the beginning of the entry lane. The feeling of expansive territory introduced at the initial approach penetrates the interiors by virtue of the well-placed roof terraces. Views into the neighboring gardens render the zoning restrictions utterly ineffectual. By reading and fully internalizing the logic of the block, Le Corbusier constructed an opportunistic site condition for the Maisons La Roche-Jeanneret. He reverses the dominant hierarchy of the typical block of this sector, making the back the front, the private public, the undesirable the most grand. Poaching off the opulence of its bourgeois neighbors, this site strategy clarifies the block structure through contrast and completely reinvents the nature of an urban dwelling in this sector of Paris.

THE TYPOLOGICAL SITE

> It is in the past that the axial laws of the work of art are found, time alone proving their durability, their *sine qua non*.[22]
>
> **Amèdee Ozenfant and Charles-Édouard Jeanneret, *Aprés le Cubisme***

The preceding quotation identifies a recurring theme in Le Corbusier's architectural work: the definition of typological standards from which all specific works are derived. By 1922, prior to beginning work on any of his commissioned Parisian projects, Le Corbusier had designed three ideal house types—Maison Dom-ino (1914–1915), Maison Monol (1919), and Maison Citrohan (1921–1922)—and had formulated his "Five Points of a New Architecture." The construction methods and formal strategies embodied in these ideal formulations constitute the basis for many of the houses he designed subsequently. Each can be seen as a version, transformation, or synthesis of one or more of these types, adapted to particular conditions of program and site.

Reyner Banham identified the vernacular Parisian studio apartment as one of the principle arrangements used by the "the younger architects to develop a new architecture...." This traditional plan configuration clearly provides the typological basis for the Atelier Ozenfant, as well as its idealized predecessors, the Maison Citrohan and Maison d'Artiste (Figure 8.13). As Banham describes:

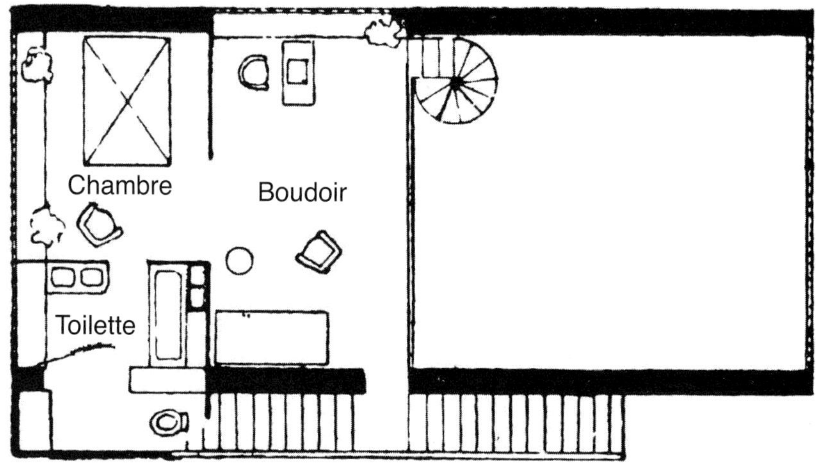

Figure 8.13. First floor plan of Maison d'Artiste. The vernacular atelier and the Neoclassical French Hotel are two distinctive domestic types specific to Paris. Particularly influential in Le Corbusier's work, the atelier found reinterpretation in the Maison Citrohan and Maison d'Artiste of 1922, shown here. Le Corbusier's fascination with type has been well documented and analyzed by historians and critics (indeed it was one of his own favorite subjects in his early writings). However, this literature has been bracketed by isolation from larger historical context. In most cases, Le Corbusier's ideal projects—his "invented types"—are presented as if plucked from the air; his work and design thinking are rarely discussed as belonging to a broader continuum of typological histories. However, a close examination of the two houses studied in this essay reveals not only their basis in Le Corbusier's idealized types, but also their connection to a more long-range typological lineage rooted in their site: traditional Parisian house plans.

> The existence of the type dates back to the previous century, when it could often be found in its pure form of a long, narrow house, its dimensions fixed by the normal dimensions of a Paris building plot. Since it was usually hard up against other buildings on either side, its windows were all on the ends, those on the more northerly end usually being amalgamated into one single expanse of glass, often two stories high and spreading from wall to wall to light the studio. The two-story studio can also be taken as a given feature, often with a storage or sleeping balcony across the back of it, reached by a spiral stair or cat ladder...[23]

Le Corbusier's transformation of this standard Parisian vernacular did not involve many steps. The overall spatial arrangement of the Maison d'Artiste, the location and size of wall openings, the partial mezzanine at the rear, even the asymmetrical disposition of openings on the façade seem to be directly influenced by the vernacular type. As applied to the Ozenfant site, the Citrohan plan prototype fuses with the Dom-ino structural model, yielding an independent structural frame that frees up the disengaged walls as "free façades." A more conventional application of this type on its corner site could have emphasized the linear studio-house layout, and the north-facing Avenue Reille frontage. This, however, would have greatly compromised the entry to (and culmination of) the Rue du Square Montsouris. Instead, rotating the east enclosing wall to align with houses on the Rue du Square Montsouris serves to pry open the typical box, resulting in a studio space greatly transformed from that of the original type (see Figure 8.9). Unlike the uni-dimensional character of the typical studio (primarily front lit with the loft to the back and two blank sides) the Ozenfant studio space becomes fully three-dimensional, lit from two fronts as well as from above by skylights. It sports two distinct lofts (the back mezzanine relating to the Avenue Reille, the front library loft relating to the Rue du Square Montsouris), each paired in plan with its own large studio window. A staged photograph of the interior (published in the *Oeuvre Complète*) reinforces the doubling of studio-type diagrams where not one, but two drafting tables stand in an "L" configuration at the center of the cubic volume.[24] Each desk faces its respective window, emphasizing the superimposition of two identical diagrams, one at right angles to the other.

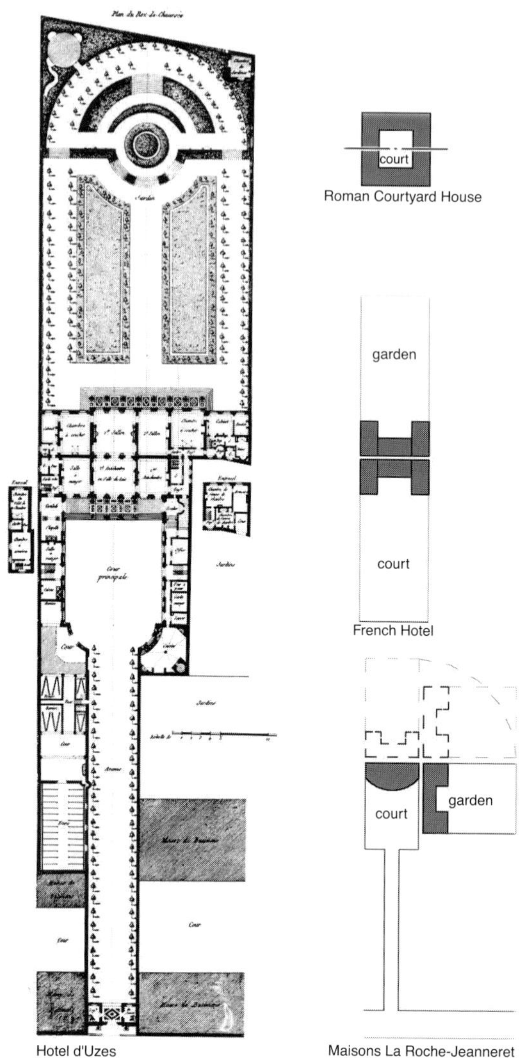

Figure 8.14. Main level plan of Hôtel d'Uzes, Claude-Nicolas Ledoux, and diagrams depicting a three-stage transformation: from typical Roman courtyard house, to French Neoclassical Hotel, to the Maisons La Roche-Jeanneret. (1) The Roman courtyard house is an altogether internalized composition; its main landscape figure—the court—is singular and interior to the plan. (2) The French Hotel plan bisects this Roman court and flips its wings to the exterior, creating two distinct house realms, each with its own exterior room: a front court and back garden. (3) The Maisons' two wings (found back-to-back in the typical French Hotel) rotate away from each other 270 degrees. The La Roche gallery, a version of a

A similar process of typological transformation and accommodation to specific site conditions can be traced for the Maisons La Roche-Jeanneret. Here, the modifications to traditional Parisian building types are a bit more complex, filtered through Le Corbusier's own prototype variations before culminating in the situated, built work. Maisons La Roche-Jeanneret present a composite of two of Le Corbusier's prototypes. M. La Roche's gallery employs the Dom-ino structural model with an adjunct wing wall in addition to the *piloti*; the residential side wing employs conventional bearing wall construction, akin to Maison Citrohan. The double height space of the major living area in the Citrohan prototype serves as the precedent for the three-story La Roche entry hall, which until very late in the design process divided the two house precincts. In final revisions, M. La Roche's dining room and bedroom shifted across this hall to the Jeanneret side, but the hall remains the grand entry to the La Roche residence.[25]

The frontal relationship of the Square du Docteur Blanche entry court to the gallery wing façade presents another instance of typological transformation by recalling the court-to-house entry sequence of a typical French Hotel plan. The Hotel, a common Parisian aristocratic house type and one prevalent in the historic Auteuil district through the nineteenth century, has a six-square plan (two rows of three rooms) fronted by an urban court and culminating in a rear garden.[26] A gate at the street gives onto an urban court—the *cour d'honneur*—which provides the foreground for the formal street façade of the house and the exterior landscape associated with the front three rooms. The rear three rooms of an Hotel plan relate to a garden at the back. The Maisons La Roche-Jeanneret exhibit an analogous set of relationships between two wings, an urban court, and a garden (Figure 8.14).[27]

Hotel's frontal wing, faces the *cour d'honneur* (here the Square du Docteur Blanche). In a somewhat perverse move, the gallery becomes the final destination rather than the entry point. The building entry at the critical joint between the two repositioned wings, and can be read either as a gap or a place of overlap. The residential wing (akin to the three rear rooms of a Hotel) rotates sideways, relating to a rear garden in section (instead of plan) since the Maisons' private *toit jardin* shifted vertically to overtake the roof of the domestic wing.

Taking full advantage of his limited building lot, Le Corbusier's *toit jardin* establishes a sectional relationship to the domestic wing directly below. From the space of this elevated garden, one occupies the tree canopy provided by the neighbor's rear gardens all around, and particularly to the west (see Figure 8.12). These same gardens also act as the house's rear garden in plan, providing light, air, and greenery by virtue of Le Corbusier's cleverly excavated second-floor, glass-lined terraces.

Tracing connections between Le Corbusier's idealized prototypes and traditional urban building typologies, and discerning how these are in turn transformed by the particular sites of built works, serves to greatly enhance an understanding of his design thinking. Far from merely implanting preconfigured, ideal types into a range of diverse site contexts (as his publication of the Four Compositions suggests) Le Corbusier's process was one of rich dialogue, interplay, and mutual influence between ideal type and specific circumstance. The absence of site information in the critical documentation of these projects makes it impossible to comprehend these works as situational—both with respect to physical location, and to historical, typological continuity. The typological site, as well as the physical site, has been suppressed by modern historiography. This is a significant omission, for at the very crux of the concept of type is the search to provide a framework for recognizing connections between works from different time periods and locations: to identify that which is essentially consistent amid superficial variations. The concept of type offers a way to think about architectural history that writers of the history of modern architecture sought specifically to deny. There is a link between the suppression of site and the suppression of typological connections over different time periods in these histories that seek to portray modern works not as developmental, but as revolutionary. Again, the emphasis rests on what is new, what is singular, and what is utterly divorced from all contexts of time or place.

THE CULTURAL SITE

The houses of the 1920s are situated within a contemporary Parisian avant-garde discourse and, in particular, within the framework of ideas extending from Le Corbusier's friendship and collaboration with the painter Amèdee Ozenfant. Together they invented the Purist aesthetic: a combination of Futurism's celebration of technology and mass-produced objects, and a particular variation on Cubism's explorations in destabilizing the traditional spatial/temporal field. This conceptual milieu reinforced Le Corbusier's fascination with the evolution of standard types and provoked his growing interest in a streamlined, machine aesthetic. It also influenced the identification and development of his "Five Points." [28]

The Purist effort in painting to deemphasize the predominance of the figure and to create greater ambiguity, transparency, overlap, and equivalence between it and a residual field, led to similar manifestations in Le Corbusier's contemporary architectural works. In this early stage of his career, his language was essentially pictorial. By rendering walls made of structural frame and infill as continuous and undifferentiated white or color-washed planes (tableaux) he created an apparent lightness and ephemerality. He was intent on abstracting constituent architectural elements to promote increasingly subtle demarcations of individual spaces and distinctions between inside and outside. He rarely simply opposed interior and exterior—whether as the threshold between rooms or between enclosed and unenclosed space. Rather, he composed his plans, like his paintings, with edges that oscillate between figure and ground. Even a distinction as important as indoors/outdoors received ambiguous definition. In the paintings, relationships between the frame and his *objet-types* give vestigial spaces a figural quality (Figure 8.15).

William J. R. Curtis provides important insight into the similar compositional strategies of Le Corbusier's Purist paintings and his architectural plans of the same period: "Remember the rectangular outline [of the painting's frame] filled with curved parts later; it is to recur in architectural plans....To compare the way in which curved partitions...have been set in the overall rectangular frame of the building, is to realize that Le Corbusier treats the plan as a sort of painting composition."[29] The "rectangular frame of the building," however, does not mark the outer boundary of the spatial composition of Le Corbusier's urban works. In fact, things get really interesting when the intense play of forms that create charged residual spaces on the interior of the building tumble out beyond the exterior walls to engage the realm of the street and surrounding context.

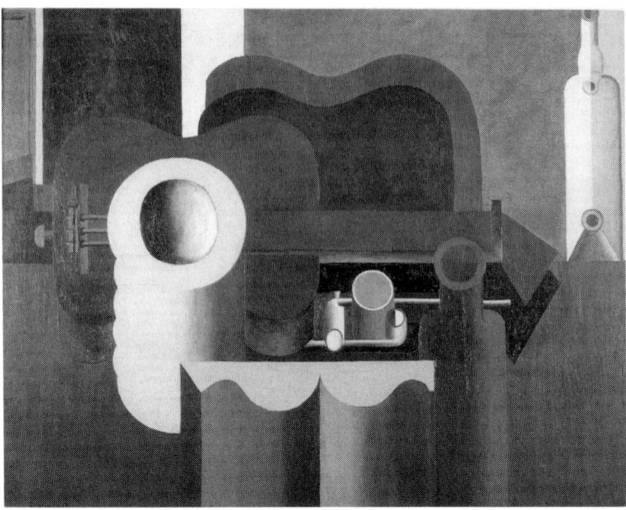

Figure 8.15. Jeanneret, *Nature morte à la pile d'assiettes*, 1920. By using the S-curve of a piano, bottle, open book, pipe, guitar (or curving wall partition), Le Corbusier insinuates the pictorial plane (or architectural space) on either side into a resonance and reciprocity impossible to achieve with a strictly orthogonal composition. His conception of modern space is not the neutral and homogenous "spatial flow" achieved by the slippage of orthogonal planes pursued in De Stijl, nor is it the even more reductive Miesian play between a grid of points and corresponding planes. Le Corbusier dismantles clear spatial oppositions, employing the play between straight and curved edges to create a series of charged residual and fragmentary spaces. There is ultimately the sense of being in or out of the overall composition, but between the two lies a series of extended and ambiguous thresholds—not a simple line (or wall) at all.

At Atelier Ozenfant, stray *objet-types* dramatically break out of the enclosing walls to engage the broader site. The exterior spiral stair in the entry court can be read as creating at least three distinct dynamic relationships between interior and exterior, between building and site. In the first, the exterior stair works in conjunction with the interior spiral stair linking the main living floor to the studio space above. The first-floor plan of the house is the most overtly figural; suggesting bottle, book, and guitar fragments (from Le Corbusier, the painter) as the origins of undulating partition walls. The only pure and complete curvilinear form within the bounds of the exterior walls, however, is the circular plan of the interior spiral stair (shown on the étage level plan drawing, see Figure 8.1). This stair begins its journey firmly lodged inside the building, hugging the east wall of the original Citrohan studio box. As this wall rotates outward—pulled by the cant of the Rue du Square Montsouris—the spiral stair appears to mobilize; it seems to spin down and out into the street space below, where it remanifests as the entry court stair. In this reading, the low enclosing wall/fence of the exterior court presents a rippling continuation of the original east studio wall, deformed and fragmented by violent dislocations but remaining firmly attached to the spiral stair in its new location. Reciprocity exists between the internal and external stair forms; they are the same figure found in different locations (both in plan and section) at the same time. Similar notions of spatial displacement and temporal simultaneity are a recurring Cubist preoccupation.[30]

In a second dynamic relationship, the spiral stair engages the larger urban surround as the figural terminus of the Rue du Square Montsouris. Walking northwest down this street, the stark, white cylindrical stair form provides a compelling reference and focal point. When nearing the end of the Rue, the spiraling sculptural element redirects the gaze vertically. This connection between a long horizontal path and a curved terminus is akin to that established between the entry lane and curved gallery façade at La Roche-Jeanneret, with one key difference: at Ozenfant, the culminating figure provides the point of entry to the house, which is promised but ultimately withheld in Auteuil.

The Atelier Ozenfant also operates as a "gate" between the monumental Avenue Reille and the smaller scale houses along the Rue du Square Montsouris. Figural elements adjacent to the site are appropriated to reinforce this reading. Here, again, the exterior spiral stair plays a prominent role. It relates to an existing building (in place since the time of the original design) situated on the opposite corner across the street. This building turns *its* corner with an opaque, sensuously cylindrical turret (Figure 8.9). The Ozenfant spiral stair and this turret together create a loosely matched pair of cylinders describing a quasi-symmetrical entry portal to the residential street beyond. Like the Ozenfant stair, much of the neighboring turret's sculptural plasticity derives from a continuous stuccoed surface. Its more traditional wall shapes the interior space of the house using conventional *poché* to define a clear boundary between inside and out. It is neither a discrete element outside the house envelope proper, nor does it partake in the decidedly modern spatial collage at play across the street. However, the purely formal correspondence between the elements is striking, given the stylistic disparity between the two buildings. In a convincing demonstration of modern architecture's ability for site responsiveness in a traditional urban neighborhood, similar basic form-types make connections despite extremely divergent time periods and stylistic language (Figures 8.16 and 8.17).

Ozenfant's double-height studio, crowned by sawtooth skylights, also exhibits Purist spatial dynamics that extend beyond the building proper. Strong reverberations between this glass-enclosed room (with

Figure 8.16

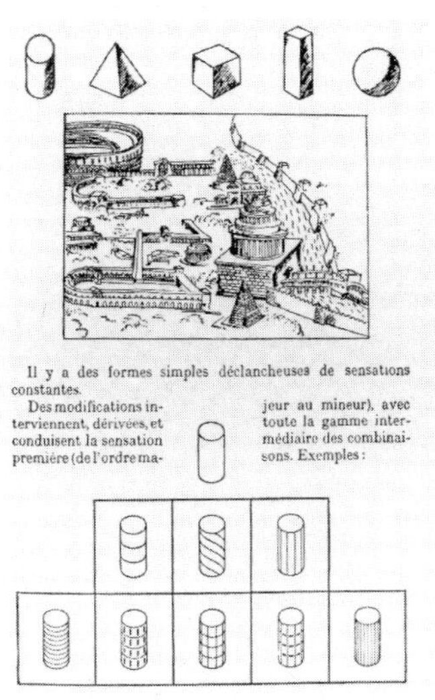

Il y a des formes simples déclancheuses de sensations constantes.

Des modifications interviennent, dérivées, et conduisent la sensation première (de l'ordre majeur au mineur), avec toute la gamme intermédiaire des combinaisons. Exemples :

Figure 8.17

Figures 8.16 and 8.17. Photograph of Atelier Ozenfant's spiral stair, and plate from *L'Esprit Nouveau* showing primary volumes, Ancient Rome and secondary articulation of cylinders. Le Corbusier's fascination with pure type-forms was apparent in all his creative efforts in this period: Purist painting, writings in *L'Esprit Nouveau*, and his early Parisian architecture. In the guise of ushering in the New Age (and closing the door on historicism), he in fact constructs a powerful link between a modernist aesthetic of pure geometrical forms and, as William Curtis describes it, the "...grand vista of Classical thought extending back through Boullée and Ledoux to Alberti and Palladio...."[31]

its rooftop projections) and the Réservoir (with its repetitive crystal towers) conjure up a large-scale urban still life composed of otherwise disparate, disjointed elements: reservoir, turret, avenue, *rue*. The tight, intense, but graceful elements of the Atelier and its site extensions bring all these pieces into synchrony, harmonizing an otherwise fragmented urban moment. In this way, specific adjacent urban elements are insinuated into Le Corbusier's Purist collage; they become part of the composition, even though they preceded it. This co-optive approach is similar to the way site elements and patterns were recognized and exploited at the Maisons La Roche-Jeanneret. There, however, the site strategy was internalized and subversive; here it is assertive and overt.

In the Auteil neighborhood of Maisons La Roche-Jeanneret, a continuous perimeter wall of houses surrounds the block to create a heavy frame for the Purist still life within. Here, the house fragments as a means to engage particular site elements. It becomes a malleable volume, to some degree inarticulate in and of itself and only completed in relation to other site features and conditions. The house alternately projects into the site (to frame a view) and recedes from it (to internalize an exterior aspect of the site, such as light, a singular tree, etc.). In the case of the gallery's balcony, a small projection affords opportunities to break through the building's outer wall and simultaneously inhabit building space and site space (in this case, the important *cour d'honneur,* where public and private space merge). The house volume undulates, inviting spatial overlap with the neighbors' gardens. The play of curvilinear walls and orthogonal frame in this project does not occur primarily within the bounds of the house as a contained, cubic volume as with most of the Purist houses (Maison Cook or Villa Stein, for example). Indeed, in this house the great majority of interior partitions are not curved but orthogonal. It is the picturesque movement and shifting of the exterior walls themselves that play against the orthogonal frame of the block and the street grid generally (see Figure 8.7).

Most notably, the gallery of M. La Roche, designed to house his growing collection of paintings by Bracque, Picasso, Ozenfant, and Le Corbusier (among others), has a curvilinear form that extends the building's orthogonal envelope outward to engage the site. This element was initially conceived as a grade level terminus to the strongly axial approach along the entry lane.[32] By lifting the gallery up on *piloti*, Le Corbusier offers glimpses of borrowed greenery beyond (underneath the structure), creating the illusion of infinite extension on a site that is actually very compact. This important change also makes the white convex curve of the gallery visible from the beginning of the Rue du Docteur Blanche approach. Had the two-story gallery remained on grade, one's prospect along the lane (which gradually slopes down 6 feet to the house) might have skimmed over its roof. This form would have appeared as gradually rising from the ground into view as one neared the building, rather than providing a constant visual reference from the entrance to the block's interior. Also, had no distant view been provided, the perceptual effects of the gallery's mathematically precise proportions would have been greatly altered. Calibrated to the slight topographic variation of the ground, the skillfully placed gallery appears as the ultimate and hierarchic destination. In this way, the Purist composition of the Maisons extends beyond the building's envelope to engage the entire block in a play of ambiguous figures and charged fields.

A SEARCH FOR NEW HISTORIES

> *Action of the work* (architecture, statue, or painting) on its surroundings: vibrations, cries or shouts (such as originate from the Parthenon on the Acropolis in Athens), arrows darting away like rays, as if springing from an explosion; the near or distant site is shaken by them, touched, wounded, dominated, or caressed. *Reaction of the setting:* the walls of the room, its dimensions, the public square with the various weights of its façades, the expanses or the slopes of the landscape even to the bare horizons of the plain or the sharp outlines of the mountains—the whole environment brings its weight to bear on the place where there is a work of art, the sign of man's will, and imposes on it its deep spaces or projections, its hard or soft densities, its violences or its softnesses. A phenomenon of concordance takes place, as exact as mathematics, a true manifestation of plastic acoustics...."[33]
>
> **Le Corbusier, "Ineffable Space"**

The preceding passage from "Ineffable Space" reveals that Le Corbusier's understanding of the formative role of site is at odds with the way architectural historiography has cast his work. The reciprocity he describes—the "concordance" resulting from a mutual influence of work and site—succinctly characterizes his siting of Atelier Ozenfant and the Maisons La Roche-Jeanneret. The many reverberations between these works and their settings are by no means accidental. Rather, they go to the heart of his view of the role of art in the world. Still, even as Le Corbusier acknowledges the importance of site to the creation of a work of art, his writings construe this relation hierarchically: the "action of the work" assumes primacy over the "reaction of the setting."

Nonetheless, the design of these houses establishes a balance between the unique work of art and its complex ground—a concordance between ideal and real, between a new architectural language and established use patterns and urban structure. Atelier Ozenfant and Maisons La Roche-Jeanneret exemplify the extraordinary subtlety and skill with which Le Corbusier sited many of his Purist villas. As such, they offer relevant models for architects who grapple with similar dilemmas today: how to reinforce continuity in dense urban contexts without resorting to ersatz contextualism, how to explore new architectural languages and new material assemblies without objectifying buildings and isolating them from their larger ground. The examples shown here, among others, provide an important reminder for contemporary architectural practice: the simple idea that a building is located in only one spot in the world—and that this site should matter. Disassociating buildings from the particulars of their sites produces architecture that is universal only in the shallowest and most alienating sense. Le Corbusier recognized the importance of the dialectic between work and setting and of a balance between specific and universal.

Few cities or buildings are more thoroughly documented than Paris and the works of Le Corbusier. Maps and aerial photographs of the sectors of Paris where Le Corbusier's projects are located are as readily available as are the ubiquitous, published versions of the building plans, sections, and elevations. Yet, no documentation exists of this architect's work as it relates to its urban site. This simple, yet huge omission in the otherwise endless sea of information and speculation on Le Corbusier is astonishing. It demonstrates the pernicious obstinacy of a narrow framing of subject matter, which goes hand in hand with the modern concept of categorization. Categorization tends to distinguish and isolate, rather than relate. The "phenomenon of concordance" referred to by Le Corbusier occurs in the interstices between building plan and city map. It is here that the story of the "action of the work" on its surround is recorded, and where the "environment brings its weight to bear." Severing this connection between work and site when documenting buildings ultimately serves to produce the impression that a connection does not exist—that the site does not matter.

Several important questions emerge from the realization that the history of these houses (and of perhaps most works of modern architecture) has been incomplete. Why, culturally, would we suppress site? How does this type of history serve ideological purposes? To what extent does it make architectural works appear simpler, more teachable? Must the idea of typology necessarily be antagonistic to site? And also: What have been the consequences of the suppression of site for architectural theory and practice?

History often replaces its own subject matter; it begins as a commentary on something more tangible (in this case, the built architectural work) and quickly becomes the prevailing referent. Subsequent criticism often tends to refer more to preceding histories than to the original objects of historical attention. Thus critical omissions quickly become institutionalized and perennial. Some of the most cogent attacks on modern architecture and its legacies would perhaps have been more accurately leveled against the historic interpretation of works than on the works themselves. In many ways, such critiques have served only to further concretize the erroneous notion that all modern architects were unconcerned with site, and that modernism itself is antagonistic to the concept of site.

Thankfully, material evidence exists in the world—the projects themselves—that pleads further study, documentation, and theorization. Such an effort requires new ways of writing history. New, more precise, working definitions of site terms need to be established.[34] The recognition of identifiable and repeatable site typologies and strategies needs to be made. A methodology of architectural analysis, akin to the one briefly modeled here, must be developed to include site issues such as topography, surrounding built fabric, relative scale, and threshold conditions, among many others.[35] Above all, certain false assumptions must be abandoned: that modern architecture is inextricably linked to a modernist conception of the city (and that it is incompatible with traditional urban form); that what counts as modern is defined by an irreconcilable break from the history of forms and ideas preceding it; that the manifestation of real projects in the world—and the departure from the ideal this manifestation necessitates—results in something lesser, more base. These myths create the context for site suppression and should at the very least be reconsidered. In doing so here, I intend to challenge architectural history to account for what it has previously missed.

Notes

1. Charles-Édouard Jeanneret, *Urbanisme*, cited in Reyner Banham, *Theory and Design in the First Machine Age* (New York: Praeger, 1960), 253.
2. Banham, *Theory and Design in the First Machine Age,* 253.
3. For example, the first point of the De Stijl "Manifesto I" states, "There is an old and new consciousness of the age. The old one is directed toward the individual. The new one is directed towards the universal," p. 39. For more on the repeated association of universality and Modernism, see Ulrich Conrads, *Programs and Manifestoes on 20th-Century Architecture* (Cambridge: The MIT Press, 1970).
4. There are notable exceptions. William J. R. Curtis, in particular, offers some of the most insightful and comprehensive historical analysis of Le Corbusier's work of which I am aware, and often refers to site conditions in describing and analyzing the projects in his *Le Corbusier: Ideas and Forms* (London: Phaidon Press Limited, 1986). I am specifically indebted to this author for his work on the Maisons La Roche-Jeanneret and Atelier Ozenfant. Tim Benton's *The Villas of Le Corbusier 1920–1930* (New Haven and London: Yale University Press, 1987) is an invaluable resource for anyone interested in the buildings of Le Corbusier's Purist Period. This book exhaustively records how interactions between the architect and his clients and builders exerted influence on the designs, providing information on how and why certain sites were selected and acquired. I have been greatly inspired by Colin Rowe's "La Tourette" in his *The Mathematics of the Ideal Villa and Other Essays* (Cambridge and London: MIT Press, 1976), 185–201; and Caroline Constant's "From the Virgilian Dream to Chandigarh: Le Corbusier and the Modern Landscape," in *Denatured Visions: Landscape and Culture in the Twentieth Century* (New York: Museum of Modern Art, 1991), 79–93.
5. Certainly Le Corbusier frequently discussed the relationship of architecture to nature and the landscape in broad terms—"l'air, lumiere, verdure..." He often referred to solar orientation and significant views in design sketches

and written commentary on his work even during the early, Purist phase of his career. But these references were typically to relatively abstract, large-scale site conditions, rather than specific and variable site elements. In the latter case, it would appear from documentation that he sought to obscure rather than to elaborate.

6. Notably the Maison Dom-ino (1914–1915), Maison Monol (1919), Maison Citrohan (1921–1922), Une Ville Contemporaine pour 3 Millions d'Habitants (1922), and the Plan Voisin (1925), among others.
7. For detailed analysis on Le Corbusier's use of staged and edited photography to achieve his propagandistic ends, see Beatriz Colomina's "Le Corbusier and Photography," *Assemblage* 4 (1987): 12. See also Kenneth Frampton's *Le Corbusier* (London: Thames & Hudson, 2001), 23.
8. Le Corbusier, *Villa Savoye and Other Buildings and Projects, 1929–1930* (New York and London: Garland Publishing, Inc.; and Paris: Fondation Le Corbusier, 1982).
9. See Carol Burns' identification of the "cleared site" in "On Site: Architectural Preoccupations," in *Drawing/Building/Text*, ed. Andrea Kahn (New York: Princeton Architectural Press, 1991), 149–153.
10. Juhani Pallasmaa, "Hapticity and Time: Notes on Fragile Architecture," *Architectural Record* (May 2000): 79.
11. Bernard Rudofsky, in his *Architecture without Architects: A Short Introduction to Non-Pedigreed Architecture* (Garden City, New York: Doubleday & Company, Inc., 1964)—along with the associated Museum of Modern Art exhibit of 1964–1965—was perhaps the first to call the architectural establishment's attention to previously unheralded vernacular traditions.
12. Sigfried Giedion, *Space, Time and Architecture*, cited in William Curtis, "Le Corbusier: The Evolution of His Architectural Language and Its Crystallization in the Villa Savoye in Poissy," in *The Open University, Arts, A Third Level Course: History of Architecture and Design 1890–1939, Units 17–18*, (London: Open University Press, 1976), 10.
13. See Folio 2, "Poissy," of the Carte des Chasses du Roi (executed between 1764 and 1807) for a representation of the site's "original" wooded state—a portion of a large forest in the terrain west of Paris and designated as the king's hunting grounds. Aerial photographs taken sporadically during World War II, and on a regular basis (every five years) beginning in 1949, are available through France's Institut Géographique National (IGN). A series of aerials of Poissy reveal the Savoye site in 1923 to be a cleared agricultural field/meadow; in 1936, the Villa Savoye appears post-construction, with saplings planted in a grid around it; by 1949, the house sits in a "clearing" amid a maturing but still clearly gridded grove.
14. John Brinckerhoff Jackson, "Concluding with Landscapes," in his *Discovering the Vernacular Landscape* (New Haven: Yale University Press, 1984), 152.
15. William Curtis describes the process succinctly: "...[by] sublimating practical concerns to a level of a sort of analogue of universal order...He now aspires to a supposedly universal grammar of design, above place and time." Curtis, *Le Corbusier: Ideas and Forms*, 53.

16. The Réservoir, over a hundred years old and clearly evident in aerial photographs taken during the 1920s, collects the waters of the Vanne, Loing, and Lunain rivers. The Hôpital, whose grounds abut the rear property line of the house to the south, is relatively new, having replaced a similarly scaled military complex existing at the time of the Atelier's design and construction. For more information on these monuments, as well as the Parc de Montsouris, see Michel Poisson, *Paris: Buildings and Monuments* (New York: Harry N. Abrams, Inc., 1999).
17. Fondation Le Corbusier document #31810; a letter to "Monsieur Jeanneret, Architecte" from "Le Chef de Bataillon Cavier/Chef du Genie de Paris (Sud)," dated April 3, 1924; and accompanying sketch sections offer a glimpse of the struggles between Jeanneret and the prevailing city and military authorities on the allowable construction along the property line of the military complex immediately to the south of the Ozenfant site. These resulted in an exceedingly awkward rear wall to the house that partially retains earth and creates a drainage ditch against the building. By trespassing onto what once were military, now hospital, grounds to reach the back of the house, one discovers elevated terrain, thick with trees and undergrowth, but almost no indication of the building's rear elevation. Low to the ground and shrouded by greenery, it is almost impossible to discern the house. See Le Corbusier, *Early Buildings and Projects, 1912–1923* (New York and London: Garland Publishing, Inc.; and Paris: Fondation Le Corbusier, 1982), 453.
18. In *Le Corbusier: Ideas and Forms*, 57, Curtis notes that "The Ozenfant Studio was a small fragment of Le Corbusier's machine-age dream…tubular railings and metal companion ladders evoked the era of steam power."
19. The built work was preceded by many alternate schemes involving various lot configurations and alternative clients, but all located in the same block. For the tortuous and fascinating history of site selection and acquisition, as well as client recruitment, that ultimately lead to the double residence for La Roche and Jeanneret/Raaf, see Benton's *The Villas of Le Corbusier, 1920–1930*, 45–57.
20. See Benton, *The Villas of Le Corbusier, 1920–1930*, 60–61. See also Curtis, *Le Corbusier: Ideas and Forms*, 72.
21. Fondation Le Corbusier document #15199 is an intriguing sketch of a preliminary scheme in its block context with neighbors' gardens labeled all along the entry lane: "jardin, jardin, jardin." This drawing makes perfectly clear that Jeanneret conceived these gardens as part of the Maisons site, part of its appropriated, encumbered terrain. See Le Corbusier, *Early Buildings and Projects, 1912–1923*, 527.
22. Amèdee Ozenfant and Charles-Édouard Jeanneret, *Aprés le Cubisme,* cited in Reyner Banham, "Paris: The World of Art and Le Corbusier," in his *Theory and Design in the First Machine Age*, 210.
23. Banham, *Theory and Design in the First Machine Age*, 217.
24. See Le Corbusier, *Early Buildings and Projects, 1912–1923,* 430.
25. See Benton, *The Villas of Le Corbusier, 1920–1930*, 60.
26. My limited knowledge of the Neoclassical French Hotel plan is entirely indebted to Michael Dennis's *Court & Garden: From the French Hotel to the City of Modern Architecture* (Cambridge and London: MIT Press, 1986),

and also to lengthy (and wonderful) phone conversations with Robin Dripps, Professor of Architecture at the University of Virginia.

27. There is evidence in the drawing archive that there was an early U-shaped scheme creating a courtyard labeled alternately *cour*, *carrefour*, and "Place de Docteur Blanche," that involved a third house sited to the east of a more fully articulated central court. See Le Corbusier, *Early Buildings and Projects, 1912–1923*, 478–480, 484, 486, 493–494.
28. See Banham, *Theory and Design in the First Machine Age*, 202–213 for an extended account of Purism's intellectual and cultural lineage.
29. William Curtis, "Le Corbusier: The Evolution of His Architectural Language and Its Crystallization in the Villa Savoye in Poissy," 20.
30. For an explicit example, see Marcel Duchamp's painting *Nude Descending a Staircase* (1912).
31. Curtis, *Le Corbusier: Ideas and Forms*, 53.
32. See Benton, *The Villas of Le Corbusier, 1920–1930*, 60–61.
33. Le Corbusier, "L'Espace Indicible," reprinted in *Architecture Culture 1943–1968: A Documentary Anthology* (New York: Rizzoli, 1993), 66.
34. For an excellent beginning, see Carol Burns, "On Site: Architectural Preoccupations," 146.
35. David Leatherbarrow exemplifies one version of this type of analysis in *Uncommon Ground: Architecture, Technology, and Topography* (Cambridge: MIT Press, 2000).

9

Neighborhoods Apart: Site/Non-Sight and Suburban Apartments

Paul Mitchell Hess

INTRODUCTION

Notions that suburbs have little spatial pattern or are composed solely of single-family housing tend to overwhelm our ability to see particular suburbs in all their cultural, social, and physical complexity. Indeed, ideas of suburbia or of the suburbs refer to a particularly generic spatial and temporal domain that is difficult to connect to conventional notions of site. Individual suburbs are real physical and historical places, but images and ideas of suburbia tend to be without place or time, and thus without site. The term *suburbia* covers all suburbs, as if they have all the same qualities and can substitute for each other across urban areas and historical periods. There is no contrasting concept of *urbia* as a generic description of city centers.[1] It is the suburbs that are "placeless," with a "geography of nowhere."[2] Single-family subdivisions, shopping centers, office parks, and freeways float in a dimensionless landscape of "sprawl." They are generic elements in a disorganized, chaotic, and unbounded landscape.[3]

Opposed to the vastness of sprawl, the idea of suburbia is also tied to a very local spatial domain, to a particular type of site: the detached house in its yard. Historians identify both house ownership and low development densities as central aspects of the American "suburban dream."[4] People consistently identify suburbs as a place for raising children and characterize suburbs as being made up of single, detached houses. The linkage of these concepts is so pronounced that, in the United States, the freestanding, single-unit house is almost always referred to as a home. A particular building type is thus conflated with a setting of domesticity and nurturing. The implication is, of course, that to live in a structure other than a freestanding house is in some sense to be homeless. Although increasingly anachronistic in terms of both family structure and (sub)urban development patterns, these images continue to persist.

In large part we remain sightless about suburban landscapes. Examining their development and planning enables us to see the complexity of suburban areas and how our notions of site depend on our frame of reference. This chapter focuses on three sites in the Puget Sound region of Washington State to illuminate the unseen spatial and cultural logics of suburban development. These Seattle-area sites are interesting because they contradict conventional notions of suburban sites and settings by containing large concentrations of apartments. Far from being chaotic and disorganized, these postwar places are highly planned, regulated, and engineered. Far from being without site, they contain multiple and overlapping sites. Far from being anomalous, they are common and integral parts of the suburban and postsuburban landscape. Although this essay is focused on Seattle, apartments and attached housing of all types constitute an important part of the postwar suburban landscape across the United States, and studying these areas has wider implications for how we see and don't see suburban landscapes more generally.[5] This chapter argues that placing multifamily housing outside or toward the periphery of our vision of suburbia has implications not just for how we see suburbs, but for how we plan and build them.

PUGET SOUND APARTMENT CONCENTRATIONS

The central Puget Sound region of Washington State has patterns of overall growth and suburbanization similar to that of many other metropolitan areas in the West and Sunbelt. Between 1960 and 2000, the population of the urbanized area containing the central cities of Seattle, Tacoma, and Everett has grown from about 1.1 million to 2.7

million people.[6] Most of this growth has been in the suburbs: 35 percent of the urbanized population lived outside the central cities in 1960; by 2000, even with some central city annexation, 69 percent lived in a vast urbanized region covering more than 700 square miles.

The growth of multifamily housing in the region, including both stacked apartments and condominium units and side-by-side units ("plexes" and "townhomes"), has similarly followed national trends. In 1960, attached units made up less than 10 percent of the housing stock in the urbanized area outside the central cities. In 2000, attached units accounted for 34 percent of the suburban housing stock and contained more than a quarter of the suburban population. This multifamily housing is not uniformly dispersed throughout the region; it is located in about one hundred small concentrations averaging less than 400 acres in area.[7]

In aggregate, the total area of these apartment concentrations make up only 8 percent of the land area of the suburban region, but contain 20 percent of its population. Dismissed as part of sprawl, the resulting gross population densities exceed those found in all but a few neighborhoods in central Seattle. Like these older Seattle neighborhoods, most apartment concentrations contain neighborhood retail stores and civic facilities within a short, walkable distance of their residential areas. Ten to thirty percent of their population is made up of people who do not identify themselves as white, making them as ethnically diverse as neighboring cities. Together, these characteristics—medium housing densities, mixed land uses, and diverse populations—reflect conventional images of urban, not suburban, neighborhoods.

SUBURBAN MAPPINGS, MISSING SITES

Multifamily housing sites are missing from most conceptions of suburban landscapes partly because conventional ways of measuring and understanding urbanized areas have obscured their identification. The high densities of apartment concentrations relative to surrounding areas of detached houses, for instance, are not captured by the common mapping tools used by planners and academics. Census tracts, forecast analysis zones (FAZs), and transportation analysis zones (TAZs)—standard geographic units of analysis used for mapping—are simply too large to capture the spatial patterning of suburban development. Although social scientists often treat and even refer to census tracts as neighborhoods, suburban tracts surrounding Seattle average almost 4 square miles in area—a much larger territory than that usually associated with walkable urban neighborhoods. At this scale, maps of the region show few tracts outside the cores of the old, central cities with residential densities higher than ten people per acre, but this is only one picture.

Remapping the urbanized area using much smaller geographic units of analysis—census blocks—shows that small spots of higher density appear scattered across both urban and suburban areas. The number of people living in areas above ten people per acre increases two and a half times from 520,00 using tracts to 1,246,00 using census blocks.

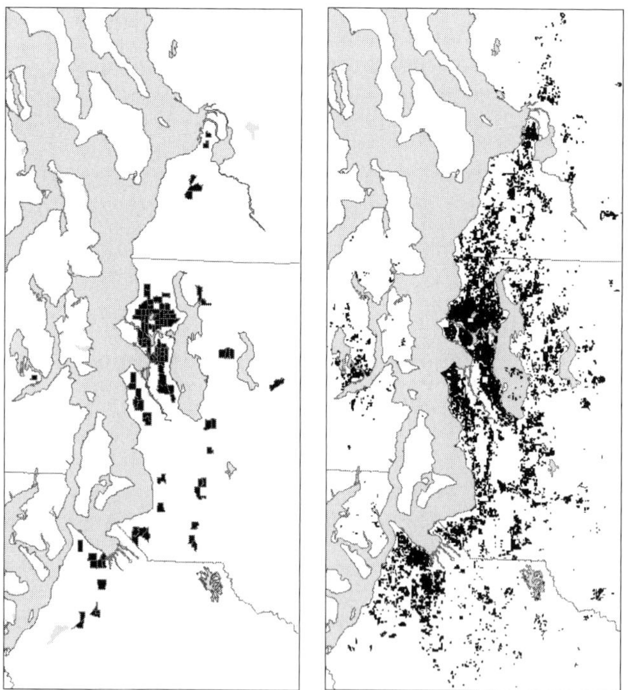

Figure 9.1. Census tracts (left) and blocks (right) with more than 10 persons per acre in the Puget Sound region.

These differences result from the ways the patterns of urban and suburban development interact with the mode of measurement and analysis. This occurs in at least two important ways. First, tract boundaries generally occur along large roadways that also tend to run through the middle of apartment concentrations. Thus, census geography *systematically* breaks up areas of higher-density housing into several tracts. Second, because tracts are large compared to suburban concentrations of apartments, they also contain large areas of other uses, potentially including low-density housing, commercial areas, and undeveloped land. When averaged together, these uses result in very low densities. In combination, apartment concentrations as a regular recurring part of suburban landscapes literally disappear from maps.[8]

Neither mapped pattern is inherently correct. Rather, comparing these mappings leads to new questions and understandings. Undercutting categorical statements about one area being more or less dense than another, differences in the spatial patterning of density become more evident. In more central areas, adjoining urban blocks tend to be similar in density, thus maintaining consistent densities across large areas. This translates as higher-density census tracts. In suburban areas, large differences in density occur between blocks and within the same census tract. In this limited respect, received ideas of the heterogeneity of the city and the homogeneity of the suburbs are reversed: measured using particular units of analysis at particular scales, suburban development is more heterogeneous than urban development. It is only when development is measured within the block, at the parcel level, that densities and other characteristics of development are obviously more varied in older, more central urban areas.

The key point is that the location of boundaries, the size of spatial units of measurements, and the methods of measurement affect the types of patterns that are understood. Patterns are not independent from the tools we use to measure them.[9] When census tracts are assumed to capture the most salient difference between urban and suburban residential densities, the resulting maps conform to and reinforce common images of the nature of suburbs and their almost exclusive association with detached houses. In so doing, these maps allow the images to go unquestioned.

APARTMENT CONCENTRATIONS AS SITES: JUANITA, CROSSROADS, AND KENT EAST HILL

Looking at apartment concentrations as sites, we see that they, too, have boundaries. These boundaries may not be precisely defined on the ground, but how we mentally map them strongly affects how we see these places. The areas of Crossroads in Bellevue, Juanita in Kirkland, and East Hill in Kent are three of the largest and most mature examples of compact multifamily development in the suburban cities surrounding Seattle.[10] Treating apartment concentrations as the locus of neighborhoods highlights them as an integral part of postwar development. As mature examples, these places demonstrate many of the characteristics rapidly developing, but not yet fully present, in many

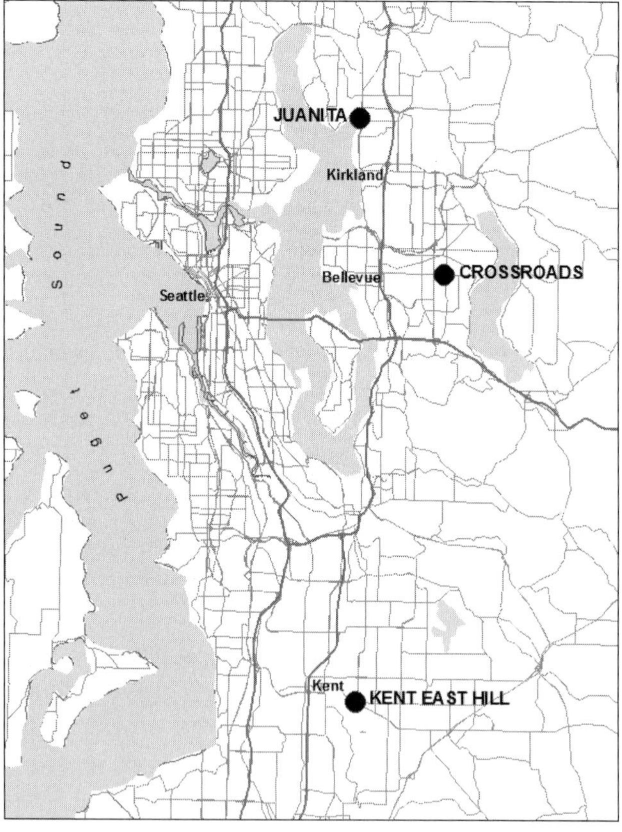

Figure 9.2. Location map.

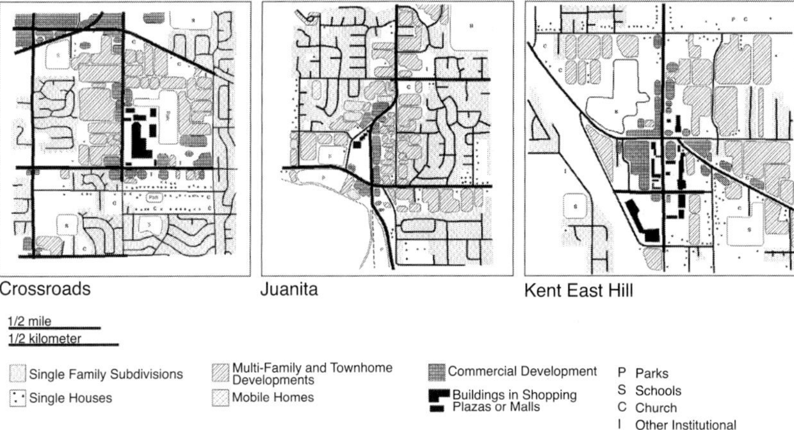

Figure 9.3. Land use patterns.

of the younger, often more anonymous multifamily areas found throughout the region.

Juanita, Crossroads, and Kent East Hill are substantial places presenting a similar combination and arrangement of land uses at odds with common images of suburban residential landscapes. Within a relatively compact area of about one square mile, the areas have three concentric rings of development with three different primary land uses: commercial, multifamily, and single family. At the center of each lies a retail area providing basic services such as supermarkets, drugstores, dry cleaners, video stores, banks, barbershops, hair salons, restaurants, and a variety of other small shops. The commercial centers vary greatly in size and configuration from a small cluster of about 30 stores in Juanita to a string of shopping plazas and commercial strips with over 110 stores in Kent East Hill.[11]

Located in a band around each retail area, multifamily housing dominates land use. Juanita contains over 2200 multifamily housing units. Crossroads and Kent East Hill each contain over 3400. In all three cases, this housing stands within a half mile from the center of their respective retail areas. Gross population densities within this area range from twelve to thirteen people per acre, similar to those found in the older streetcar-era neighborhoods in the region.[12]

In Crossroads and Juanita the ring of multifamily housing is surrounded by a further ring of detached houses. In Kent East Hill, the third ring of development consists of small farms, large-lot houses typical of the suburban–rural fringe, and a few small single-family subdivisions. Institutional and community facilities such as parks, churches, fire stations, and schools, can be found anywhere in these three zones, with elementary schools located within areas of detached housing.

This arrangement, a retail center surrounded by two rings of medium- and lower-density residential land uses, creates neighborhoods providing a range of daily services, and the numbers of apartments establish a population dense and large enough to support these services. Total populations in Juanita, Crossroads, and Kent East Hill exceed 5300, 7000, and 7300 people respectively. These aggregations of people and housing units situated close to daily convenience services are typically associated with more urban, prewar neighborhoods. Juanita, Crossroads, and Kent East Hill, however, resemble many others apartment concentrations in the suburban areas of the Puget Sound. They must be seen, therefore, as a common type of site, a part of, and not anomalous to, suburban development.

SITE SEQUENCING

These types of sites emerged, not as separate or distinct areas, but as part of the general suburbanization of the region dating to the late 1950s and early 1960s. Juanita began as a park and resort area on Lake Washington with a small amount of retail located at a main intersection by 1960. As was common in the pre–World War II period, some single-family development occurred with separate individual and institutional actors subdividing land and building houses over a number of years. By 1965, though, Juanita began to take on its present pattern. A small shopping center was built north of the main intersection, and subdivisions were constructed in a ring of land located at the edges of the area, away from the new commercial development. By this time, housing construction took place along with land subdivision, with one builder constructing dozens or scores of houses. The remainder of the 1960s saw continued small-scale commercial development in the center, and the undeveloped land between the commercial area and the outer ring of single-family housing began to be filled in with multifamily housing. The amount of development increased after 1970 and was mostly complete by 1980.

In Crossroads, the development sequence was similar, but the pace of infill more rapid and the scale larger. The origins of Crossroads are closely connected to one of the region's first large-scale housing subdivisions, Lake Hills, located near the city of Bellevue.[13] By the late 1950s, Lake Hills consisted of over 3000 houses on new curvilinear streets to the south and east of Crossroads. By 1960, the discontinuous road network along the public land survey section lines was completed to create the crossroads that gave the area its name. At this time the subdivision's developer established the modest beginnings of the shopping mall, and the first apartment complex was also constructed. By 1970, the formerly outdoor mall had been enlarged and enclosed and large areas of multifamily housing were established, with most complexes in place by 1980.

In Kent East Hill, the process skipped the phase of single-family subdivision, going directly from a rural landscape to an area of relatively dense commercial and apartment development. Located on a plateau above the nineteenth-century agricultural town of Kent, the East Hill area was in use as either pastureland or orchards before urban development. By 1960, as is common in suburban fringe areas, a few single-family subdivisions were established with a dozen or so new lots accessed by straight cul-de-sac streets built directly from main service roads. These lots were filled with owner-built houses over the course of several decades. In contrast, retail and multifamily development proceeded rapidly, starting just before 1960 and continuing apace through the 1970s, 1980s, and 1990s.

In all three cases, commercial and residential development is closely linked and mutually supporting. The closest spatial link exists between multifamily development and retail areas. In all cases, multifamily housing was developed immediately adjoining retail uses. Single-family houses, where they exist, are placed behind multifamily development and away from retail uses. Generally, these patterns were established first with single-family housing, then with retail services, and last with multifamily housing. Thus displaying a common underlying logic, the separate types of development within the sites are comparably patterned and sequenced both spatially and temporally.

DEVELOPMENT AND DIVISION

A close correspondence to historic land ownership and division illustrates the fundamental social logic of this land use arrangement. During most of the first half of the century, lot patterns were fluid as individual landowners speculated in the sparsely settled land at the outer fringe of the region's few cities. Parcels were subdivided, aggregated, and resubdivided in new patterns of paper plats that legally established streets, lots, and blocks, but were often never developed and had little actual impact on the land. By the 1920s, average lots size ranged from 10 to 30 acres in the three areas, certainly large by urban standards, but small considering that substantial development did not occur until decades later. In contrast, very large, section-sized lots owned by railroad and lumber companies, cities, King County, or Washington State were located just outside of the areas later developed with apartments and stores.

In the postwar period, these sites were attractive to vertically integrated companies seeking to mass produce entire "communities" with economies of scale, which could not be achieved on small, scattered sites.[14] In Crossroads, for example, the company that developed the Lake Hills subdivision acquired several square miles of contiguous land. In Juanita, where the land was already more finely divided when postwar development took place, single-family subdivisions took place on smaller lots than in Crossroads, but followed the same pattern with subdivisions occurring on the largest lots, located furthest from existing roadways. The relatively small amount of detached housing in Kent East Hill is also partly explained by older lot patterns. With truck farms serving the Seattle market, land in the East Hill area was dedicated to agricultural use and was more finely divided than either Juanita or Crossroads. In addition to its longer distance from the region's core city, these lots were less suitable for the large-scale single-family development practices of the early postwar period.

Multifamily development did not strongly reshape land division patterns. Rather, such development occurred on lots that already existed before World War II or on simple divisions or aggregations of these lots. The largest multifamily complexes developed on lots almost 20 acres in area, with average sizes more in the range of 3 to 4 acres. The size of these lots fits into a gradient of predevelopment lots that corresponds to current land uses. The smallest lots found along existing roadways were eventually dedicated to retail and commercial uses. The largest lots, the locus for single-family development, were located furthest from existing roadways. The medium-sized lots, located in between, were used, with little modification, for apartment development.

The temporal sequencing of single-family, retail, and apartment development, the spatial arrangement of these uses relative to each other, and they way that these patterns fit with existing land division patterns begins to tell the story of how integral apartment areas are to the production of postwar suburban landscapes. Juanita and Crossroads started as neighborhood commercial centers serving an existing market of newly established single-family subdivisions. Commercial uses were located on main roads where accessibility was greatest. The development of large, protected subdivisions took place on large lots located away from these roadways. Multifamily complexes were built concurrently with commercial development, but occurred on less accessible medium-sized lots that were seen as too small and too close to commercial uses for single-family housing. In Kent East Hill large lots suitable for postwar subdivisions did not exist, but apartment development was nevertheless relegated to an area around a growing commercial center. In all three areas, multifamily zones provided a larger market for the retail stores and acted as a buffer between single-family subdivisions and commercial development. These areas of higher-density housing do much more than contradict the image of low-density, single-family suburbia; they act as a shield that actually helps create the protected zones of detached housing so central to the image.

APARTMENTS APART

Apartment areas were integral to the production of postwar suburban landscapes, but they were rarely treated as integral parts of neighborhoods. Instead, each complex was conceived as an independent site with minimal connections to surrounding development. Their design reinforced their treatment as compounds, and the resulting inward-oriented environments remain unknown to anyone other than their residents and the people who service or visit them.[15]

There are several basic configurations of suburban multifamily housing in the United States, with a basic division between side-by-side plex-units (or townhomes) and stacked apartments (including condominiums). However, they share many characteristics and can be seen as generic "housing products." Townhomes are one- or two-story units attached in rows with individual ground-level entrances. Garden apartments, the most common form of suburban multifamily housing, are typically three stories tall with walk-up units. Stair entrances located at several points along buildings each provide entry to six units, two per stair landing. Through-units, spanning the full depth of the building, occur in both types. Living rooms and other internal formal spaces are placed away from parking lots and sometimes overlook shared lawns at the "back" of the buildings. In Juanita, Crossroads, and Kent East Hill, some complexes have up to 400 units, and housing densities range from about 10 units per net acre in the lowest-density townhome developments, to more than 35 units per acre in some garden apartment complexes. Average net densities are about 20 units per acre.[16]

Complexes have private parking and driveway systems that penetrate deep into the interior of the very large blocks on which suburban multifamily housing tends to be located. In contrast to single-family subdivisions, where gateways mark entrances and legally public streets are treated as a private realm, these private systems can feel anonymous

Figure 9.4. Garden apartment entrances off a parking lot.

and public because meeting unrecognized people is a common occurrence in large complexes. Nevertheless, driveways do not connect between complexes and, configured as either loops or as a main feeder road with branching cul-de-sacs, all traffic enters and exits complexes at one, or at most two, points along public streets. In large developments these public–private connections may be busy enough to warrant their own traffic signals. Although they rarely have sidewalks, these entrances are used by pedestrians as well as vehicles.

Little apparent relationship exists between building sites, building types, or the type of driveway and parking systems used. Buildings, driveway systems, and shared open spaces each take up, roughly, one-third of lot areas. Small apartment buildings seem to be strewn haphazardly across the site. Fences typically mark lot lines, although different developments with people of similar socioeconomic status may be open to each other. Otherwise, design decisions seem to bear no relationship to the conditions of adjoining parcels. One suspects that apartments were designed by people who saw a property diagram but never visited the site or considered its context. Rather than pooling green spaces, units in one development overlook the parking areas of the adjoining development. Units next to parks orient toward small internal spaces with parking lots placed along the park.

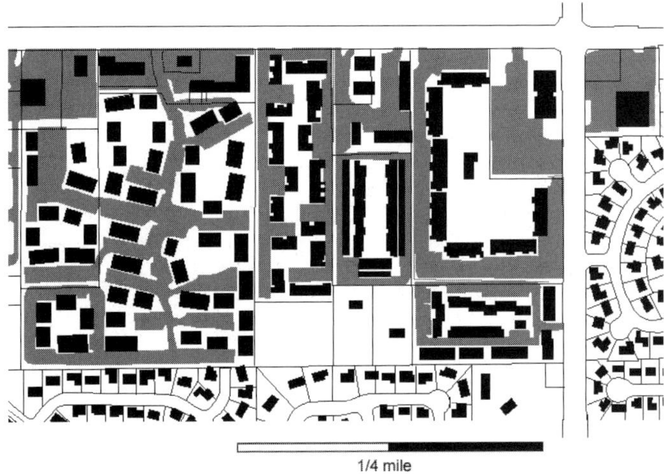

Figure 9.5. Site layouts with parking (gray), buildings (black), and open space (white) for an area of garden apartments and townhouses in Crossroads.

APARTMENTS APART *AND* A PART

The treatment of multifamily complexes as independent sites with little connection or regard to surrounding development reinforces a stereotypical image of sprawl as disorganized and disconnected, in that complexes are treated as abstract development modules plugged into public street systems with no indication of any kind of area planning. However, the strict arrangement of land uses, especially in Juanita and Crossroads, into retail, medium-density multifamily, and low-density single-family zones is just too neat and too similar to zoning principals and twentieth-century neighborhood planning models to accept this interpretation. Ideas based in town planning must be seen as guiding the design and development of these places, working in conjunction with land division patterns and development practices. In combination, these reflected prevailing cultural attitudes about what constitutes appropriate housing environments for families.

The development of zoning as a legal and standard planning tool, for instance, was closely tied to both suburbanization and protecting single-family areas from other uses.[17] The landmark 1922 Supreme Court decision establishing the constitutionality of zoning, *Euclid, Ohio v. Amber Realty*, specifically mentioned apartment houses as "parasites" that "take advantage" of the "residential character" of single-family districts in reasoning to support the decision. Spreading throughout the country, a hierarchy of zoning practices assigned the most preferential status to single-family zones. Courts in many states accepted that apartments may and should be used to buffer single-family residential areas from nonresidential uses.[18] The spatial arrangement of land uses found in the three areas under discussion clearly reflect these zoning principals.

During the same period that zoning was established as a standard planning tool, this land use arrangement of employing apartments to protect single-family areas from other uses was also central to neighborhood planning models, particularly Clarence Perry's 1929 neighborhood unit proposal.[19] In simplified terms, Perry proposed that residential neighborhoods should be organized around elementary schools and other community facilities and that they should be bounded by, rather than divided by, major roadways. Intended to be a flexible concept, the geographic area of a neighborhood unit could correspond both to the number of households needed to support the school and to the urban location and density of housing types used. Neighborhood units could be composed of all kinds of housing types, including very dense multifamily buildings. The most commonly seen and copied formulation of the concept, however, appears in a classic diagram of the principle in which the neighborhood unit describes a 160-acre area strongly oriented toward single-family housing. Neighborhood retail uses and apartments also appear, but they sit apart from the single-family core and its central school. In particular, retail stores with apartments behind are pushed to the edge of the neighborhood and located along the major roadways, especially at intersections. Apartments and stores, although perhaps necessary, are physically placed at the edges, peripheral to the vision of neighborhood life.

The neighborhood unit remained a powerful planning model and was still in use by the vast majority of professional city planners in the United States until at least the late 1960s, forty years after it was first proposed.[20] King County was no exception. Although not mentioned by name, the short King County comprehensive plan of 1958 clearly relies on the concept. In the plan, the "ideal neighborhood" is described as "made of a group of families." The "ingredients" for a neighborhood are "a rather solid pattern of homes, linked by quiet streets and centered on an elementary school....A small neighborhood shopping location may be spotted near the edge of the neighborhood."[21] The much more ambitious 1964 plan also relies on the concept, which is embedded in its illustrations and text. In the residential development policies, for instance, the plan states that "stable residential areas should contain pleasant homes" and that "residential areas are best formed in elementary school *neighborhood units* which are bounded by prominent physical land features, major elements of the circulation system, and other more intensive land uses." In contrast, the plan states that multifamily areas "shall always be located functionally convenient to a major or secondary arterial highway" and that they may be "logically developed adjacent" to shopping areas.[22] These policies emphasize a particular vision of the neighborhood unit in which single-family zones are seen as the center of a stable community life, and multifamily and commercial development are seen in more functional terms and as linked.

These planning ideas, and the ideals they encapsulate, closely fit the suburban apartment concentrations around Seattle once one shifts the boundaries of how they are looked at and defined as sites. The major difference between the conventional neighborhood unit and the depiction of apartment areas offered here is not in their overall land use patterns, but rather in how their centers are defined. Treating retail areas surrounded by apartments as the center of analysis relegates single-family housing and associated schools to the periphery—exactly opposite from the neighborhood unit concept. Treating intersections where retail uses cluster as centers simply combines the corners of several neighborhood units across large streets. Using a more urban notion, it treats major commercial streets as focal points where people and activities come together rather than as the dividers of neighborhood units. Indeed, many apartment concentrations are found where arterial streets meet along national survey grid lines, precisely where the corners of four 160-acre neighborhood units would adjoin. The pattern varies a great deal because each area has an individual development history, but, as a general organizing principal, apartment areas strongly conform to a sort of *inside-out* neighborhood unit model. Analogous to using different census boundaries to measure suburban densities, redrawing the boundaries of suburban planning models, in effect turning them inside out, opens up new questions about how suburban sites are conceived and perceived.[23]

STREETS AND AUTOMOBILES APART

Street networks reinforce the separation of single-family housing; they show that multifamily and commercial concentrations were not considered as a focus of community activity. In single-family development, the subdivision process encourages new public streets to access the relatively small lots required for separately owned detached houses. Over time, developers learned to minimize the amount of land devoted to expensive, non-revenue-producing roadways, and by the late 1970s most subdivisions were built with loop- and cul-de-sac-type street systems that created no through routes and few if any blocks. Multifamily and single-family zones frequently meet along fenced, landscaped boundaries in the middle of the resultant superblocks, but, whenever possible, entrances to subdivisions are placed well away from those of multifamily housing, often on entirely different arterial streets.[24]

Suburban apartment and retail development utilizes large lots that do not require subdivision and are not, therefore, subject to one of the main tools of development control. Lots are accessed directly from arterial streets, and developers, as a rule, do not create any new public streets at all. As a result, in Crossroads and Kent East Hill some commercial and multifamily lots extend a full quarter-mile into blocks. In Kent East Hill one block measures 138 acres, and even though the area contains a huge shopping district with thousands of housing units, the current block structure originates from before 1960 when the area was still in agricultural use. Only one new public through street was built in more than forty years of development in order to access new apartments. Likewise, in Crossroads the two blocks containing the majority of stores and multifamily units measure almost 200 acres. Only in Juanita, where single-family development takes up a larger area, are blocks smaller, averaging about 15 acres. Still, this is six times larger than average block sizes found in older Seattle neighborhoods developed at similar densities.

As with the strict patterning of land uses, sparse street networks reflect planning models as well as development interests. In the nineteenth century, critics started to attack the American tradition of laying out cities with an orthogonal grid of streets and lots, as monotonous and unnatural, even unhealthy. By midcentury, curvilinear street patterns suggesting romanticized rural landscapes were adopted in some higher-income, planned suburbs such as Olmstead's plan for Riverside, IL, but most subdivisions continued to rely on grids. This began to change in the 1920s when automobile traffic became a part of daily life and fine grids of streets were subject to a new criticism: they were seen as inherently dangerous. Urban grids allowed through traffic almost everywhere, with small blocks creating huge numbers of intersections and an attendant potential for traffic collisions.

In 1929 two solutions were proposed to this perceived problem, one by members of the Regional Plan Association of America, and one by the Russell Sage Foundation. The first, Perry's neighborhood unit, was based on the creation of protected neighborhood areas within a much larger grid of wide streets.[25] The other was Clarence Stein and Henry Wright's model neighborhood of Radburn, NJ.[26] Stein and

Wright pushed the separation of neighborhood areas and traffic further than Perry, placing their housing away on cul-de-sacs that penetrated true superblocks. The roadless block interior was used for parkland, community facilities, and a pedestrian walkway system entirely separated from auto traffic.[27] For the most part, however, ideas from Radburn were only partially applied during the massive wave of suburbanization that took place after World War II.

Beginning in the mid-1930s and extending into the postwar period, the Federal Housing Administration (FHA) publicized the plan of Radburn as an important model. The FHA worked directly with developers to redesign subdivisions; because it indirectly influenced developer financing, it was very influential.[28] The promoted designs however, were so stripped down so as to make the connection to Radburn almost unrecognizable. Central ideas—providing community parkland and protected pedestrian networks—were dropped entirely. The FHA advocated large blocks and curvilinear streets to create better communities and, significantly, to yield large cost savings in comparison to traditional grids. As shown in Juanita, Crossroads, and Kent East Hill, one result is the use of the old rural roads as the basis for new suburban superblocks.

These enormous superblocks do protect single-family development from through traffic, but outside of these protected zones, they are places to move automobiles, not to build neighborhoods and communities. Areas that concentrate people and activity arguably should be supported by the most well-developed infrastructure, but instead, the superblocks with multifamily housing and commercial uses have skeletal street systems compared to areas of low-density single-family housing. Despite continual road widening, traffic congestion here is endemic.[29] Even though large numbers of people live right next to retail centers, indirect walking routes, discontinuous sidewalk systems, and wide, heavily trafficked roadways discourage walking. Analogous to the normalization of block sizes that has occurred in some urban areas, detailed studies of informal pedestrian paths in these places show some modification of the block structure.[30] In spite of the hostile environment, a surprising number of residents do make “the land use–transportation connection” by walking between multifamily areas and the retail centers.[31] Carved into the ground—in, around, and through

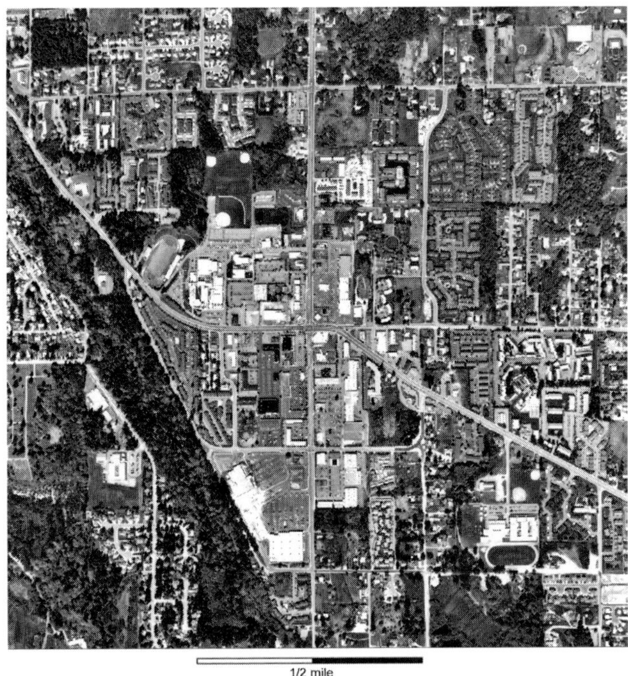

Figure 9.6. Kent East Hill from the air. Note arterial streets on the old rural road network.

fences, retaining walls, and other pedestrian barriers—their paths illustrate the deficiencies of the formal street system.

SIGHTING SUBURBAN APARTMENTS AS NEIGHBORHOODS

In terms of both land use patterns and street systems, suburban apartment concentrations illustrate a close correspondence between early-twentieth-century planning models, the application of standard planning tools such as zoning, and the interests of mid- and late-century developers. Planning and planning ideas helped shape the development practices evident in these places, but they did so in close conjunction with developer interests and cultural attitudes. As such, suburban apartment concentrations must be seen as integral to how suburban landscapes are built and structured. They belie ideas of suburban landscapes as disorganized or as dominated by single-family residential uses. The almost singular emphasis on protecting single-family areas from traffic and "nuisance land uses" helped create concentrated areas of apartments and retail stores between such protected zones. These medium-density, mixed areas share many attributes associated with urban, not suburban, neighborhoods.

Unlike their more urban counterparts, however, these places were conceived as edges, not centers. They have a tightly structured neighborhoodlike land use program, but despite the best attempts by residents, they remain largely disconnected places. Compared to their urban counterparts, the land use mix is coarse, the size of their parcels is enormous, and the street and block systems resemble areas that are still rural, albeit with wide, heavily trafficked roadways. They might be termed *resultant neighborhoods*: ones that were never planned, designed, or developed to work as cohesive places. In other respects, they should not be called neighborhoods at all. The term *neighborhood* is generally reserved for areas that are recognized as distinct places based on special character or identifiable group of inhabitants.[32] One of the most striking aspects of suburban apartment concentrations is precisely their invisibility. Their existence remains hidden by institutionalized modes of professional analysis, by development practices, and by planning models.

Recognizing these places is important for a number of reasons. Increasing the density and mix of land uses in suburban areas has become a key goal of smart growth policies in many parts of North America. Juanita, Crossroads, and Kent East Hill suggest that many, albeit unnoticed, suburban places already exist with substantial densities and housing and stores in close proximity. Since these places likely do not create the kind of transportation and social benefits that smart growth policy hopes to achieve, they suggest furthermore that attaining goals of reduced auto congestion and enhanced walking, bicycling, and public transit will require more than pursuing abstract notions of density and mix. New planning tools will be needed to create finer-grained street networks, complete sidewalk systems, and improve connections between development parcels. These are essential elements of community design missing from the zoning and subdivision regulations used to shape suburban development.

Despite smart growth policies, the types of development patterns evident in suburban apartment concentrations continue to be replicated. They can be seen in master planned development, where the arrangement of land uses, the configuration of street systems, and the design of building types are much more tightly controlled by a single developer than is possible with government planning tools applied to separate development proposals that take place over time. These patterns even show up in New Urbanist communities, despite their stated objectives of integrating land uses and connecting streets. A band of apartments immediately adjoins the rather conventional suburban shopping plaza in Kentlands, MD, for example. These apartment buildings are neither historicist in architectural style, nor are they located on the well-connected street system belonging to the more predominantly single-family areas. Despite other important innovations in Kentlands, this concentration of multifamily housing replicates mid-century suburban models with apartments kept apart from single-family zones. It is necessary to understand the origins and social logics of these models to both change new patterns of development and redesign old ones to create connected neighborhoods.

The advocates of New Urbanism have gone a long way toward bringing issues of community design into the fore of suburban development to help achieve these ends, but much remains to be done. Rather than implementing New Urbanist principals in large developments at the far edges of metropolitan areas, we need to look more closely inside the enormous existing areas of already urbanized suburbs. Juanita, Crossroads, and Kent East Hill offer three large and mature examples from the scores of other apartment concentrations found in the urbanized region around Seattle. Similar forms exist across the country. These are significant places, partly because of the substantial numbers of people living in them, and partly for what they say about suburban development practices, suburban lifestyles, and our images of suburbia.

All these places could be improved as neighborhoods and communities, but first we need to refine our images of the suburban landscape. Suburbs are more than a dimensionless realm without site and more than the locus of single, detached houses. Redescribing suburban sites as complex, multiple, and overlapping allows for the revised understandings necessary to improve areas of multifamily housing and shape them as neighborhoods. This effort to see suburbs in a new way takes a first step in acknowledging that roughly one-third of suburban Americans in metropolitan areas call their apartments home.

Notes

1. There is, however, the notion of "the inner city," oxymoronically, another aspatial term of place used to refer to very poor areas housing ethnic or racial minorities and often associated with drugs, unemployment, and crime. Thus, like suburbia, the term has strong social and political stereotypes attached to a generic environment.
2. E. C. Relph, *Place and Placelessness* (London: Pion, 1976); James Howard Kunstler, *The Geography of Nowhere: The Rise and Decline of America's Man-Made Landscape* (New York: Simon and Schuster, 1993).
3. P. Blake, *God's Own Junkyard: The Planned Deterioration of America's Landscape* (New York: Holt, Rinehart and Winston, 1979).
4. K. T. Jackson, *Crabgrass Frontier: The Suburbanization of the United States* (New York: Oxford University Press, 1985); R. Fishman, *Bourgeois Utopias: The Rise and Fall of Suburbia* (New York: Basic Books, 1987); R. Harris, *Unplanned Suburbs: Toronto's American Tragedy, 1900 to 1950* (Baltimore: Johns Hopkins Press, 1996).
5. According to U.S. Census data and definitions for urbanized areas of over one million people, almost 36 percent of the housing units outside central cities are found in some kind of attached unit. Although these attached units contain smaller households than average, they house just under one-third of suburban Americans.
6. U.S. Census of Population and Housing, 1960 and 2000, data for the Seattle and Tacoma urbanized areas. The 1960 data is the first to use the definition of urbanized areas that is still in use. The extent of what constitutes the urbanized area has changed over time. The Seattle-Tacoma-Bremerton Consolidated Metropolitan Statistical Area contains about 3.5 million people.
7. A. V. Moudon and P. Hess (2000). "Suburban Clusters: The Nucleation of Multifamily Housing in the Suburban Areas of the Central Puget Sound," *Journal of the American Planning Association* 66(3): 243–264.
8. See P. Hess et al. (1999). "Measuring Land Use for Transportation Research," *Transportation Research Record* 1674: 11–31 (1999). Note that using blocks brings these area/boundary issues down to a smaller scale, but does not eliminate them. These issues would also apply to social characteristics. To the degree that certain social, economic, ethnic, racial, or household structure groups are also associated with apartment areas—something almost certainly true—our understanding of suburban social segregation will be affected.
9. In geography and spatial statistics this is called the modifiable areal unit problem. It has been long known in these fields, although it is rarely dealt with

explicitly. In architecture, urban design, and planning, the problem is rarely acknowledged at all.

10. Data used to understand these areas include property atlases and aerial photographs available for five- to ten-year increments over a period of more than four decades. Field data on physical form and design features was collected in association with previous research by P. M. Hess, "Pedestrians, Networks, and Neighborhoods: A Study of Walking and Mixed-Use, Medium-Density Development Patterns in the Puget Sound Region," Ph.D. dissertation, University of Washington (2001).
11. Juanita is currently being developed as a "mixed use" center, but that is the subject of a different mapping of contemporary suburban landscapes.
12. P. M. Hess, "Pedestrians, Networks, and Neighborhoods: A Study of Walking and Mixed-Use, Medium-Density Development Patterns in the Puget Sound Region," Ph.D. dissertation, University of Washington (2001).
13. Bellevue, incorporated as a city in 1952, is now the state's fourth largest city in terms of population (about 110,000 by the 2000 census) and is the region's second largest employment center after Seattle.
14. M. R. Wolfe, *Locational Factors Involved in Suburban Land Development* (Seattle: Department of Urban Design and Planning, University of Washington, undated); M. Weiss, *The Rise of the Community Builders: The American Real Estate Industry and Urban Land Planning* (New York: Columbia University Press, 1987).
15. The way these complexes are designed and laid out within sites is almost invisible in the planning and design literatures. Carl F. Horowitz, *The New Garden Apartment: Current Market Realities of an American Housing Form* (New Brunswick, NJ: Center for Urban Policy Research, 1983), (twenty years ago!), is an exception. Their design origins lie in the great experiments in new suburban form in the years before the Great Depression. It is noteworthy, though, that Clarence Stein's design for Radburn, for example, is incomparably more famous in how it influenced single-family subdivision, than is the design for Baldwin Hills Village in Los Angeles, arguably the founding type for garden apartments (and for which Stein was a consulting architect).
16. Note that the densities of these development types are understated compared to their urban counterparts where streets are public, and, therefore, net densities include only buildings and their associated open spaces.
17. R. Fischler (1998). "The Metropolitan Dimension of Early Zoning—Revisiting the 1916 New York City Ordinance," *Journal of the American Planning Association* 64(2): 170–188.
18. D. R. Mandelker, *The Zoning Dilemma: A Legal Strategy for Urban Change* (Indianapolis: Bobbs-Merrill, 1971).
19. C. A. Perry, "The Neighborhood Unit," in *Neighborhood and Community Planning, Regional Plan of New York and Its Environs vol. 7* (New York: Russell Sage Foundation, 1929).
20. T. Banerjee and W. C. Baer, *Beyond the Neighborhood Unit: Residential Environments and Public Policy* (New York: Plenum Press, 1984).
21. King County Planning Commission, *Comprehensive Plan for King County, Washington* (Seattle, 1958), 3.

22. As discussed in the introduction, the term *homes* is still a euphemism for single-family housing. King County Planning Department, *The Comprehensive Plan for King County, Washington* (Seattle, 1964), 111. My emphasis.
23. The variation in the pattern occurs because each apartment concentration has a different development history. One significant overall difference with neighborhood units is that the densities of typical suburban single-family areas developed after WWII can rarely support a school in such a small area. Also, and not incidentally, planning for schools has been institutionally separate from county and city land use planning, making coordination difficult.
24. Within the superblocks, the separation of single-family and apartment zones is reinforced by strict landscaping ordinances required for multifamily development. These ordinances create physical barriers and visual screens between the two uses. See K.-J. Kim, "Regulatory Impacts on Suburban Residential Form: A Case Study of Bellevue, Washington," Ph.D. dissertation, University of Washington (1992).
25. Although often attributed to Perry, the neighborhood unit idea was actually formulated earlier, with a fully articulated version by William E. Drummond Johnson some 20 years previously. See D. Leslie (2002). "Origin of the Neighborhood Unit," *Planning Perspectives* 17: 227–245.
26. C. S. Stein, *Toward New Towns for America* (Cambridge: MIT Press, 1966).
27. Note that Radburn closely paralleled the neighborhood unit in the arrangement of large streets framing protected areas of houses and community facilities. Rarely acknowledged in the planning and design literatures, Radburn has apartments located at the back of commercial facilities at the main corner of the superblock that was developed. European modernists also proposed superblocks for similar reasons, though they applied this "new" system of circulation to neighborhoods with much greater density than American reformers.
28. K. T. Jackson, *Crabgrass Frontier: The Suburbanization of the United States* (New York: Oxford University Press, 1985); M. Weiss *The Rise of the Community Builders: The American Real Estate Industry and Urban Land Planning* (New York: Columbia University Press, 1987).
29. W. Kulash et al. (1990). "Traditional Neighborhood Development: Will the Traffic Work?" *Development* 21(4): 21–24.
30. A. Siksna, "A Comparative Study of Block Sizes and Form," Ph.D. dissertation, University of Queensland (1990); P. M. Hess, "Evaluating Pedestrian Environments: Proposals for Urban Form Measures of Network Connectivity, with Case Studies of Wallingford in Seattle and Crossroads in Bellevue, Washington," Master's thesis, University of Washington (1994); A. Siksna (1998). "City Centre Blocks and their Evolution: A Comparative Study of Eight American and Australian CBDs," *Journal of Urban Design* 3(3): 253–283.
31. In good weather, daytime walking rates vary from 30 people per hour walking into the small center of Juanita, to over 100 people per hour walking into the large, but relatively compact center in Crossroads. See P. M. Hess et al. (1999). "Neighborhood Site Design and Pedestrian Travel," *Transportation Research Record* 1674: 9–19. These walking rates are about one-third of those found in older, urban neighborhoods in the region with simi-

lar residential densities and retail uses. The "land use transportation connection" is a commonly used phrase in the planning literature. This literature has not, however, examined these kinds of places. Examples where the phrase is used just in the title include T. Moore and P. Thorsnes, *The Transportation/Land Use Connection* (Chicago: American Planning Association, 1994); R. Cervero and J. Landis (Fall 1996). "The Transportation–Land Use Connection Still Matters," *Access* 7: 2–10; P. W. G. Newman and J. R. Kenworthy (1996). "The Land Use–Transport Connection: An Overview," *Land Use Policy* 13(1): 1.

32. S. B. Flexner and L. C. Hauck, eds., *The Random House Dictionary of the English Language, Unabridged* (New York: Random House, 1987).

The Twin Towers, World Trade Center, New York City.

10

Study Areas, Sites, and the Geographic Approach to Public Action

Peter Marcuse

This essay takes up three related concepts: site, study area, and area of concerns. The first two are in common usage in architecture and urban planning; the third is not, and this essay argues that it should be—indeed, it should be the starting point for professional involvement in any project. As commonly used, *site* simply refers to the bounded piece of property on which a particular project is to be undertaken;[1] the extensive ramifications of the term, suggesting meanings and implications that go far beyond this common understanding, comprise the subject matter of this book. This essay, however, focuses on the other two related terms. For urban planners, a *study area* is generally defined in terms of a given geographical unit—a neighborhood, street, or zoning district, usually selected on the basis of a problem presented by the client—poverty, blight, conflicting proposals, congestion, environmental quality—that is then given a geographical definition. I use the term *area of concerns* here to denote the set of problems a given project is intended to or should address. "Area of concern" may be read as a "potential study area," but leaving open the question of whether it should be geographically defined. I say "intended to or should" deliberately, because I conclude with a normative statement of the appropriate approach for professionals in dealing with sites and study areas, an approach that may frequently differ from that in common planning practice, and I use the approach taken in planning for the World Trade Center site as an example of what I mean.

The three arguments made here are:

1. A study area should be defined for any project not only *from the inside out*—that is, not only from a viewpoint concerned with the development of the site and asking what factors outside the site need to be studied to ensure a successful project—but also *from the outside in*—that is, asking what concerns in the community in which the site is located may be addressed by a project on that site.[2]
2. A study area is only for convenience defined as a geographical, a physically bounded, area. It should be defined so as to include the areas of concerns of the community for which the project, and its alternatives on that site, may be relevant. The initial step for professional action is the definition of the relevant *areas of concerns,* which should then be translated into one or more study areas only for methodological convenience.
3. The determination of appropriate *areas of concerns* is both a technical matter (how might the site practically be used?) and a normative matter (what are the most important concerns a project at that site might address?). The resolution of the normative issues can largely rest on the ethical commitments of the design professions.

Architects and planners face somewhat different situations, in these regards. Written from the point of view of a planner, this essay addresses issues faced specifically by planners and architects in the public employ. Whether the normative approach suggested here has applicability in the private sector also will be taken up at the end of the discussion.

The parameters used to determine what should substantively be of concern in defining study areas for purposes of intervention remain markedly under-theorized, even though they have a significant effect on how sites are developed. For architects, the area of concern is often simply named the "site," defined as the parcel or lot owned by a client: a geographically bounded, legally defined piece of physical property. I argue here that an *a priori* focus on neither site nor study area should be accepted without serious examination, and that the criteria for the selection of either deserve much greater attention in both professions than they usually receive. I end with the preliminary suggestion that in determining a study area for a particular site, professionals should begin "from the outside in," and I outline a set of criteria appropriate for planning practice, which may apply in parallel if not identical fashion to an architect given a site to develop for a client.

The two concepts—site and study area—are certainly related, but their relationship is complex. In some cases, the definition of a site may begin with a given physical location, and a study area may then follow from the determination of a particular physical, social, or economic impact (for example, if contextual design is important, a study area may be defined by the surrounding buildings; if the proposed development may pollute, the area over which pollution may be expected). In other cases, the process may begin by the definition of a study area based on the geographic locale in which a particular problem exists, and only then of a site, a particular location, where the problem may be best addressed (for example, if pollution in a particular neighborhood is the concern, the neighborhood will be the study area, and the source of pollution thereafter determined as the site for action). But, as one examines even these conventional approaches in more detail, difficulties arise. If starting from a given site and working to determine the study area, how broad a context should be considered? What in the context warrants study: Height of buildings? Building form? Social characteristics? History? Aspects of all these things, within the practical limits of funding? The possibilities are open ended, and each may require a quite different formal definition of a study area. If starting with the study area, even the point of departure often remains cloudy; few problems are confined within clear-cut boundaries, and even if they are, the causes may well lie outside those boundaries. Pollution, perhaps heaviest at point A, will have effects in a gradient around that point, making the borderline difficult to define. The cause may well be outside the affected area, across a river, upstream, or somewhere else quite far afield. Further, the definition of the causes of the stated problem may dictate quite different study areas: if the problem is health, or inadequate housing, or unemployment, its cause may lie in a hospital, a school, a job market—quite removed from the location of those experiencing the problem. *Study area* is as complex a concept as *site*.

Surprisingly, the concept of the study area is hardly explored in the planning literature, even though most planning projects begin by its use. Most planning studio presentations in most planning schools throughout the country—I dare say throughout the world—start with the presentation of the facts about the study area, and zero in from that to the specific object of the studio. Yet one looks in vain through the index of any standard planning treatise for the term "study area." One does find references such as "the surrounding residential area,"[3] or "the relevant physiographic features,"[4] or claims that the scope of a land use survey should depend on "the size of the area, the size of the planning staff, and the time available,"[5] or "the targeted neighborhood"[6]—the selection of the target coming (perhaps understandably) from some source other than a study. Provisions in many zoning codes require formal notice to be given to all those within a quantitatively specified linear distance from the parcel for which a change is requested, but those requirements are concededly arbitrary rather than performance-based. They are not predicated on any conceptualization of an area of impact. In the many treatises on data collection and use for planning, one might expect to find detailed discussion of the area for which such an effort should be made, but one does not. At best one finds suggestions to start by defining "the areas…[that] the decision makers can control."[7]

The following list attempts to categorize briefly some alternative ways of defining a study area in general use by planners today, trying to make explicit the concepts adopted (usually implicitly) and how varied the results might be if one definition is selected over another.

By legal jurisdiction—either governmental boundaries or area of formal power, as with a quasi-governmental organization (although few problems mesh neatly with such lines, and few such areas are homogeneous, so that their use as units of analysis will tend to conceal significant differences within them)[8]

By topography, as with a flood plain or wind shadow (although these vary over time and intensity)

By the boundaries of a physical ecosystem (but such boundaries are generally very wide and their limits vary with the issue and are essentially arbitrary)[9]

By present (and/or predicted) users of a given or proposed facility (with the obvious danger of circularity)
By the level of intensity of a given problem (with establishment of an arbitrary cut-off)
By the concerns of a particular interest group, such as a real estate board or a neighborhood association (often internally contradictory)
By socially accepted definitions of neighborhood or community or urban or metropolitan area or region (bearing in mind that such definitions are essentially arbitrary, even if grounded in quantitative models such as the Shevsky-Bell social area analyses so popular in the 1950s, and that their use often creates a self-fulfilling prophecy, as well as failing to deal with those aspects of the problem outside the thus defined boundaries)[10]
By the availability of data (thus census tract lines frequently determine the precise locations of study area boundaries)[11]
By the preconception of the planner, or the ambition of the architect or developer (the most frequent, if the truth were told?)
By the location of the stakeholders (although this nebulous concept is often circular—if stakeholders are sought within the study area, and only within the area, then how can the study area be defined by the stakeholders?)

The definition of a study area can be seen as a subset of the problems involved in trying to define a problem or formulate a solution to a problem, in geographic terms. The first difficulty lies in establishing the criteria by which the relevant geographic boundaries are set. The second lies in the usually implicit and hidden assumptions being made about the nature of the problem and its confinement to such boundaries. Pierre Bourdieu addresses both of these issues in philosophical language, first suggesting the importance of social space, and then questioning its role vis-à-vis physical space:

> The structure of social space shows up as spatial oppositions, with the inhabited (or appropriated) space functioning as a sort of spontaneous symbolisation of social space. There is no space in a hierarchised society that is not itself hierarchised and that does not express hierarchies and social distances, in a form that is more or

> less distorted and, above all, disguised by the naturalization effect produced by the long-term inscription of social realities in the natural world.[12]

The danger lies precisely in ignoring the implications of the naturalization effect for social space, by assuming that an area of concern can be intuitively (i.e., "naturally") defined in geographic terms: the assumption that social space will always be congruent with some physical space. As a result, hierarchical relations of physical space are ignored, almost always at the expense of those at the bottom of the hierarchy.

It follows that the definition of the concerns to be addressed, or the *area of concerns,* must precede the definition of the study area, not the other way around.

As I write this, the World Trade Center in New York City is perhaps the most talked about site in the world,[13] from the point of view of architects and planners.[14] The definition of the areas of concern to the various agencies dealing with this site makes a fascinating study in the benefits and pitfalls associated with defining areas for purposes of planning and design. We may assume, probably counterfactually, that each line drawn around a geographic area for planning and policy purposes marks the result of careful study—that it can be treated as a study area, and even perhaps a delineated area of concern for treatment. A review of the process would make it appear that the logic has gone from *site* to *study area* to *area of concerns*. The difficulty is that various geographic areas have been identified for a disparate set of treatments, each apparently based principally on the physical relation to the site, with one or more study areas identified only thereafter. None of the extensive documentation of the planning process gives any indication of exactly how geographic boundaries were drawn, what studies led to them, and how the concerns they were supposed to meet were defined. The steps in the process leading to boundary definitions are simply elided in almost all cases. Nothing is presented to suggest that the various boundaries drawn for different purposes—the jurisdiction of different public bodies, the area in which investment will be subsidized or city zoning procedures overridden, where residents are entitled to compensation for loss—have been in fact subject to study.

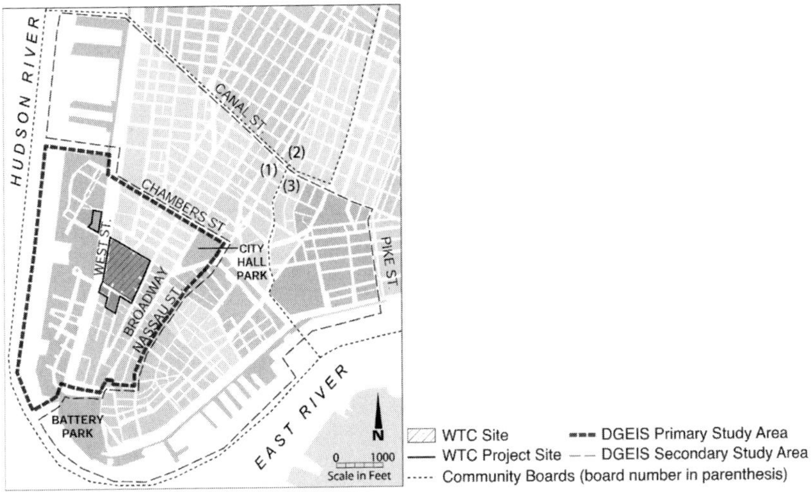

Figure 10.1. Study Areas and Communities in Lower Manhattan.

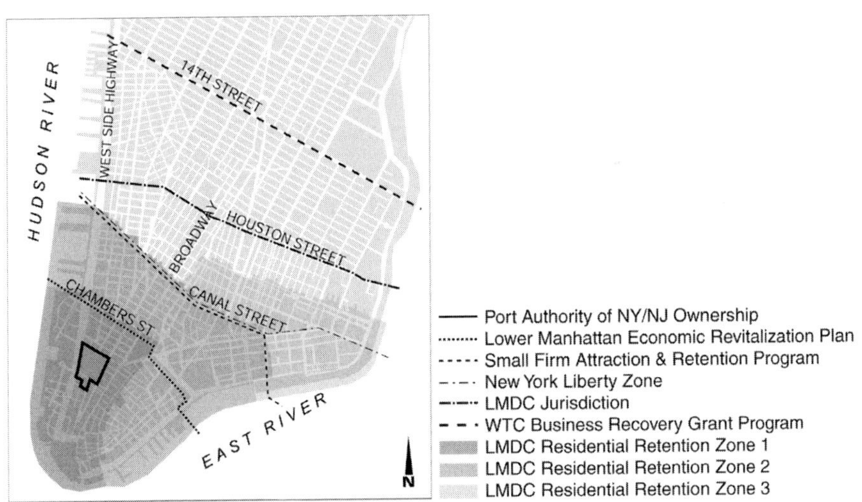

Figure 10.2. Study Areas and September 11 Program Areas.

Consider the following three maps. The first (Figure 10.1) shows the boundaries of the generally recognized communities in lower Manhattan, areas conventionally understood as having a common character. These boundaries are at two scales. At the neighborhood level, grey tones show the commonly recognized residential neighborhoods, defined partly by ethnicity (e.g., Chinatown, Little Italy), partly by the commonly recognized dominant usages (e.g., City Hall, Financial District), and partly by geographically defined image (e.g., Soho, Tribeca). Apart from these latter two, the boundaries among neighborhoods blur more than such lines would suggest; thus Chinatown is expanding into Little Italy, the limits of the emerging residential district have yet to be firmly established. At a slightly larger scale, the map shows the boundaries of the lower Manhattan Community Boards, the legal subdivisions created by the city as the basic unit of government in the city charter. These boards serve to advise the city government on issues of land use and public services in their respective areas, and play a significant role in political decision making in the city. As such, they would serve as a natural set of study areas for purposes of any activity affecting lower Manhattan.

The second (Figure 10.2) shows the boundaries of areas established by a variety of agencies dealing with planning and reconstruction after September 11, generally guided by the Lower Manhattan Development Corporation. It depicts formal and legally binding eligibility areas for the implementation of various governmental programs. The map also shows the legal jurisdictional boundaries of both the Lower Manhattan Development Corporation and the Port Authority of New York and New Jersey. Figure 10.2 does not show eligibility for Federal Emergency Management Administration's Mortgage and Rental Assistance Program (which has a component extending over all of Manhattan). It also omits other FEMA programs and specific Small Business Administration programs that are simply not geographically confined, but instead extend to all those affected by September 11, no matter their location.

Figure 10.1 and Figure 10.2 use different graphic conventions to show the World Trade Center Site, the World Trade Center "Project Site," and the Primary and Secondary Study Areas, all designated by the Lower Manhattan Development Corporation and shown in its Draft Generic Environmental Impact Statement. The lines defining the site and the two study areas were clearly not drawn to reflect either common neighborhood definitions or political boundaries (in Figure 10.1) or the planning and implementation of the governmental programs already underway centered around the aftermath of September 11 (in Figure 10.2).

Figure 10.3, prepared by New York New Visions, a voluntary group of architectural, design, and planning professionals that came together immediately after September 11, 2001, to assist in the replanning effort, shows the regional impact of September 11 and the centers that this responsible professional group considered necessary to take into con-

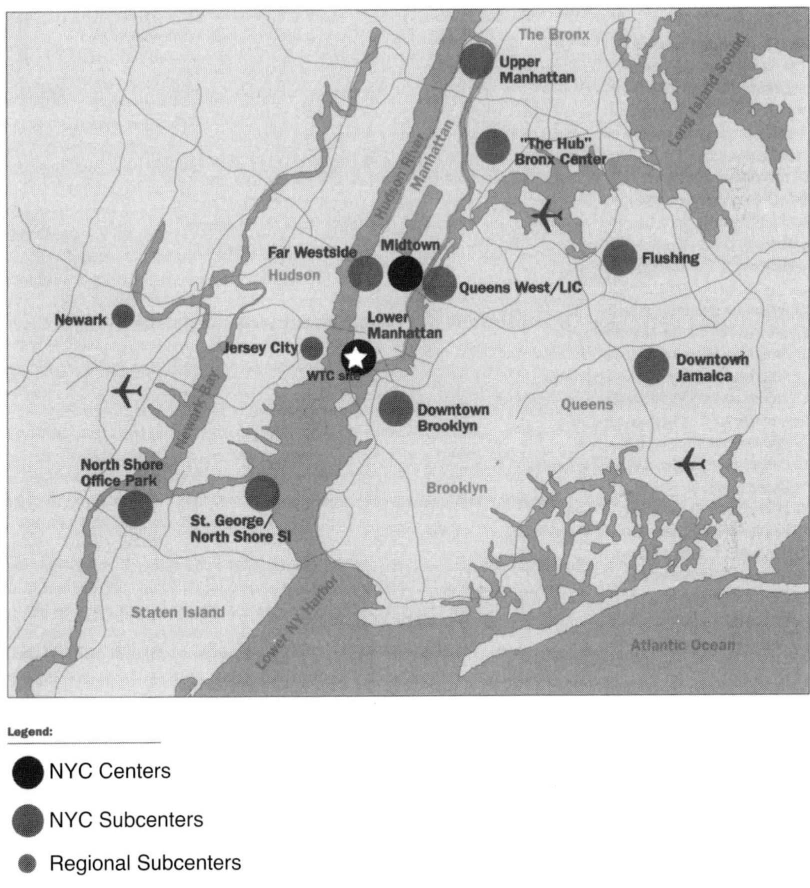

Figure 10.3. Regional Embeddedness of the World Trade Center Site.

sideration in such an effort. This describes the regional context in which the World Trade Center site was and remains embedded. Neither the definition of the site nor of the study areas makes it possible to take into consideration any of the impacts on the region nor these regional centers.

But what should be the *areas of concern* for the World Trade Center site, and how should they be defined and bounded—if indeed geographical definition is appropriate? The answer is by no means obvious. One can perhaps list the considerations.

The World Trade Center complex occupied 16 acres at the edge of the Financial District in lower (southern) Manhattan. Clearly much more than those acres is involved in everything that happens there. Defining the area of concern affords a fruitful opportunity to look at the issues involved in any reuse proposal. It turns out that multiple areas of concern exist because multiple concerns are involved, some congruent, others not, all operating at quite different levels. Let me enumerate a few.

PHYSICAL CONCERNS: BEYOND THE PARCEL

We start, almost automatically, with a physical definition of the immediate area of concern, which will, in any possible approach, be part of both the limited physical site for action and the study area: Ground Zero. Sixteen acres? But even that is not so simple. From an engineering point of view, the platform on which the buildings stood depends for its strength on supports located outside those 16 acres. The pedestrian bridges crossing West Street, one boundary of the area of concern, were essential components of the Center. The utility infrastructure radiates out in almost all directions. Had the area of concern been as it was before the World Trade Center was built, the waterfront might have provided at least one clear edge to the west; that can hardly be maintained today, now that Battery Park City has been built. So the definition of the area of concern, from an engineering standpoint, must be much more than the limited 16 acres the building complex actually occupied. In fact, as time progresses and more information becomes available, the boundaries of the physically impacted area change: one building, formerly considered not at risk, and therefore not within Ground Zero, was deemed so unsafe as to require demolition as late as September 2002. An exact delineation of a physical area of concern can only be established after substantial further investigation; such a physical definition can only be hypothesized at the beginning. The important thing is not to assume a definition at the outset, but to see what physical area of concern emerges from the exploration itself.

Significantly, the newest coalition of civic groups concerned about the future of the World Trade Center site has named itself "Beyond 16 Acres." In its meetings this coalition's area of concern seems limited to lower Manhattan, but that limitation raises sharply the question of what the boundaries of the real area of concern should be. The Civic Alliance comments on the Draft Environmental Impact Study,[15] and even more explicitly its comments on the Draft Scope for the DGEIS, make many of the same points raised in the following section, although in a more limited fashion.[16]

HISTORICAL CONCERNS: TEMPORAL LIMITS

It is conventional to look at the history of an area of concern when beginning its analysis. The history here is fascinating and goes back a long way. The area was originally a Native American village, then part of a thriving port, then a center for the electrical industry and a home for a disparate mixture of immigrant workers, predominantly Arabic, before it was cleared for the World Trade Center in 1970. It abutted a set of piers, part of the busiest port in the world in its day, which were obliterated when fill from the excavation of the area was dumped in the Hudson. During the period of the Twin Towers' existence, the area was the western anchor of the Financial District. On September 11, 2001, it was the scene of one of the worst atrocities ever to occur on United States soil, outranking, for instance, Pearl Harbor by almost 10 to 1 (although paling by comparison, for instance, with the massacres in Rwanda, or the slaughter of native Americans in the early days of the nation's settlement).

What aspect of this history remains relevant today? Without doubt, the atrocity of September 11 cannot be ignored. Perhaps a memorial is appropriate, perhaps a monument, or an archive, or a reproduction—some way of communicating the story of those who died there. Certainly something. Ghosts reside there, and they will not go away. An open memorial competition held in late 2003 generated 5201 entries; a winnowing process undertaken by a group of prominent jurors resulted in a selection meeting a number of these possible objectives. The program called for a memorial confined to the actual limits of the World Trade Center itself. Since what happens on that site clearly has repercussions for what could happen adjacent to it, the rigid site definition of the competition had to be sprung, and such "off-site" factors as underground transportation access and above-ground sunlight and shade brought into play.

How about the rest of the history, going back in time? The Arabic character of the prior residents and users carries a symbolic weight today. They were displaced by actions of the state, with essentially no compensation, certainly not for disrupted lives, jobs, networks, and attachments. Can this be woven into the considerations to affect the area's reuse? What about other earlier residents, and earlier users? The port-related functions of the area of concern had critical importance in the first decades of the twentieth century and in much of the nineteenth; they comprise part of the history of the area. Should they be respected today? Are they part of the "historical area of concern?"

Again, the answer cannot be given at the outset, or in the abstract. First, an understanding of the issues that the project raises as well as the issues it can address must be reached; only then can a determination of the relevance of its history be made. The historical area of concern thus depends on what the historical exploration actually reveals, how people today relate to various parts of the past, and the possibilities of incorporating these views. The boundary of the historical area of concern needs to remain open until the exploration has been undertaken. The definition of the area of concern in time is as important as its definition in space, and the two are linked.

PLANNING CONCERNS

What of the planning history of the World Trade Center? It surely involves examining the original proposed site for the project, on the

East River. Other buildings (and parks, open spaces, and highways) exist there now. Again, ghosts surface. An alternative history of the World Trade Center, what might have been and where: these constitute a counterfactual, but nonetheless, relevant area of concerns.

Politics have been critical in the development processes leading to the configuration of the area of concern. If religious ideology counts as "political," politics arguably produced the area of concern in its present state. Politics certainly produced the Twin Towers; the story of Governor Nelson Rockefeller's role in the center's development has been graphically told. Today, intense political interests abound. Much of the political leadership of the city (and perhaps of the state and nation) is committed to a very rapid reconstruction schedule—as a symbol of the resilience of the city, and presumably a reflection of the effectiveness of their leadership. But the parameters of the area of concern in which these political interests are vested extend beyond the 16 acres of the World Trade Center itself. There is talk of the revitalization and reconstruction of the Financial District as a whole, an area of variously defined limits, certainly including damaged buildings in the vicinity of the 16-acre parcel, but probably other office buildings as well, such as those needing to be upgraded to Class A status or converted to residential uses if the Financial District is to be developed to its maximum. Where to draw the line?

MARKET CONCERNS

When we come to the economic definition of the area of concern, the difficulties multiply. No doubt a critical opening question is what the demand for space in any of the various possible developments of the 16 acres might be: what we might call the area of concern as private real estate. (While the Port Authority of New York and New Jersey is the owner of the title to the land, its lease to a private development group for 99 years in July 2001, makes the latter effectively the real party in interest in ownership.) To properly assess the area of concern as private real estate, the market for real estate (including both demand and supply sides) must be appraised. How large is the area of concern, thus considered? When David Rockefeller, as president of Chase Manhattan Bank, undertook the construction of his 53-story modern office tower on the eastern side of the Financial District in 1955, he was intensely interested in the way this building would be affected by the overall development of the entire district. He thus considered the construction of the World Trade Center, at the western end of the District, to be critically relevant to his own area of concern to the east. By the same token, his building on the eastern end should be considered within the real estate area of concern of the 16 acres to the west.

Further, as a matter of a competitive real estate location, within what property market must this area of concern be considered? It is certainly competitive with midtown Manhattan; indeed, the entire effort resulting in the construction of the Twin Towers can be explained largely as an effort to gain ground in the competition with midtown. Metrotech Park, in Brooklyn, has benefited substantially from the loss of World Trade Center office space; certainly placing it within the same market as this is written. So, for that matter, are Stamford, CT; Jersey City, NJ; and White Plains, NY. The firms that quickly relocated their offices from the World Trade Center to these locations after September 11 are unlikely, at least in the short or medium run, to be looking for space again at or near the 16 acres. To the extent that private businesses and private developers will be involved in the reuse of the World Trade Center area of concern, the real estate market at least as far afield as these cities must be considered part of the private real estate definition of the area of concern.

Other aspects of the economy of the area of concern—specifically in relation to employment, job creation and growth, tax-paying ability, and contribution to the economic health of the city's workers—produce yet another definition of the area of concern as economic location. People (over 50,000 of them) did work within the 16 acres, and presumably at least some (perhaps not the same ones), perhaps 100,000 or more, were quite directly involved with activities there. The Fiscal Policy Institute did a careful study on the distribution of those jobs. The three big categories are finance, services, and retail—the first highly paid (on average), the latter two lowly paid. So the employment area of concern contains at least retail, service, and finance jobs. Those extend well beyond the 16 acres, beyond the Financial District, and even beyond lower Manhattan to the rest of Manhattan as well as the other four boroughs (as Fernando Ferrer tried to argue during the last Democratic mayoral primary, garnering 48% of the vote in the process). For those in finance, the job area of concern extends well into the suburbs of New York City, as far as Stamford, suburban New Jersey, and Westchester County.

Thinking about the area of concern in these terms raises yet another issue, generic to many of the definitions discussed here. There are locations competitive to the 16 acres—whether one looks at them as employment areas with a concern about the holders of the jobs lost or as areas affecting real estate (or, as cultural areas of concern involving the cultural past or present to which the 16 acres relate)—and certainly there are other important locations if the concern lies with a reassertion of democratic values and democratic communication. Competitive locations exist in all cases. Considering the World Trade Center as a historic area of concern, for example, the recent and even not-so-recent past could be preserved, recalled, and engaged in other settings. Many major monuments (the Vietnam Veterans Memorial being the latest national example) and many commemorative institutions (for instance, Holocaust museums) do not get physically sited where the events they present actually occurred (although in most cases those actual locations memorialize their histories as well). In fact, the World Trade Center historical area of concern only partially depends on location; immigrant communities that once existed there now reside elsewhere, the workers that perished there lived elsewhere, the public servants who died in the rescue operations came from fire stations and other bases located elsewhere. In each case, the specific history of the events at the World Trade Center area of concern can also be dealt with at other locations—fire stations, police stations, hospitals—located elsewhere. With the real estate area of concern, midtown Manhattan, Metrotech, and the Jersey City waterfront equally constitute areas of concerns of financial jobs; the entire city comprises an area of concerns for employment of service and retail workers. A comprehensive view of any project for the 16 acres must take into account, and include within the scope of its studies, alternative and/or supplemental locations.

SOCIAL CONCERNS

Loss of lives, loss of jobs, and loss of homes are some of the most egregious consequences of the attack on the World Trade Center. Many programs undertaken by the Lower Manhattan Development Corporation address the consequences. Figure 10.1 shows the eligibility areas used to determine who may benefit from the assistance programs specifically geared to small business. Similar geographic boundaries have been established for programs directed at residents whose homes were destroyed by the attack, and still other boundaries delimit where people are entitled to assistance for job loss. However, most of those who lost their jobs lived far outside any of the areas included on Figure 10.1, and even outside the study areas depicted on Figure 10.2. Geographic definition of eligibility for various remedial programs may facilitate administration of those programs, and it may reduce the need to examine each case on its own merits, but it does not make a great deal of sense where the concern being addressed is not geographically limited. Perhaps abandoning the idea of geographically defined study areas for social concerns would be the better way to go in such cases.

DEMOCRATIC CONCERNS

The final area of concern I want to consider here (although there are surely others) is that of democratic consideration and decision making. The processes of open and participatory planning, of democratic decision making, focus—in ever-changing patterns—on specific locations, around which the communicative and conflictual processes of civil society and public life swirl and congeal. For the World Trade Center in particular, this comprises a critical aspect of the area of concern today. Is it to be defined by a group of the thirty largest developers in New York, meeting in closed session with the mayor? Is it to be deemed an area of concern for review by the city's planning commission, or does that group function, as its chair has recently told its members, merely to deliberate and consider, but not to plan or suggest? Are the key participants simply the title owners to the property and the lease-holders (and their sub-lessees and their sub-sub-lessees)?

Perhaps the ultimate and most important concern that should be considered in defining the areas of concern of any project for the World

Trade Center site should be its nature as a democratic focus—as an opportunity to exercise the full breadth and depth of democratic life, with all its glories and all its warts. What will be built there, in physical terms, is certainly important. But in the end, how the outcome of the rebuilding process will be seen, used, appreciated, or rejected ultimately depends largely on how people feel about the process by which it gets realized. Every area of concern is socially constructed, not physically determined. Certainly the World Trade Center site and its surroundings today are not defined in the public consciousness simply as a physical location, but also as an area of social concern—of concern with history, with real estate, with employment, with democracy. The limits of these concerns are also socially constructed, not physically determined. Openness to examining these aspects of any proposed project on the World Trade Center site, viewing them as subjects of democratic decision making rather than as involving issues that can be arbitrarily limited to one or more specific geographic location is critical to any proper planning or design approach.

The World Trade Center development project provides but one instance of the complications involved in defining sites, study areas, and areas of concern for a particular project. Two other examples, one involving the national urban redevelopment program, the other involving contemporary empowerment zone legislation, consider the effects of the geographic definition of a site or project area, when implicit assumptions are not carefully thought through, producing quite unexpected consequences.

When first authorized in 1949, the urban redevelopment program defined areas eligible for Title I assistance as needing to be "blighted" and "predominantly residential." The boundaries of Title I sites were thus determined by conditions within the sites themselves; a broader study area was useful only to establish that boundary. This rigid geographic limitation came under attack from two directions. Some people criticized the predominantly residential focus; those critics, like Robert Moses in New York, became adept at defining and redefining a blighted area to conform to whatever goals they wanted to achieve.[17] Others wanted to broaden the scope of the program beyond clearance to include rehabilitation and consideration of other reuses; among them were the drafters of the Workable Program requirement, which for the first time, required consideration of the entire city as an area of concern, establishing the need for rehabilitation or clearance on the basis of a citywide survey of conditions.[18] In practice, the attempt to promote consideration of a serious study area before embarking on renewal turned out to be "a well-known farce."[19]

The evolution of the study areas required by federal legislation after the adoption of the Workable Program requirement would make a fascinating study. They varied from those requiring, in the late 1950s, General Neighborhood Renewal Plans, intended to define areas for action but instead developed after such areas were already (somehow?) established;[20] to requiring Community Renewal Programs in 1959, reincarnated as Neighborhood Development Programs in 1968; to asking for Community Action Programs in the antipoverty period of the late 1960s; to the establishment of Model Cities Neighborhoods in the Model Cities legislation of 1966. I would suggest that a careful study of the legislative language would find no guidelines for how to approach the beginning of the effort to define areas eligible for treatment under that legislation; they provide a definition of the eligible treatment area, which becomes, *ipso facto*, the study area.

The consequence of this approach can be seen in the latest progeny of this line of legislation: the empowerment zone provisions.[21] They include a very specific definition of the areas eligible for empowerment zone designation, based on census statistics dealing with poverty. Not coincidentally, African-Americans are represented disproportionately in 90 percent of the areas designated as empowerment zones. The conceptual correlation between the designation of eligible areas and a rigorous definition of the ghetto is sharp, and the overlap with definitions of an underclass is also strong. The rigid establishment of geographic boundaries by internal criteria, without allowing for use of a study area that would factually establish the parameters of the problem to be addressed and the location of the resources necessary for its treatment, is crippling. This view of how an attack on poverty ought to be carried out within an artificially geographically defined area results in further strengthening the walls of the ghetto, making the areas initially equated in practice with ghetto conditions even more of a ghetto.[22]

CONCLUSION

The very definition of the geographic area to be examined or treated constitutes a critical element in the determination of what will ultimately be done there. In good planning practice, that area is deduced from analysis of a study area, whose own boundaries, however, are too rarely conceptualized. In legislation, the relevant geographic area is generally simply defined by quantitative demographic or economic criteria, without reference to a broader examination of the locus of the problem or the resources for its treatment. For architects, the area of concern is often simply the parcel owned by the client, sometimes with one eye on immediately surrounding physical structures. And yet little attention is generally given to the method of defining the area that should substantively be of concern. Though the definition of that area can make a major difference in the result, the conceptualizations involved are very much under-theorized.

Discussion of essentially similar problems in various branches of planning and social science literature include the following.

The process of determining scope in environmental reviews is probably as close to a technically mandated requirement for defining a study area as can be found now in practice.[23]

The discussion of what groups or areas to include in cost-benefit analysis and other evaluation procedures raises similar problems.

The importance of scale, receiving increasing attention in the literature of geography in particular, is directly related.[24]

The age-old but ongoing and quite unresolved issues in the definitions of *urban*, *region*, and *metropolitan area* raises these questions also.[25]

Is it possible to generalize, then, from these diverse approaches to a very complicated question? How should a study area be defined for any particular site, or any particular project? Or, in the terms used here, how should the areas of concern for a project be defined, as they provide the basis on which study areas will subsequently be determined?

I believe at least two major alternatives can be outlined. One begins at the site and works from the inside outward; the other begins on the outside, with the affected community, and works inward.

Certainly the most prevalent in practice is to begin from the inside, with the site—the location of the projected action—and work outward. The client owns a particular piece of land, or the City Planning Commission is acting to deal with a particular problem or proposal that affects a particular location. Multiple sites might be examined for the location of a particular project (a home, a business, a museum, a waste disposal facility), and external factors may weigh heavily in a choice. But when it comes to a selection among the possible sites, the evaluation proceeds from the inside out: Does the location of that site meet the client's needs? Will there be adverse effects on surrounding areas that must be considered from the point of view of the project? (The editors may mean this by "area of effect.") Are there impacts on the site from the outside that must be considered? (The editors may mean this by "area of influence.") If so, the study area must encompass the locations outside the site that may impact it; but it will be the impact on the site, the impact seen from inside, that will count.

The alternative begins by looking at the site from the outside, to evaluate the function it performs in the broader community. What are the greatest needs in the community, and how might a project at the site best assist in meeting them? What is the best potential use for the site, or sites like it, in terms of community needs? Are there major concerns about the number of jobs created, temporary or permanent? Is the identity of the community a concern, and how might alternative proposals affect it? Is the tax base a key concern? How will alternative uses relate to the general plan for the community, or should the plan be modified because of the potentials of the site? If there is public investment involved, is this the best use of those funds (an important question for private clients also).

Defining a study area by looking in from the outside presents the most difficulties. At least four obstacles will arise: the definition of community, the scope of the task, the weighing of alternative concerns against each other, and the client's wishes. Each obstacle (except perhaps the last) can be overcome in practice.

First, definitions of community abound. These are an issue of scale, and depend on the magnitude of the project and the formal tools available to decision makers to influence it. Rarely will the realistic scale be larger than the city, although for very large projects it well might be. In any case, the feasible scale for examination must be limited by the public jurisdictions in authority. That authority may be actual and formal or potential and informal (a state generally may have major influence over what happens within a city, but only exercises its full powers in very rare instances). The practical definition of community thus must be largely political and significantly legal.

Second, the difficulty of the scope of examination within the study area must be taken into consideration; there is no point defining a study area so large that resources are not available to examine it. What can be done will of course vary according to each case. The best way to begin is with a scan: a quick overview of the possibilities, the concerns that stand out, what logic and experience suggest would be important, what existing pressures have highlighted. Scanning, which has a long tradition in planning theory and public administration,[26] should cover potential issues, as well as an initial feasibility review of what can be usefully examined. Even if it is only possible to call attention to the factors not being examined, this at least should always be done.

Third, concerns conflict: one party's environmental concern influences another party's real estate value; some prioritize jobs over open space, others do not; some are concerned with through transportation, some with local traffic pacification; some want market rate housing, others subsidized. Balancing competing concerns is the subject of innumerable discussions in planning theory and public administration. One approach sees the planner/designer's role as seeking consensus. The approach of involving all stakeholders might be seen as a means of achieving consensus, but might well simply be a way of clarifying where the power lies and going with it. And of course the very determination of legitimate stakeholders already prejudges the outcome: Over what area of concern are stakeholders to be invited?

There is an answer to these questions, at least for professionals concerned with the ethics of their work. The *Code of Ethics* of the American Institute of Certified Planners (AICP), for instance, states:

> A. A planner's primary obligation is to serve the public interest. While the definition of the public interest is formulated through continuous debate, a planner owes allegiance to a conscientiously attained concept of the public interest, which requires these special obligations:

1) A planner must have special concern for the long-range consequences of present actions.
2) A planner must pay special attention to the inter-relatedness of decisions.
3) A planner must strive to provide full, clear and accurate information on planning issues to citizens and governmental decision makers.
4) A planner must strive to give citizens the opportunity to have a meaningful impact on the development of plans and programs. Participation should be broad enough to include people who lack formal organization or influence.
5) A planner must strive to expand choice and opportunity for all persons, recognizing a special responsibility to and for the needs of disadvantaged groups and persons, and must urge the alteration of policies, institutions and decisions which oppose such needs.
6) A planner must strive to protect the integrity of the natural environment....[27]

The concerns that obligate planning and planners thus are not determined by the particular constraints of the site, but by the need to see it as part of an area of long-term concerns that includes related decisions elsewhere. Decisions as to what area of concern should be taken as a study area, and who the relevant stakeholders are, must be taken from the outside in, with a particular eye for the interests of disadvantaged groups, environmental quality, and the other requirements of professionally ethical conduct.

That leads to the fourth obstacle, which may realistically present the greatest difficulty in the proper definition of a study area: the wishes of the client. Not many private clients will take interest in looking at a site from the outside in, beginning with an analysis of the general problems of a community for which that site may play a role. Most clients have concern for the feasibility of a particular project: the private sector mandates profitability; in the public sector the nature of the problem to be addressed generally comes from public decision makers. A professional may therefore be caught in a dilemma: either follow the wishes of the client, or follow the dictates of the *Code of Ethics*. With a private client solely concerned with self-interest, the dilemma can come down to taking the job, using such influence as the professional may have to broaden the concerns of the client, or rejecting the job altogether. In the public case, the choice should not be so difficult. Any public agency should be concerned to look at the wide scope of issues affecting any given project, or that the project might affect; certainly the ethical obligation of comprehensiveness would dictate this for a planning agency. The earlier statement by the then American Institute of Planners, forerunner of the AICP, holds:

> The professional planner owes faithful, creative, and efficient performance of work in pursuit of his client's interest, but also owes allegiance to a conscientiously attained concept of the public interest and a primary commitment to maximize opportunity and expand the extent of choice available to those restricted by social, economic, personal or other constraints. When a professional planner considers that planning policies, instruments, organizations or institutions are not in the interests of those intended to be served by the planning process, he must strive diligently to ensure that they are altered to reflect such interests.[28]

The obligation is not to succeed, but to try, diligently.

Apply these ideas to the lower Manhattan case: The community whose interests are involved here is very broad. To begin with, we have the national community. Viewed comprehensively, what happens at the site of the direct physical damage invokes the national interest primarily because the events that occurred there had supra-local, national, and indeed international origins. It is, in a sense, coincidental that New York was involved. The goal was clearly to make a statement about the United States' power, in this case financial power, and the World Trade Center simply provided the symbol of that national/international relationship. This has particular relevance to decisions affecting the memorial and the extent to which (or the way in which) the site is used to confront that supra-local issue. But that national/international interest is barely reflected in the competition guidelines for the memorial established by the Lower Manhattan Development Corporation. Instead, the entirely legitimate concerns of a much narrower community—those who lost persons close to them in the attack—takes preeminence, to the significant exclusion of broader interests.

At the more local level, the state of New York does not have a discernibly separate interest in the definition of the area of concern here. As legal "parent" of the city, the state (and indeed the federal government) may well wish to assist the city in a matter of grave difficulty. That presumably benevolent interest should entitle the state merely to see that its contributions are not wasted; it does not give the state any separate interest from that of the city in what happens at the site. Given this logic, the governor's extensive involvement in decisions affecting the site is inappropriate. The legitimate concerns of the state are no different from those of the city, and should be subsumed under those of the city.

Taking the city of New York as the community whose concerns should represent the beginning of planning for the World Trade Center site—taking the city as the study area—is appropriate. Such a definition is only geographic as a matter of convenience; almost all the concerns relevant to planning for the site are found or represented within the territorial limits of the city. For example, the concerns of those connected to individuals who died in the attack on September 11 are important for what happens on the site. Most lived within the city of New York. But that hardly bears on the nature of their interest; almost as many of those killed lived in New Jersey as in New York. Yet by examining interests within New York City, the parallel interests of those without will also surface.

The question of appropriate public investment (and encouragement of private investment) poses a major issue in planning for the World Trade Center site. What study befits that question? The state hardly seems a major concern: the suggestion by Governor Pataki to use federal funds directed at September 11 issues to fund a rail route between New York City and Schenectady was laughed out of serious consideration. On the other hand, some months before September 11, 2002, Senator Schumer had convened a committee of thirty-two to examine the long-range potential of investment in subcenters in New York City, locations outside downtown Manhattan where major centers of business activity might be supported, such as Jamaica in Queens, the Hub in the Bronx, or central Brooklyn. What happens in lower Manhattan clearly has relevance for what happens in those other locations. The precepts of the AICP *Code of Ethics* are:

Special concern for the long-range consequences of present actions
The inter-relatedness of decisions
Expanding choice and opportunity for all persons, recognizing a special responsibility to the needs of disadvantaged groups and persons

If the precepts are to be followed, the study area must encompass these locations outside downtown Manhattan and permit inclusion in the planning of considerations of how investment at the World Trade Center site would affect employment at these other locations, who would be affected, what their needs were, and so on.

The best way to define this area of concern, however, is not solely in geographic terms. The national interest is not circumscribed by geography. Those affected by the individual deaths of September 11 are not geographically identifiable. Nor are those who lost their jobs. Looking broadly at the community in which the site is located, the interests of the disadvantaged cannot be essentially geographically described, although they may live or work in geographically concentrated areas. Each of the lines drawn around specific geographic areas, as shown in Figure 10.1, reveals the inadequacy of the geographic basis for defining a particular area of concern. The geographical definition is merely shorthand for an economic, social, or psychological concern.

Area 1 is the site itself, the area of direct physical damage. Even it cannot be defined *ab initio*, for the extent of physical damage needed detailed examination. Determining whether a given building (for instance the Deutsche Bank building immediately to the south of the World Trade Center site) was within an area of demolition and clearance, rather than repair and rehabilitation, required extensive investigation, and was in fact only resolved, some two and a half years after September 11, 2001. Thus, Area 1 concerns extent of direct physical impact; that performance criterion must determine its boundary.

Reviewing the areas drawn by the Lower Manhattan Development Corporation, FEMA, the city, and other concerned groups, reveals that the setting of boundaries stems from, and is a surrogate for, the confrontation with social, economic, physical, and individual concerns not in fact circumscribed by, although perhaps concentrated in, geographic space. Even concerns most logically linked to particular locations (e.g., residents of lower Manhattan) could alternatively be defined as residential concerns linked to the negative effects of September 11. If Area 1 in Figure 10.1 represents a cut-off for consideration of those concerns, then the bias of the designation becomes clear: on one side of the line, compensation, on the other, none. The distributional effect, the impact on "the disadvantages" that are supposed to be a special responsibility of planners, is dramatic. In this particular case, a gradient of incomes and "advantage" moves from the World Trade Center site to the northeast, and the line designating Area 1 favors the better-off contained within at the expense of those less well-off outside. A serious study area taking as its concern residential difficulties must be much larger than Area 1, and should arguably include all those within the city whose residential security has been affected by September 11. If such an area needs geographic definition, that can be done only after the broad area of concern has been examined. Even then, the examination will disclose that some of those affected lived outside the city: many in New Jersey, some in Connecticut, and a few well beyond the borders of the state of New York. Their concerns also need to be included.

The same analysis will show that, for each of the other areas outlined in Figures 10.1 and 10.2, the definition provides a weak substitute for an analysis and a set of policies that would be generated from beginning with a much wider study area. The secondary study area shown in Figure 10.2 includes Chinatown and those of its residents affected by September 11. One type of impact stems from location: much of Chinatown, due to its position, directly felt the smoke and ashes following the attack, and all of it suffered from the ensuing difficulty of access. Others suffered—were affected—in ways less locationally specific: jobs lost, breadwinners killed, markets gone. The issues that define the secondary study area also make it appropriate to define a much larger study area in which all those similarly affected can see their concerns addressed.

The transportation hub proposed for lower Manhattan, Calatrava's new winged design, is the most dominant feature of the planning thus far detailed and involves a huge investment: two billion dollars. A key component provides direct rail link to JFK airport. As far as is known, the study area used to arrive at the current proposal considered primarily the possible paths through Queens to the East River, the possible crossings of the river, and the connection to other transit lines at

Fulton Street and the site itself. But looking from the outside in, the first question would be: What is the appropriate role of a transportation hub at this site? An examination of the transportation network in New York City and its region would raise questions such as: Is the site a better location for a terminus of a JFK line than midtown Manhattan? With limited funds, is a Second Avenue line a better investment than a JFK line? How do either compare with an upgrading of the subway system as a whole, or with bringing LIRR lines into Grand Central Terminal, or upgrading commuter rail to New Jersey, Westchester County and above, or Connecticut? This study area should be regional and should consider the range of geographic impacts of these alternatives, not just the impact on the site itself or on the primary and secondary study areas.

Practically, many of the concerns inevitably involved in this project either conflict or, given limited resources, require prioritization, so that a useful listing of areas of concern can guide study and implementation. Again, The *Code of Ethics* of the AICP provides guidance. Paragraph 4, quoted earlier in this section, stresses citizen participation, which would be important in cases just such as the World Trade Center. Such participation has in fact taken place, through massive outreach efforts by the Civic Alliance, the Municipal Arts Society, and many other private volunteer civic groups. The Lower Manhattan Development Corporation has also held various public hearings, of much more limited scope, and is not bound to take into consideration, much less abide by, any of the resulting areas of consensus. Formal participatory processes provided for in the charter of the city of New York—its Uniform Land Use Review Procedures, hearings before the City Planning Commission and the city council, and so on—legally have no binding force under the legislation creating the Lower Manhattan Development Corporation. Similarly, the City Planning Commission has not shown itself particularly desirous of getting involved, except very belatedly and then only to limited questions of street configuration within the site itself. Nevertheless, the right way to define areas of concern for a project such as this, and priorities among them, would certainly call for a broad and effective process of citizen participation.

The result, in the World Trade Center case, would begin with a map similar to Figure 10.3, prepared by New York New Visions shortly after September 11, 2002, to show the real extent of the places affected by that event and needing to be considered in any planning to deal with its consequences. Looking from the outside in, this would be the starting point.

How then should a study area be defined, using the general principles set out in this essay and the lessons from the lower Manhattan case? The process should begin with a consideration of the concerns affected by a project, looking at the site from the outside—that is, its position in the wider community or communities in which it is located or which it affects. An orderly scan of alternatives should be undertaken. Priority should be given to those concerns, goals, and values to which the planning and design professions are dedicated, including the interests of the disadvantaged, environmental protection, and social equity. Participation in that scoping process should be as widespread and democratic as possible. A study area can then be defined that permits adequate consideration of the concerns identified and evaluation of their relationship to what is proposed for the site. For that purpose, the boundaries of a study area should not be taken as more than a convenient way of looking at concerns that in many cases may not be geographically bounded at all. Definition of a geographic study area is simply a surrogate for definition of the concerns to be studied.

The concerns of a site, viewed from the inside out, should not dictate the study area. Conversely, the concerns of the community in which a site is located should determine what area involving the site should be studied, viewing the site from the outside in, and even before that, what areas of concern should be taken into consideration, whether geographically defined or not. Broad and effective public participation can help determine those concerns; for professionals the interests highlighted by professional ethics—for the disadvantaged, environmental protection and social equity—should have prominence. In the planning of a project, it should always be remembered that the boundaries of a geographically defined study area serve simply as surrogates of convenience for the analysis of the human concerns found within, but often also without, those bounds.

Notes

1. See editors' introduction, "Why Site Matters" (in this volume).

2. The distinction is roughly equivalent to that made by the editors in their introduction to this volume in speaking of areas of effect and areas of influence.
3. John M. Levy, *Contemporary Urban Planning* (Englewood Cliffs: Prentice Hall, 1988), 133.
4. F. Stuart Chapin, Jr., and Edward J. Kaiser, *Urban Land Use Planning*, 2nd ed. (Urbana: University of Illinois Press, 1979), 254.
5. William I. Goodman and Eric C. Freund, eds., *Principles and Practice of Urban Planning* (Washington, D.C.: International City Managers' Association, 1968), 108.
6. Donald A. Krueckeberg and Arthur L. Silvers, *Urban Planning Analysis: Methods and Models* (New York: John Wiley & Sons, 1974), 194.
7. Frank S. So and Judith Getzels, eds., *The Practice of Local Government Planning*, 2nd ed. (Washington, D.C.: International City Management Association in cooperation with the American Planning Association (APA), 1988), 94.
8. The point is strikingly illustrated by a comment of David Johnson, of the University of Tennessee, on a Brookings report speaking of a net transfer from "the Northeast" to "the Southwest." Johnson points out that the fallacy here is that the study area is so gross that it conceals internal inequalities within the Northeast region, due to averaging of high incomes and low incomes. Communication with the author, David Johnson, November 2002.
9. See, for instance, Leonard Ortolano's *Environmental Regulations and Impact Assessment*, a reference Ellise M. Bright kindly provided.
10. Dan Abramson brought this aspect to my attention in commenting on note deletion in "Local Areas of Vancouver," by B. W. Mayhew of the Research Department of the United Community Services of the Greater Vancouver Area, January 1967 (Revised January 1970). This report outlines the method used in Vancouver, B.C., to divide the city into smaller units appropriate to the distribution of social services. The relevant citations he provides are Wendell Bell and Eshref Shevsky, "who identified urban sub-units in the San Francisco Bay Area" (no full citation given). There were two other relevant citations: D. Foley "The Use of Local Facilities in a Metropolis," in *American Journal of Sociology* 56:3 (November 1950); and W. H. Form et al., "The Compatibility of Alternative Approaches to the Delimitation of Urban Subareas," in *American Sociological Review* 19:4 (August 1954).
11. Thus Chapin and Kaiser, supra, list as a "major requirement" the selection of an "area officially used for reporting census information," 116.
12. Pierre Bourdieu, *La misere du monde* (Paris: Editions du Seuil, 1993), English trans. *The Weight of the World* (London: Polity Press, 1999). The translation here is from "Site Effects," *Quaderns* S.S.234 (2002): 33.
13. I have written about aspects of 9/11 and the reactions to it in several places. See, for instance, Peter Marcuse, "What Kind of Planning after September 11? The Market, the Stakeholders, Consensus—or…?" in Michael Sorkin and Sharon Zukin, eds., *After the World Trade Center: Rethinking New York City* (New York: Routledge, 2002), 153–162; "On the Global Uses of September 11 and Its Urban Impact," in Stanley Aronowitz and Heather Gautney, eds., *Implicating Empire: Globalization & Resistance in the 21st Cen-*

tury World Order (New York: Basic Books, 2003), 271–286; "After the World Trade Center: Deconcentration and Deplanning," *Quaderns d'arquitectura i urbanisme* 232 (2002): 38–45, also in Spanish, "Despues del World Trade Center: Desconcentracion y Desurbanismo," *Quaderns d'arquitectura i urbanisme* 232 (2002): 28–37; and "Urban Form and Globalization after September 11th. The View from New York," *International Journal of Urban and Regional Research* 26(3): 596–606.

14. It should not go without comment that many people in the world have problems that are even more pressing than those in New York City, hard as that may frequently be for us here to imagine.
15. See *Civic Alliance Response to the Draft Generic Environmental Impact Statement (DGEIS) WTC Memorial and Redevelopment Plan*, March 9, 2004 (New York: Civic Alliance).
16. See Civic Alliance to Rebuild Downtown New York, *Comments on the Draft Scope*, at *http://www.civic-alliance.org/pdf/0804CivicAllianceEISresponse.pdf*.
17. Moses's attitude was summed up by Guy Greer ("City Planning: Battle of the Approach," *Fortune* 28 [November 1943]: 164–165), quoted in Mark Gelfand, *A Nation of Cities: The Federal Government and Urban America, 1933–1965* (New York: Oxford University Press, 1975), 423: "the way to solve problems is to attack the sorest spots at dawn without presuming to try to plan in terms of the whole community."
18. The proposal, and the term, comes from Miles Colean's *Renewing Our Cities* (New York: Twentieth Century Fund, 1953), and was adopted by President Eisenhower's Advisory Committee on Housing, and incorporated in the *Housing Act of 1954*.
19. Gelfand, supra, 214.
20. Hawaii legislation, selected at random, is typical; it authorizes its redevelopment agency "to prepare a general neighborhood renewal plan for urban renewal areas," but nowhere states how such areas shall be established. See Section 53–55, Hawaii *General Statutes*. In New York State it authorizes "to prepare or cause to be prepared a general neighborhood renewal plan for an area consisting of an urban renewal area or areas, together with any adjoining areas having specially related problems." (*General Municipal Law*, § 554 [16, 17]).
21. Part I of Title XIII, Chapter I, Subchapter C of the *Omnibus Budget Reconciliation Act of 1993*: "Empowerment Zones, Enterprise Communities, and Rural Development Investment Areas."
22. For a more detailed discussion, see Peter Marcuse, "Federal Urban Programs as Multicultural Planning: The Empowerment Zone Approach," in Michael Burayidi, ed., *Urban Planning in a Multicultural Society* (Westport, Conn: Praeger, 2000), 225–234.
23. For a discussion of the broad issues, see Gordon E. Beanlands and Peter N. Duinker, *An Ecological Framework for Environmental Impact Assessment in Canada* (Halifax, Canada: Institute for Resource and Environmental Studies-Dalhousie University, 1983).
24. See Erik Swyngedouw with N. Heynen, "Urban Political Ecology, Justice and the Politics of Scale," *Antipode* 34(4) (2003): 898–918.

25. The issues in definition of neighborhood are, it seems to me, somewhat different, for there the effort is precisely to delimit and define narrowly, not to examine broad effects.
26. For a more general discussion, see Andreas Faludi, ed., *A Reader in Planning Theory* (New York: Pergamon Press, 1973); and Scott Campbell and Susan S. Fainstein, eds., *Readings in Planning Theory*, 2nd ed. (Oxford: Blackwell, 2003).
27. *AICP Code of Ethics and Professional Conduct*, Section A.
28. *The Social Responsibility of the Planner, General Guidelines*, Section 2.

Manhattan Skyline.

11

Defining Urban Sites

Andrea Kahn

How does an urban site gain design definition? What delineates its boundaries? How does it engage its surrounds? What determines its scale? This essay works through the problem of site definition as a necessarily indefinite task, especially when looking at terms of site definition in urban design. As used here, *urban site* makes double reference to both the whole city and limited sites within it, since even the smallest urban design intervention always speaks to the project of city-building writ large, and defining applies to both a process and its outcomes. At issue are means of site definition in urban design as well as the site knowledge they produce.

In design discourse, the qualifier "urban" attaches to the concept of site to no significant effect. This should not be the case. When representing urban sites, or relationships between sites in urban situations, designers draw on concepts, terminologies, and graphic conventions that pertain to all kinds of sites, in general. Common terms (*place*, *ground*, *context*, *scale*, *location*, *boundary*, etc.) remain largely indiscriminate with respect to differences in setting or settlement conditions. Without benefit of language expressly applicable to urban sites, their definition, as a subset of sites in general, remains tied to notions of property and ownership, to a physically delimited and containable parcel of land. A site is defined as urban adjectivally, based either on geographic milieu (an urban design site refers to a limited place within an already established urban area or to an urban area in its entirety) or physical size (urban design sites are presumed to be larger than architectural sites and smaller than regional ones).

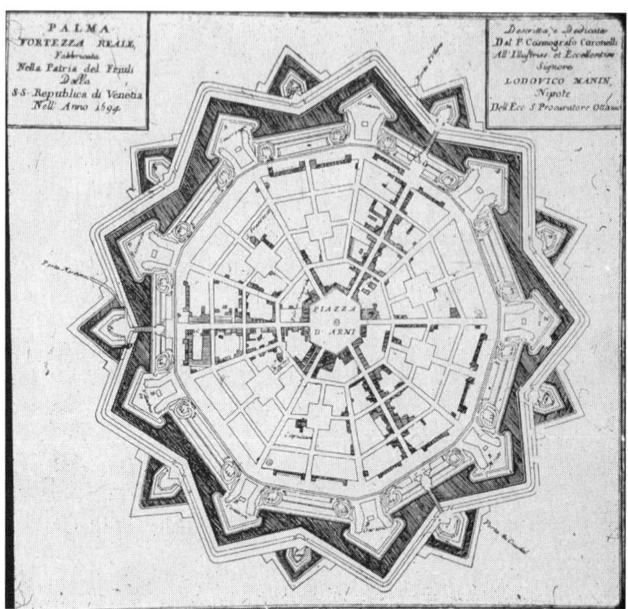

Figure 11.1. Anonymous, Palmanuova Plan, 1713.

To frame a site in explicitly urban terms, I use examples from New York City to lay out an operationally based definition concerned with what a site "does" in the city rather than what (or where) it "is." Then I turn to the role of representation in the site definition process. Finally, I conclude by offering up new terms to address the complexity inherent in urban sites. These terms provide conceptual tools applicable to urban analysis as well as urban design. By representing sites as having multiple boundary conditions and multiple scales, they frame a new conceptual model for describing, interpreting, and analyzing places slated for urban design intervention.

DEFINING URBAN SITES

> The point is not that drawing boundaries is somehow impermissible...but that the permeability of those boundaries has to be constantly reasserted; more than this, that the space in which they are drawn is not a simple plane. Each side folds over and implicates the other in its constitution.[1]

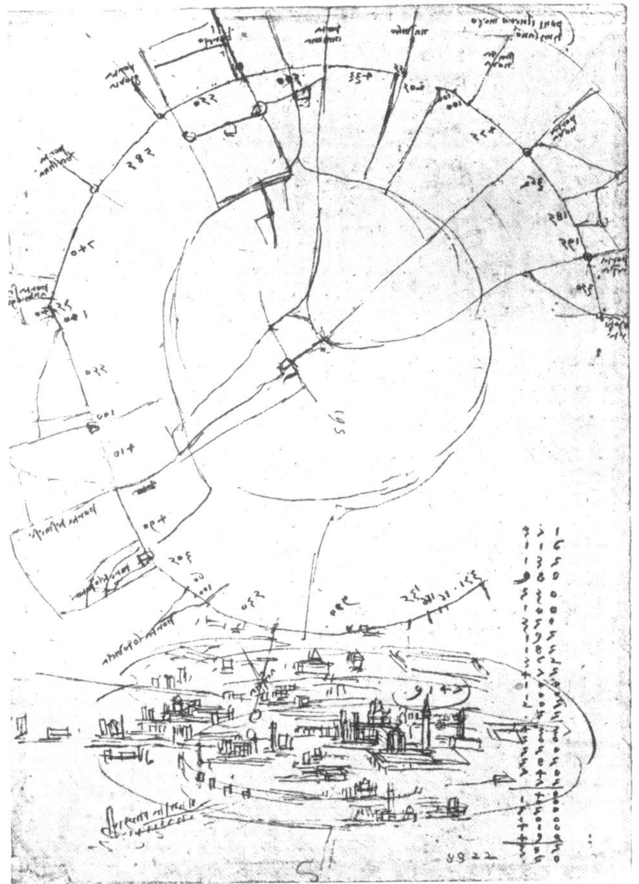

Figure 11.2. Leonardo da Vinci, View of Milan, sixteenth century.

Two drawings, a 1713 anonymous plan of the ideal Renaissance plan of Palmanuova, and a sixteenth-century Leonardo da Vinci sketch of Milan, register an often-overlooked but significant distinction in the way designers define site limits as well as how they understand site scale. The Palmanuova plan depicts the urban site as a clearly bounded place. In this walled enclave intended to be impenetrable to attack, the city is described as a fixed object in an open field. The drawing's centered composition, inset textual inscriptions, and heavy dark lines enclosing fortifications reinforce the reading of a city figure afloat in empty space. The plan strongly delineates inside and outside. Inside the walls of this city rendered as discrete object, everything sits carefully contained in its proper place.

In stark contrast, da Vinci's sketch swirls with the movements of many trajectories crisscrossing an unbounded space. Radiating lines activate the drawing's surface, projecting an image that extends outward beyond the edge of the page. Neither the bird's eye view at the bottom nor the plan above inscribes full enclosure. This drawing, which depicts a set of active interrelations, makes it impossible to locate the edge of the city. What lies inside its boundary and what lies outside is unclear. The limits of this urban site cannot be pinned down in the horizontal or the vertical dimension. Its boundaries remain porous, its figure incomplete.

Comparing these historical images illustrates an important difference between an idea of site linked to conventional notions of place and one disentangled from notions of limited location. The single Palmanuova plan conceives the city as stable and rigidly bounded. The composite sketch of Milan shows an active setting with permeable limits, an urban site comprised of many overlapping spaces. In Leonardo's image no border divides site from situation. Rather than equating boundary with a line of separation, this sketch encourages viewers to ask how an urban site is linked to its outside. Instead of creating divisions that frame simple enclosures, as Palmanuova does, the looser and more porous image of Milan offers an alternative conception of site limits and scale. It captures the complexity found in actual urban situations.

Consider, for example, a high-density residential project on a large lot extending north from 56th to 72nd Street, on Manhattan's Upper West Side. Understood narrowly as legally owned property, this site—developed by Donald Trump—obviously has a fixed boundary line. However, since the urban impact of his development reaches well beyond the edge of his parcel, when considered in urban terms, the significance of this legal perimeter diminishes greatly. Trump City's urban site includes not only the ground under the residential towers, but also those areas affected by their construction. For instance, a subway station three blocks to the east required renovation to accommodate the expected load of thousands of new commuters, and a waste treatment facility eighty blocks to the north in Harlem was built to bear the infrastructural burden of Trump's high-density towers.

Forcing changes to New York City's subway and sewage systems, the property limits of the Trump site are hardly impervious to the many forces that ultimately establish the project's urban condition. Adopting an operational definition of the site—based on how it works in, with, through, and upon its urban situation—alters the understanding of Trump City's "limits."

Treating urban sites as operational constructs recasts their boundedness. Instead of demarcating simple metes and bounds, defining urban site limits requires accounting for co-present, but not necessarily spatially coincident fields of influence and effect. Urban sites encompass proximate as well as nonproximate relations, physical as well as nonphysical attributes.[2] As settings for interactions and intersections that transgress abstract property divisions, urban sites are conditioned by, and contribute to, their surroundings.

Times Square, in New York, easily fits such description: a place whose identity is comprised by interactions between a global circuit of entertainment (the Disney Corporation, Condé Nast), a metropolitan crossroads of commercial developments (Broadway and Seventh Avenue), and a local district of direct and imaginary engagements (Broadway shows, Madame Tussaud's Wax Museum, ABC's *Good Morning America*, the minimal remains of an erstwhile thriving sex industry). The specificity of this urban site is construed through an array of co-present but not coincident operations. Its *reality*—or, more accurately, its *realities*—are constituted through the experience of radically shifting programs in constant interaction. What defines Times Square as an urban site is a function of the crossings of spatial networks, each with its own degree of spatial extension. The determination of its boundary—or again, more accurately, its boundaries—depends on how far afield these networks, and their influence, reach. As an urban site emplaced in numerous local, global, metropolitan, and regional settings, Times Square is tied into diverse scaling processes at one time. While it provides a particularly vivid example of the multiscaled site, urban sites—wherever they are located and whatever their size—will be similarly constituted.

Hell's Kitchen, lying just two blocks to the west, operates at just as many scales. The area is at once a residential neighborhood, a commercial district, and a nodal intersection of transportation infrastructures. It is the locus of a national highway system (entering midtown Manhattan through the Lincoln Tunnel); regional, cross-country, and international bus lines (arriving at and departing from the Port Authority Terminal); a metropolitan public transit system (subways and buses); global speculative ventures (proposed large-scale development on the far West Side); citywide commercial markets (specialty food shops, restaurants catering to immigrant taxi drivers); local communities (Hell's Kitchen neighborhood, with its own association). Numerous fields of operation converge at this one place, each involving different scales of activity. As such, the scale of this site cannot be characterized as singly or simply urban. Rather, this place operates at local, metropolitan, regional, national, and global scales. As an urban site it is scaled through a set of dynamic functions created by fluid interactions between many differentially extensive processes.[3]

Embedded within, and constitutive of, so many framing contexts, such multiscalar urban sites open to diverse interpretation.[4] They are saturated with difference, permeated with irreducible diversity: heterological, to borrow a term from Mikhail Bakhtin.[5] They offer up myriad dimensions for consideration (economic, social, historical, physical, political, haptic), each of which situates the site within a web of specific associations. In terms of their limits and their scales, urban sites present designers with shifting and potentially conflicting identities. As such, they are best characterized as resulting from "a matrix of forces, impossible to recoup and therefore impossible to resolve."[6] They are crisis objects that destabilize our certainty of the real.[7]

Urban sites are dynamic rather than static, porous rather than contained, "messy" like da Vinci's Milan sketch rather than "neat" like the ideal plan of Palmanuova. Defining them in design terms thus does not come down to establishing some unique identity of a limited physical place, but quite the opposite. It involves recognizing the overlay and interplay of multiple realities operating at the same time, on the same place. How designers give definition to these multivalent and multiscalar urban design sites, however, remains an open question.

REPRESENTING URBAN SITES

> However forcefully the real and the represented world resist fusion, however immutable the presence of that categorical boundary line between them, they are nevertheless indissolubly tied up with each other and find themselves in continual mutual interaction, uninterrupted exchange goes on between them...[8]

Given an operational definition of urban sites as multiscalar, heteroglot settings for interactions and intersections, how do designers think through their complexity and multivalence? This question raises the issue of site study and with it the means, methods, and modes of site definition processes. As in any design process, ideas of site come through making. Designers confront the challenge of defining urban sites through a creative process of representation.

The artifacts of this process, representations such as drawings and models, do not simply illustrate what designers think about (in this case, the city); more profoundly, they reveal how designers think. The identities of an urban site can be construed many ways. Mappings can present each "reality" separately and attempt to position each in relative terms as a function of shared descriptive and analytic parameters (scale, drawing type, categories of information, etc.). Or they can project a heterogeneous urban condition by utilizing representational techniques that actively combine distinct parameters. By bringing different realities into contact and establishing methods to chart their interplay, the process of site representation works as the staging ground of site thinking. It is a place of assembly and a point of departure for constructing relations between and across different forms of site knowledge.

In common usage, *representation* is a word loaded with meaning; it has political, philosophical, symbolic, and aesthetic dimensions, visual and nonvisual connotations. Even in the relatively focused vocabulary of design, *representation* is a term subject to misunderstanding. Used as a noun, it refers to things made. Used as a verb, it refers to a process of making. But these two meanings still do not make the full extent of representation's role in site definition apparent. Representation is a conceptual tool that orders understanding of the multivalence of urban

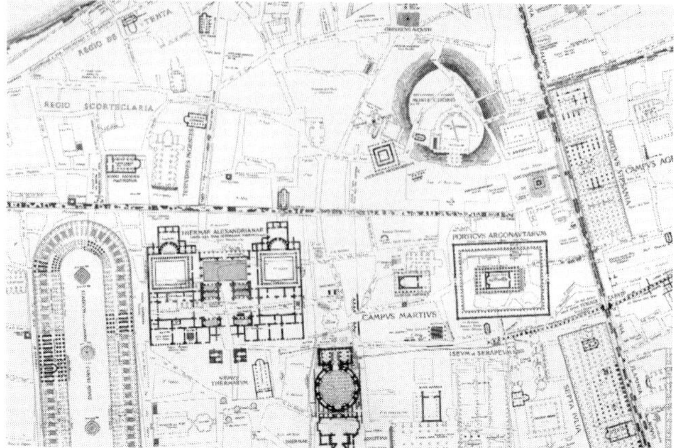

Figure 11.3. Rodolfo Lanciani, *Forma Urbis Romae*, Plate 15, 1893–1901.

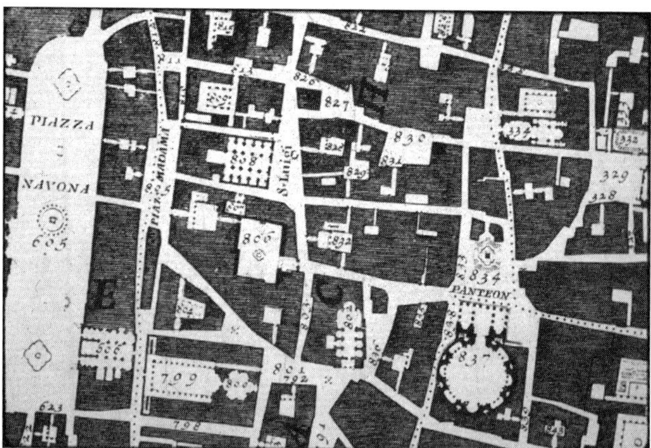

Figure 11.4. Giambattista Nolli, Rome Plan, 1748.

sites. It is a means of literally thinking through their many realities—presencing as well as positioning them in relative terms.

Site representations propose working hypotheses for comprehending and testing working definitions of urban site. To grasp the full import of this idea, one first has to recognize the expansive potential of representation: that in the most profound sense, representation is not about depicting reality, but about making knowledge. For design, it is a mode of conceptual operation, a process of knowledge formation. More than simply amassing and organizing facts, figures, and impressions of a given condition, the descriptions and analyses that designers produce actually generate the knowledge necessary to engage a given condition as a site. Site representation is not a matter of getting a reality right as much as a matter of constructing forms of knowledge that can cope with multiple realities. In this sense, site drawings, models, and discourses are never mere second-order redescriptions of some preexisting condition as much as they are evidence of thought in formation, a thought about what the urban site might be.

At the most basic level, representation gives definition to the urban site because it is a process in which different ideas of site settle down or settle in—perhaps an idea found through urban history, as in Rodolfo Lanciani's *Forma Urbis Romae* mappings or, perhaps a idea based on city form, as shown by Nolli's well-known figure–grounds of the same city. Each mapping proposes an identifiable site reality, because each operates as a distinctive mode of site thinking. To ask which of two representations depicts the real site is meaningless, just as it makes no sense to ask which of two ways of thinking is correct. Distinct site representations produce different artifacts, but each artifact instantiates a similarly dialogic and creative performance, an "experiment in contact with the real."[9] Site representations construct site knowledge; they make site concepts manifest by design.

FIVE CONCEPTS FOR URBAN SITE THINKING

For urban design, site concepts matter. More than merely discursive, they act as powerful tools to structure site thinking. Yet, without language to discern between different kinds of sites, the ways designers represent and engage with urban sites cannot be situationally derived. Generic concepts only allow for generic site thinking. But design discourse has no specifically urban site concepts on offer. The five new terms outlined in the following sections conceptualize sites in meaningful ways for urban design.

Mobile Ground

Much of urban design, as a field of design action, involves framing constructive conversations among different interests and agents in the city. To be effective, designers at work on projects with urban aspirations must account for and negotiate between many players invested in the future of a particular locale: workers, owners, neighbors, and builders; politicians, developers, and bankers; preservationists, ecologists, and economists, to name but a few. Each interested party construes the urban design site according to its own terms, adopting its own preferred modes of representation.* They all claim to know it, but one player's knowledge rarely conforms to the knowledge held by others. Different lenses filter these understandings.

As concerns shift back and forth between various takes on the same place, these oscillations define a variable field where the constructed and the real are not opposed.[10] They inscribe a *mobile ground* where urban sites are understood as dynamic and provisional spaces, as points of departure to parts unknown rather than places of arrival of fixed address.[11] Conceiving of urban sites as mobile ground foregrounds their provisional condition, reminding designers that sites remain subject to change beyond their control. On mobile ground, urban design actions are best considered in strategic terms—focused on framing urban relations and structuring urban processes.[12] Mobile ground describes a space of progression, slippage, and continual revaluation, where diverse realities tip over, into, and out of each other. It is where site boundaries and site images shift, bend, and flex, depending on who is looking.

Site Reach

The issue of scale is key to the definition of urban sites, influencing how designers understand the context of their work and how they define the geographic extent of their areas of concern.** Because urban sites participate in many differently scaled networks at once, talking about an urban scale, as a singular measure or the attribute of some entity,

* "Multifamily housing sites are missing from most conceptions of suburban landscapes partly because conventional ways of measuring and understanding urbanized areas have obscured their identification. The high densities of apartment concentrations relative to surrounding areas of detached houses, for instance, are not captured by the common mapping tools used by planners and academics. Census tracts, forecast analysis zones (FAZs), and transportation analysis zones (TAZs)—standard geographic units of analysis used for mapping—are simply too large to capture the spatial patterning of suburban development." P. Hess, "Neighborhoods Apart."

** "The definition of a study area can be seen as a subset of the problems involved in trying to define a problem or formulate a solution to a problem, in geographic terms. The first difficulty lies in establishing the criteria by which the relevant geographic boundaries are set. The second lies in the usually implicit and hidden assumptions being made about the nature of the problem and its confinement to such boundaries." P. Marcuse, "Study Areas, Sites, and the Geographic Approach to Public Action."

obscures the multiscalar condition of urban sites. Urban locales register on multiple scalar networks, in some cases at different times, in other cases simultaneously. *Site reach* measures the extent, range, and level of interactions between a localized place and its urban surroundings. It gauges vicinities of exchange and intersection between places, reciprocal and nonreciprocal relations, inscribed within and contributing to co-present urban spatial networks. For urban design, the concept of site reach proposes a much-needed alternative to a conventional, nested, and hierarchical model of scale that identifies different scales with differently sized territories, and as such obscures the multiscalar condition of urban sites. Urban sites are constructed by a complex overlay of distinct but interrelated uses, boundaries, forms, and temporal sequences. In any given locale, variously scaled interactions establish a unique set of linkages to other places. The reaches of a site depend on the spatial and operational extension of those associations and connectivities that tie it to other places. By situating any limited place within the space of the city as a whole, site reach reinforces the fact that any urban design intervention, no matter how limited in physical scope, participates in a project of city-building writ large.

Site Construction

Although considered a predesign activity, site analysis inevitably prefigures and reflects design intentions.* The logics and values structuring initial site observations are always and already prescribed by ideas about the future modifications imagined for a place, and conversely, the analysis process initiates a way of thinking about place that resonates through all subsequent phases of design.**

* "As often as not, an architect's description of an existing context will soon underpin a subsequent series of decisions to intervene in that context. A characterization of context smuggles into the design process a set of confirming values camouflaged as a description of existing conditions and observed facts; the details of any description of context will usually indicate whether the speaker aims to respect or reject it." S. Isenstadt, "Contested Contexts."

** "Site analysis, at a large scale and recorded through detached rational mappings, has given way to site-readings and interpretations drawn from first-hand experience and from a specific site's social and ecological histories. These site-readings form a strong conceptual beginning for a design response, and are registered in memorable drawings and mappings conveying a site's physical properties, operations, and sensual impressions." E. Meyer, "Site Citations."

In urban design, more often than not, sites are actively produced. *Site construction* is a site study process that yields a designed understanding of site through consciously selective viewing. The site definitions it produces are distinct from the design decision that results in establishing project boundaries (the determination delimiting where design actions physically take place).[13] This site study method embraces design agendas and asserts the interpretive basis of any site viewing process.

To define a site as urban, the process of site construction accounts for multiple fields of influence and effect, each with distinct spatial limits that in concert construe a territory of design concern. It recognizes, but does not attempt to reconcile, heterogeneous urban orders and logics. By not oversimplifying site complexity, this method of site study initiates and supports nonreductive urban design actions. These site analyses underscore the multivalence of urban sites, making of it a key issue for urban design attention. Regional, metropolitan, and local architectural; moving or static; large and small scale; close and distant: each vantage point brings different aspects of a site to light and each way of organizing site information (politically, economically, formally, historically, spatially, etc.) results in a distinct site configuration. Individually, these expose a predilection toward some combination of the city's myriad characters.* Drawn together, the many approaches begin to approximate the multivalence built into the urban landscape. Rather than conceive of sites as having one single bounding condition, site construction posits that site boundaries shift in relation to the position—the physical location and ideological stance—of their beholder. It dispels the illusion of the city as either containable or controllable by hypothesizing the urban situation as a porous and shifting space.[14]

Unbound Sites

Any design action for a limited site in a city is at once influenced by, and has consequences for, the city as site. The impossibility of isolat-

* "Part of preparing a place to become a site involves the formation of new narratives. Familiar to anyone who observes real estate development is the narrative onslaught that begins almost immediately as developers and real estate brokers tout the benefits, for example, of their proposed apartment building, its compatibility with urbane lifestyles, and its prestigious address. Planners and designers are complicit in this process. Their presence indicates a seriousness of purpose and even inevitability to the project. Their reports and images portray and publicize the new place. The first act of real estate development is the narrative remaking of the site." R. Beauregard, "From Place to Site."

ing one urban locale, operationally, from its surrounds, lends urban design its inherently public dimension, and acknowledging this public dimension prompts a critical reassessment of how site boundary is typically understood in design. Irrespective of whether rights to a limited development parcel are privately, publicly, or jointly held, design actions in urban contexts have consequence beyond narrowly construed limits of legal metes and bounds. The unbound site uncouples the definition of site boundary from notions of ownership and property. It views site limits as open to configuration according to various forms and forces of determination.* Rather than drawing a line between urban and site (equating boundary with a line of separation) urban designers need to ask how many ways sites are linked to an "outside," to spaces, times, and places beyond their present and immediate control.** Defining site boundary in terms of a single property line produces a circumscribed figure, contained, isolatable, and controllable (the site defined as entity under design control). Designers need instead to recognize border porosities and to treat scale as a measure of boundary permeability. In this sense, the urban site is unbound by virtue of its having many different structuring limits simultaneously in play, not because its boundaries are simply effaced. Urban sites are comprised of multiple fields (areas under design control, areas of influence and areas of effect) each delimited according to its own operational horizons.[15]

---

* "Grounds operate with great nuance. They resist hierarchy. There are no axes, centers or other obviously explicit means of providing orientation. Single, uncomplicated meanings are rare. Instead, there are open networks, partial fields, radical repetition, and suggestive fragments that overlap, weave together, and constantly transform. Within this textural density edges, seams, junctures, and other gaps reveal moments of fertile discontinuity where new relationships might grow. Relationships among grounds, are multiple, shifting, and inclusive. They engage the particular and the concrete rather than the abstract and the general." R. Dripps, "Groundwork."

** "Over the past thirty to fifty years, theories in the science of ecology have been reconsidered in at least three major areas: first, with regard to whether local ecosystems can be considered "closed" to larger-scale flows of materials and energy or whether the influences of these larger flows should be considered integral to local systems (I will refer to this as the spatial scale paradigm shift); second, in the degree to which local and regional history influences contemporary ecosystem dynamics (i.e., the temporal scale shift); and third, in the explicit consideration of physical landscape patterns as an important component of ecosystem functioning (i.e., the pattern shift). These developments have broad implications for ecologists who now think differently about relationships between local observations and events (or local spatial arrangements) and relationships that are neither local nor recent." K. Hill "Shifting Sites."

Urban Constellation

Context is what the site is not. Yet urban sites exist and participate in many contexts.* How, then, to define the confines of urban sites? The traditional idea of context implies that sites derive definition from their larger situation. Seeing a site "in context," however, depends on maintaining a clear distinction between inside and outside, thereby obscuring the difference between the boundaries of a building lot and the limits of an urban site.

At once a concept and a process, *urban constellation* blurs the line between context and site by demarcating site interactions across multiple fields of urban operation. It refers to a dynamic relational construct—formed by myriad interactions between variable forces (physical, social, political, economic, etc.) animated across multiple scales (as embedded in local, metropolitan, regional, and global spatial networks)—and the process through which that construct is defined. The process of urban constellation involves integrating knowledge of local place-based urban characteristics with knowledge of larger-scale spatial logics that underlie contemporary urbanism in all its forms. It problematizes the received idea of context as some outside, impassive backdrop.

Constructing urban constellations is not simply a matter of enlarging the contextual frame through which a particular place may be viewed. Rather, the concept of urban constellation requires that designers situate their urban sites in multiple contextual, or scalar, frames simultaneously. Constellations foreground context itself as a variable. Further, by projecting site and context as mutually implicated in the other's constitution, urban constellations reinforce understandings of site as a relational construct.

---

* "Few cities or buildings are more thoroughly documented than Paris and the works of Le Corbusier. Maps and aerial photographs of the sectors of Paris where Le Corbusier's projects are located are as readily availaable as the ubiquitous, published versions of the building plans, sections, and elevations. Yet, no documentation exists of this architect's work as it relates to its urban site. This simple, yet huge omission in the otherwise endless sea of information and speculation on Le Corbusier is astonishing. It demonstrates the pernicious obstinacy of a narrow framing of subject matter, which goes hand in hand with the modern concept of categorization. Categorization tends to distinguish and isolate, rather than relate. The 'phenomenon of concordance' referred to by Le Corbusier occurs in the interstices between building plan and city map. It is here that the story of the 'action of the work' on its surround is recorded, and where the 'environment brings its weight to bear.'" W. Redfield, "The Suppressed Site."

DEFINING THE INDEFINITE

The concepts outlined in the preceding sections consider urban design sites as relational constructs. In so doing, they oblige relational site thinking. They invite designers to consider how urban design sites differ from architectural ones on more than simply locational or dimensional grounds, emphasizing that limited locales in cities incorporate urban processes, systems, and logics that qualify and extend to the city as a whole.

In lieu of adopting topology (or topography) to generate schematic site representations, these new concepts set up a site definition process grounded in tropology.[16] Slippages in meaning between the terms intentionally figure urban sites as dynamic and processive. Their purpose is not to stabilize meaning, but to challenge the very idea of a stable urban site. These tools frame a new conceptual model for thinking about, and thinking through, urban sites. They construe the process of urban site definition as one of defining the indefinite. Instead of defining site in a narrow lexical sense, these concepts activate gaps between sign and meaning to characterize urban sites as spatially elastic and temporally provisional. Each recasts received ideas of boundary and scale in a slightly different way, yet all rebound around the same underlying point: that for urban design what matters is gaining understanding of the city *in* the site.

Notes

1. Derek Gregory, *Geographical Imaginations* (Cambridge: Blackwell, 1994), 72.
2. Melvyn Webber, "Urban Place and Non-Place Urban Realm," in M. Webber et. al., *Explorations in Urban Structure* (Philadelphia: University of Pennsylvania, 1964).
3. Neil Brenner has written extensively on the issue of scale and scaling processes. For a discussion of urban scale, see "The Urban Question as a Scale Question: Reflections on Henri Lefebvre, Urban Theory and the Politics of Scale," *International Journal of Urban and Regional Research* 24 (2000): 361–378. For a discussion of the fluidity of scale, see Erik Swyngedouw, "Neither Global nor Local: 'Glocalization' and the Politics of Scale," in K. Cox, ed., *Spaces of Globalization* (New York: Guildford Press, 1997), 137–166.
4. See Nigel Thrift on the definition of context as "active" and "differentially extensive" in *Spatial Formations* (London: Sage Publications, 1996), 3.

5. On heterology, see Tzvetan Todorov, *Mikhail Bakhtin: The Dialogical Principle* (Minneapolis: University of Minnesota, 1998), 56.
6. On heteroglossia, see M. M. Bakhtin, *The Dialogic Imagination,* trans. C. Emerson and M. Holquist (Austin: University of Texas Press, 1981), 291.
7. The notion of the city as a "'crisis-object' which destabilizes our certainty of 'the real'" comes from Robert Shields, "A Guide to Urban Representation and What to Do about It: Alternative Traditions of Urban Theory," in A. King, ed., *Re-Presenting the City: Ethnicity, Capital and Culture in the 21st Century Metropolis* (New York: NYU Press, 1996), 227.
8. M. M. Bakhtin, *The Dialogic Imagination*, 254.
9. Gilles Deleuze, *Foucault* (London: Athlone, 1988), 12.
10. On the constructed and the real, see Bruno Latour, "Whose Cosmos, Which Cosmopolitics? Comments on the Peace Terms of Ulrich Beck," *http://www.ensmp.fr/~latour/articles/article/92-BECK-CK.html* (April 2004).
11. "Places are best thought of not so much as enduring sites, but as moments of encounter, not so much as presents, fixed in space and time, but as variable events, twists and fluxes of interaction." Ash Amin and Nigel Thrift, *Cities: Re-Imagining the Urban* (Oxford: Polity Press, 2000), 30.
12. See my Aarden Hank, "Nomadic Thoughts 1: LA" *LAFORUM Newsletter* (September 1992): 5; and "Nomadic Thoughts 2: NJ," *LA FORUM Newsletter* (February 1993): 7.
13. On determining urban design site boundaries, see Edmund Bacon et al., "The City Image," in Elizabeth Geen, Jeanne R. Lowe, and Kenneth Walker, eds., *Man and the Modern City* (Pittsburgh: University of Pittsburgh Press, 1963).
14. For a more extensive discussion of site construction, see my "From the Ground Up: Programming the Urban Site" in *Harvard Architectural Review* 10 (1998): 54–71.
15. For a more elaborate discussion of the different areas of a design site, see the editors' introduction, "Why Site Matters."
16. On the theory of tropes, see Hayden White, *Metahistory: The Historical Imagination in Nineteenth-Century Europe* (Baltimore: Johns Hopkins University Press, 1973), 31–38.

12

High-Performance Sites

Carol J. Burns

DYNAMIC ROLE OF THE SITE IN BUILDING

Not fixed or static, the role of the site in the design disciplines has altered over time. This essay, an exploration of the changing status of site in design and construction of buildings, assumes the site to be both material reality and a cultural construct. As a material reality, the site endures in lowly earthiness, but as a living form it regenerates continuously in triumphant potency. As a construct of culture, the site is comprehensible only insofar as it is touched by human practices. We know the site because we make and shape it, socially, economically, and politically. Both of these viewpoints, realist and idealist, inform my argument, which traces three fundamentally dissimilar renderings of site in architecture. The first characterization of site is that of source for building materials and energy for construction. The second depiction is that of repository for building materials and energy imported from far afield. Finally, drawing on an emerging environmental impetus, the site is portrayed as linked interdependent systems combining intrinsic and extrinsic resources. These versions of site have risen to importance, respectively, in three different eras: the first beginning in prehistory and continuing today; the second beginning with industrialization and modernism; and the third beginning in the present time, characterized in developed economies as postindustrial. Though distinctly dissimilar, each version retains its currency today. Examining them provides insights into the dynamic status of the place of site in design disciplines as ascribed within changing social norms and professional values.

SITE AS A SOURCE OF MATERIALS AND ENERGY FOR BUILDING

For centuries, local sites provided the materials used in construction. Materials were limited to those readily available in nature: stone, clay, wood, straws and grasses, sod, masonry, concrete, and elemental metals. Some basic chemical transformations had been understood for thousands of years, including, for example, brick and tile from clay and concrete from cement, lime, and aggregate. However, few such transforming combinations were in use before the mid-nineteenth century.[1]

Transportation was difficult and expensive prior to industrialization. Therefore, construction materials typically came from locations on or near the building lot. The immediate or proximate site served as stock for basic material supply. The plot provided space for stockpiling and storing materials both preceding and following extraction or harvesting. The construction site—the area disturbed and transformed by building the structure—served as the platform for building fabrication. The energy for building—fuel for construction as well as human food sources—was limited and came, similarly, from the immediate area.

Autochthonous construction, using materials and building practices at hand, has remained remarkably unchanged for centuries. Techniques developed through trial and error, were handed down through craft and tradition. Construction, transportation, and craft all took time and evolved slowly.

The effort invested in making anything—a city, a house, a piece of furniture—was too significant to waste. The cost of materials was a greater component of economic value than the direct labor costs of building. Every artifact therefore was used, reused, and adapted until it wore out, and even then the parts were recycled. This mode of production conformed to the economic pattern of traditional societies: circular consumption sequences in which parts fit into interlocking wholes, each necessarily as efficient as possible. Vernacular buildings surviving to the present provide striking material evidence of deep abiding connections between places and human artifacture.[2]

In the vernacular approach, the operations of a building also functioned as an integrated system. Dynamics between building and site provided input for the building system, with the building fabric mediating between internal and external climates. Each aspect of the physical building fabric—the orientation of elements, the weight and thickness of walls, the size and placement of windows—fits together in interlocked relationships with processes of nature bearing on the site, including the sun, the wind, atmospheric pressure, and precipitation. Slow in production, simple in operation, the building and the site functioned as one integrated system. This simple design was intended to optimize the potential for comfort and habitability, though these were difficult to attain within the limits of available knowledge and technique.

This model—direct integration of site and building materials and energy—persists widely today. It depicts the available approach to building for the still-significant portion of the world's population that has not undergone industrial modernization. Within developed economies, these local rudimentary practices inform small-scale operations and structures, including the self-help programs supported by government in many emerging economies and, to a degree, the do-it-yourself ethos of renovation in North America. Fundamental aspects of this basic knowledge inform but do not fully comprise what is later described here as high-performance sites.

SITE AS A DEPOSITORY OF MATERIALS AND ENERGY FOR BUILDING

In the late-nineteenth century, an explosion in new technologies and materials began to transform architecture and construction. Materials and composites invented during this period include steel and reinforced concrete. Development of new materials continued to accelerate in pace, including a plethora of synthetic and sheet goods in the 1950s and continuing to the present day with new and expanded categories such as reinforced plastics, new adhesives, and alloys and metals including titanium. These goods typically require considerable transformation and processing. With origins in elementary matter extracted from the earth, construction materials increasingly take form and shape through industrial processes.

The development of new construction materials has depended on related parallel advances in transportation technologies. The harnessing of steam power in the early-nineteenth century brought with it mechanization, urbanization, the factory system, and product economies of price. Raw goods shipped by rail and steamboat supplied producer and consumer markets within and across regions. In the immediately ensuing phase of industrial revolution, electric power accompanied mass production, mass consumption, and the continual search for economies of scale.[3] Production and consumption of new construction materials depended on more elaborate transportation networks.

Though the building site remained a platform for construction, the source of materials and the site of fabrication for building components multiplied and dispersed. Specific geographic areas took on specialized roles, some as the source for resource extraction, others as the locus of processing, and still others as the location of labor for assembly or fabrication. The materials and components of buildings were gathered and assembled from across numerous sites of accumulation prior to delivery to the construction site. Concurrently, material production became rationalized with respect to standard building systems, and the formulation of building codes became more uniform. Thus, mechanization in conjunction with seemingly unlimited access to fossil fuels superseded the locally based handcraft approach of producing building materials and components. The direct labor cost became a greater component of economic value than material costs of construction. Production of goods and materials for all sectors occurred easily and, arguably, to excess.[4]

The invention of machinery for heating, cooling, and ventilating buildings led to innovations in controlling the interior environment in ever-larger structures, including new building types, such as the skyscraper. However, by the time of the Modern Movement in Europe, as Reyner Banham describes, the use of this new technology for "improved environmental quality was most ruthlessly sacrificed on the altar of a geometrical machine aesthetic and the honest expression of everything."[5] The vernacular model of differentiated structure to mediate between interior enclosed space and exterior site space was repudiated, for ideological rather than practical reasons.[6] Le Corbusier said, "Every nation builds houses for its own climate. At this time of interpenetration of scientific techniques, I propose: one single building for all nations and climates."[7] Le Corbusier's advocacy of what came to be known as the International Style carried into the building's interior climate as well: "The buildings of Russia, Paris, Suez or Buenos Aires, the steamer crossing the Equator, will be hermetically closed. In winter warmed, in summer cooled, which means that pure controlled air at 18 degrees C. circulates within forever."[8] Admitting that "Le Corbusier's position of unrivalled esteem among architects makes him too convenient a target for criticism," Banham posits Le Corbusier as

> no worse than the rest of his generation....The whole generation was doubly a victim; firstly of an inability of its apologists and friendly critics to see architecture as any more than a cultural problem, riding upon a conventional view of function that had not been related to twentieth-century needs; and, secondly, of its own (apparently willing) submission to a body of theory more than half a century behind the capabilities of technology, still preoccupied with problems—such as the use of metal and glass in architecture—that had been propounded...and effectively solved by an earlier generation.[9]

With this as introduction to Le Corbusier's concept of *machines à habiter*, Banham examines in detail the mechanical and environmental dimensions of several buildings by Le Corbusier, along with his awareness of environmental problems, characterizing them as a "machine-age aesthetic."[10]

Developments in technology for control of building environments proceeded in a series of piecemeal solutions responding to piecemeal problems, evolving so that buildings today, worldwide, have mechanical systems to mediate between human beings and local climate, providing for habitability and comfort. Building mechanical systems often must compensate for factors in a building's orientation or fabric—poor siting or excess glazing—that have not been designed from an environmental viewpoint. This approach prioritizes invention and propagation of sophisticated "state-of-the-art" equipment. Increasing mechanization, including the invention of computer controls in the 1970s, reinforces the commitment to sealed interior building environments.[11] The site, exteriorized from the experience of the building, is also repositioned in sensibility and social norm. This site has become a source of discomfort.

Buildings have become more technological, as an increasing portion of building cost, often as much as 50 percent, goes toward mechanical systems, rather than toward the fabric of enclosure—structure, walls, and roof. Emphasizing mechanical systems and functional independence, the currently prevalent model of building depends on a linear metabolism, by which fossil energy goes in and waste and energy are expelled. The building operates as a collection of different unrelated systems.

For market-based buildings designed by architects, conventional design processes tend to reinforce the tacit understanding of the site as a source of discomfort. Methodologically, designs are schematized and developed sequentially from architect to engineer to subconsultant. The process of design, having become more specialized and splintered, delivers buildings that, designed as if isolated from their sites, consume more energy. Among those designing different aspects of the building, the architect has remained focused on the appearance of things.[12]

BUILDING WITH SITE: HIGH-PERFORMANCE DESIGN

Many today—including building owners, contractors, environmental groups, professional designers, and research institutes—question the performance level of typical development and construction practices in relation to the environment. The critique of standard practices does not call for a return to traditional construction as that would address neither practicalities nor ideals. Though vernacular architecture does the best with material at hand, in comparison with "modern urban standards of scale, amenity, safety and permanence...vernacular architecture is often unsatisfactory."[13] Rather, energy- and resource-efficient projects that reap meaningful cost savings, including important benefits, that are commonly known as "green" or "sustainable." Here, the characterization of such projects as "high-performance" speaks to a new understanding of the relationship between building and site within environmental design: the observance of limitedness in an economy of means within an industrial framework.[14]

In brief background, the Rio Earth Summit in 1992 brought together heads of state who committed their nations to exploring ways of achieving "development which fulfills current needs without compromising the capacity of future generations to achieve theirs."[15] Three principles of sustainable development ground this concept: consideration of the "life cycle" of materials; increased use of natural raw materials and renewable energy sources; and reduction in the materials and energy used in material extraction, transportation, product manufacture and use, and disposal or recycling of waste. Though the Rio summit marks the rise of more widespread awareness of these issues, consciousness of the need for an environmentally based architecture had been growing for decades.

As early as the 1970s, following the first global oil embargoes, a number of designers, mostly in housing and small-scale cultural and institutional buildings proposed environmental alternatives. Pioneers of low-technology green structures include Joachim Eble in Germany, who designed projects in timber, and Sverre Fehn in Norway, with projects using earth. The most notable proponent of a low-technology approach is Paolo Soleri, working in Arizona with a concept of *arcology*—a fusion of architecture and ecology that proposes a highly compact urban form using indigenous materials—that can well be characterized as within the first model described here, "site as source."

At the opposite end of the technology spectrum, architects including Norman Foster, Renzo Piano, Richard Rogers, Thomas Herzog, Francoise-Helene Jourda, and Gilles Perraudin came together to form the READ Group—Renewable Energies in Architecture and Design. The group received official recognition and backing from the European Economic Union in 1993 at a conference in Florence.[16] The landmark eco-tech buildings to date are the Commerzbank Tower in Frankfurt and the dome of the remodeled Reichstag in Berlin, high visibility projects both designed by Foster and Partners. Media coverage of path-breaking projects has had a positive effect mobilizing support as others follow in their wake. Various techniques used in these projects, such as double-skin glazed façades, have been applied to other, smaller projects with considerable success. The promise of the highly technological approach remains to be more fully pursued, particularly regarding temperature control in summer and energy saving in winter.

Between the extremes of high- and low-tech design, an emerging middle way is distinguished by well-considered combination of traditional materials and innovative industrial products. As early as the 1970s, Gunter Behnish produced buildings and urban projects integrated with landscape. Stefan Behnish characterizes the position of Behnish, Behnish and Partner this way:

> There are basically two schools of sustainable architecture. The Norman Foster school, where environmental problems are solved by bringing in technology; and the Soleri school, which rejects technology. We fall somewhere between these two; but my sympathies are more towards Soleri. I don't want to go back to the stone age, or to change the way we live now—but so long as we are prepared to accept that we will be warmer in summer and cooler in winter, then I am convinced that we can achieve an acceptable level of comfort by following the laws of nature.[17]

The U.S. Green Building Council has begun to suggest the direction of a middle path in the United States. This consortium of building owners, suppliers, contractors, government agencies, architects, engineers, and others formed in 1993 with the purpose of promoting a mainstream change in the industry toward sustainable facilities. The group developed an uncomplicated rating system to evaluate building practices, LEED (Leadership in Energy and Environmental Design). Created through a consensus process, LEED is seen as a transition document to help move the U.S. building industry toward more sustainable practices. Formally introduced in 2000, the system measures performance relative to a series of prerequisites and credits in five areas: sustainable sites, water, energy and atmosphere, materials and resources, and indoor environmental quality."

Updated regularly, it is rigorous, transparent, and easy to use. Design team members track progress toward earning a LEED rating, with no need for specialty consultants. The system includes four levels of performance depending on the number of credits earned, and design teams must verify that all the prerequisites and at least 40 percent of the credits have been met to get a basic rating (bronze). As such, the system functions to promote and guide comprehensive and integrated high-performance building design. Most of the credits are performance based (rather than specification based, as are most building codes), meaning that they measure the degree of improvement relative to a recognized standard, rather than requiring the use of specific strategies or technologies.

Within the hierarchy of factors in high-performance design, issues of siting a structure play a central role. In a guidebook to sustainable design written under the auspices of one of the largest architectural firms in the United States, the itemization of "Ten Simple Things You Can Do" includes nine items that refer to the site (the tenth advocates recycling).[18] High-performance design draws on principles used in older building practices. Manipulation of land features, building forms, and exterior materials takes the climate into consideration in order to get the most out of a site and building fabric *before* drawing upon electrical and mechanical assistance from mechanized energy-driven systems.

High-performance design favors "appropriate technology" over sophisticated "state-of-the-art" equipment. Sophisticated building components now conventionally available—such as wired building components or highly technical windows—increasingly address hybrid functions, manifold demands, and complex requirements. An integrated or whole-building design approach requires thinking about the building, its materials, its components, and its site as a series of interlinked and interdependent systems. In this sense, the building is conceived not as an object but as a set of processes interacting within and across the processes of the site. In this model, a single design refinement might simultaneously improve the performance of several building systems.

Basic objectives of this approach include maximizing operational energy savings, providing healthy interiors, and limiting the detrimental environmental impacts of building construction and operation. Compelling side benefits include improvements to occupants' health and well-being attributed to better daylighting, artificial lighting, and indoor air. Worker productivity-gains in a number of completed high-performance commercial structures have been documented in measures that dwarf the combined capital, operations, and maintenance cost expenses.[19]

Because such benefits are difficult to quantify, the full value of high-performance buildings can be underestimated by traditional accounting methods that do not recognize "external" costs and benefits. High-performance building cost evaluations should address, in some measure, the economic, social, and environmental benefits that accompany green design.

Building construction costs, similarly, do not measure the adverse environmental impacts of construction-related activities. Today's design decisions have local, regional, and global consequences. According to the Worldwatch Institute, almost 40 percent of the 7.5 billion tons of raw materials annually extracted from the earth are transformed into concrete, steel, gypsum board, glass, and other building materials. One quarter of the annual wood harvest is used for construction. At the level of building operations, globally, buildings use about 16 percent of total water withdrawals; in the United States that amounts to about 55 gallons per person daily. Buildings consume about 40 percent of the world's energy production and produce about 40 percent of the sulfur dioxide. The high cost of inefficient practices carries into the interior environment. Indoor air pollution constitutes one of the top five environmental risks to public health, found in up to 30 percent of new and renovated buildings. Many industries have a growing appreciation that sound economic and environmental choices are not mutually exclusive, but instead are compatible, even interdependent. This suggests that high-performance building practices increasingly will be market driven as the economic advantages of environmentally sound design and construction gain recognition and support.

Continued development of lightweight, high-strength, high-performance materials offers the prospect of economy, efficient transport, reuse, and less waste. The development of new materials has continued to accelerate in pace. Existing categories of materials have transformed and expanded (such as titanium, aluminum, and ceramics). New categories of materials have emerged (including polyaramids such as Kevllar and Goretex, or foamed materials. A vast array of new composite materials holds potential for high performance (reinforced plastics, polymers threaded with glass fiber, or thin films applied to fabrics). Producing the materials and fabricating them within architectural components requires environmental and technical controls exceeding those provided at the construction site. The trajectory of materials development suggests a continued increase in off-site fabrication of building components delivered to the site as prefabricated elements or modules.

The emergence of high-performance design prompts reconsideration of models for design decisions. The old decision model based on factors of cost, quality, and schedule, mandated the protection of the health, safety, and welfare of society; the emerging model also considers the health, safety, and welfare of the environment. Issues of ecology consider the local site as well as the local environment. In this sense, light, air, and solar inputs can be deployed as building resources, and though inexhaustible, are similar to the use of resources extracted within the preindustrial model of building.

High-performance outcomes demand a much more integrated collaborative approach from architects, engineers, and other designers of a building project. A unified, more team-oriented design and construction process brings together various experts early in the goal-setting process. This interdisciplinary approach, in effect, quickly coordinates various types of professional expertise at the start of a project, rather than in sequential development, making a departure from past practices. During design development, input from users and operators can accelerate progress, eliminate redundant efforts, engender commitment to decisions, reduce errors, and identify synergistic opportunities.

Within the high-performance model, the site of the building is considered reiteratively at many scales: at the scale of ecology and multiple generations, at the scale of the property, at the scale of the building, and at the scale of building systems and components. These are integrated across the site, and linked on out to regional and global scales. Conceived not as objects, the site and the building systemically are brought into existence together. The new methods have created a number of different sites in design: one that is intellectual and based on prior principals of design methods and forms; another that is based on a site seen as ecological, but without constitution as a physical locality; one, along with others not listed here, called the physical site.[21]

THE UNSETTLED SITE

At stake here is an understanding of architecture as participating in a world of living systems and entities. The organization of cultural/physical systems is not reducible to a set "base" or "core" of patterns or structures, or to such structures found "behind" contexts or settings. Rather, in this view, order in design is embedded within dynamic context. Design includes the processes by which participating components organize local lived situations. These mutually constitutive dynamics include processes, which are living entities, being constituted by the very processes of living.

Dynamics regarding site performance have been articulated here in the terminology of professional design. In further opening up this territory for future rethinking of relationships in design, frameworks established by theorists in other disciplines offer concepts and terminology for describing and analyzing mutually empowering relationships. Material can be explored within those disciplines that have articulated a mutually constitutive approach to understanding living systems, traditionally including the biological sciences, philosophy, and the social sciences.[19] The number, range, and breadth of disciplines that bear on this subject speak to the multiple registers of the site.

Conceptualizing architectural sites within processes of living change, this argument begins with the premise that the site is both a cultural construct and a material reality. The two exist in parallel, but they are not, and never can be, the same thing. Both halves of this double definition implicate dynamic change. They define from the outset that site is not settled.

As models, the notions of site outlined here—as source, as depository, and as interdependent systems—are sufficiently at odds to suggest that they are mutually exclusive. In the physical world of sites, they can and do coexist. Duration and overlap of these notions of site show that new developments of different times overlay those of prior eras, without canceling or negating each other. Unlike ideology, which moves to exclude alternative positions, the environment incorporates contradictions.

As a relational process within a physical, spatial, and cultural framework, a site is not a bounded, fixed, or even singular entity. In questioning the stable ground plane as a firm site for architecture, so too does the object building inserted in an abstract landscape come up for critical reconsideration. The unsettled site—conceived as the building and the site in a set of interacting processes—means that even the most amorphous or degraded setting, including the ubiquitous commercial strip, can yield meaningful content for design.[20] This view of design extends beyond production to the complete life cycle of that which is produced.

Methodologically, this view advocates for dissolving, not reinforcing, boundaries between thinkers and makers. Rather than focusing on design or engineering of artifacts, the goal is the design of processes. Tools for thinking and for learning therefore should be based on simulation or modeling rather than simply on representation. Through this can be discovered new relationships with natural and social processes and histories, including but not limited to new relationships with the ground.

Notes

1. Issues of building materials are discussed in relation to fabrication on and off the site in Stephen Kieran and James Timberlake, *Refabricating Architecture* (New York: McGraw Hill, 2004).
2. See, for example, Bernard Rudofsky, *Architecture without Architects* (New York: Museum of Modern Art; distributed by Doubleday: Garden City, NY, 1964).
3. An abbreviated history of these forces as related to the built environment can be found in Peter Rowe, *Modernity and Housing* (Cambridge: MIT Press, 1993).
4. For a more detailed critical assessment of cultural factors contributing to environmental sustainability, as well as the wide variety of architectures claiming it, see Susannah Hagan, *Taking Shape* (Oxford: Architectural Press, 2001).
5. Reyner Banham, *The Architecture of the Well-Tempered Environment* (Chicago: University of Chicago Press, 1984), 125.
6. Hagan, 106.
7. In Banham, 159.
8. In Banham, 160.
9. Banham, 143.
10. Banham traces what he describes as Le Corbusier's abandonment of the attempt to extract symbolic values and cultural performance from the application of advanced technology—along with the common-sense orientation of all-glass walls to construction in the early 1930s of the Cite de Refuge and, more notably, the Pavillon Suisse.
11. Hagan, 106.

12. Several architects have taken up the issue of the site as conceptual material for project. These include, for example, Steven Holl, with a notion of "anchoring"; Stanley Saitowitz, who has designed a set of geological projects; and Peter Eisenman, who has worked across a complex of site-inspired concepts and metaphors. Notwithstanding the concern with site phenomena and tectonics, these projects tend to work with site at the level of image.
13. James Marston Fitch, "Vernacular Paradigms" in ed. M. Turan, *Vernacular Architecture* (Sydney: Avebury, 1990), 267.
14. The nomenclature of performance, with connotations of measurability, supersedes and subsumes the various and conflicting interpretations of "green" and "sustainable" architecture. For example, the *High Performance Building Guidelines,* published by the City of New York Department of Design and Construction (April 1999), were written to support additional collaboration required for high-performance buildings defined as those that measurably "maximize operational energy savings; improve comfort, health, and safety of occupants and visitors; and limit detrimental effects on the environment."
15. In Dominique Gausin-Muller, *Sustainable Architecture and Urbanism* (Basel: Burkhauser, 2002), 13.
16. For a more detailed discussion of the history and issues of the environmental movement, focusing especially on European practice, see Gausin-Muller.
17. In Gausin-Muller, 17.
18. Sandra Medler and William Odell, *The HOK Guidebook to Sustainable Design* (New York: John Wiley & Sons, 2000).
19. Salient references from the social science include: Pierre Bourdieu's perspective of "habitus" and "practice"; Anthony Giddens's exploration of relationships between agency and structure; Martin Heidegger's phenomenological perspectives; Maurice Merleau-Ponty's focus on social life as lived; and formulations of indexes, indexical meanings, and "referential" meanings offered by Charles Peirce, Wesley Jakobson, and Jane Bachnik.
20. I use the term *unsettled* with different meaning than does Wendell Berry in *The Unsettling of America,* in which his concern for land focuses on agribusiness. However, this text shares with his the understanding that the land and the products of the site—artifacts as well as agriculture—are the fundamental expressions of culture.
21. I am indebted to Ed Robbins for this formulation.

Engaging the Field

William Sherman

FIELDS IN FLUX

In the field of physical design, disciplines evolve. As ideas change about what design entails, the relationships between design disciplines transform as well. Ever since the early Renaissance moment marking the birth of modern abstraction, when Leon Battista Alberti codified *disegno* as a formal operation, architecture and landscape architecture have been defined in formal terms, distinguished from each other based on their associated scales, and materials, of operation. Today, however, we look at design differently, calling such distinctions into question. We comprehend design as operating at many scales simultaneously, and understand design materials in terms of performance rather than appearance. A common concern for ecology has altered design thinking, binding disciplines together in significant new ways. The boundaries formerly dividing areas of design concern become places of fertile cross-disciplinary invention.

Architecture and landscape architecture comprise part of this field in flux. Designers in both areas now investigate the materials and workings of cultural and ecological networks at multiple scales, challenging previously accepted disciplinary limits. Through a close reading of the contemporary city, new relationships between ecological processes and cultural practices become evident. For example, environmental transformation or deterioration cannot be considered as separate from socially and economically determined patterns of land use.

More often than not, the assumed boundary between architecture and landscape architecture has been identified with the line of the building envelope. This gross oversimplification masks great complexity. How designers construe where the building meets the land has profound implications. Recasting the terms of boundary definition from the formal to the processive undermines oppositions such as the living and the inert, the ecological and technological, the dynamic and the static. Once these presumed antonyms have been recast as inescapably intertwined phenomena, the limits of technology to control dynamic forces become evident. In this fluctuating territory, architects and landscape architects start to recognize that the world cannot simply be subjugated to human will. Here, disciplines do not control separate territories of operation: each must recognize the knowledge offered by the other. The engine of this intellectual invention—the new interaction between the two disciplines—is driven by a new model of design. We are being driven to work together because the way architects and landscape architects have historically defined their respective territories of operation does not provide to either the tools needed to deal with contemporary challenges. From interaction between diverse perspectives, new understandings emerge that alter both disciplines from their limits to their cores.

In the past, explosions of knowledge associated with modernity produced increasingly rigid institutional and disciplinary boundaries. This was reflected in a century of ever-narrowing academic disciplines and professional responsibilities. Today, new areas of inquiry, from bioengineering to nanotechnology, are having an opposite effect. As breakthroughs occur and understanding advances, fields lose their previously clear delineations, leading to new forms of professional and disciplinary collaboration. Rigid boundaries define what it is necessary to know based on what is already known; disciplines slide into obsolescence when they cease to produce meaningful invention. Pliable boundaries suggest possibilities for what could be known; disciplines can be reenergized in the face of new knowledge. Typically this process is incremental, but there are times when a radical reordering occurs.

RECONCEIVING INFRASTRUCTURE

For the past hundred years, change in the design fields has been manifest in formal terms. The incessant search for new form has been supported by the evolving technological apparatus of modernity. The process of abstraction that characterizes modern thought finds a physical analog in the vast infrastructures created to parallel and stabilize dynamic ecological systems. These infrastructural systems replace the temporal processes and spatial limits of a tangible place, allowing discrete works of design to disengage from their local surround. As a result, these projects stand seemingly absolved from accounting for their cultural and ecological impacts. The essential processes that structure human engagements with the physical world have been reduced to a resource delivery system, reflecting a predilection rooted in modernity for the ravenous consumption of the present tense, without consequence beyond the moment. The long-term impact of our technologically driven, consumer culture necessitates a critical reconsideration of the failings of this modern apparatus as a precondition for design.

With the shift to a dynamic conception of form and a new engagement with time-based processes, design has repercussions at many scales. No work can be conceived independently of the human and natural processes that form its context. The infrastructure that made possible the last half-millennium of urbanization was conceived as a one-way system providing a predictable flow of resources in lieu of nature's volatile processes. It delivered the stability required for economic and cultural progress. This modern infrastructure implies dependence, though, on a fragile premise; stability breeds reliance on increasingly vulnerable centralized authorities. The freedom to invent new form was thus predicated on a false sense of security.

In response to a changing understanding of design—as driven by process rather than form—infrastructure may now be reconceived as a multidirectional field rather than as the inherited model of a highly centralized (figural) flow. Instead of passively expecting services to be delivered, we now have the opportunity to take on the responsibility for the true costs of consumption. Reshaping the relationship between infrastructure and ecology has political and social consequences, potentially leading to more equitable forms of urbanization.

This argument points up an ethical dimension to design. The disciplines of architecture and landscape architecture can actively assert a positive common mission with respect to how a culture constructs its world. This shift does not diminish the importance of form to design's endeavors. Rather, formal invention acquires a new role. It becomes the medium through which novel ways of engaging the world are made manifest; new possibilities take form, constructed in support of a web of shared values.

New modes of collaboration lie at the heart of this changed intellectual setting. Ways of thinking no longer constrained by historical assumptions about established boundaries between disciplinary or professional knowledge foster cultural invention. In this field, the physical site has particular resonance as a simultaneously ecological, infrastructural, and cultural construct. Inextricable from the act of design, the site is at once a product of the imagination and a catalyst for new intersections between and across habits of mind. This new field of engagement provides the setting for, and is expanded through, the essays on site collected here.

Biographical Information

LUCY R. LIPPARD

Lucy R. Lippard has published over twenty books on contemporary art and culture. The most recent ones include *The Lure of the Local* (1997) and *On the Beaten Track* (1999). She has been a columnist for the *Village Voice*, *In These Times*, and *Z Magazine*, and was the co-founder of Printed Matter. She has a black cat and lives in Galisteo, NM, where she edits the community newsletter (for eight years).

HARVEY M. JACOBS

Harvey M. Jacobs holds a joint appointment as Professor in the Department of Urban and Regional Planning and the Gaylord Nelson Institute for Environmental Studies at the University of Wisconsin-Madison. His research and teaching focus on public policy, theory, and philosophy for land use and environmental management. He is the editor of *Private Property in the 21st Century: The Future of an American Ideal* (2004) and *Who Owns America? Social Conflict over Property Rights* (1998). His writings address how societies define property, and the policy structures they develop to manage the relationship between private and public rights in property.

ROBERT A. BEAUREGARD

Robert A. Beauregard is Professor of Urban Policy at the New School University in New York City. He writes on urban development and redevelopment, urbanism, and urban history with particular attention to theory and issues of representation. Recently he published a second edition of *Voices of Decline: The Postwar Fate of U.S. Cities* (2003) and, with Sophie Body-Gendrot, edited *The Urban Moment: Cosmopolitan Essays on the Late 20th Century City* (1999).

ROBIN DRIPPS

Robin Dripps is the T. David Fitzgibbon Professor of Architecture at the University of Virginia, where she has taught for more than thirty years. During that time she was Chair of the Department of Architecture and founding Director of the Program in American Urbanism. Her research on the structure of myth as a fundamental basis for architectural form has been published recently as the book, *The First House: Myth, Paradigm, and the Task of Architecture* (1997). Dripps has also written about theories of construction and the critical role of the detail, as well as the role of nature in urban design. Her architectural work has been exhibited internationally and published in leading architectural journals.

ELIZABETH MEYER

Elizabeth Meyer is a landscape architect who has taught at the University of Virginia School of Architecture since 1993. She has lectured and published extensively on modern landscape architectural theory and criticism. Meyer's writings have appeared in anthologies and journals including *Landscape Journal, Process Architecture*, and *Places*. Ms. Meyer, a licensed landscape architect, has worked on urban landscape design, historic preservation, and campus planning projects. Much of her design practice involves collaboration with architecture firms.

KRISTINA HILL

Kristina Hill is Associate Professor at the University of Washington in Seattle, where she teaches landscape architecture and urban design with an emphasis on ecological functions. She co-edited *Ecology and Design: Frameworks for Learning* with Bart Johnson (2002) and taught urban design at the Massachusetts Institute of Technology before moving to Seattle. She currently chairs the design and construction committee of the Seattle Monorail Project Board of Directors, and she is at work on a book about landscape urbanism in the Pacific Northwest.

SANDY ISENSTADT

Currently Assistant Professor of Modern Architecture at Yale University, Sandy Isenstadt has written about postwar reformulations of modernism by Richard Neutra and Josep Lluis Sert, visual polemics in the urban proposals of Leon Krier and Rem Koolhaas, the history of refrigerator design, picture windows, real estate appraisal, and the fate of architectural memory in an information age. His history of the visual enhancement of spaciousness in the architectural, interior, and landscape design of the American house is being published by Cambridge University Press.

WENDY REDFIELD

Wendy Redfield is Assistant Professor of Architecture at North Carolina State University in Raleigh, and principal in the firm OTA Archictecture. Her interest in architecture's relationship to the land characterizes her teaching and her creative work. Ms. Redfield has delivered papers at conferences nationally and internationally, and has mounted exhibits on the subject of site representation and analysis. Ms. Redfield edited *Modulus 20: Stewardship of the Land* (1991). She is currently engaged in research on the siting of Le Corbusier's early work, and in the design of private commissions in her practice.

PAUL MITCHELL HESS

Paul Mitchell Hess is an Assistant Professor at the Department of Geography and Program in Planning at the University of Toronto, where he teaches courses in urban design. His research focuses on suburban development patterns, development control and planning history, and transportation, especially pedestrian travel. Current projects include the planning history of the Toronto metropolitan area and the transformation of the suburban landscape with high-rise apartment blocks in the early post–World War II period. His work has been published in *Transportation Research Record* and the *Journal of the American Planning Association.*

PETER MARCUSE

Peter Marcuse, a lawyer and urban planner, is Professor of Urban Planning at Columbia University, in New York City, where he has taught since 1978. Involved with urban policy for many years, he has worked in various capacities in city governance and was in the private practice of law for more than twenty years before joining academia in 1975. With a focus on social justice, the main theme of his current work concerns the meaning and impact of globalization on housing and on urban social spatial patterns in comparative perspective.

ANDREA KAHN

Andrea Kahn has been on the core faculty of the Master of Architecture and Urban Design program at Columbia University since 1992. She also teaches at Yale University. Her writings and research focus on the roles of site representation and site analysis in the urban design process. She has taught in many architecture programs in the United States, and has lectured widely in the United States, Europe, and Australia. In addition to her many journal publications, she is the contributing editor of *Drawing/Building/Text* (1991).

CAROL J. BURNS

Carol J. Burns, an architect and academician, is a partner at Taylor & Burns Architects, in Boston, MA. Built projects by her firm have been exhibited and published internationally. She has taught at Harvard and MIT for fifteen years and, as a visitor, at Yale, University of Virginia, and elsewhere. Her research in practice and teaching focuses on buildings and the spaces between them, relating architectural theory to professional and social practices and to evolving urban form. She has written on professional education and practice, housing, and the site as a factor in design. Burns is contributing editor of *Thinking the Present* (1990) and *Perspecta* 21 (1984).

WILLIAM SHERMAN

William Sherman is Chair of the newly formed Department of Architecture and Landscape Architecture at the University of Virginia. He is also Associate Professor in the Department of Architecture and a practicing architect. His research and teaching have long focused on the relationship between architecture and the city, from the perspective of the cultural responsibilities of technology. In his prior role as Associate Dean for Academics, he worked to create new relationships between faculty in the School of Architecture's four fields, both among the departments and across University grounds. In his current position, he is developing the intersections between the curricula of the two design programs. He has received a number of awards for design from the American Institute of Architects and his work has been published in *Progressive Architecture* and *Architecture* magazines.

Figure Credits

Page xi	Courtesy of Carme Pinos
Page xiii	Courtesy of Glenn Murcutt
Pages 3–18	Images generously provided by the artists
Page 5	Photograph © Agnes Denes; Commission: Public Art Fund, New York City
Page 15	Courtesy of the artist. From *In the Place of the Public: Airport Series* (Ostfildern-Ruit: Cantz Verlag, 1998)
Page 38	Photograph by David W. Hess
Page 79	Courtesy of the Kröller-Müller Museum, The Netherlands
Page 92	Photograph by Elizabeth Meyer
Page 104	Courtesy of Harvard Map Collection Composite image by Elizabeth Meyer and Robin Lollar
Page 105	Model by Elizabeth Meyer and Katie Towson
Page 107	Model by Elizabeth Meyer and Robin Lollar
Page 110	Composite image by Elizabeth Meyer and Robin Lollar
Page 130	Photograph by David W. Hess
Page 156	Photograph by Andrea Kahn
Page 167	Figure 7.1 Courtesy of Venturi, Scott Brown and Associates, Inc.
Page 170	Courtesy of Robert A.M. Stern Architects
Page 173	Courtesy of Gehry Partners, LLP
Page 184	Photograph by Wendy Redfield
Page 187	Courtesy of 2004 Artists Rights Society (ARS), New York: ADAGP; Paris: FLC
Page 188	Courtesy of 2004 Artists Rights Society (ARS), New York: ADAGP; Paris: FLC
Page 191	Courtesy of 2004 Artists Rights Society (ARS), New York: ADAGP; Paris: FLC

Page 195	Drawing by Ellen Weinstein
Page 196	Photograph and section drawing of Atelier Ozenfant courtesy of 2004 Artists Rights Society (ARS), New York: ADAGP; Paris: FLC
Page 198	By Ellen Weinstein
Page 199	Courtesy of 2004 Artists Rights Society (ARS), New York: ADAGP; Paris: FLC
Page 201	Courtesy of 2004 Artists Rights Society (ARS), New York: ADAGP; Paris: FLC
Page 202	Courtesy of 2004 Artists Rights Society (ARS), New York: ADAGP; Paris: FLC
Page 203	Courtesy of 2004 Artists Rights Society (ARS), New York: ADAGP; Paris: FLC
Page 206	Courtesy of 2004 Artists Rights Society (ARS), New York: ADAGP; Paris: FLC
Page 208	Drawing by Ellen Weinstein
Page 212	Courtesy of 2004 Artists Rights Society (ARS), New York: ADAGP; Paris
Page 214	Courtesy of 2004 Artists Rights Society (ARS), New York: ADAGP; Paris: FLC
Page 248	Photograph by Andrea Kahn
Page 255	Drawings by Matthew Priest
Page 257	Courtesy of New York New Visions
Page 280	Photograph by Andrea Kahn
Page 283	Copyrights Biblioteca Ambrosiana Auth. No F 074/04

Index

C

D

E

F

G

H

N

S

T

U

V

W

Y

Z